"¡San Zapata!" Ix[...] [...]d almost round with fasc[...]

The vast room was [...] rock laced with gold, and in the torchlight the gold made the walls gleam in streaks like tongues of fire. The ceiling was at least thirty feet above them. There was a dark wooden table ten feet long, set with a golden plate, silver utensils, and a red carnelian goblet. A thick yellow tallow candle stood in a golden, three-foot-tall candlestick in the center of the table. There were four wooden chairs around the table and a long stone bench beside the wall to the companions' left. In the wall opposite them was a stone doorway.

"I don't like this one damn bit," Matsemela's face twisted in a dark scowl as he evaluated the oversized furniture. "Whoever they are, they're bigger than Ixtpan." Matsemela was eager to find a way out and did not care who had once lived inside this mountain—unless, of course, they came back while he was there. He started toward the closed door on the far side of the room, Topsannah and Paradox right behind him.

At that moment, there was a great grating sound of stone against stone, and the twelve-foot door slowly opened.

Paradox let out a high-pitched squeak. Topsannah gasped. Matsemela cursed. And Ixtpan stood frozen in a cross between horror and fascination as the creature entered the room.

Fully eight feet, it was taller than Ixtpan, with a heavy muscular build. It gave off a very strong odor that made Paradox wrinkle her nose. It was naked except for a breechcloth of gold beads. Its feet were tremendous, easily a foot and a half long. It stood erect on two legs like a man, and its long face and narrow, slightly slanted, dark eyes looked human—but its face and body were covered with long, thick brown hair, almost like that of a bear. It uttered a menacing growl and pounded its huge fists against its massive, hairy chest, then snatched Paradox—the smallest of the group—from the floor.

Paradox screeched loudly and punched the hairy creature in the right eye. It raised its arm to hurl her against the wall.

"Sasquatch!" Topsannah yelled. She and Matsemela were at Ixtpan's side, all three of them about to jump the creature to try to free the helpless itzaur.

The creature froze in midswing, holding Paradox suspended over its head, her moccasined feet kicking it in vain.

Other TSR™ Books

STARSONG
Dan Parkinson

ST. JOHN THE PURSUER:
VAMPIRE IN MOSCOW
Richard Henrick

BIMBOS OF THE DEATH SUN
Sharyn McCrumb

RED SANDS
Paul Thompson and Tonya Carter

ILLEGAL ALIENS
Nick Pollotta and Phil Foglio

THE JEWELS of ELVISH
Nancy Varian Berberick

MONKEY STATION
Ardath Mayhar and Ron Fortier

THE EYES HAVE IT
Rose Estes

TOO, TOO SOLID FLESH
Nick O'Donohoe

THE EARTH REMEMBERS

Susan Torian Olan

Cover Art
JOHN and LAURA LAKEY

TSR, Inc.

for
ANITA MARIE OLAN
with all my love

and, of course, for
TEXAS

I want to thank the following people without whom it would not have been possible for me to write this book: Norman Bendicksen, Karyl Lee Figueroa, Pat McGilligan, Sarita Olan, Dr. Alfonso Ramirez, Cristela Cano-Romero, Prescilliano Romero, Peggy Standing Deer, and Marie Torian. I especially want to thank Robert Thaxton, who knows and understands the true and complex history of our continent.

THE EARTH REMEMBERS

Distributed to the book trade in the United States by Random House, Inc. and in Canada by Random House of Canada, Ltd.

Distributed in the United Kingdom by TSR Ltd.

Distributed to the toy and hobby trade by regional distributors.

ADVANCED DUNGEONS & DRAGONS, AD&D, DRAGONLANCE, and ENDLESS QUEST are registered trademarks owned by TSR, Inc.
PRODUCTS OF YOUR IMAGINATION is a trademark owned by TSR, Inc. ™ designates other trademarks owned by TSR, Inc.

First Printing: December, 1989
Printed in the United States of America.
Library of Congress Catalog Card Number: 88-51732

9 8 7 6 5 4 3 2 1

ISBN: 0-88038-778-5

TSR, Inc.
P.O. Box 756
Lake Geneva, WI 53147
U.S.A.

TSR Ltd.
120 Church End, Cherry Hinton
Cambridge CB1 3LB
United Kingdom

THE EARTH REMEMBERS;
THE EARTH SPEAKS;
THE UNDERSTANDERS OF WHAT IT SAYS
ARE THE HUMBLE ONES—IN MEXICO,
   AT LEAST.

J. FRANK DOBIE
TONGUES OF THE MONTE

PRONUNCIATION GUIDE

Some of the words and names in this book are in Spanish. Others are in Nahuatl, the language of the Aztecs (A.D. 1244 to 1521). Just as English and Spanish developed out of the Latin of the Roman Empire, Nahuatl developed out of the language of the Toltecs (A.D. 900 to 1168) and of the Teotihuacános before them. The civilization of Teotihuacán in the Valley of Mexico (100 B.C. to A.D. 700) was to this continent everything Rome was to Europe. It was an empire that spanned the continent, that endured for eight hundred years. From Teotihuacán came the languages, the culture, the religion of pre-Conquest North America. We do not know the language of the Teotihuacános or of the Toltecs, but we can infer that they were similar to Nahuatl, just as the English of Chaucer is similar to our English today. Words in Nahuatl are generally pronounced as they are spelled. The accent falls on the second to last syllable unless otherwise indicated by an accent mark.

Cuahtémoc — Kwoh-TAY-moc
Ixtpan — ISHT-pan
Quetzalcoatl — Ket-sahl-CO-atl
Teotihuacán — Tay-oh-ti-wa-CAHN
Tenochtitlán — Tay-noch-tit-LAHN
Tezcatlipoca — Tes-caht-li-PO-ca

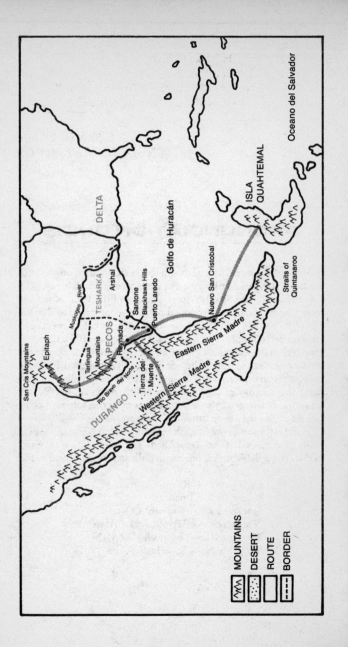

BOOK I

BEHOLD, ALL THINGS ARE BECOME NEW.

PAUL
II CORINTHIANS: V, 17

CHAPTER 1

CROSSING

The cloud-shrouded eastern *cordillera* of the Sierra Madre rising out of the desert was a welcome sight to the lone rider approaching the mountains from the southwest. They were gray, as he remembered them, and eerily veiled in the high-altitude haze. He reined his black mustang to a halt and looked in reverence, momentarily forgetting both the *federales* behind him in the south and the occupation army ahead of him in his homeland on the north side of the Rio Bravo.

The light of the setting sun filtering through the airborne desert dust colored the sky in shades of red and purple as the rider turned his horse toward the mountains. The air was still and hot, with not so much as the slightest whisper of wind to cool the land.

The rider looked like a cross between two legendary figures—a Texas cowboy and a *Mexicano* vaquero. Which is essentially what he was, having spent the first eighteen years of his life in Pecos Territory, the western part of the ancient land of Texas, and the past five years south of the river in exile, mostly in Durango, a nation made up, according to legend, of several of the northern *estados* of Old World Mexico. Though the old nations were a thousand years gone, their achievements had yet to be equaled and they were remembered and evoked in legend, song, religion, politics, and fashion.

The crease across the top of his wide-brimmed gray hat was in the characteristic style of Pecos range riders, but the brown eagle feather and rattlesnakeskin headband were *puro Mexicano*. The arrows in his deerskin quiver were cut from Durango dogwood, and the bow over his left shoulder was made of Pecos bodark. The alkaline desert dust covered his loose white cotton shirt, and his blue denim pants had faded nearly to white. A chunk of polished black volcanic obsidian, a gift from a Yaqui *compañero*, hung from a leather thong around his neck. His boots were made of bisonhide and crocodileskin. He had worn these particular boots for six years and they were very scuffed, cracked, and torn. And they were as much a part of him as his sun-bronzed skin.

He rode easily, like a man used to living on horseback, through the black brush, passing nopal, or prickly pear cactus, as tall as live oak trees, through fields of spike-leafed maguey, a forest of ten-

foot-tall yucca, and deep, dry arroyos. And through the ruins of
the human past. Occasionally he passed a long-abandoned dwell-
ing, its roof gone, its adobe walls crumbling into the desert. On
some, traces of their timeworn blue or white paint were still
visible.

Once he started climbing into the mountains, he even saw the
remains of a shack made of Old World tin, now well rusted, so isolated it had miraculously escaped the scavenging of later generations that had lost the ability to work metals. Now, in the rider's
own time, metals were in use again, though humans had yet to
discover how the people of the Old World used their powerful
magic to create the metal called *acero*, or steel. The only steel on
the continent was that which remained from the glorious past.

As he traveled into the sierras, the rider began to relax. He was
reasonably sure he'd lost the Durango *federales*, having given
them the slip two days before; and what he had to face on the
other side of the border was still far away. The brutal beauty of the
land was a perfect backdrop for what was going on in his mind as
he made his way toward *el norte*—painful memories of the homeland across the river he'd left five years before, half a step ahead of
soldiers who were searching for him to kill him, fragmentary plans
of what he would do when he returned.

He wondered how far he'd get once he crossed—assuming he
made it to the river. More than once he told himself he must be
loco for going back to Pecos. I'm as good as dead on the other side,
he thought. But it still beats the hell out of going on the way I was.

Days passed and he was long out of water. He became dizzy and
weak and sun-drugged, and was beginning to hear the voices of
friends long dead and to see ghostly images in the sand, when he
caught sight of the old mission.

The nearly bare mountaintop looked as white as snow in the
eerie half light of dusk, the time, as the vaqueros say, when no
man recognizes his brother. He smiled at the idea of snow, because these mountains had never been touched by frozen water.
They had rarely been touched by liquid water, either. For thousands of years this land had been called *Tierra del Muerte*, the
Land of Death.

There was virtually no water to be found in this vast mountain-
ous desert that lay in the northern *República de Durango*, the
great nation directly south of Pecos Territory, across the Rio Bravo.
The sun burned there with murderous intensity, and the days were
so hot that the rattlesnakes crawled only at night. This mesquite

desert of sun-bleached gray, green, and brown, all blending into
one in the heat haze, had been crossed many times over thousands
of years—by warring armies, by vanished nations, and by nomadic
horsewarriors. But most often, the *Tierra del Muerte* had been
crossed by individuals alone, all of them driven by some version or
another of hope, fear, or rage, many of them carrying great riches
in gold, silver, or currency—but none of them carrying anything
more precious than a canteen or gourd of water.

The arched doorway and adobe walls of the mission reminded
the rider of the Alamo. He had made the pilgrimage—a ritual sacred to all descendants of the ancient Texans—to the shrine in the
old port city of Santone on the coast of the *Golfo de Huracán*
when he was ten years old. Santone, if legend could be believed,
had once not been on the coast but two hundred miles inland, in
the center of Old Texas. The holy shrine itself was surrounded by a
square mile of blackened, twisted ruins—like the changed coast-
line, the result of war in another epoch. The pilgrimages to the
Alamo had been made for centuries, having arisen as a custom
during the Dark Ages that followed the destruction of the Old
World. Seems like it was a hundred years ago, Zaco and I were
there at the Alamo, the rider thought, remembering how dark
and cool it had been inside the earthen building. Might as well
have been another lifetime. In reality, it had only been thirteen
years since he and his adopted brother, Apizaco Two Creeks, had
knelt inside the centuries-old building where legendary gods and
heroes of antiquity, such as St. Davy of the Coonskin Cap and St.
Bowie of the Curved Knife, had, according to the stories that had
been passed by word of mouth for generations, offered their lives
in blood sacrifice for liberty.

The epoch of the Old World, the time in which the venerable
Texans had died at the Alamo, had been an age of wonders and
miracles, and was regarded with such intensity that, even centuries after its downfall, its scattered, random remains formed the
basis for the related endeavors of mythology, religion, and politics
across the continent of Noramica. And scattered and random its
remains certainly were, for the Old World had been so thoroughly
destroyed by a Great War a thousand years before the rider's time
that very little was actually known about it, a circumstance that
led to a great deal of conjecture, argument, and outright lying
among archaeologists, historians, priests, magicians, and politi-
cians of succeeding generations.

In the way of people who lived on a land that had already seen greater glory than could ever be matched, the people of the rider's world felt the events of the epic past—as they imagined them to have been—almost as strongly as if those events had happened only recently. Songs were sung, stories recited, services held, and glasses raised because of events known only from ruins and legends. Men, women, and children fought and died in the name of heroes and gods such as St. Davy of the Coonskin Cap, Falling Eagle, San Zapata, Quetzalcoatl, Guadalupe, Cristos, Juarez, and St. Elvis of the Last Days—dim memories whose reality had been long forgotten, if in fact they had ever been real at all.

Many historians labeled Texas and Mexico, or *Mexica*, as nothing more than the mythology of primitive peoples and asserted that no such places had ever existed. But the people of both Pecos Territory and the *República de Durango* proudly claimed descent from the civilizations of those mythological nations.

The mission's adobe walls were cracked in many places. The man knew the building could well be deserted, possibly having been abandoned centuries before. Like the Alamo, it had been built in an ancient era by a religion and a government both as dead as the coyote and bison bones in the desert.

But there were signs of current habitation on the mountain: a shack known as a *jacale*, made of mesquite limbs daubed with mud, two sun-bleached bisonhide tipis, and a small corral, also made of mesquite limbs, that held a bare-boned gray mare, two black mules, and a blue-haired goat whose orange eyes blazed like burning embers in the night.

Nobody here but maybe the padre and a dirt farmer, the man thought as he reined in his horse outside the mission. He saw no sign of *federales* or bounty hunters, observing only a couple of Comanche or Athaba trading families camped beside the mission. Hell, what does it matter if the *federales* are here waiting for me? he thought. The horse and I need water bad. *Asi es la vida*. That's life.

He dismounted and tethered the horse to a mesquite hitching post. Mesquite was a popular wood in the southern quadrant of Noramica, because it was virtually the only tree that could live in the sun-baked desert. The hillside was otherwise bare but for a few forms of desert plants—prickly pear cactus, maguey, and several twisted mesquite trees no higher than the gray brush.

The wooden mission door opened with a shrill, creaking sound. The man reached for the jaguar bone handle of his obsidian knife. A slight breeze blew, gently rustling the mesquite leaves and stirring up the dust.

"*¡Bienvenido!*" A tall, broad-shouldered man in a long black cassock stepped through the arched doorway. He was holding a yucca broom, which he leaned against the fractured adobe wall. His black hair and beard were long, flowing over his shoulders and chest. And his skin was unusually fair, almost stark in the un-earthly light of dusk. "How can I help you, vaquero?" he said in Spanglish, a universal language throughout the southern quad-rant of Noramica. He held out his hands, palms up, showing the visitor he was unarmed.

"The horse and I need water, Padre." The man's slow drawl was made even slower by his painfully dry throat. He let go of his knife and took off his hat in a gesture of respect. The dying sunlight caught the gold streaks in his long brown hair. After a moment, he staggered toward the mission door, moving with the stiff, bow-legged gait of a man who'd been on horseback for days. "They call me Cimarron. Cimarron Langtry. Coming from Hacienda Hildalgo, down south in the western Sierra Madre."

That was not the whole truth, but he did not dare trust a stran-ger with the rest. There were many throughout the land, priests among them, who would kill one of the bandit general Diego Laredo's men without a second thought, and Cimarron had rid-den across Durango with Laredo's vaqueros for the past three years. The fact that the man was a priest, even one who appeared to be unarmed, did not mean Cimarron was safe. Not by a long shot. Many priests hid knives in their wide sleeves and swords in their long cassocks. "If there's a well or a spring, I'd be obliged if you'd point me to it." He put his hat back on and held out his right hand, a sign of goodwill since time immemorial.

The padre took the visitor's hand in his own and grasped it forcefully, looking straight into his visitor's dark brown eyes. "The names you carry should bring you the protection of the gods and spirits of this land. Cimarron—for the sacred homeland of the Tserokee Tribes—and Langtry—for the shrine of Old World Texas that bears that name. The spirits and gods are certainly with you, my son, for the Mission Santa Guadalupe Tonantzin does have wa-ter from a deep well. Sit a while and I will get water for you and for the horse." The padre gestured to a wooden bench inside the doorway and went to draw fresh water from the spring.

Inside the chapel was an altar and above it hung a picture lit by three candles. It was a painting on canvas of a beautiful, dark-skinned woman wearing a long blue veil covered with golden stars. He had seen her image before—Santa Guadalupe Tonantzin. "Our mother," the people had called her for thousands of years. Her origins were long forgotten, but she was, nonetheless, a powerful symbol of survival in the face of overwhelming destruction. And theirs was a land that needed gods of survival.

Cimarron breathed in the cool air inside the mission as though it were water quenching a deep and desperate thirst. He brushed some of the dust from his hat and from his long hair, then leaned back against the cool wall and closed his eyes.

The padre appeared and handed him a red pottery mug of water.

Cimarron drained the mug in one long drink. "*Gracias*, Padre. You've saved my life, and I'm in your debt."

In the torchlight, the padre realized the gaunt and haggard traveler was younger than he had thought at first. It was the lines at the corners of the man's dark eyes, crinkled as though from the habit of constant watchfulness, that made him look older. And there was a hardened, distant look about this one, unusual in someone younger than thirty. That the visitor lived much of his life in sunlight was clear—his skin was bronzed darker than his gold and brown hair. "*De nada*," the padre said. "You owe me nothing, my son. But it seems that most who pass this way are either running from or pursuing someone. Have I saved your life tonight only for someone else to take it *mañana*?"

"I guess I'll have to live 'til tomorrow to find out." Cimarron grinned, and when he did the dust that caked his skin cracked like dry dirt. "*¿Quién sabe?*" The expression meaning "who knows?" had passed intact from the great tribes of Old World Mexico through the nations and languages of a millennium.

And so another one crosses the great river, the padre thought sadly. Always they go either to kill or to die. And the way things had been going north of the river, under the iron rule of the Tesharka Confederation of Territories, it was most likely this young man was going to Pecos to die. The traders and exiles who passed his way told him that even the land itself was dying north of the Bravo. The Confederation, as it was commonly known in all the languages of the continent, continued to spread south and westward, stripping woodlands and resources and enslaving the people as it went.

Tesharka, the capital state of Guvnor Baines Winchester's growing empire, more than five hundred miles northwest of Pecos, was said to have once been a beautiful, rolling land of pine forests and lakes. Legend held that in archaic times it had been part of glorious Texas itself, an eastern part, somehow separated from the rest by a different geography and a different history long since lost in myth and fantasy. The legends also told of another time, before the Great War, when the land of Tesharka had been worked by slaves, as it was in the present. Now, when the passing traders and exiles spoke of Tesharka, they spoke in hushed voices of a flat land where the bare soil blew away in the black wind.

Cimarron rose wearily and started toward the door. He stumbled and swayed but caught his balance quickly by grabbing the granite bowl of water blessed by the padre.

"Rest here, my son. I can see you have ridden long and hard. You are in no condition to go on. Take sanctuary here for the night. Sleep for a while. I'll wake you before the dawn."

"*Muchas gracias*, Padre, but you don't know me. You don't know what I've done." For just a moment, the light seemed to fade from his dark brown eyes. "Or what I'm going to do. I've killed. More times than I can remember. And I'm going to kill again. Any right I had to sanctuary . . . I gave it up a long time ago." He reached out for the door, but the room began to spin around him.

The padre was surprisingly strong and caught hold of Cimarron before he could pass out where he stood. "The mission is a refuge, nothing more. You will find neither condemnation nor absolution here." He helped his visitor lie on the mesquite bench and sat close beside him. "Remember, *hijo mio*, the earth teaches us how to survive. Just look to the mesquite tree. The ancient king Quetzalcoatl created the mesquite when this land belonged to the Toltecas, twenty centuries ago." The padre's eyes clouded over, and he stared silently at the blank adobe wall in front of him, then continued in heavily accented Spanglish. "Mesquite roots go down deep, a hundred feet and more, to find water. Once rooted, there is no digging them out. And the tree is armed with sharp thorns. It is hard for anyone or anything to kill it. We who come from this land must be as the mesquite to survive."

Cimarron laughed. He'd spent five years trying to tear out his own deep roots and had failed badly at it. Then he reached up and grabbed the padre by his arms. "How long's the ride to the Pecos border from here?" There was a savage look in his eyes.

"More than a hundred miles. Three days' hard ride in this country. But sleep well before you decide to cross the Rio Bravo, my son. Security on the border is tight. In the western San Cris Mountains, a young shaman many are calling a prophet has commanded the defeat of four companies of Confederation cavalry. Many people from across the continent flock to him—and the army has orders to assume any refugees it comes upon are going to join his rebel army and to kill them on sight."

"What do you know of this prophet, Padre?" Cimarron's voice was barely a whisper, his eyes half closed.

The padre paused before answering. "Only that many say he has within him the spirit of an ancient warrior who has returned in this time to save this land from those who would destroy it." He sighed wearily. "You must understand, *hijo mio*, how dangerous it is for you to go near the border. Not only does the man in the San Cris Mountains challenge the Confederation. In the South, Diego Laredo and his vaqueros threaten the government of Durango, a powerful ally of the Confederation. The stability of the Confederation is threatened, and Guvnor Baines Winchester wants his borders closed. He has army units patrolling all the borders, along with the usual border patrol. There's a bounty of a hundred jadas being paid for scalps brought into the garrison over at Reynada on the other side. These are hard times in which we live, and the bounty's sure to have the scalp hunters and the soldiers sharpening their knives and spears. This is no time to cross into Pecos."

"I've got to go back, Padre. I've got to get back to Pecos. There's something I have to do." But his haunted eyes closed and he fell almost instantly to sleep.

"This land never frees her children, *hijo mio*. When she calls to you, you must return, no matter what the sacrifice." The padre spoke the words sadly, thinking not only of the stranger lying in front of him, but also of the young shaman far away in the San Cris Mountains. He covered the sleeping traveler with a red and black striped *sarape*.

How many times had lone riders stopped at Mission Guadalupe Tonantzin in his long years there? the padre asked himself. Many came five years before, when the Confederation army put down a rebellion in Pecos Territory. The repression had been particularly fierce in Reynada, the territorial capital. Many desperate survivors of the doomed insurrection against Winchester's colonial government had fled south of the river and then scattered into the jungles, deserts, mountains, and valleys of the southern quadrant of the continent. Since that time, only a few travelers came each year to the isolated mission. Some heading north of the big river, some heading south, none ever willing to say why. Always they came in an endless ebb and flow. As it had been for thousands of years.

The padre made the ancient sign invoking the power of creation over the young man, moving his right hand in the pattern of a cross, a symbol dating back long before the fiery death of the Old World, the period believed to have been the Golden Age of human history. The horizontal bar of the cross represented things of the earth and flesh—things mortal—and the vertical bar represented those of air and spirit—the eternal.

When the padre returned to check on his guest two hours later, both the man and his horse were gone. He shook his head sadly while stroking his long black beard.

* * * * *

Cimarron Langtry passed several rock-covered mounds as he continued on his way to the border. They were unmarked graves of people desperate or driven enough to cross the frontier. The land was dotted with whitened fragments of bone, as the sky was covered with silver stars: the jawbone of a coyote; the massive skeletons of several bison, their six-foot horns having been long ago carried off to be made into weapons, utensils, or jewelry; the fractured bones of a four-foot itzaur, the slightly reptilian chimpanzeelike creatures that lived in adobe settlements out in the desert west of the Terlingua Mountains of far western Pecos. All the skeletons lying among the yucca and mesquite were reminders of how often the price of traveling this land was life itself.

He stopped, pushed his wide-brimmed gray hat up off his forehead, and looked up at the vast domed panorama of the pitch-black night sky strewn with burning stars. "By all the *santos* of the Alamo, I'm almost home," he said aloud to the Western Star, as if the bright star by which he judged distance, direction, and time were a person or a god who could hear and understand him.

It's taken me a long time to get back to Pecos, he thought. Five years. A lifetime. But, by all the gods, I sure learned how to fight in Durango. And I stole five years of life I damn near didn't have.

Cimarron had spent those past years south of the Bravo in a land made up of deserts and rain forests, mountains and coastal plains, brush country and cloud forest. It was known in the folklore and mythology of the Old World as *Mexica* or Mexico, the name still used to refer to the southern quadrant of the continent.

For most of those five years he had been in the nation of Durango, where most of the people lived in isolated cities and tribes or on the great haciendas of the mountain country. The government in the old city of Parral had never fully consolidated power, even with its considerable army, known by the ancient term *federales*, a word whose actual origins were long lost in history. The population was scattered and diverse. And there were also the wastelands in Durango, as there were in Pecos and across Noramica. Some, like the harsh deserts, were the work of nature, and some, the *tierras quemadas*, or burned lands, where the earth was black and no form of life could survive, the result of warfare in a past epoch when people had such powerful magic they could destroy the land itself forever.

Much of the continent of Noramica remained uncharted. Only a few intrepid explorers had ventured farther west than the foothills of the San Cris Mountains and no one knew what lay there or beyond. In the East lay Delta Territory and beyond it was an unmapped land of swamps and forests. Only a handful of Old World cities remained north of the ancient ceremonial religious center at Memphis, where hundreds of pilgrims annually flocked for the late summer festival of St. Elvis. The northern half of the continent had been so decimated in the Great War that most of it was one vast *tierra quemada*, still uninhabitable, causing horrible sickness and certain death for anyone venturing there. Consequently, most of the people and much of the history of the northern half of the continent had been lost completely and irrevocably.

As Cimarron approached his homeland, he thought back over his years south of the river. He had spent his first year after fleeing from Pecos roaming the jungles three hundred miles south of Durango. He remembered that year as a haze of leaves and vines and tribes of dark-skinned people with parrot and toucan feathers of red, green, gold, and black in their hair—and great pyramids and elaborate temples whose builders had vanished many centuries before.

Then, for a year, Cimarron had ridden the buffalo trails with the vaqueros in the western range of the Sierra Madre in Durango. He enjoyed working with the vaqueros and came close to being happy in his time with them.

When he had fled from Pecos, he had sworn as he swam south across the Rio Bravo that he would be back before the earth had circled the sun again. But it had not worked out that way. For so long, he thought, I couldn't think, couldn't feel, just forced myself to stay alive day to day. Minute to minute. Living on *mezcal* and *pulque*. Then I found the open range. The riding was good, and the vaqueros were good, and I could face the sun coming up in the morning. Sometimes I could even sleep without the dreams coming. But, it wasn't enough. I kept moving, kept drinking, kept picking fights with men who should've been able to kill me. Until Diego Laredo himself picked me up dead drunk in the street outside that cantina in Xicalamanca. That was luck, he thought, I didn't deserve.

He laughed out loud, remembering the first time he had come face to face with the bandit leader whose name struck terror in the hearts of people across Durango and beyond. Cimarron had been too drunk to be afraid that steamy-hot day three years earlier, when he looked up from where he lay in a dusty gutter and saw that distinctively mustached brown face with coal-black eyes glaring from under a wide-brimmed brown hat. He had seen too many wanted posters across Durango and beyond with that face on them not to know who he was dealing with—the most notorious bandit *jefe*, or chief, of his time, who was accused of having killed hundreds of people. Through a fog of fiery *mezcal* Cimarron recognized Diego Laredo, who rode at the head of a gang of bandit vaqueros while calling himself the general of an army of liberation. Laredo's vaqueros had struck across the five–hundred–mile expanse of northern Durango, robbing, killing, and occasionally doing actual battle with the *federales* of Gen. Carlos Cortezhijo de Huerta, who had ruled with an iron fist, a vicious army, and a corrupt treasury for thirty-eight long years.

Cimarron had heard a good deal about Diego Laredo, much of it in *corridos* that were sung in cantinas across the land. The vast majority of the folk songs were about Laredo's killing someone or another, most often a *federale*. The bandit general had, according to the *corridos*, killed his first *federale* at the age of sixteen, twenty years earlier, and had been an outlaw ever since. *El Tigre del Norte*, the Tiger of the North, he was called. His followers said Laredo was a liberator who robbed the rich to give to the poor. By other accounts, he was a bandit who simply robbed everyone, rich, poor, or otherwise. Cimarron soon found out for himself that Diego Laredo was indeed a bandit, by accompanying him in the robbery of several large haciendas. And, indeed, some of the loot was distributed to the poor, which made Laredo, in Cimarron's opinion, if not a liberator, at least as close to it as anyone in that part of the world was likely to see.

Fighting suited the young fugitive from Pecos, and he did it well, killing with speed and proficiency. "With a vengeance," Diego Laredo had said approvingly. Soon Cimarron rode at Laredo's side as they attacked haciendas, government supply trains, and villages they believed to be supplying government troops. Before long, Cimarron was directing raids on his own.

Three years after Cimarron joined it, Laredo's army, now numbering thousands of peasants and vaqueros, had marched victoriously into the city of Nueva Torreon, the strategic key to northern Durango, and Laredo was on his way to becoming president of the *República*. Unless General Huerta's good friend and ally, Guvnor Baines Winchester of the Tesharka Confederation, sent his army to fight on the side of the *federales*. Intelligence reports of a massive Confederation troop build-up in Reynada, the capital of Pecos, indicated Winchester might be planning to do just that. And Winchester was already supplying Huerta's forces with swords and spears of iron and bronze, and arrows tipped with bronze or copper, weapons that gave them a great advantage over vaqueros armed with obsidian knives, spears, and lances, and arrows tipped with flint.

But Winchester's army had its own problems. In the lands west of Pecos, a young shaman that people were calling a prophet had defeated four companies of Confederation cavalry near the San Cris Mountains. And the Comanches, the great horsewarriors of the grasslands, kept the cavalry busy by chasing them across the plains. As long as the Confederation was tied down to the west, it could not move south to Durango, and therein lay Cimarron Langtry's purpose in returning to his homeland.

His reasons were simple enough on the surface. He had volunteered to investigate the strength of the northern forces, looking for ways to sabotage them, as well as looking for allies against them. He had said in his slow Pecos drawl, "I'm a natural for this one, *mi General*. Someone has to go north of the Bravo. And there's no one who knows that land—or the people—the way I do. *¿Quién sabe?* Maybe there'll be some way I can help out. I've learned a thing or two from you that might come in handy." He had laughed hard when he said those words. And the general, a dark-skinned man with legs that seemed too short for his stocky, muscular body, had stroked his long mustache and sadly agreed, knowing he might never see the young vaquero again in his lifetime.

But you knew why I really had to go back to Pecos, Diego, Cimarron thought. *La verdad.* I couldn't go on with my life, is what it came down to. There're things you just can't live with. What happened in Pecos five years ago was like that for me. Vengeance is what you and I both live by, so I know you understand. Hell, *la venganza* runs so deep in our culture, it's practically our religion. He smiled, remembering that last somber conversation, smoking corn shuck cigarettes with the man called *El Tigre del Norte* by the light of a few burning embers.

Diego knew, Cimarron was certain, that he had volunteered to go because he had his own business to take care of in Pecos. Diego had said it himself. "Sooner or later, no matter how far you go or what you do, you'll have to go home. If you do not face your past, it will destroy you and those around you." Cimarron shivered in the desert heat as he remembered those words.

Suddenly, he was brought back to hard reality by a faint hiss and a steady, rapid clicking. Rattler, he thought, recognizing the sound of a deadly poisonous snake half a second before his horse reared up frantically in a blind panic. He struggled for control as the mustang reared higher. When it came down, it fell, the beast's left foreleg having broken with its own force, and rolled over. Cimarron narrowly missed falling under the horse, scrambling clear just in time. He was on his feet in another second.

His fingers moved by distances no longer than the length of grains of sand as he reached for the black obsidian knife that hung from his leather belt in a snakeskin sheath. His breathing was so shallow it caused scarcely a vibration in his lithe and muscular body. He sensed the precise second at which the snake drew back to strike, and in that instant he jumped out of its way, twirling behind it in an arc and slicing off its head from behind in one fast move.

A rustle of wings whipped the air around him and Cimarron saw a large black vulture snatch up the body of the dead snake and devour it.

He sat down on the sandy earth, shaking from the adrenaline that raced through his system. He slit his horse's throat with one fast thrust of the obsidian knife. "Sorry," he said aloud to the dead animal, "but it's easier for you this way, amigo."

The rest of the journey would have to be on foot. He set one foot in front of the other, walking north, alone.

The soft whisper of the Rio Bravo was clear, like a beacon of sound among the other noises of night on the border—the mournful wails of the coyotes, the occasional hoot of an owl, or a ripple of bat wings in darkness broken only by the stars and the half-moon. Cimarron Langtry heard the familiar rhythm of water rushing over rocks long before he could see the Rio Bravo, which lay just over the scrub-dotted, low rolling hills ahead of him. The sound of running water was more than a sign he had reached the border—it was the sound of survival. As it had been for thousands of years.

"By St. Davy's coonskin cap, there it is," he said aloud, as he looked from the top of a low ridge on the riverbed twisting like a black serpent through the land.

At the river's edge, he dropped to his knees and drank the water of the Rio Bravo deeply, his earth-brown eyes closed. Then he took a small pottery vial from his shirt pocket and dipped his fingers in the black tar in the vial and ran them through his long golden brown hair. Rubbing tar through his sun-streaked hair would keep it from shining in the moonlight and from revealing him to the Confederation's border patrol, which guarded the river's northern bank. He looked back to the south, at the land that had become as much a part of him as his golden brown skin and his slow Pecos accent, and his lips silently formed the word, "*Adiós.*"

It was time to cross. Crossing this river was a ritual thousands of years old, and at that moment Cimarron felt the weight of those years, of all the people who had passed through these waters, many of them fugitives and refugees like himself. He knelt on the bank for a moment before diving into the rushing water.

There must've been a hell of a lot of snow in the San Cris Mountains this year for the Bravo to be this high, he thought. Only when the snow melted in spring high up in the mountains northwest of Pecos did the river run this high. Hell, years ago he'd seen it shallow enough to walk across. Some had even called it the Big Ditch.

The dark waters swirled around him, buffeting him with tree branches and small rocks being carried down from mountains in the far Northwest, washing away the Southern earth from his body. In the water of his homeland, Cimarron's mind replayed the last day of his old life, before he fled south of the border, watching helplessly as soldiers fired arrows at his friend, Apizaco. The memory was as vivid as the bone-chilling water around him, just like the dreams. He had watched Zaco die a thousand times in his dreams, always in slow motion, always with the same sensation of time coming to a crashing stop, of a whole lifetime lived in one moment.

Finally, near collapse from battling the powerful current, the returning exile dragged himself out of the river, and he lay on the sandy soil, gasping for air and feeling his muscles contract painfully. Cimarron caressed the carved ebony handle of his knife and, gazing up at the vast canopy of stars, laughed as he felt the sharp tip of its obsidian blade.

He rested a moment, adjusting to the strange reality of being in the foreign land that was his home. Looking around, he noticed that the northern bank looked and felt a lot like the southern— open and wild and free. Wind-twisted mesquite, patchy scrub, *ocotillo*, barrel cactus, and prickly pear scattered about the land.

Cimarron pulled off his buffalohide and crocodileskin boots and shook them upside down to remove water and a small fish from them. He pulled the boots back on and realized he'd lost his hat in the river. Damn, he thought. I liked that hat. He knew he would have to get another as soon as possible because the sun over Pecos could be deadly. He headed off toward Reynada, up the river. He still had a long way to go—as long as a week on foot— but crossing any closer to the heavily fortified territorial capital would be suicide.

Cimarron had not gone far, when he stumbled over something and saw in the moonlight that it was a human skull. Nearby he saw a pile of human bones, clearly the remains of many bodies. Even in the dark he could see the bodies had been hacked to pieces and then left to feed the vultures.

Just then he heard the sound of camels traveling over sand. Scalp hunters! he thought. Or worse—soldiers. Cimarron scrambled into a gully, pulling a dead mesquite tree over him. He heard the barking of the pitlos, the enormous gold, tan, and gray dogs bred from wolves over generations to be savage killers, which were used to guard the border against rebels, bandidos, smugglers, and horsewarriors.

When the two ferocious dogs came tearing through the mesquite barrier, Cimarron, in one swift motion with his obsidian knife, slit the throat of the first to come at him. He wasn't so lucky with the other one. It had his right arm in its mouth and its teeth were tearing into his muscles before he could kill it with a long thrust under its belly. Worse, he felt the brittle obsidian knife break when it struck one of the animal's ribs.

With the two dogs lying dead beside him and his knife broken, he looked up into the grinning faces of three soldiers who patrolled the far-flung frontier, all wearing the bronze hoop armor vests of the army of the Tesharka Confederation.

*   *   *   *   *

The bronze hoop armor made a characteristic clanking sound when the Confederation soldiers moved, giving rise to the derisive name called them by the conquered peoples of Pecos: Clankers. Over the hoop armor they wore buffalohide vests, and beneath it blue cotton shirts and pants. Rawhide chaps and thigh-high buffalohide boots completed the uniform. They carried with them bows and arrows, iron knives, bronze axes—and thick, intricately carved wooden clubs, which at that moment each of the three standing before Cimarron was fingering happily.

The nation these soldiers served, Tesharka, had emerged as a continental power roughly a hundred years earlier under the formidable leadership of Gen. Beauregard Winchester. With the use of swords of ancient steel, General Beau had transformed a minor territory into the most feared nation on the continent and crowned himself "Guvnor" in Tesharka's capital city of Arshal, more than five hundred miles northeast of Reynada.

The story of Tesharka and how it had emerged as the greatest power in northern Noramica since before the Great War was known in legend and in song. Under the leadership of the eccentric but dynamic Guvnor Baines Winchester, General Beauregard's son, the Tesharka Confederation had come to dominate much of the central and southeastern continent of Noramica, forcing other territories and tribes into its expanding empire with its superior weapons and tremendous armies. It had been fifty-nine years since Baines Winchester had succeeded his father, General Beau, as guvnor of the Tesharka Confederation of Territories. General Beau had been content to control and exploit the nation of Tesharka—in fact, it was he who began the process of stripping the pine forests for which the land had been famous since before the Great War. But his son wanted more and was determined to get it. From Tesharka Baines's armies moved north and conquered Muskogee, exterminating most of the indigenous population as they did so. From Muskogee they moved on Smokey Mountain to the north. Then they seized the cotton-growing territory of Delta to the east. In each conquered territory, the woods and minerals were stripped and taken to Tesharka, leaving the land dead and barren. The people of Delta were brutally enslaved and forced to work in the cotton fields. Then the formidable army moved south to Pecos.

Pecos, an independent nation for two hundred years, had resisted for four years, but ultimately fell to the superior weapons of the invaders twenty-six years before Cimarron's birth. Half the nation's population had died in the war or was killed by the plague the invaders brought into the land. The Confederation army had burned the corn and wheat fields and had slaughtered the buffalo so the people would starve.

An entire generation had perished in the conquest and its aftermath, and the survivors were understandably traumatized. But then a new generation, Cimarron's generation, was born, nourished in secret on the sacred past and willing to try to liberate its homeland. The people, many of them young, rebelled in the capital city of Reynada and across the territory in an act of great but futile daring. They were horribly crushed by a large imperial army, strengthened by conscripts from all the territories, including Pecos itself, and armed with weapons of iron and steel.

The nation of Tesharka was blessed with vast quantities of iron ore and also with great deposits of Old World metals, such as steel and chrome, which had apparently been stored there—or perhaps dumped, some radical historians speculated—before the Great War. These metals had given the Confederation army, under the command of the decisive, ambitious, and cruel Gen. Absalom Ironheart, a distinct advantage over the other peoples of the continent. Winchester ruled his empire from his fortified capital, and Ironheart commanded the army in the field. And where the army went, the slavers and tax collectors soon followed. The slavers took the people of the captured lands to work in the mines in the North or in the cotton fields of Delta in the Southeast. The tax collectors took everything that could be carted out of the territory. The soldiers killed anyone who got in their way—and now Cimarron Langtry had gotten in the way of three of them.

Even with his right arm bleeding where the dog's teeth had torn deeply into his flesh, Cimarron fought with a vengeance and managed to deck one of the soldiers before the other two knocked him to the ground with blows from their heavy clubs. They kept beating him long after he could no longer fight them. Before Cimarron Langtry had been in Pecos an hour, his blood was flowing into her earth again.

"Just another heathen savage," one of the soldiers, a fat man wearing a coonskin cap, said as he put Cimarron's bow and quiver of arrows over his own left shoulder. "Kill him. I'll get his scalp so we can claim the bounty in Reynada." He drew a sharp flint knife from a woven sheath attached to his colorful fiber belt and grabbed and twisted a handful of Cimarron's tarred brown hair in his left fist. His tall, skinny partner took a short hemp rope from his belt and laughed.

Cimarron could not move. The three of them had him pinned down. He felt the rope around his throat tightening, cutting off his breath. He felt the blade touch his scalp.

Suddenly something streaked through the darkness, whistling past them.

Then the soldier dropped his flint knife with a groan and fell to the ground, trying futilely to pull an obsidian-tipped arrow from his heart. A swift bronze spear struck the soldier who had been strangling Cimarron. The third soldier looked about wildly, not knowing even in which direction to flee. Before he could make up his mind, he was struck down by an arrow.

The three camels ran off toward the west, where they could roam free with the wild herds in the western desert.

By then the sun was just rising, turning the eastern sky pink and bright blue, while the western sky was still as dark as night. Cimarron looked up, and in the filtered light of morning he saw three camels above him, a rider on each. Feathers and shells hung from the camels' leather bridles and their tooled leather saddles were set over colorful, striped blankets.

On one camel sat a man who was clearly a professional warrior. The mercenary was an intimidating figure with broad shoulders and thick muscles, chocolate-brown skin, curly black hair, thick, expressive lips, a wide, flattened nose, and angry brown eyes. He looked as if he could easily take on a jaguar or two and win. The man wore a vest of copper scale armor over tattered red and gold robes, and a round helmet of bone and leather—in a style Cimarron had seen in Durango worn by traders from the continent Afria across the East Ocean. The sunlight flashed on the curved blade of the iron dagger the warrior held ready to throw, and a gold handled sword hung in a silver sheath from his leather belt. He looked at Cimarron contemptuously and spat in the dust.

On the camel beside the warrior rode a man taller than many of the adobe buildings in Pecos. The giant was almost seven feet tall—though he was also very slender. The long bow he carried was taller than most men of his time. His gray-streaked black hair was long, thick, and disheveled, giving him a slightly wild look, and his skin was a deep bronze, almost as red as the clay of Durango. He wore a white cotton tunic with its hood thrown back, brown leather trousers, and rattlesnakeskin boots. His narrow, obsidian-black eyes were slightly slanted, and his face was long, with a high forehead.

The third camel knelt, and a small, slender woman wearing a dark green shawl that covered her hair and obscured her face, dismounted and ran toward Cimarron. As she bent over him, the shawl fell from her head and he looked at an apparition in swirling colors. Her hair was coal black, thick, and hanging nearly to her waist, her skin golden brown. Her catlike eyes were iridescent golden green, like the three-foot-long tail feathers of the quetzal bird that was revered as a symbol of life by many tribes on both sides of the Bravo for thousands of years. The quetzal's green feathers changed hues in the light, and the woman's eyes had that same quality, transforming from green to gold to blue to lavender as he looked at her.

Her white cotton blouse, decorated with embroidered white ruffles, barely covered her brown shoulders. Her skirt was woven green cotton with three turquoise stripes near the hem, which hung just above her ankles. An amulet of ancient silver shaped like a butterfly hung on a silver chain around her neck. Set in the long-tarnished silver was a spiral, like the inside of a conch shell—the symbol of the eternal cycles of life and death, creation and destruction—inlaid in turquoise. Along with the chain and amulet, she wore a long strand of tiny stones of a hundred kinds and colors, all of them sparkling in the early morning light, that hung almost to her waist. Half a dozen tiny pouches of silk, fiber, and animal skin hung from long ribbons and chains around her neck—medicine bags they were called by the Pecos tribes. She seemed to glow from all the colors with which she surrounded herself.

Curandera, Cimarron thought, seeing all the stones and amulets. Healer. *Bruja*. Witch. He groaned, reached out to the woman, and passed out in the dirt.

"Ixtpan, *puede usted* help me? We may be able to save this man," the woman called to the giant, speaking in Spanglish with a rhythmic accent. She was using Spanglish, which along with Comanche and Sign Language was a universal language in the southwestern part of Noramica, out of deference to the warrior. Between themselves, she and Ixtpan spoke a much older language. Spanglish was very unlike Angelina's native language, and she used it awkwardly as she was mentally translating the words from her own tongue as she spoke.

The *curandera* knelt beside the unconscious refugee. He was young, she noted, with sun-bronzed skin and tar-darkened brown hair. The lines of his face were lean and hard, with prominent, angular bones and deep hollows in his cheeks. His lips were stretched

tight with pain. He was of average height, and though he was
thin, his muscles were well developed, rounded, and glistening
with sweat—and streaked with blood. "He is a well-trained warrior who has seen many battles," she said as she tried to stop the
bleeding from his right arm with the hem of her green shawl.
"Like you two, he has taken life many times."

"Angelina, I know how you feel about killing." The giant was
tired of having this conversation with Angelina. He knew very
well that she believed the taking of human life was an insult to nature and the power of creation. It was a notion with which he had
little patience. "Those border guards would have killed this man
for his scalp if I had not fired that arrow. Would you have us watch
them scalp him, *compañera*?"

"No. . . ." She paused, deep in thought, her fingers feeling
the pulse on Cimarron's neck.

"Matsemela, make yourself useful for once and help Angelina." The giant made absolutely no attempt to hide the irritation
in his heavily accented voice. Like Angelina, he spoke a highly in-
flected, almost musical tongue, and Spanglish did not come easily
to his lips. "I must learn if our enemies are near."

"*¡Basta!* I've had just about enough of this," the helmeted warrior said, getting down from his camel and grumbling in a voice
that seemed to rumble from his insides. "I should leave you both
smack in the middle of this wasteland and head straight back for
civilization. You know the only reason I haven't dumped you yet,
señorita, is because that overgrown baboon, Ixtpan, has it arranged so I don't get the other half of my pay until I deliver you to
those loco rebels holed up at Epitaph in the San Cris Mountains,
and I need the money to go looking for the Lost Cienfuegos Gold
Mine, which I believe is out that way. But I can't use the other
thousand jadas if I'm dead, now can I?"

He angrily jerked his bronze spear from the body of one of the
soldiers and wiped it clean of blood on the body's own vest. "Why
did you have to shoot off that arrow and get us mixed up with that
stranger?" he demanded of the giant. "He's no one. He's worse
than no one. Look at those boots and that bandana. He's a godfor-
saken cowboy." The cow was a weak and puny creature that
roamed the prairies of the Old World like the buffalo. In Cimarron's time, cows were extinct, though the term "cowboy" had remained in the Spanglish language of the western frontier.

"He has a right to live," Angelina answered before Ixtpan
could, her voice sharper than either man had ever heard it. She

felt oddly cold even in the bright morning sunlight. There was something hauntingly familiar about the man who lay dying on the sand in front of her, something that evoked an uneasy sense of recognition. "If you do not approve of what Ixtpan did, why then did you kill one of these border guards with your own spear?"

The mercenary pulled a thick corn shuck cigar from inside the leather pouch he carried over his left shoulder, and struck a flint to light it. "I threw that spear because this overgrown ape here," he gestured menacingly at the giant, "had already started the fight. And, besides, I can't stand the sight of those Confederation army jackals. This continent used to be a hell of good place to live. Bastards like these," he pointed to the dead border guards, "are making a mess of it. Now, the best we can do for this poor soul here is to send him on to whatever afterlife he believes in—and get on our way before more of these half-witted slugs show up. You both knew there was a war going on out here when you set out on this loco journey. That's what happens in wars—people die. This guy is just one more. He's nothing to us. Let's go." He took a long drag on the cigar, as though to call an end to the tiresome conversation. He reached into his pouch of soft, dark leather and withdrew a map drawn on a piece of yellowed maguey parchment.

Angelina spoke rapidly, her rhythmic accent sharpened by anger. "I will not leave this man to die here." She held her silver and turquoise amulet in her left hand, her fingers caressing its surface almost desperately. "I cannot abandon someone I can save. If I scorn the energy of life, it will abandon me."

Matsemela Nyakir grunted in annoyance and continued studying his map. He had a hard time with the woman's otherworldly mysticism—and an even harder time with her story that she was journeying to the San Cris Mountains to heal some crazy rebel leader. He was skeptical about the whole story—with him, skepticism was a way of life—but he did know from his contacts in mercenary circles that the survivors of a hundred lost battles had migrated from the Four Sacred Directions to the San Cris Mountains in southwestern Noramica, where the pueblo dwellers along the Rio Bravo and the horsetribes of the plains were in rebellion against the Confederation. That much was true. The remnants of tribes and rebel armies across half of the continent had gathered around an apparently demented young shaman they called the Prophet. They had taken refuge in an archaic pueblo, a relic of a long-gone era, known as Epitaph. They certainly gave that place the right name, he thought.

Ixtpan gritted his teeth to keep from saying something absolutely vile to Matsemela, whom he did not completely trust. Unfortunately, he realized, a hired warrior was necessary, since he and the woman were traveling through land that had not seen civilization in hundreds of years—if ever. He mentally scolded himself, not for the first time, for bringing Angelina on this journey.

But he had been desperate. Falling Eagle, the man so many people across the land were calling a prophet, was ill, always in pain, often unconscious, and unable to lead his people—as an army of thousands gathered to the east against them. Ixtpan needed a healer and there was none like Angelina in the world, so he had journeyed by land and sea for a month to reach her. When he told her of Falling Eagle's suffering, Angelina insisted on going to heal the young shaman whose life was being slowly but steadily drained by a mysterious, agonizing illness.

She was young, barely twenty-one, when he took her from her home, the city of Tamoanchan, high in the mountain cloud forest of the *Isla Quahtemal*, an island off the southern coast of Noramica. In ages past, the Isla had been part of the mainland of Noramica. Now the island was cut off, surrounded by the perilous waters of the *Golfo de Huracán* on the east, the Western Ocean on the west, the Straits of Quintanaroo on the north, and the *Océano del Salvador* on the south.

Angelina had led, Ixtpan realized, a very sheltered life, growing up in the temple with the *tlamantinimi*, or Wise Ones, of her people, under the tutelage of High Priestess Xochi, a woman who had, Ixtpan fervently believed, a truly holy spirit.

Though Angelina was highly developed psychically and spiritually, Ixtpan knew she had absolutely no experience in practical matters and could not, in his estimation, really comprehend the dangers they faced—in spite of the horror and violence she had already experienced while traveling north toward Epitaph. Nor could she understand just how much was at stake in Epitaph, in spite of his warnings to her and to the high priestess that there was great danger there. Oddly, it was Xochi, an elegant woman with long red-streaked black hair she always wore piled high on her head, who had made the final decision that Angelina should accompany him, no matter what the risks. Angelina, Xochi had said, must meet Falling Eagle and give him the butterfly-shaped turquoise medallion her people had guarded for two thousand years. Their meeting, Xochi had said, would fulfill an ancient prophecy. Ixtpan had sworn to Xochi he would protect the young priestess with his life—and Ixtpan preferred the thought of death to the thought of failing Xochi in any way.

Now, again, Ixtpan regretted his decision to bring Angelina north. She was just too innocent, too impressionable, too vulnerable. And worse, Ixtpan thought, Angelina's religious vows forbade the taking of another human life under any circumstances, while, on the other hand, the Confederation army was made up of people who thrived on killing. For that matter, the frontier itself was populated by people who gave as little thought to killing other humans as to swatting flies. There was just no help for it—they needed the uncouth mercenary for protection until they reached Epitaph.

He waved his arms over his head and called out in a deep, singsong rhythm in a language of his own. A camel belonging to one of the dead soldiers returned immediately at a gallop. It approached the humans and stood silently, as though waiting for a command. Ixtpan gently patted its neck, speaking and crooning in a guttural language the camel clearly understood, both the man's black and gray hair and his white tunic blowing slightly in the gentle western breeze.

While Ixtpan was conversing with the camel and Angelina was trying to stop the bleeding from a cut above Cimarron's right eye, Matsemela surreptitiously stole a glance at another map he carried. This one, drawn on a piece of dried deerskin, was smaller and had been rolled inside the larger one. The reddish brown lines showing the river and the desert and the great mountain range west of Pecos were written in the pictographs that were a common language on the frontier and through the southern territories. Someone had drawn an "X" on the map—in the mountains where Angelina sought her prophet—and the words were scrawled: Lost Cienfuegos Gold Mine. The words and pictographs were hard to read because the mapmaker had drawn them using his index finger and his own blood, instruments less precise than the quill and ink. They were heading into the San Cris Mountains—where the Lost Cienfuegos Gold Mine lay, waiting to be found again.

Matsemela smiled to himself and slipped the map under his scale armor vest, into the pocket in his cotton shirt over his heart. He thought, I said I'd get you there, lady, and I will. And then I go for the mine.

"The camel tells me the Confederation cavalry is setting out from Reynada—under the command of Colonel Reno Bismark,

the Butcher of Abilene himself." Ixtpan took the woman firmly by
the shoulders, causing her long black hair to shimmer around her
in the sunlight. "They know you are here in Pecos, Angelina. And
they know we're going northwest to Epitaph. There is an army of
thousands coming after the Prophet. And they seek to stop us
from reaching him while he still lives."

"¿*Verdad*, Ixtpan?"

"*Si, compañera*. We are in great danger here." He removed a
polished stone axe from the dead soldier's saddle and stuck it into
his belt. With a wave of his hand, he dismissed the camel to run
off after its two companions.

Angelina felt the young man's pulse. It was faint and growing
more rapid. There was little time. She lowered her voice so that
only the giant could hear her words. "He *must* survive. And I will
not abandon him to the vultures."

The large black vultures were already circling overhead.

"C'mon!" growled Matsemela.

"The mercenary is right for once, Angelina," Ixtpan said. "We
cannot take this man with us. He would only slow us down. And
moving him now would quickly send him on to his gods."

"His pulse has stopped." Angelina put her ear against his chest.
Her tears reflected the light so that her green eyes flashed with
hues of blue and purple. "His heart is not beating. Ixtpan, *por
favor* . . ."

"No!" the giant said, emphatically, taking her arm to pull her
away from the dying stranger. "The last time you healed someone, you nearly died for it. Remember what happened in Nueva
San Cristobal when the good people of the town saw your healing
powers? They tried to burn you as a witch. I will not risk that happening again. We gave this man a chance at life. If the gods want
him to live, let them heal him."

Cimarron Langtry was, in what remained of his consciousness,
looking into a bright, clear light, a light that seemed to have no
source, at the end of a swirling black tunnel. Inside the light there
was no pain. Inside the light there was peace. He knew the light
was death and he knew he was moving steadily toward it. With all
his remaining strength he dug his fingers into the earth of his
homeland.

CHAPTER 2

UNDER
THE FIFTH SUN

As the sun rose higher in the sky, the air got hotter and hotter and the land itself began to bake as a Confederation cavalry platoon searched the area north of the Rio Bravo a hundred miles upriver from Reynada. There were two dozen mounted soldiers in the unit sweeping the area and three more units were in the field, all of them searching for an unlikely trio: a *curandera*, a giant, and a mercenary.

The unrelenting heat made the earth and the air blur together as though they were one shimmering element. And the land was unrelenting. There were patches of three-foot mesquite trees and scrub brush and cacti so thick anyone riding through them would be cut to pieces. Other than the hardy desert plants, there was nothing else but the entire expanse of the wide golden horizon in every direction. And there was no wind at all.

The wide open space of the land of western Pecos was unnerving to many of the Confederation army soldiers, particularly those who came from Tesharka and the colonies to the north and who would never—no matter how many years they spent in Pecos—get used to the heat or the land. The soldiers in the cavalry platoon were all sweating in their uniforms and were so covered with dust they looked like the mummified remains of the Ancient Ones sometimes found in the Southwest.

"You've got to be bred in this country not to be killed by it," the old doctor who traveled with the army had grumbled time and again over some soldier's dead body. The week did not pass that at least one of them fell from his saddle from the heat sickness that sent a person into the sudden convulsions that inevitably preceded death.

The heat and dust and days spent on horseback combined to make the soldiers quick to use their weapons—bows and arrows, bronze swords and knives, and stone clubs. Only the officers carried the much-treasured steel swords. The obsidian and other stone weapons still most common throughout the known parts of Noramica were no match for steel.

The army of the Tesharka Confederation had found conquest

relatively easily for one hundred years—until it tried to go beyond
Pecos into the deadly lands to the west. There it suffered a stunning defeat at a place called Isleta, at the hands of a vast array of
forces led by the young warrior many people were calling a
prophet. The Prophet's forces had been armed with ancient
magic, according to the rumor going around in the army. The
Clankers' general, Cal Olivera, had died at Isleta along with all of
his men. Olivera had been a popular, if overconfident, young officer, and, to a man, the army wanted revenge for his death and
even more for his ignominious defeat. And for the first time, the
soldiers wondered among themselves if they might be facing some
weapon greater than their own.

Three soldiers rode together, talking as they searched the horizon for any sign of their quarry. They had known each other, had
fought together, since coming out to Pecos from Tesharka to put
down the rebellion five years earlier. In spite of all their time
there, the land and its people were still alien to them.

"I hate this place and I hate the people more," a bony, red-
faced private named Billy Ray Haggard declared in his flat Muskogee accent to the corporal next to him. Billy Ray had been in the
army ten years and was still a private. He'd gone into the service,
as doing a stint in the army was euphemistically called, at fifteen.
Now, at twenty-five, he looked twice his age.

"Me, too," laughed a tall man with golden curls hanging below
his wide-brimmed white hat. "But, damn, we've had some good
times out here, now haven't we, boys?" He held the rank of lieutenant, but he did not wear the military uniform, preferring
buckskin instead.

The simple fact of the matter was that in the way of professional
soldiers, these men had become addicted to the soldier's life,
needing both the violent action and the social position it afforded
them. Being a member of a conquering army was not without its
advantages.

"We seen some action, that's for sure," Billy Ray responded,
with a wide grin that revealed two missing front teeth. "But do
you think we'll see any real action soon? Hell, it's too hot to fight
out here."

The corporal riding beside him, a short, round-faced, black-
skinned man named Noji Aliota, bit off a large chaw of tobacco
and kneed his golden palomino. "You bet we will if we run into
the Comanches. And sure as dust we'll come upon Comanches.
Or have them come upon us. I remember back in San

Angelo . . ." He was ten years older than his buddy Billy Ray and had worked as a hired sword in Muskogee before joining the Confederation army fifteen years before.

"Enough with the reminiscences," said the man with golden blond, curly hair. "We're in for some action, all right. Colonel Bismark has orders from the capital to go on and take Epitaph. We'll be moving out from Reynada in a few days. Taking Epitaph won't be easy at all."

"Just a bunch of crazy savages out there, Amos," responded the corporal, his sun-furrowed, dark face reflecting his disgust at the prospect. "Hell, boy, we'll ride through Epitaph as easy as riding through a bunch of prairie dogs."

"No," said the blond-haired man who went by the name Amos Crimsonleaf, "those folks at Epitaph, they're folks who've lost everything—their homes, their land, their people. And I don't give a buzzard's gizzard what people are saying about this Prophet fella's magic. People get like that, they'll do anything. Taking them is going to be real, real hard. But, you know, I'm kind of looking forward to it."

"Hell, Amos," Noji said, spitting out his tobacco, "you just like killing folks."

"I admit it," Amos replied. "Always have."

*   *   *   *   *

"*¡Basta!* I will do what I must." Angelina's voice was almost a hiss and her green eyes were narrowed like those of a jaguar about to spring. Her almost-animal fury startled both Matsemela and Ixtpan into silence. She touched Cimarron's forehead, and closed her eyes in deep concentration. She began whispering an incantation in a language not spoken in the land of Pecos for two thousand years. Then she began to moan and sway as though she felt the young man's pain.

Cimarron opened his eyes and began to tremble violently, but he did not see the three travelers around him.

A brown-skinned young man with long black hair runs through dirt streets among the shattered adobe buildings. A dozen soldiers are running after him, so I'm firing arrows. He grabs a cedar post and leaps up to a red-tiled roof. And then he jumps straight at his attackers, a copper knife gleaming in his hand.

Cimarron cried out, "Zaco, no!" and then fell as still as death.

Angelina shuddered and pulled away, exhausted and shaking her hands as though they had been burned. She pressed her ear to the young man's chest. "His heart beats, but the blood still flows from his veins inside his body. He is in great pain—in his body and in his soul."

Ixtpan lay back against the large, round base of a yucca and wiped his sweat-covered face with a green handkerchief made of tightly woven reeds, respecting Angelina's need to heal the stranger. If she felt so strongly that the man must live, he reasoned, then perhaps her god was directing her, perhaps it was not chance but divine intervention that caused them to come upon the vaquero just as the border patrolmen were about to kill him. Ixtpan would accept her choice to try to save the man—at least for the moment. "Go slowly, Angelina. You are a gifted *curandera* and your powers are strong, stronger than any of the others of these latter-day humans. You can save him, but do not let whatever ghosts haunt him drain you. I promised High Priestess Xochi I would protect you. . . ."

"*Silencio*," she whispered. "*Comprendo*." Angelina took Ixtpan's bronze hands in her own, raised them to her lips and kissed them. Then she pulled a small leather pouch, embroidered with geometric designs in blue, black, red, and white silk, from inside her blouse. From the pouch she took three tiny gemstones—a blue star sapphire, a ruby, and a piece of gold citrine crystal—and a small mortar and pestle made of polished rose quartz. She handled the stones tenderly, stroking them with affection, her fingers lingering over the citrine, the stone of health, the stone that drew toxins from a human body.

She laid the pouch, the pestle, and the gemstones gently on the earth next to Cimarron, then stood over him and began to sway as though to some rhythm only she could hear. Holding her arms outstretched to the rising sun, she began to recite the ancient words with which to draw the energy of life, her long green skirt swaying around her slender legs.

Ixtpan pulled a golden pipe from inside his bronze breastplate and began to play an intricate, haunting tune that fit perfectly with Angelina's words and motions.

Matsemela groaned in annoyance. "In the name of every foolish god ever imagined, I never did see any point to religion," he muttered. "And this is downright crazy." He turned angrily away from Angelina and Ixtpan and went on studying his maps. He might as well, he figured, use this time to consider what route to take if he decided to ditch his companions.

Angelina did not hear Matsemela's complaint or anything else.

She was lost in a ritual whose origins were thousands of years old; her energy and her will were concentrated on the dying vaquero and on the ancient forces she could summon to heal him. "In four epochs, life has been created and destroyed on this planet. The end of each epoch has been marked by a time of great darkness, as if the sun itself had died. The Ancient Ones believed the sun that appeared when the long darkness finally passed had been new-born.

"In the beginning, under the first sun, the Sun of Earth," Angelina continued. She knelt beside Cimarron and sprinkled sand from the earth on which he lay into the rose quartz mortar.

Angelina's turquoise-green eyes rose to the skies that were lighting up with red and pink and blues of a hundred shades. "The second sun was the Sun of Air." She held the mortar in front of Cimarron's face so he breathed into it. Then she pressed the butterfly-shaped amulet to his lips.

"The third sun was the Sun of Fire, the element of the God of Fire and War, Tezcatlipoca, the god who has brought the destruction of each civilization born of this land." She dropped into the mortar the blue star sapphire, the red ruby, and the piece of gold citrine crystal, gems which held within them the fires of the creation of the universe. She reached, as an afterthought, into another medicine bag and pulled out a bloodstone, which she added to the stones in the mortar. The bloodstone was a green quartz that got its red flecks, according to legend, when it was splattered with the blood of a god named Cristos as he hung dying on a wooden cross. For centuries, healers had used it to stop bleeding. Angelina ground the tiny stones with the quartz pestle, crushing them as though they were sand.

Now Matsemela was suddenly wide-eyed with interest. Those stones were too hard for the average person to crush so easily to grains. He was himself a very strong man and it would have taken him far more effort than it was taking the seemingly frail Angelina. He felt a chill creep up his spine.

Cimarron opened his eyes, slipping in and out of consciousness, hearing strange words echoing in his brain. He saw the woman, like a vision in glowing colors, pulling him away from the clear light. He tried to understand what was happening but gave in and let the pain and exhaustion wash over him.

"The fourth sun was the Sun of Water." Angelina walked to a cactus that grew among the limestone rocks on the riverbank. The plant's fine white needles covered the cylindrical green cactus like exquisite lace.

Ignoring the spikes even as they pierced her fingers, causing them to bleed, she broke off a cactus flower with three rows of petals, each a different shade of red, and placed it in the quartz mortar. Then, murmuring thanks to the spirit of the plant in a musical language of her own, she broke off the needle-covered tip and put it in the mortar. Her own blood stained the cactus needles.

"This plant of the harsh lands contains water created under the fourth sun." The inside of the cactus held water, and as Angelina began to grind it with her rose quartz pestle, the liquid was forced out of the plant fiber and mixed with the crushed stones. She continued grinding the elements together, mixing them with the water and air.

"But then the fifth sun, *El Quinto Sol*, the Sun of Movement, was born. Movement balances the elements and creates from them the spark of life that is self-generating. The Ancient Ones personified the balanced union of matter and spirit in the image of the god, Quetzalcoatl, the Feathered Serpent, the symbol of the union of earth and air, the essence of life. Quetzalcoatl gives life, and Tezcatlipoca, the God of War, destroys it in an endless and inescapable cycle."

Ixtpan put his pipe down for the moment and spoke, his voice slow with great sorrow. "We continue to call this sun, our sun, *El Quinto Sol*, even though there has been an episode of greater darkness and destruction than any of the Ancient Ones who counted the rise and fall of great civilizations as the passing of suns could have imagined. A little over a thousand years ago, during the Great War, humans themselves released the Fire God, the god Angelina's people call Tezcatlipoca, from within the earth with far worse destruction than had been seen on this planet in over thirteen thousand years." Ixtpan's voice was angry, his black eyes blazing. He was thinking not only of the fools who had destroyed the Old World, but also of his own race, who had themselves discovered the secret of the Fire God. "They changed the face of the planet. Mountains became rivers of molten earth. Rivers flowed in *flamas*." He picked up the pipe and began playing his solitary rhythm again.

Angelina's green eyes filled with tears and she touched the giant's shoulder as though seeking solace, then continued. "Yet, when life should have died out, it burst forth from the scorched earth. Many creatures and races of humans died in the Great War, but others came forth from areas once isolated to cover the land again. The fire released your ancestors, the Paleoricans, the race born of the earth of Noramica, from the Ice Mountains, where they had been imprisoned for thousands of generations and allowed you to be alive in this time, *mi compañero*," she whispered to Ixtpan.

The Paleoricans had disappeared from the face of the earth thirteen thousand years before, leaving only a few oversized human fossils and some old legends about a race of giants who had built the first pyramids by levitating tremendous stones, the only evidence of what was once a great civilization.

"Yes," Ixtpan said softly in a language that was old when mastodons, saber-toothed tigers, and giant sloths still roamed Noramica, "the ice and the fire gave a handful of my people another thousand years in a world wholly transformed from the one they had known. But, unlike many of the tribes of southern Noramica who were able to crawl out of the rubble of the Old World and repopulate the land, there were too few of us to survive beyond a few generations. Now, I am the last of a once-great race, an afterthought of time, who would give anything for just one glimpse of what the world was like so long ago, when my race covered this continent from coast to coast." And, he thought, I am tormented by the knowledge that my own people left the seeds of destruction scattered about this continent, hidden beneath the idols of the god who destroyed them—and by the knowledge that others, too, seek those horrible idols that release mushroom clouds of fire and make the sky grow dark and the land turn cold, as if the sun itself had died.

The slender woman took a long, slim golden chain from around her neck. On the chain hung a clear crystal, which Angelina held up to the sun, and the stone broke the light into all colors of the spectrum. She held the mortar so the rainbow light would strike its contents. "Through the crystal, which is the frozen essence of the stars, the light is broken and released in life-creating motion."

Angelina rubbed the now-hot crystal in her hands. Then she waved her hands over the mixture and tiny rainbows flickered from her fingertips like the lights from a prism. Streaks of the whole spectrum of visible colors danced around her, swirling around the quartz mortar. The mixture took on a bright glow, with all the colors of broken light, and then dimmed and cooled. She rubbed the mixture of the elements over Cimarron's heart and the rainbow lights again flickered from her fingertips and danced over his body.

Above them a majestic eagle appeared, soaring high over the earth. The eagle dipped low, flying in an arc directly above Angelina and Cimarron, then glided off in the direction of the southern mountains.

The expression of pain left Cimarron's face, and soon he was sleeping naturally, safe for the moment from pain and from memory, the bleeding inside his body stopped.

Only then did Ixtpan put his pipe away.

When Angelina rose, her green shawl and long green skirt were stained red by the earth on which she had knelt, and she was trembling from the ordeal of transmuting energy and from the pain she had absorbed from the man's body.

"Every soldier, sailor, and priest in this land is looking for us." Matsemela took the healer's arm to steady her. He had in the past few moments gained, if not a new respect, at least a new interest in Angelina. The woman had claimed to be a healer, but he had never seen a healer do anything like what she had done. If she could crush stones and stop a man from bleeding, what else might she be able to do? He took Angelina firmly by the shoulders and snapped, "I said I'd get you to the San Cris Mountains alive, and when I make a deal, I keep my part of it. I'm not going to let your softheadedness get you killed. At least not yet."

"We cannot leave this man defenseless here." Angelina's voice was weak, and she was fighting dizzying disorientation, her small body trembling.

"We can't risk our lives for some lowlife trying to sneak into this country through the back door. Whoever this guy is, if he's traveling this land, he's a real desperado of some kind. And you can bet there's no sin he hasn't committed."

Angelina slumped weakly into Ixtpan's strong arms, drained of all energy by the healing and further weakened by a desperation she herself did not understand. He picked her up as though she were a child and turned angrily to Matsemela. "I suppose you think you're virtuous, you whose sword is for hire to the highest bidder. You do not spit unless you get paid for it. Who are you to judge Angelina? Who are you to judge this man? After all, his destiny may one day be linked to our own."

Matsemela bit meaningfully on the cigar and rolled his silver eyes to the heavens. "Not likely. Clean the guy up pronto—if you must—then we're getting the hell out of here. Remember, it's that pathetic madman hiding out in the San Cris Mountains she's

come to heal, not some nameless stranger. If you want my help—
and I believe you do with the Clanker army behind you and the
Comanches ahead of you—we do this my way."

Ixtpan opened his mouth to respond, but Matsemela silenced
him in sign language with an insulting comment on the virtue of
the giant's mother. The sweeping, rapid hand and finger movements were, like Spanglish and Comanche, a common language
on the frontier. Then the dark-skinned warrior began walking
slowly along the riverbank with his back to his traveling companions, his right hand on his elaborately carved golden sword hilt.

The giant set Angelina down, resigned to the fact that their
chances of survival without the mercenary were scant at best.

Angelina's strength returned quickly this time—sometimes
healing someone seriously ill or injured would leave her weak and
feverish for days—and she quietly took the dry gourd canteens
from the bodies of the ill-fated soldiers. She filled them in the
river, along with a large buffalohide canteen she wore tied to her
waist.

Ixtpan carried the young man to the narrow shade of a limestone bluff and three short mesquite trees, then went to tend to
the animals. "Angelina," he called, turning back to her, "I know
you don't approve of killing, but give him this to defend himself.
Now that you have given him back his life, give him a chance to
keep it." He handed her a small dagger with a handle of elaborately carved black ebony—and a blade of sacred *acero*. The steel
knife was a precious relic of the Old World. It would have fetched
a fortune on the black market, where Old World relics went for a
steep price. Ixtpan had unearthed it on his first archaeological dig
forty years before, when he was sixteen, and had carried it ever
since. Since Angelina had stopped the young man's bleeding, Ixtpan reasoned, the gods must want him to live. Consequently, he
would help the young man in the only way he could. He had never
been much good with a knife anyway.

Angelina used the dagger to clean the tar from Cimarron's hair
and yucca root for soap to wash his hair and face. She cleaned
Cimarron's wounds and bandaged his arm with fabric she cut
from her shawl.

It was not enough to stop the bleeding from the wounds. If left
untreated, poisons would develop in the wound that would
spread through the blood and kill the victim. Ixtpan brought
Angelina some of the padlike prickly pear cactus leaves, also
known as *nopalitos*. She carefully peeled them with the steel dag-

ger and packed the external wounds with the sticky cactus flesh. The cactus flesh would draw the poisons from the wounds. She left peeled *nopalitos* covered with a large swordlike maguey leaf beside Cimarron so that he could change his bandages when— if—he regained consciousness.

Then Angelina took a small green glass vial from one of the many small pouches she wore on ribbons around her neck. From it she poured jasmine water on his forehead, on his chest, his arms, and legs to repel rattlesnakes. Then she cut off a piece of buckskin from a large bag she carried slung over her camel's back, and, using hemp thread and a needle carved from a jaguar bone, she fashioned it quickly into a pouch. She filled it with water and laid it, along with a dried gourd filled with *posole*, ground corn mixed with honey, beside Cimarron. In it she placed ten jadas, the round jade coins used for money throughout the territories and the frontier.

From a brown leather pouch she took a small piece of turquoise and put it in his pocket over his heart. Turquoise was Quetzalcoatl's stone and she hoped to bring the young man the protection of the god whose teachings her people had followed for over two thousand years. Then she hesitantly placed the handle of Ixtpan's steel dagger in Cimarron's right hand. Matsemela and Ixtpan were saddled up and waiting to ride on, but Angelina lingered, looking at the young man. She bitterly regretted having to leave him in such a precarious and helpless condition. She bent over, kissed his forehead, and whispered, "Live, stranger."

He opened his deep-set brown eyes and looked straight at her. Cimarron saw her large, catlike green eyes, her olive skin, her long black hair, and the long earrings of white onyx beads that swung like flashing sunlight beside her face. His wide lips opened in a weak half-smile. "*Gracias, mi salvadora. ¿Quién eres?*" he asked, wondering wildly if he were alive or caught up in some death vision.

"I am only a dream. I am not of your world." She touched his lips with her fingertips. "I will pray for you."

"Save your prayers, *señorita*," Cimarron whispered hoarsely, "for someone who still has a soul." His sins were too many, he knew, for anyone's prayers to help him now. His dark eyes closed and he moaned softly in pain.

Matsemela had grown impatient and had come to fetch Angelina. "A vulture told your big friend there's an army squadron barely an hour east of here. We're leaving now, and we have to leave this guy here." He took her firmly by the shoulders and led her away from the injured vaquero. "He'll be dead by nightfall, sooner if he's lucky," Matsemela said with a laugh. "And so will we if we don't get the hell out of here. We've wasted too blasted much time already." He lifted the nearly limp Angelina onto the back of her kneeling camel.

Ixtpan took the reins of Angelina's camel to guide it, since he feared she would be unable to. Angelina's face was streaked with tears as they rode away from the rising sun and Ixtpan was worried about what was going on in her mind. But he was more worried about the proximity of the Confederation army.

And so the travelers resumed their journey northwest—a journey that would take them more than five hundred miles across two deserts and two mountain ranges before they reached the San Cris Mountains and the prophet they sought.

Cimarron Langtry tried to get up, to follow the strange woman, but his strength failed him and he collapsed. As he slipped back into darkness, his fingers gripped the rippling handle of the steel dagger, and he struck it hard into the sandy ground, as though he were stabbing an enemy.

*   *   *   *   *

Angelina had ridden for days in silent meditation—all the way from the Rio Bravo—and Matsemela was sick of it. Why should some down-and-out saddletramp concern her so much? he wondered. There was just no figuring this one. Women in general were incomprehensible and Angelina was weird to boot. That healing mumbo jumbo made him nervous, and Matsemela, who was famous among the mercenaries of the continent for his nerves of steel, had *never* been nervous in his life.

Of course, Matsemela thought, this trip is pretty depressing. There's more human than animal bones lying along the old Comanche Trail. Damn trail's white with powdered bones in places. Maybe that's got her spooked. Someone who doesn't like killing's got no business traveling *this* frontier. He reminisced as he rode along about the fate that had led him to abandon his home continent of Afria and seek a new life in Noramica twenty years before. He had, of course, heard the stories from other traveling mercenaries that Noramica was a strange place. But where was I to go when I had to leave Lagos so fast? he asked himself, as he had many times before. I should've gone east, across the Sahara Grasslands, that's what I should've done. And kept going all the way to

Tibet. But, no, I had to go west, across the East Ocean, then across Noramica. And now I'm here on the far side of Pecos. It might as well, he thought, be the far side of hell.

Western Pecos was a land of wild and dangerous beauty. The colors were vibrant: the deep blue sky, the red sun, the golden light reflecting off the hot white sand. Red and purple and gold mesas and gigantic black rocks. Green and gray desert plant life— barrel cactus, nopal, *ocotillo*, yucca, maguey, and here and there a short mesquite tree.

Matsemela wiped the perspiration, dust, and alkali from his face with a torn black silk handkerchief, then reached into his leather map case and took out a piece of hardened and dried buckskin on which someone had drawn a map. He slowed his camel's pace while he consulted the sketches and pictographs.

"Ah," he said with heartfelt relief. "We'll be coming to Comanche Springs soon." He was cheered immensely by the prospect of finding food, drink, and different companionship.

"This map had better be more accurate than the last one we followed." Ixtpan's dark eyes darted suspiciously over the horizon to be sure Matsemela was not leading them into some new disaster.

"Is it *my* fault if things change in the world?" Matsemela roared, startling his camel. "Some of those maps were drawn when the earth was still hot from the Great Fire! So what if a few things changed over the years?"

"You irresponsible, opportunistic *cabrón*. . . ." Ixtpan had a tendency to lapse into various ancient epithets when his temper was provoked.

Angelina snapped, "*¡Basta!* I cannot stand this bickering between you two anymore. I must concentrate my energy for the Prophet. . . ."

"We're going to get all the way to the San Cris Mountains and that poor sap will already be dead. Not that I care, as long as I get paid." Matsemela was mentally cursing the day he got mixed up with the healer whose words made no sense whatsoever to him and the eccentric giant who fancied himself a travel guide. Then again, he reminded himself, the pay was good—and the opportunity even better. He had no money to stake himself on an expedition to find the Lost Cienfuegos Gold Mine in the San Cris Mountains. He had won the map to the lost mine in a poker game but had no means of financing his way north.

One day that odd-looking giant entered Jorge's Cantina in the old port city of Matahuela and asked if there was anyone willing to sell their sword for hire. Of course, Matsemela was more than willing. Having the annoying giant offer him pay and transportation to the San Cris Mountains was practically a miracle. It's destiny! he had thought joyfully at the time he took the job. He was, however, beginning to wonder just what destiny had in store for him if it sent him off into some of the most hostile terrain on any continent.

He noisily stuffed the map back in its case, took out his silver flask, and turned the flask upside down to demonstrate what he already knew only too well—that it was empty.

Fortunately, this time Matsemela and his map were proven correct, and at the top of Dead Goat Hill the three travelers stopped and looked down on the small frontier town of Comanche Springs, shimmering in the heat haze.

"And do you know anything at all about this town?" Ixtpan asked as he nudged his camel to kneel. "Do you even know where we are?"

"Listen, lamebrain, I always know where I am. Just because an old map was wrong—"

"Wrong!" Ixtpan yelled. "Wrong! Your map led us straight into what must be the biggest tar pit in recorded history! I hope someday to lead a paleological team there to look for fossils! There we were, fifty miles west of that silly shrine to Saint Lillie, in that pathetic village called Langtry on the Rio Bravo, in the middle of *nowhere*, and suddenly we are confronted with a tar pit three miles across! And you said we were about to find an oasis! Those maps of yours are worthless! Not worth the parchment and leather they're drawn on!"

"You overgrown ape! Let's see how well you do at getting us where we're going. . . ." Matsemela was off his camel and rolling up his sleeves.

"If you told me the earth was round, *cabrón*, I would say somebody had better sail around it and look."

"Enough!" Angelina had tremendous powers of concentration developed through years of training, but the bickering between the mercenary and the giant was getting to her. "We are here. And, as Matsemela and his maps say, there is a town nearby. If there is a town, then there must be water. And we need water, for we have far to go before we reach the sierras we seek. Ixtpan, *por favor* wait here and keep watch for anyone following us. Consult the calendar stone. Be sure we understand the dates correctly. . . ." She seemed about to say something else, but thought better of it. "Matsemela and I will go to the town and buy water and salt—and find out where we are."

"*Maravilloso*. Finally I will have a moment's peace," Ixtpan said, sitting down on a black lava rock and absent-mindedly taking out the oscelotskin bag that contained his intricately carved jade calendar stone.

"None of that superstitious nonsense until I'm outta here." Matsemela made a rude gesture with his spear for emphasis. "That's nothing but a carved rock. It can't tell you anything about the future."

"This calendar has told the people of this continent the cycles of time for thousands of years. And this calendar—" His voice dropped lower— "tells us that in this year the power of the ancient gods will be felt again in this land."

"Right," Matsemela said contemptuously. "You keep right on looking to that damn rock for your future. But while you're at it, keep your eyes open. This is no place to meditate. Out here the army's not our only problem. There are bandidos out here. And Comanches."

"Do not be absurd." Ixtpan spoke in the tone one might take with a dull-witted child, his fingers appreciatively caressing the calendar stone that held within its intricate designs the keys to the circular patterns of human history that had governed the rise and fall of so many nations and races. "What would bandidos want with us? We do not have anything to steal. And the Comanches are nowhere near. They live hundreds of miles north of here, on the Sea of Grass."

"Don't bet on it." Matsemela laughed as he mounted his kneeling camel. Ixtpan could hear his deep laughter even after the warrior and the healer were out of sight.

*   *   *   *   *

Ixtpan made camp in a dry arroyo surrounded by red- and gold-streaked sandstone near the top of Dead Goat Hill, where he would wait while Matsemela and Angelina went about buying water and gleaning information.

Soon the giant was enjoying his solitude. "That imbecilic lout gives me a headache," he muttered to himself as he made a meal of mesquite-cooked rabbit with agave strips. "But civilized people such as ourselves need protection out here among the barbarians."

He sensed the presence of a Gila monster, a red-and-black poisonous lizard of the Southwest, which he snatched up before it was close enough to detect his presence. He ripped off its wings, tossed it on the fire, and wolfed it down. This is the first time I've been really full since we left Tamoanchan, he thought.

I miss my work as an archaeologist, he thought wistfully, wiping a strand of his thick hair out of his face and reflecting on the life he had lived. He had enjoyed the contemplative yet active life of an archaeologist—seeking to understand the past, to understand what had happened during those millennia his race was gone from the land. Such a sad history it has been, he reflected, and yet I find peace in uncovering it.

It was a peaceful life—until I journeyed into the sacred San Cris Mountains, searching for the ancient idol of the Fire God that my people left in that land over thirteen thousand years ago, he thought.

He had found the idol deep in a ceremonial pit, called a *kiva*, far beneath an ancient pueblo now known as Epitaph. And had met the man he was certain the gods had sent to guard the idol—Falling Eagle, Cuauhtémoc in the old language.

A prophet they're calling him, Ixtpan thought, a sorrowful smile softening his long face. They cannot imagine how right they are. He is that and much more. He is a man who has lived before, and he is that most developed of spirits—one who has full memory of his past life. "*Pobrecito*," Ixtpan muttered sadly. "How sad for him that the pain of that other life is always with him."

He reflected on what an odyssey his own life had been, from his obsession with the past, a life as an archaeologist, trying to uncover what little he could about his own lost race, to his quest to find the deadly Fire God idols left by his people, to aiding the rebels in the San Cris Mountains, all of it tied together by the man he was taking Angelina to heal. He burned some sage on the fire and hoped the sweet smoke would carry his prayers to the gods, prayers that Angelina would be able to save Falling Eagle from the pain that tormented him day and night, that she could keep him alive long enough to fulfill his destiny.

¿Ay, mi compañera, Ixtpan thought, what have I brought you to, Angelina? You come from a people isolated for so many centuries. And now you face a world that must seem to you shamefully barbaric—as well it is. I'll do all I can to protect you, *hermanita*, but your destiny was determined long before your birth. And there is no escape from destiny. Not for any of us. As I told you before we left Tamoanchan, *We, all of us alive today, are only living out an ancient saga, one beyond our understanding. Our destiny was determined long ago. As the Ancient Ones believed, we are* but players on Tezcatlipoca's stage. Tezcatlipoca, or Dark Mirror as he also was called, was, according to Angelina's belief, a god who manipulated the affairs of human life for his own amusement and to provide himself with a never-ending supply of the source of his life—human blood. He was known to Ixtpan's race as the Fire God.

As the sun began to set and the burning land to cool, Ixtpan again took out the oscelotskin pouch that contained his calendar stone. "Is another of the eternal cycles of life near its end?" he asked, almost wistfully, as he felt the carvings on the green jade stone. Even a spirit as powerful as Falling Eagle's may not be able to help this time, he thought. Perhaps, Ixtpan reasoned, the return of Falling Eagle's spirit was only a sign that another epoch was nearly over, as his death in another life marked the end of the epoch of his own race, the Aztecs.

*   *   *   *   *

As the soldier of fortune and the healer entered Comanche Springs, the air was hot and still. Not so much as a breath of wind blew on the flat ground at the base of the Terlingua Mountains. The town was only a way station for the desperate: prospectors, scouts, settlers, and outlaws; consequently it was not much to look at.

A scrawny black dog chased two squawking chickens down the dirt street that cut through the desolate settlement. Something hung from a mesquite limb in the hot, still air. It was the skeleton of a man, picked clean of flesh by the vultures and left hanging in the sun. A hanging corpse was such a common sight on the frontier that most people paid one about as much attention as they would a rolling tumbleweed. As they rode past the body, Angelina murmured an incantation for the dead as she fingered a clear, double-terminated crystal she wore on a long green silk ribbon.

There were a handful of small, one-room adobe dwellings, a few cabins of mesquite daubed with mud, a half-dozen sun-bleached buffalohide tipis, four or five shacks, and a wood-slat building easily identifiable as a jail by the bronze bars in the windows. A mangy camel, two small horses, and a mule were tethered by a watering trough outside a building made of adobe—and something else Angelina could not quite make out.

However, once closer she took one good look at the building of adobe combined with the unidentifiable material and realized immediately what had made Matsemela, whose keen knack for locating refreshment and companionship was legendary in his own time, so eager to visit Comanche Springs.

"I'll handle this," Matsemela said to Angelina beneath a swinging wooden sign that featured the carved likeness of a grinning armadillo and the words "Armadillo Saloon." He pushed open the swinging doors and stood glaring in the doorway.

Every hand went for a weapon as Matsemela and Angelina entered the room. The saloon was surprisingly crowded, but as the spring that gave the outpost its name was one of the few sources of water in the area, it tended to draw everyone passing through that part of the continent. They came traveling west to the frontier and the Sea of Grass, or south to the sierras of Durango, or even north to the mountains. Everyone eyed everyone else for a minute and then, uttering a collective grumble, went back to solitary drinking or talking among themselves.

The Armadillo Saloon was an ingenious structure that took its name from the shell of a long dead armadillo that actually formed the entire back wall. Of course, it had been cleaned of flesh and hair and dried in the baking sun years before by Slim, the bartender and owner, who had finally seen a use for the giant animals' shells—as building materials. It only took one of them to make a wall.

A long cedar table was set up across the back wall, and on it were pottery bottles of liquid refreshment, gourds filled with *posole*, and prickly pear *tunas*, as the sweet, liquid-filled cactus fruit had been called since before antiquity, fried in bison fat and served on wooden platters. The floor was dirt and the ceiling was held up by cedar beams. In a corner, a dark-haired woman knelt, grinding corn with a stone *metate*.

On the walls hung several sets of buffalo horns and a stuffed mountain lion head, its mouth open in an eternal snarl. The animal trophies made Angelina's stomach turn. She trembled, catching the end of a pine table for support with her right hand, her long green skirt rippling around her ankles. With her left hand she grasped one of her many small pouches of stones. It was a blue cotton bag filled with a small chunk of obsidian for emotional detachment, a multicolored agate for acceptance of circumstances, and a round piece of green jade for courage.

"What can I get you, strangers?" Slim the bartender asked from his rocking chair behind the cedar table as he finished rolling a corn shuck cigarette, struck a flint, and lit it. He held a flint spear across his lap and at his feet was a copper axe.

"Two mugs of your best *pulque*, *mi amigo*!" Matsemela helped Angelina to a chair at one of the piñon wood tables for the customers.

There were five tables in the room, all occupied. Matsemela and Angelina sat across from a woman and her child. The woman had the look of so many who lived on the frontier: her skin dried and deeply lined by the hot air and bright sun, her brown eyes dulled from having seen far too much in life. She wore a long, faded gray cotton dress. The child wore a faded blue calico shirt and skirt, a fringed tan buckskin vest, and a blue calico bonnet so large it hid her head and face. By her size, roughly four feet, she looked to be about ten years old.

Three prospectors, all dressed in lizard skins and covered with so much dust they defied any classification as to age, race, or sex, drank and mumbled among themselves.

At a table in the far corner of the room sat a man and a woman, both dressed in patchwork—a combination of scraps of hundreds of fibers and skins popular among the poor. The man had silver hair and skin the color of ground cinnamon, and he seemed to be shivering in spite of the heat. The woman's arms were around him, her head on his shoulder, her long black hair hanging over his heart as though it could protect him.

Then there were two buffalo trail riders, the men who drove the herds of the giant animals north to market. They wore clothes of tan woven cotton that looked as though several herds of the beasts had run over them. One had long black hair streaked with gray. He sat staring into his pottery mug. The other, a tall man with ruby-red eyes and white hair so short it stood on end, strummed a guitar and hummed softly to the rhythm. At a far corner of the table sat a Comanche trader—identifiable by the long black hair that hung in braids wrapped with strands of deerskin, red-bronze skin, short stature, and beaded buckskin bags and clothing. The Comanche held a pottery mug of sage tea in his left hand and his stone tomahawk in his right.

A man in a long brown cassock of rough homespun cotton, its hood thrown back, revealing a face as pale as death and long matted hair the color of the blowing sand outside, sat at the remaining table. His orange eyes were wild with the haunted look of a man who had seen monsters staring at him from blank walls and shifting sand dunes. A rope belt tied his cassock, and from it hung his *pitero*—the small flute played by clerics of the Brotherhood of

Darkness. Matsemela uttered a curse under his breath when he saw the flute and recognized the man as a member of the ancient brotherhood. These guys can be real trouble, he thought, instinctively laying his hand on the golden hilt of his sword. It was the doctrine of the members of the Brotherhood of Darkness— *penitentes* they were still called by some on the far frontier—that only through physical pain could the soul be redeemed. And they had been known to force the unwilling to redemption.

However, it had been a long journey, and the mercenary was not about to let the presence of any sort of priest—even a member of the Brotherhood of Darkness—spoil his evening, so he set out to relax and have a good time. As he raised the pottery bottle of *pulque*, a milky white liquor made from fermented maguey, to his lips, one of the prospectors at the next table raised his own in Matsemela's direction and said in a drunken slur, "To the health of the guvnor."

"To Guvnor Winchester," several voices murmured reflexively. "May he live long."

Matsemela grunted irritably, muttered, "Live long, indeed," under his breath, and raised his pottery mug, returning the toast without a word. The guvnor, Baines Winchester, was already at least seventy-nine years old and was said not to look a day over fifty. It was whispered that he kept his health and his looks through diabolic rites of blood sacrifice and the powers of a mysterious priest. Matsemela laid his long bronze sword, its golden handle decorated with a carving of an entwined water lily and a serpent, on the table at his right hand, and set his spear at his left.

Angelina purchased the water to fill all their canteens, both skin and gourd, along with a month's supply of salt, and went out to load up the two camels. When she returned to the room, she was hoping to get her escort to leave quickly, having seen him *borracho perdido*, dead drunk, on more than one occasion. But it was not to be.

Matsemela was filling his silver flask, his wine pouch, and a couple of gourds while recounting a story about the time, back twenty years when he was new to the continent, when the irate father of a young lady with whom he had been too friendly in Delta had chased him all the way across Pecos in a sandstorm. Having already discovered that there was no stopping the man once he got started, Angelina ordered a drink and sat down beside him. She took off her quiver of silver arrows and set it and her bow down beside her, then took a small deep purple amethyst from her pouch and pressed it into his left hand.

"What's that?" he demanded, fearing more hocus-pocus.

"*Una amatista.* The amethyst prevents drunkenness."

Matsemela snorted, tossed the gem into his pocket, thinking it might be of some monetary value, then resumed his story as though he had not been interrupted.

As Angelina sat sipping her unfermented cactus juice from a red pottery mug, she looked at the mother and child across from her. Poor things, she thought. What a rough life they must be having on the frontier. "Excuse me, *señora*," she asked, trying to be friendly, "how old is your little girl?"

"Little girl? What little girl? Oh, this? This is no *niña*." The woman pulled back the calico bonnet. "Where you been, girl, that you ain't seen one o' these?"

The woman's voice had the distinctive twang characteristic of the people of western Pecos, and Angelina found her accent hard to understand. But she gasped in surprise at the sight of the little green face, the large, round black eyes, and bulging forehead. The creature was about four feet tall, with short forearms and five clawlike fingers on each hand. Its skin was finely scaled and with a shimmering quality. "What is it?"

"Why, honey, it's an itzaur," the woman answered, surprised.

Itzaurs lived—as was generally known—only in the desert west of the Terlingua Mountains. Some, because they were intelligent enough to perform simple household tasks and manual labor, were captured by humans and used as servants on the frontier. Owning an itzaur had even become something of a fad in the capital, where their owners dressed them in velvet robes and paraded them on silver chains through the streets.

"How come you ain't seen one before?"

"Uh, well, . . . I mean . . . *si*, I have seen them," Angelina stammered, anxious to hide her ignorance from strangers.

Matsemela had been listening and wondered not for the first time where this woman had been hiding all her life that she knew so little of the world. Probably been out in the wilderness meditating with some bunch of sun-baked clerics, he thought. But he whispered patiently to her, as though to a child, that the itzaur was a highly evolved reptile, of some limited intelligence. Rather like a smart ape.

The itzaur grinned at Angelina and went on munching fried prickly pear *tunas*, which it held in its green clawlike fingers. Angelina grasped her double-terminated crystal as though for protection.

"She dances," the woman said, as if to explain the creature's presence. "Real pretty. Miners up in the mountains toss coins. We been all through these parts, me and her. By the way, her name's Paradox."

"Well, let's see," one of the prospectors yelled out, pulling an old copper mouth harp from inside the filthy skins he wore and beginning to puff a little tune. The bison driver picked up the rhythm on his guitar.

The woman, who identified herself as Maude Three Stars, pulled out a goatskin tambourine and began tapping it against her knee.

Paradox hopped to her feet, kicked off her leather-strip *huarache* sandals, and began twirling happily to the rhythm. Most people in the bar started clapping along, relaxing with the entertainment.

But then a voice bellowed, "Sin and corruption! Sin and corruption! The itzaur is the creature of *el diablo*. And dancing a sin of the flesh!"

Matsemela was no animal lover. Far from it. He would have preferred to eat the creature rather than watch it dance, but the clerics of his time annoyed him. Over the centuries, they had fallen into a pathetic state, wandering the continent, preaching doom and destruction, serving no particular purpose Matsemela could discern but to annoy people. And the Brotherhood of Darkness was the worst of the lot.

The cute little itzaur was standing still in the middle of the room, tears forming in its black eyes and rolling down its round green face.

"Leave it alone," Matsemela said in a voice that could freeze a tar pit, his fingers eagerly closing around the handle of his sword.

The priest rose, his eyes wild. He smelled of rotgut hooch so strong that it could have been used to varnish the army's wicker shields.

Without saying a word, Slim, the bartender, rose very slowly. He simply waved his spear at the mercenary and the priest as though he were shooing away mosquitos. The priest sat, chastened but stewing in silence. Matsemela loudly ordered another *pulque*, and Paradox returned to her place beside her owner, her recent distress apparently forgotten.

The young man huddled with the long-haired woman at the back table spoke up. "Where do you travel from?" His eyes constantly darted to the door and the saloon's one window.

Angelina opened her mouth, but before she could say a word, Matsemela answered the question. "New Shiloh. I am escorting this lady to meet her betrothed, an officer in the territorial army." He cast a dark look at Angelina to keep her from saying otherwise.

"Army?" the young man asked. "Is it near here?"

"Not that I know of." Matsemela took a long drink.

*   *   *   *   *

Ixtpan chewed on piñon nuts as he stared reflectively at his jade calendar stone. A brilliant bolt of lightning cut through the bright blue early evening sky. And from within the earth he felt a distant rumbling.

Suddenly he felt the presence of many animals, more than normally traveled in herds this far south. "Horses! And humans!" Before the thought had fully formed in his mind, Ixtpan was on his feet, running up Dead Goat Hill.

The sun was setting in colors of flaming gold and red on the horizon before him. The scene below was worse than he could have imagined. The tiny town of Comanche Springs was being surrounded by two companies of territorial cavalry. At least a hundred men on horseback, armed with bows and arrows, axes, spears, maces, and knives, were encircling his companions.

"By all the ancient gods," he muttered angrily, "now I've got to contend with a barbarian army!" He had his longbow and arrows, but all he could hope to do with them was shoot a few Clankers before the rest of them got him. And that would not do himself, Angelina, or the Prophet any good. He looked about desperately for some means to help—or at least warn—Angelina. Then he noticed the large red boulder behind him.

CHAPTER 3

BACK HOME

Cimarron Langtry heard a sound he'd have sworn was a jagged sword striking stone, that seemed to be coming from inside his own head. Looking up, he was momentarily blinded by sunlight. Suddenly a huge black monster rose up in front of him, blotting out the horizon.

It was only an eagle rising from a prickly pear cactus on a rock near him, carrying a struggling, writhing rattlesnake in its beak.

Cimarron closed his eyes against the harsh sunlight and tried to remember what had happened. He didn't know how long he had lain in the shade of the rocks near the river. It all seemed like a bad dream. But here he was, lying in the dirt, feeling as if he had been stepped on by a bull buffalo. He touched his right arm, which was burning as if it were on fire, and felt the fiber bandages tied in place with strings of buffalohide. His fingers closed over the carved handle of the steel dagger that lay beside him. He had seen steel before, had fought against steel weapons. Only a handful of people in the world possessed it, and most of them were in the army of the Tesharka Confederation. As he examined the dagger more closely, he saw that the dark wood handle was shaped and carved in intricate patterns of spirals within spirals.

Was she real? Cimarron wondered, remembering. Was she a *curandera*? Or something else, more than a healer? He knew many people of the time considered a *curandera* to be in reality a *bruja*, or witch. And witches were the servants of ancient gods who demanded human blood and practiced destructive magic. But this woman had stopped the flowing of his blood from his body. Without her he would be nothing but vulture-cleaned bones bleaching in the sun by now. Whatever else she was, she was a *milagrosa*, a woman with the power to create a miracle. And she had done it for him, a fact that surprised him as much as finding himself still alive.

It was a good thing he had only to reach out to pick up the canteen of water and the gourd of ground corn, because he was still dizzy and weak. The food and water made his head stop throbbing and his vision clear. Finally he was able to stand with some hope of not falling promptly on his face. He stuck the steel knife in the snakeskin sheath on his brown leather belt. He was grateful the woman had left him the knife, since his own had broken. Zaco gave me that knife, he thought as he looked at the one that lay broken among the dog's bones. He was tempted to retrieve it, even as broken and useless as it was, but he rejected the idea. On land like that of southwestern Pecos, you just don't carry anything you can't use.

Cimarron started walking upriver toward Reynada, his first destination, but turned at the top of the first ridge and looked back at where he had crossed into Pecos. "*Bueno*," he said aloud with a grin, seeing that the *zopilotes*, the large black vultures, had already devoured the carcasses of the border guards, leaving only their bones and bloodstained, tattered uniforms in the sand by the river. He felt profoundly grateful to the strange trio of travelers who had saved his life and killed his enemies, and he wondered if he would ever get a chance to repay them.

As he made his way west, he stumbled on sharp and jagged rocks and mesquite spikes, and fell several times under the blistering sun. "I sure as hell wish I hadn't lost my hat in the river," he muttered more than once. A person needs a hat under a sun as fierce as this. In spite of the heat, his weakness from his wounds, and the danger he faced in his homeland, the land drove him on. He drank it in like a man dying of thirst drank from a cool stream.

The path homeward took the returning exile over the rolling hills and through shallow, twisting valleys filled with bluebonnets so thick they looked like patches of water. Heavy spring rains must have soaked the earth to bring out those hundreds of flowers. They would bloom only a week or two and then be turned to dust by the dry, hot air. But on Cimarron Langtry's day of homecoming, the hillsides were covered with patches of pinkspirit and groves of gold huisache, yellow retama, and pale green mesquite trees. And the yuccas.

The blooming yuccas stood out like giant white flames in the darkness. *Velas de Dios*, candles of God, the people of this land had called them since long before the Old World burned. The slender plants, with rough tan stalks and spiky green leaves, stood as tall as the tallest warriors, and the white petals formed a flower shaped like a candle flame, half again the height of the tree. The yucca blossoms, spread out through the sea of blue and pink and gold and green, seemed to Cimarron to light his way to his hometown, Reynada.

For days he walked westward toward Reynada, the two-century-old capital city of Pecos Territory, surviving on water-rich prickly pear *tunas* and an occasional jack rabbit or coatimundi he killed with the steel knife. He was used to walking long distances, as were most of the people of his time, many of whom had crossed half the continent on foot. When he had fled Pecos five years before, Cimarron had walked two hundred miles south of the border before he managed to steal a horse from some poor cactus farmer who lived at the base of the eastern Sierra Madre. And he had walked halfway across the *Tierra del Muerte* with Diego and his people the summer before. Half the soldiers and *soldaderas* had died—and more than half the horses. After that experience, walking for a few days across southern Pecos seemed easy.

He approached the old outpost called Snake Flats, where he had had friends in the old days, before he left Pecos. Once a thriving trading center, it had now become a ghost town with tumbleweeds blowing through its silent, dusty streets.

In what had been Snake Flats, the bodies of the dead, picked clean by the vultures, still lay where they had fallen. The town had not fallen to the Confederation army or the roaming horsetribes. The buildings, mesquite plank and adobe, were still standing, not burned by the Clankers. No skeletons lay in the streets with the horsewarriors' feather-tipped arrows still among their bones. Snake Flats had died of plague. The evil spirits that carried the plague were believed to linger in an area, even after the people were dead, so Cimarron hurried away from the empty town.

The sky was lit up with gold and amber as he neared the top of Zaragoza Bluff. Cimarron had always heard that there were no skies like those over Pecos, but he had forgotten the impact of the sky in that part of the continent.

For the first time he realized just how truly, deeply homesick he had been for the past five years, how much the place itself had drawn him back. South of Rio Bravo, he had seen mountains and jungles, palaces and temples, rivers and oceans, bright sun and eternal mist, creatures that defied imagination and description, but nothing—none of it—had ever looked as beautiful to him as the green-gold bluff and the red-gold skies over Pecos at that moment—before he reached the edge of the bluff and looked down on Reynada. He could see everything from the bluff, but remain hidden from the view of those below by jagged white rocks.

The alabaster courthouse in the heart of the ancient trade center shone white in the sun and still dominated the city. It had—miraculously—escaped the Clanker onslaught in the final days of the rebellion, when most of the city had burned. Around the courthouse was the square, or *zócalo*, where the market had been conducted for generations. From the bluff, the square looked like a solid mass of people and animals.

He looked on the colorful marketplace, the ornate buildings made of red and black volcanic *tezontle*, imported from south of the Bravo, and the adobes that shone almost white in the sunlight. Half the city had been reduced to rubble during the rebellion, but where familiar adobe buildings had stood, there now were new ones. The new buildings were built not of *tezontle* or adobe, but of the painted wood planks popular in Tesharka. Cimarron smashed his right fist into his left hand at the sight of his rebuilt hometown.

Reynada had been a large city for generations. It was, as it had been for more than two hundred years, a trading center at the crossroads of a continent. Merchants came across the continent. Priests, mystics, and seers came from the world over; from Ticonderoga to Huitchita, from Vinland to San Cruz, from Ciowacan to Pokipsie. Settlers and prospectors came from all the provinces and territories.

There must be fifty thousand people here now, Cimarron thought incredulously. *And it looks like about twenty thousand of them are Confederation* soldados. "Winchester's Clankers." He spat the derisive term aloud, his brown eyes narrowed with hatred.

The glow of the red afternoon sun lit up the soldiers' shining metal weapons. He could see their bronze hoop armor and the gleam of sunlight on copper, silver, gold, bronze, and iron. Just north of town he could see a massive wood-and-stone fort, long adobe-and-wood barracks, and camel and horse corrals. He realized clearly that the intelligence reports of a military buildup in Reynada were accurate.

The buildings around the *zócalo* were close together, but the others, homes of sheep ranchers, buffalo herders, and cactus farmers, were spread over the northern side of the valley, all the way to the Blackhawk Hills to the north and to Buckhorn Gulch to the west. He could see the Blackhawks, eerie dark hills that shone with streaks of red in the sunlight. They had been created, as legend had it, by the changes in the earth from the Great Fire that killed the Old World, and looked like no other hills Cimarron had ever seen in his hundreds of miles of travel. Throughout the valley, were scattered *jacales*, mesquite limb huts daubed with mud, and a handful of buffalohide tipis.

The *zócalo* was still ablaze with color and activity, as it had been for the centuries of the city's existence, the streets around it packed tight with shoppers, merchants, refugees, and slaves from every part of the territory and beyond. People from throughout Pecos, and even from neighboring territories—as well as from Durango in the South—came to sell their goods in Reynada's market. Cimarron could pick out the many-colored woven garb of the people from the mountains northwest of town, the colorful feathers and buckskins of those from the desert in the far West, and the scant but colorful breechcloths and sarongs of the people from the humid, sandy coast of the Southeast.

Funny, he thought, they all come here for market, but they can never get together to drive out the invaders. His memories of fighting people from the other captured territories, even from Pecos itself, during the rebellion still caused him to clench his fists and set his jaw tight.

Women knelt on the ground outside some of the sun-baked adobes, grinding corn and chocolate on the stone *metates*. Some things never change, Cimarron thought. Then his eyes focused on the ornately carved wall of the old courthouse in the center of the square. Suddenly five years melted away as if they had never happened.

An arrow strikes a young man dressed in white. He falls as other arrows strike him, his blood running into the dusty street.

Cimarron shook himself violently as though the flashback were water that could be thrown off. He was surprised and disturbed by the intensity with which he had suddenly found himself reliving the past. The flashbacks were far more vivid than memories, with all the intensity of the actual experience. They had, over the past years, driven him to desperation, drink, and violence. He reflexively reached for his knife, and his right hand grasped the carved ebony handle of the steel dagger. As he clasped the knife handle, he chased the shadowy images from his mind and forced himself to go on assessing the changes in his hometown.

He had learned in the southern mountains to make himself invisible by blending in with his surroundings, and he found an outcropping on the rocky bluff where, shielded by the red rocks, he could hide until he could enter Reynada under cover of darkness. His location gave him some protection from sentries who patrolled the outskirts of town and, at the same time, a clear view of anyone coming his way.

The colors changed around the city as the sun set and the nearly

three-quarters moon came out. The foothills looked blue in the
moonlight and the mountains beyond them pitch black. He
watched the Western Star, whose path told the people when to
plant and when to reap, the star that many people from the world
over had followed to reach Pecos in centuries past. Gazing at the
stars that shone down on his homeland, Cimarron leaned back
against the hard stone and fell asleep, with a large green and red
iguana snapping at fireflies nearby. And on this night, as on so
many others before, he was tortured by dreams of the dead and
dreams of killing.

Some nights he'd wake up in sweat, reaching out to nothing—
having been dreaming of reaching out to stop Apizaco as he ran
off into the darkness, stopping only once to look over his shoulder
and smile with that ironic half-smile of his. Other nights Cimarron would wake up trembling, having dreamed of stabbing and
stabbing and stabbing an unending line of Clankers and
federales. And no matter how many of them he killed, more rose
up to fight him until he opened his eyes in desperation to make it
stop. On this night, he dreamed yet again of his friend Zaco, as
much his brother as if they were of the same blood, running
through the streets of Reynada, and he woke up moaning, as he
had so many times before, "Forgive me, Zaco. *Lo siento*. I'm
sorry."

* * * * *

In the moments of the first faint rays of dawn, Cimarron
climbed down the bluff and headed into his old hometown. He
meandered the dusty streets, still limping and unsteady on his
feet from his encounter with the border patrol. He was hoping to
blend in as merely another street beggar or dream-touched wan-
derer, of which there were many in Reynada. His clothes were in
tatters and he was certainly dirty enough to play the part. No one
ever looks closely at someone with nothing. It's the perfect disguise, he thought.

The dusty streets were crowded with shoppers and merchants,
government officials and priests. And lots of soldiers. Refugees
from all the provinces filled the avenues. Many lived in the
streets—there were children who had known no other home but
Reynada's dusty gutters. Beggars, many of them hideously scarred
by the plague or otherwise deformed or mutilated, pulled at Cimarron's shirt and thrust their hands in his face. A young woman sat
in a debris-filled alley, trying to nurse a dead baby. There was pal-

pable tension in the crowd, a volatile combination of fear, anger, and defeat that Cimarron could feel all around him.

Cimarron caught sight of a platoon of soldiers escorting a group of rag-clad slaves through the back streets of Reynada. He could tell they were slaves because they were filthy, emaciated, and bound with copper chains. One of the soldiers was saying, "It's beautiful up there in the mountains. I tell you, you'll love it in the mines."

Cimarron stopped and looked at the old courthouse up close. The last time he had seen it seemed only five minutes—instead of five years—before. A large white marble statue of a man stood under the live oaks by the front entrance. "Sam Houston," Cimarron murmured respectfully. He reached for the rim of his hat to tip it to the hero of the long-gone tribes of Old World Texas, but remembered he had lost his hat in the Rio Bravo. The Clanker army had destroyed a lot of the cultural and religious artifacts of Pecos, but it had not dared touch the statue of Sam Houston, who was regarded as close to a god by the people of his land. Through their mythology of Texas, they kept alive the memory of a time when they had been free.

Though Texas had been destroyed, possibly even before the Great War, Cimarron, like all the young people of his age, had been raised on stories of Houston and the others, such as Travis, Crockett, Seguin, Bowie, Zapata, Villa, Guadalupe, O'Reilly, and One-Reed. Even though they were only stories, legends passed on by word of mouth from long-dead nations, they helped shape his generation's vision of the world and their place in it— and of what its world demanded of them.

Being back in Pecos brought back a lot for Cimarron. Not the least of it was the constant and inescapable presence of history.

Walking into a trading post, he was momentarily blinded by the darkness of the cavernous room. There were a dozen other shoppers in the store, buying supplies for their ranches or for expeditions to look for gold in the West. Cimarron purchased a sarsaparilla with one of the coins the strange woman healer had left him, and savored its sweetness. He had loved the drink as a child and had not had any in the five years of his exile. He bought two plump green *jalapeños* and ate each of them whole, chasing them down with a swallow of sarsaparilla. He loved to feel the heat from the peppers flood his body, and the pottery sarsaparilla bottle felt cool and smooth. He had become used to drinking from gourds, canteens, or—most often—his hands.

There were tables covered with the latest in weapons of both stone and metal. Cimarron, who was good with a knife, admired a table covered with knives and daggers of all sizes, of copper, bronze, and iron. But none was anything like the dagger the woman at the river had left him. None had a blade of steel.

Other tables held pottery: jars, pitchers, mugs, spoons, pipes, and whistles, most made from the common red clay of Pecos, but some in the black pottery from far-off Oaxaca, which was popular among the wealthy. Kitchen utensils for sale included bone spatulas and copper skillets with wooden handles.

Every kind of merchandise available on the frontier was for sale at the trading post. Tallow candles. Coffee. Tobacco. Woven cotton and wool fabrics. Horsehair lassos. Leather whips.

Drinking the sarsaparilla, Cimarron wandered around the store, picking up snatches of conversations. An old man dressed in dark furs was buying mastodon hunting picks, communicating with the clerk in the sign language that was common across the frontier. A woman in blue gingham purchased burlap for wrapping cactus to be transported north as food. A man who looked at first to be ancient, but on second look was evidently little more than twenty, was saying the Lost Dutchman mine had been found, out in the Jicarilla Mountains this time. Two filthy children dressed in prairie dog skins ran up and down the aisles, making a dreadful racket and annoying everyone.

Two men who looked to be buffalo trail drivers were talking in whispers while looking over the branding irons. Cimarron managed to catch a bit of their conversation.

"Bandidos hit the last army payroll riders," a stoop-shouldered man in a wide-brimmed, silver-trimmed black hat was saying. "Second time this month."

His dust-covered companion replied, "They strike and run across the river or into the hills. So far, the army hasn't been able to catch them." Both men laughed as though they shared a great joke.

A priest dressed in a torn and filthy cassock of coarse maguey fiber stood in a corner, screaming to no one in particular that the end of the world was at hand and that the time had long passed for even repentance to be of any use. "Any day," he swore in both Spanglish and sign language, "you will look into the gray dusk and see skeletons grinning back at you! As the Ancient Ones foretold, *los muertos* will walk again and the last day of life on the planet will be at hand."

And a well-dressed traveler, a trader carrying many woven packs and wearing the loose, embroidered cotton robes of the Zephyr tribe, declaimed to a few shoppers standing near the masto-donhide tipis, "Oh, he's dead this time. I heard it from the lieu-tenant in Sandringham, and he heard it on the best authority. Oh, yes, the Prophet is dead. Really dead this time." His curly gray beard bobbed up and down, as if for emphasis.

Cimarron's whole body tensed. He had hoped to investigate the Prophet, the man who supposedly had wiped out four divisions of Confederation cavalry, as a possible ally for Diego. Damn, he thought, that Prophet *hombre* can't be dead, not yet.

"We've heard that five times already this year," a young woman wearing jaguar skins answered derisively. "People say the Prophet can't die. He's immortal."

So it's only a rumor, Cimarron thought. He remembered that, though much of the frontier was sparsely populated, with dis-tances of hundreds of miles between cities, rumors could spread across it with the speed of a prairie fire.

"Archaic superstition. . . ."

"They say he's been killed a dozen times—and yet he lives!" The tall miner emphasized his point by waving a handy copper lantern angrily in the merchant's face. "Sorcery! That's what it is. *Malo*."

"You are right about that. The man is evil, all right." The trader stuck his lower lip out.

A tall, dark man with the deeply lined skin of a buffalo trail driver said, "Out north o' Glorieta, folks tell that the Prophet's come back from the past to do battle with Guvnor Winchester."

"Ridiculous," sniffed the merchant. "No, you can be sure that crazy young man who calls himself a prophet is dead this time—or soon will be. Colonel Reno Bismark, the Hero of Abilene, will lead a massive force of our army out to the San Cris Mountains to bring back the body and finish off the rest of the renegades. They'll stick your prophet's head on a pike outside of town. Then see who dares stand in the way of progress and civilization."

Cimarron choked on his sarsaparilla.

Col. Reno Bismark, he thought, his mind flashing on memo-ries of a childhood friend, of a boy with copper-colored hair who had run through the streets of Reynada after a rubber ball with him and Zaco, of a young man he'd played *pelota* with a hundred times. So, his old friend, Reno Bismark, had become a Clanker colonel and would be leading an expedition west soon—an expedition to destroy the Prophet. Cimarron felt as if he had been kicked in the gut. The bitter irony of it all made his head spin.

He inspected the supply of the new two-sided iron swords, trying to calm himself until he could think clearly. Then he noticed a large board hanging on the wall behind the counter. On it hung the inevitable wanted posters. Most of the people he had grown up with were probably dead, he knew, killed by the army, the plague, or the land, but he could not help smiling when he saw Ray Barnstow's picture staring down at him from faded maguey parchment. And Penny Crowfeather. Both of them wanted for sedition, treason, insurrection, robbery, and murder.

"Somethin' interest you in them posters, boy?" a deep voice with the characteristic accent of Tesharka asked him loudly.

Cimarron turned and found himself face to face with a red-faced army sergeant who stank of alligator fat—a popular mosquito repellent that had the added advantage of repelling humans. Cimarron grimaced in disgust, his right hand moving slowly toward his knife. "No. Just passing the time out of the sun, officer. I'll be on my way."

"See that you are. Reynada is a civilized town now. We don't need no barbarians dirtying it up." With that, he seized Cimarron by the collar and threw him out into the dusty, noisy street.

By high noon, Cimarron was nestled in a shaded corner of the town square, leaning against a cedar post that supported a roof of semicircular red tiles over the long adobe cantina. A good position from which to pose as a beggar and a good position from which to observe his old hometown.

The square was packed with people displaying goods for sale in the bustling *mercado*. Each merchant displayed merchandise on a blanket about three feet square, often with colorful geometric patterns and designs woven into it.

Animals were everywhere. Many people led or rode their beasts—camels, donkeys, or horses. Burro-drawn wagons hauled corn from the west, firewood from the mountains in the north, and oranges from the southeast valley. Chickens ran loose, cackling through the streets, narrowly avoiding being stepped on by the people and the larger animals. Wild dogs ran among the people, and Cimarron could see a pack of hyenas lurking on the outskirts of town. He noticed that many of the animals were so thin that their ribs showed through their hides.

Cimarron rose and wandered down the avenue. The streets and spaces among the blankets were choked with people, and Cimarron was jostled repeatedly—by a burro drawing a small wooden wagon, by several venders sticking everything from green and red chiles to arrows dipped in rattlesnake poison in his face, and by an *jorobado*, or hunchback, dwarf dressed in short leather pants and a flower-embroidered shirt, who played a wooden flute. Beggars, none of them more than ten years old, followed Cimarron through the streets with their hands outstretched. Soon the youthful beggars gave up, realizing he had nothing to give them, and went after a man in long, flowing red-and-white-striped robes, who was trying to lead a heavily burdened camel through the market.

The air was filled with the enticing aromas of buffalo fajitas, rattlesnake slices, armadillo steaks, and javelina chops sizzling over many fires. An old man in a high silver turban and purple breechcloth sold dried gulf fish that hung from a pole beside him. A woman dressed entirely in black robes, with a black veil that hid her face, sold jaguar skins spread out on a blanket. A group of women in the colorful woven dresses of the mountains sold iguanas, whose rubbery flesh was used in chile pepper stew.

A man in a wide-brimmed black hat with a silver hatband displayed a small selection of Old World artifacts—bits of the precious metals whose original uses were no longer identifiable, chips of the magic stone called concrete, pieces of marble statues—some of them allegedly parts of statues of Sam Houston and the other gods and heroes of the past—all of them selling for a virtual fortune—to a group of black-robed priests. Old World relics, believed by many to contain within them the spirits or magic of the people of the fabled past, were highly coveted and sold at tremendous prices, both legally and on the black market. A foot-long piece of blackened granite, with the mysterious expression "August, A.D. 2039" carved in it, was priced at fifty thousand jadas. A three-inch-long piece of wood, its traces of white paint still barely visible, was advertised as a genuine relic from the guitar of St. Elvis and was for sale at the exorbitant price of one hundred thousand jadas—a price it would surely fetch, since relics of the famous white guitar had been known to heal the sick and raise the dead. The trader even sold tiny bits of the colorful, hard material called plastic for five thousand jadas apiece—more money than most people could make in two years. It's funny how much money folks'll spend to buy a scrap of a dead world, Cimarron thought.

Jewelry merchants displayed shining stones and beautifully worked metals. A young man who wore his red hair shaved on the sides and standing on end down the center of his head stood beside a pine table with several stones from the mountains. A woman with short, snow-white hair displayed some of the jaguar bone scrimshaw that appeared to be the current rage among the military officers, government officials, and well-to-do traders—the only people who could afford it.

A few well-dressed individuals had green and brown itzaurs trailing behind them, carrying their purchases in their clawlike hands. They've made slaves of those poor, stupid creatures, Cimarron thought angrily.

Refugees from every corner of the territories and beyond had been driven into the city by the army, famine, and the plague. The city, once lovely and open, was now filthy and crowded.

Hundreds of voices blended into one loud cry: "Buy here!" "Buy here!" "Best price on black pottery! Direct from Mescalero!" "Fresh berries from Bastrop!" "Feather weavings direct from Lost Hope!" "Bobcat skins!" "Slothskin rugs!" "¡Pulque! First-rate *pulque*! Sure to take the chill out of a cold evening on the range!"

By the Abaddon Wall a group of priests in tattered maguey fiber robes were preaching to a group of children and three dwarfs—who appeared from their orange gowns and bald heads to be monks from the East.

Cimarron turned down an alley, and it was then that he saw it. Someone had tried to scrape off the red paint, but the symbol that had been painted on the wall was still unmistakable. It was a five-pointed star—the Lone Star, the symbol of old Texas. It was the image on the blue background of the Pecos flag. Cimarron looked long and hard at it. He leaned against the opposite adobe wall, then slowly sank to the ground, drawing his knees to his chest. He bent over, his head resting against his knees, his face buried in his arms.

Two women wearing colorful, striped *sarapes* walked past him. He overheard one of them comment, "They say the *curandera* is here among us, the one whose magic was strong enough to put out a fire in San Cristobal when the padres tried to burn her as a *bruja*. She will heal the Prophet and he will lead an army out of the west to free the land, as has been foretold since the gods created time. . . ."

Cimarron was startled to hear talk of a powerful *curandera* and wondered if the women could be referring to the black-haired woman who had healed him beside the river. And he needed to find out more about this prophet who'd whipped the Clankers so badly. He got up and started after the two women, following them out of the alley and onto the square. Then a platoon of Confederation foot soldiers wearing bronze hoop armor over blue cotton uniforms came marching through the square. Cimarron stepped into an arched doorway, out of the soldiers' view.

Two of the soldiers stepped out of line and helped themselves to the corncakes being sold by an old woman in the red and black garments of the highland Chimayo tribe. She objected and one of them hit her with his spear handle. From an abobe wall, a flash of black and blue lightning hurled itself against the soldier. This particular lightning bolt, Cimarron noted, punched and kicked furiously.

"You son of a ground sloth!" the figure yelled.

The soldier was instantly on the ground, possibly thinking he must have been jumped by ten rebels. Actually it was only one boy.

Damn it, Cimarron thought. He told himself that if he got involved by defending the boy, he would blow his chance of slipping back into town unnoticed, and that he would probably end up in jail, if not dead. But I can't sit and watch the kid be hauled off, he thought angrily. They'll kill him.

Cimarron jumped up and pulled the second soldier off the boy, knocking him out with one fast, well-directed punch. The boy kneed the other soldier in the groin and was about to strike him when Cimarron slugged the man with a hard right, sending him sprawling, unconscious, to the ground. Cimarron grabbed the boy by the collar and took off running. The rest of the squad was on its way back through the square. They saw their men in the dirt and immediately ran after the perpetrators.

The boy ran fast, surprisingly as fast as Cimarron, who had run up and down mountains while living in the south. Cimarron turned into an alleyway between two adobe buildings. The boy hollered, "No! This way," and jerked him into the squadron's line of vision.

Cimarron swore violently. He would have kept cursing, but the ground opened up at his feet and he fell in.

They were in some kind of deep dirt pit, sheltered by a large building.

"This is my turf, and I give the orders down here," the boy snarled, turning to Cimarron. "You follow me and don't try no heroics." He rolled a boulder between them and the pit's entrance and gestured for Cimarron to follow him through a dark, narrow tunnel that went into the ground.

Since he could hear the shouts of the squadron leaders right above them and had no intention of letting them catch him, Cimarron lay in the dirt and followed the strange boy into a narrow tunnel. Soon they came to a wall of rock.

Great, Cimarron thought. By St. Bowie's knife, we're trapped here.

But the boy forced his fingers beneath the rock and suddenly it rolled to the side, revealing another dark and narrow passageway. Once on the other side, the boy pressed a stone in the wall, and the rock rolled back, hiding the tunnel from anyone who could follow them that far.

They crawled, sometimes flat on their stomachs, through the narrow, shallow, and pitch-dark tunnel until Cimarron felt as if he had eaten a ton of the red dirt of Pecos. The tunnel wound around so many times it was confusing, and he lost all sense of direction. The wood planks that supported the tunnel scraped his flesh, still bruised from the beating at the border, but he kept following.

Finally the tunnel widened into a small cavern. Though it was a relief to stand, Cimarron still had to bend over because of the low ceiling. The boy reached over and picked up a flint off a tree trunk table. He struck the flint and lit a small candle, revealing dark walls of earth from which the room had been carved.

"We stay here 'til the gang gets 'em off our tail. Believe me, any minute now those sloths will have a lot more to worry about than us," the boy said. "Meantime, I'm Stether Delgado. Make yourself at home." He gestured with a sweep of his hand at a woven reed mat on the floor. "Oh, yeah—and thanks."

"So this is the furniture, is it?" Cimarron sat lightly on the mat.

"It is, and we're proud to have it. We don't need no cracks from an outsider." He looked older close up—but sixteen at the most. He wore a faded brown cotton shirt and black cotton pants. His boots were knee-high, fringed buckskin. He was fair-skinned and so thin, almost frail, that it was hard to believe that, only moments before, he had deliberately jumped a heavily armed soldier. His hair was coal black, and he used the jelly from an aloe plant to make it stand high before it fell in a long cascade to his shoulders. A multicolored scarf was wound around this head and a gold hoop earring hung from his right ear. His eyes were a clear, bright blue, like the morning skies off the southern coast. In a flying flash, he had made a fierce impression. Standing still, he looked like an angry child.

The underground cavern was rocked by the sound of screaming and running feet from above, quickly followed by the unmistakable sound of crackling flames and then the sound of a large wooden building collapsing.

"There goes the army's supply depot across the square," the boy said, laughing so hard he held his sides. "That was our real target. You mixed yourself up in *my* diversion, old man." The boy laughed until tears rolled down his face.

* * * * *

Inside the saloon, the mercenary was holding forth. "I tell you the world's going to the dogs. Paris is nothing but a teaming pest hole these days. Worse than Detroit. Not that there's anyplace better. Myself, I came originally from Lagos, on the northeast coast of Afria. Left there, must've been twenty years ago, maybe more. Who keeps up with the years, anyway? Oh, Lagos was a great town, seaport and all—'til we got this do-gooder king. He ran off the pirates and closed down the waterfront bars and . . . uh," he paused, noticing Angelina's eyes widening with interest, "well . . . other places my comrades and I used to enjoy. It was becoming a real cultural center. With universities. Even an observatory. Scholars started arriving in droves." He shuddered at the memory. "That's when I hit the road. When civilization's on the way in, buckaroos, you can be sure Matsemela Nyakir's on his way out. How else would I've ended up in this pathetic . . ." His train of thought was broken by the sound of many animal hooves. He and Angelina exchanged knowing glances so fast the others never noticed.

Matsemela jumped up, sword in hand, and grabbed Angelina by the arm so hard that her long black hair spun around her. "Ah, my friends, this sweet child and I must be in New Shiloh before the sun sets on another day. Thanks for everything," he said, moving away from the direction of the door.

"What's going on?" One of the prospectors jumped up, waving his bronze axe. An arrow flew through the window and he fell to the packed-dirt floor with blood spurting from his throat. By then, everyone in the tavern was on their feet with a weapon in hand. But it was too late.

A deep and powerful voice—a voice accustomed to command—called out, "This is Colonel Reno Bismark of the army of the Tesharka Confederation of Territories. You've got some escaped slaves in there, Jivaro Jaguar and Tamara Redwolf. Send them out. Cooperate and no one will get hurt."

"Slave?"

"¿Esclavo?"

Voices murmured throughout the room as everyone looked at everyone else, wondering who the army was after. It didn't take long to figure it out. The couple who had been sitting huddled at the back table were embracing each other. The woman faced the rest of them, tears running down her face, and said, "Yes, we are the ones they want."

"Okay, then you get on out there and give yourselves up," Slim the saloonkeeper said, pointing his flint spear menacingly at them.

"If you send us out there, they'll kill us," Tamara cried.

"You can die in here or out there, and we'd a whole lot rather it be out there." Slim was firm, and the other patrons backed him up with grunts and threatening gestures with their weapons. "Nobody leaves a mess in my saloon."

Angelina's wide, almond-shaped eyes were flashing in shades of violet and metallic blue. She had seen the work of the army of Tesharka. She and her companions had passed the ruins of the once-beautiful ancient city of Del Rio on the Bravo. She had seen the burned remains of the adobe and marble buildings, the grass growing through the broken streets, the skeletons of the dead lying where they had fallen. "You cannot turn these people over to those soldados!" She spoke up so forcefully, it startled Slim—not to mention Matsemela. "You know they will kill an escaped slave."

"Too bad, ain't it," Slim replied. "But business is business, and I can't have no trouble here. So git."

"And what will they do to us once they have their slave?" Angelina asked quietly.

"We'll take our chances." The priest pulled out a flint knife and pointed it at the slave's heart.

Suddenly the scene was interrupted by a strange, loud rumbling and the sound of horses scattering. Before anyone in the saloon had time to even speculate on what unspeakable weapon was being sent their way, a huge red boulder came crashing through the armadillo-shell wall. The pine tables, pottery mugs, and plates of posole went flying. The three prospectors were knocked over by their table. The itzaur jumped out of the path of the boulder, missing it by inches. Slim was less fortunate. The bolder struck him directly, killing him instantly. Maude Three Stars ran out the door of the saloon and was struck by a dozen Confederation arrows.

As the walls began falling in, Matsemela grabbed Angelina's arm. "Let's go. Stick with me."

"¿Qué? What are you saying? We cannot leave these people. . . ."

"The hell we can't!" Matsemela tossed the healer over his shoulder and carried her out of the crumbling building.

The boulder had broken the line of cavalry that had the saloon surrounded, and the soldiers were running around in confusion. Thinking they were under attack from the hills, they pulled back momentarily. Matsemela's well-trained eyes spotted the break, and he ran for it.

Matsemela was a big man, but his size did not slow him. He could run as fast as a man half his age—which, on that particular night, was a good thing. They made it to the boulders at the bottom of the foothills of the Terlingua Mountains, where they were sheltered from the searching eyes of troopers.

Angelina screamed, "What are you doing?" She was clutching one of her embroidered leather bags of stones and feathers to her heart, desperate to summon the protective energy within it.

"Saving your life. Now lie low and shut up."

From the rocky cliff they saw and heard it all. Soldiers rushed the Armadillo, dragging the surviving patrons—the priest, the three prospectors, the two bison trail riders, the Comanche trader, the black-haired cook, and the fugitives, Tamara and Jivaro—out.

Both Angelina and Matsemela knew immediately which soldier was in command. Reno Bismark, the young colonel from Pecos who had already made a name for himself in military circles by subduing a rebellion in his own homeland, was easy to pick out. He was tall and broad-shouldered, with long hair and a mustache, both the color of molten copper. He wore a wide-brimmed blue hat trimmed in gold and a vest of bronze hoop armor over a blue uniform. He rode a magnificent blue-gray stallion with a shining silver mane and tail, larger than any horse Matsemela had ever seen.

"So these are the ones who've given us so much trouble," Bismark said as a soldier threw Jivaro and Tamara to the dirt in front of him. Tamara fell face down, and Jivaro lay over her, trying to protect her. "We can't have slaves trying to escape," the colonel said with a laugh, drawing his long steel sword. "Sets a bad example." His blue eyes shone like the blade's steel as he surveyed the young couple helpless before him.

Matsemela kept dragging Angelina up the jagged rocks that were the beginning of a deadly and little-explored mountain range, but her eyes kept returning to the scene outside the saloon. The ground beneath them was rough and tore their clothing and skin.

The screams of Bismark's victims echoed throughout the hills, like the wailing of the ghosts of all the vanished, ancient races of the land, as the Clankers cut down with their iron swords all those they had routed from the Armadillo Saloon. The two bison trail riders tried to resist, fighting even after they had received mortal wounds.

"Don't look down there." Matsemela put his strong arm around Angelina's waist and lifted her to the next ridge.

But she did look back—in time to see the colonel himself stab Jivaro, once, then again. Jivaro rolled over, dying. Tamara lay trembling on the ground beside the man she loved. Bismark slowly raised his sword and said, "This is what happens to traitors." Then he plunged the weapon into her heart and laughed long and hard.

"The next rise is only a few feet away." Matsemela grabbed Angelina and pulled her along.

Crawling around boulders and scrambling from one ridge to the next, they made their way steadily up the hill. But the sounds of the massacre carried mercilessly across the land, and they could not help looking back. They witnessed the destruction of Comanche Springs.

"Bring the fire!" Reno Bismark commanded, and a sergeant stepped forward carrying a small stone oven in which a fire burned. "Burn this pestilence!" Another soldier stepped forward with a dozen arrows and lit the tip of each in the fire, then passed them on to camel riders near him. The colonel waved his right arm, and his soldiers shot the burning arrows into the remains of the saloon, which immediately burst into flames. Then they shot burning arrows into every building of Comanche Springs. The people were forced from their homes by the flames—and when they ran out of the burning buildings, they were cut down by the slashing swords of the cavalry.

Within minutes the whole town was ablaze, and the town of Comanche Springs belonged only to its ghosts.

Angelina shuddered as she heard Colonel Bismark proclaim his victory to his assembled troops.

"This is a great day in the holy struggle to bring civilization to this continent, and you can all be proud of your part in it. Today we have destroyed barbarians who stood in the way of our sacred destiny to unite this land from coast to coast under the Tesharka Confederation's leadership."

"Will even Ixtpan's prophet be able to stop this madness?" Angelina laid her head against Matsemela's broad chest and clutched the turquoise medallion as though it could stop the killing or help the dead. The medallion, two thousand years before, had belonged to the greatest prophet of her own people, and she sought the help of its powers now.

An unexpected sound below them made both Matsemela and Angelina jump, ready to fight or run. Matsemela, so it seemed, was not the only one to have seen the opening in the ring of cavalry made by Ixtpan's boulder.

The mercenary uttered a groan and several rapid curses, and Angelina cried out in surprise as Paradox climbed onto the rocky ledge next to them.

"Let's get the hell out of here," Paradox said in a strange voice that managed to be both high-pitched and rasping, surprising Matsemela into an unaccustomed silence. Her round green face was set in an expression of barely controlled rage, an impression heightened by the furrows in her bulging forehead. "Follow me."

Neither Matsemela nor Angelina moved.

"You *are* a creature of evil." Matsemela had seen dozens of itzaurs, and not one of them had ever spoken a word.

"Just because we don't waste our breath talking to you brainless humans . . . Look, you two can follow me or you can wait for that barbarian's soldiers to find you. The choice is yours." With that, Paradox began climbing the boulders behind them and suddenly disappeared, seemingly into a wall of red rock.

Angelina and Matsemela looked at each other, wide-eyed in amazement.

Angelina took off after the childlike, two-legged creature in the blue calico skirt and fringed buckskin vest.

Matsemela followed, cursing bitterly in several languages.

* * * * *

For Cimarron Langtry there was no going back after the encounter with the Clankers in Reynada, particularly once the army's sup-

ply depot went up in flames and he had been seen striking a soldier in the middle of the marketplace. Hundreds of Clankers were
combing every inch of Reynada and its environs for the perpetrators, and maybe one of them had gotten a good look at him before
he and the kid gave them the slip. Cimarron had no choice but to
follow the boy—who did, at least, have a route out of the city that
was not observable. I'll lie low for a while, then head west, Cimarron thought. Or slip back into town. Maybe one of these days, I'll
learn to control myself. Who was the kid to me that I should've
gotten mixed up with him? he asked himself.

Cimarron and Stether Delgado followed the tunnels for hours,
then emerged north of Reynada. When the boy promptly led him
to two hidden and tethered horses, a pinto and a bay, Cimarron
decided to stick with him.

"Let's go, buckaroo. Or do you want to head off on foot?"
Stether jumped on the bare back of the pinto.

"All right, kid, you're on," Cimarron responded, mounting
the bay.

They rode west for two hours to the blackened, twisted Blackhawk Hills, a freak formation, not of nature but of the Great War,
when mountains had crumbled and flatlands had been pushed
into mountains. They made their way along narrow, hidden pathways, where the mesquite grew not as a tree, as it did elsewhere,
but as a shrub barely a foot high, snaking all over the ground, its
long spikes waiting to cut anyone passing by. Stether took a long
bronze sword, its point broken off, from a sheath tied to his saddle
and hacked a path for them in some places.

"We were through this way last week," Stether said, grimacing
as he hacked at the thorny plant, swinging the broken sword from
on horseback. "This damn stuff grows back as fast as you cut it
down."

Finally, in a concealed clearing surrounded by jagged black
walls half a mile high, they dismounted, leaving the horses tethered. Stether approached the rock wall and grabbed a bundle of
dead mesquite.

"By St. Elvis's blue shoes!" Stether cursed as the mesquite
thorns pierced his hands.

Cimarron started to intervene but stopped dead in his tracks,
startled to see that where the dead mesquite had been was the
three-foot-high entrance to an old mine. "What's this, kid?" he
asked. "Don't tell me we're going in there?" The wrinkles at the
corners of his brown eyes deepened as he surveyed the opening in

the black mountain wall.

"I am, and so are you, unless you want to wait around for the Clankers. Just follow me."

Cimarron was sorely tempted to get back on his horse and keep going, but the sound of many horses' hooves nearby caused him to change his mind.

"Let's go," Stether said. He ran and untied the horses, slapping the rump of one to send them both off at a gallop, hopefully misleading whoever was approaching them. "Sounds like an army. Our people would've given a signal."

Cimarron reluctantly followed the boy into the dark mine.

Once inside, Stether reached out and pulled the bundle of mesquite limbs back over the small mine opening. He left the broken sword by the mine entrance. It would only be in his way from here on.

Another hour later, after more crawling through old tunnels, Cimarron was muttering, "I should've let those Clankers have you!" A wooden plank splintered beneath him and slivers pierced his hands, arms, and knees. "How long ago were these infernal tunnels dug?"

"This one?" Stether replied. "I'd say around a hundred years ago. These mines've been shut down since before I was born. Guess all the silver was gone. The narrower tunnels, some of them are recent. We connected some of the mine tunnels ourselves."

"By St. Bowie's knife, this plank must have been laid before my grandparents—whoever the hell they may have been—were born."

"You don't know who your people were?" Stether asked, grunting as he pulled himself through a narrow passageway on his knees and elbows.

"No. Just that they came from Pecos." Some of Cimarron's Comanche friends told him they saw a Comanche soul in his eyes. His *compañeros* from Durango told him they saw the blood of their ancestors in his brown skin. When Dezcalzo Two Creeks had found him as an abandoned infant, he had been wrapped in the Pecos flag. That flag was his only legacy, and even in his childhood he had taken to heart all the things it stood for: independence, honor, and reverence for the land. He came from Pecos, a descendant of the tribes of Texas, and that was all that mattered to him. Beyond that, he knew nothing of who or what he was, and he did not really care. This matter-of-fact attitude about his background was common among the people of the frontier, many of whom were unaware of their own origins, as well as many who knew but preferred to forget.

"Well, I knew mine," Stether said softly, pausing for a moment in the darkness. "Clankers killed them, my parents and my brother, and they carried off my little sister five years ago when they took Puerto Laredo."

Puerto Laredo, a great seaport where the Rio Bravo emptied into the *Golfo de Huracán*, was an ancient city, tracing its heritage to before the Great War, when it was far inland. According to legend, the city only became a seaport when the Great War caused the seas to rise and the gulf waters covered hundreds of miles of land that had once been part of Texas.

"I'm sorry, kid. Really." So he's a Pecos boy, Cimarron thought. Just as I figured.

"It's over and done," Stether answered.

Cimarron had badly scraped the skin off his hands, elbows, and knees from the hours of crawling through rock and earth over wooden planks, rock, stone, and dirt. The rough, often narrow, tunnels had further shredded his clothes and torn his boots. His whole body hurt, and he was still weak and dizzy from his near-fatal encounter with the border patrol at the river.

He could see it all as if he were detached from himself, as if he were an observer watching his life from a distance and trying to make sense of it. At the moment, he didn't see much sense. He felt as if he must have gone miles following a crazy kid through the dark tunnels and dusty, stale air. Sometimes they seemed to go almost straight down and sometimes straight up through the endless maze. And sometimes Cimarron would have sworn they were turning around and around like the wooden barrels he and his friends had rolled through the dirt streets of Reynada when they were kids.

About the time Cimarron figured they would never see the outside world again, he saw a light, very small but bright. Well, that's a surprise, he thought. The light was still a long way ahead, but he knew he could reach it, and knowing he could get there gave him strength to go on. It reminded him of the light he'd seen when he lay dying by the Rio Bravo. But that light had no source. This light, he realized as he squinted and looked ahead through an opening in the rock wall, came from a star. When he smelled and felt fresh air, he was, for that brief moment, almost sorry he had underestimated the boy.

Then, just before they reached the small opening, Stether

stopped and spoiled the illusion by whispering, "This is the most dangerous part, ahead of us."

"Why didn't I figure that?" Cimarron growled, his hand on his steel dagger.

"Are you with me or not?" Stether turned, holding a small bronze knife directly between Cimarron's eyes.

Cimarron didn't flinch. "We both hate the Clankers, so I reckon that puts us on the same side. Doesn't it?" He could not control the fierce glare he fixed on the boy.

"For now." Stether put the weapon away. He crawled on for a few feet until he was near the mine opening. He leaned back against the rock wall and gulped the fresh air. Then he pushed his scarf up above his forehead and looked out on the night sky. "Clankers wiped out our main tunnel a couple weeks back. Burned it. Took out four of our best people. We had to make a fast change to hit the supply depot—and these tunnels are the best we could do."

"Where are we?" Cimarron's voice was suddenly, surprisingly, calm, almost gentle, as he sagged against the tunnel wall, drew his knees up to his chest, and closed his eyes.

"In the Blackhawks. Pretty far up. It's still desolate out here, even with the fort and the government in Reynada. But they still send patrols sometimes. Some of our folks oughtta be keeping them pretty busy in a box canyon by now. . . ." He took out a corn shuck cigarette from a shirt pocket, struck a flint to light it, and inhaled deeply.

Stether offered Cimarron a cigarette, which the man refused.

"Tombstone Canyon." Cimarron grinned, and his face softened in the dim filtered light.

"How'd you know? You from around here?"

"Maybe. I guess y'all know the hidden passage out of Tombstone through the caves?"

"Yeah. So you are from these parts."

"Get me out of here alive, and maybe I'll tell you about it, kid."

"There's an open path along the canyon wall. It's not far, but we're sitting ducks to anyone watching from below—or above. If you slip, well, it's a long way down, so hang on."

"Hang on to what, the loose rocks?"

"You got it, pardner. Hang on, lay low, stay a few paces behind me. Makes it harder for them to spot us. And not a sound. No matter what happens to either of one us." Stether slipped out into the night air.

Cimarron gave Stether a six-foot head start, then slipped out behind him. He mechanically watched the bottoms of the boy's buckskin boots as he inched along the open ledge. He could see, even in the starlight, that he and the boy were high up in the hills. The Blackhawks were nothing compared to the towering Sierra Madre, but they were high enough that there'd be no surviving a fall.

They made their way slowly and carefully across the cliff to rocks several feet away that offered them shelter. They were drenched in sweat from the effort of crawling through the tunnels, and Cimarron shivered in the night air.

Just as Stether was about to reach out and touch the rock sanctuary, an arrow flew past him and bounced off the sandstone only inches above his outstretched hand. Both young men froze, pinned down and defenseless. Only their ears told them what was happening around them.

Another arrow shot through the air. They could tell by the sound that this one was not aimed in their direction. Someone was firing at their attackers. They dared not move a muscle.

In less than a second, they heard another whistling noise, then a man's scream, the sound of a body striking the ground with great impact—as if after a long fall—and the sound of a running horse. Then they heard the same sounds repeated.

An arrow hit the wall just below Stether and then another whistled by, followed by another scream, another fall, and another horse running off into the hills. And then silence. Cimarron instinctively looked up.

At first he saw no one on the ledge above them, but then he caught the glint of silver and realized he was looking up into a pair of large, round eyes. The person was as dark as the night and consequently was practically invisible—until she stepped to the edge of the ridge and the moonlight shone directly on her. She held up a dark wooden bow with a brown eagle feather attached at one end. In her other hand she held an arrow. Cimarron knew she could shoot them both before they could possibly reach shelter. She raised her bow.

But instead of firing at them, she only held up the bow and waved it from side to side in some kind of greeting or salute to Stether, then turned and disappeared.

Stether made it into the rocks, Cimarron right behind him. They were hidden by the earth again.

Cimarron heard a strange noise, soft and muffled, like crying or gasping. For a moment, he thought the boy must have been hit by one of the arrows. But he quickly realized Stether was biting his lip to keep from laughing out loud.

"You're warped, kid. People south of the river say we're crazy up here in Pecos, and they're right."

"She's our best archer," Stether said proudly.

"Who in the name of all the saints of the Alamo . . . ?"

Stether rested against the tall red rocks to catch his breath. "Her name is Iphigenia."

The cavern reminded Cimarron of the massive prehistoric temple in Taotitlan—huge and dark. It had been created by opening an old mine shaft and bracing it with old timbers. He could make out the presence of several people. A handful of torches and a couple of hand-held copper lanterns where corncobs burned cast a flickering orange light. We're deep inside a good-sized hill, he thought. It's probably Cotula, the highest and widest of all the Blackhawks.

"This is home," Stether said jovially, waving his right arm at the growing crowd in the cavern.

The pupils of Cimarron's brown eyes widened as he grew accustomed to the light, and he realized the cavern was filling with people. "All right, you little bastard, who are you?"

"The Clankers call us bandidos. We're from all over Pecos, all over the continent."

Stether laid a hand firmly on Cimarron's shoulder, as though reassuring a younger brother. "Most of us'd be dead already, and the rest would be stealing and begging in the streets, if we weren't here together. A gang can steal a lot more than one kid can. A gang doesn't have to beg. And, by St. Elvis's blue shoes, we do hurt the Clankers. They need those supplies brought in from the North, and we manage to stop a few of them. How do you think we've armed ourselves so well?" He laughed, and Cimarron realized the light was gleaming off weapons of iron, bronze, and copper all around him.

Cimarron was surrounded by at least a hundred people and more were coming out of the narrow tunnels. He blinked in astonishment when he realized the youth of the people surrounding him. Some of them are hardly more than babies, he thought, realizing that some could be no more than ten. The kid is the oldest one of the bunch.

They were urchins from all nations and tribes of the vast continent, in all sizes and all colors of the rainbow. One boy had bronze skin and black hair and wore coyote skins; another boy, barely three feet tall, with tan skin and short, curly brown hair, wore a deerskin breechcloth; a pretty girl with long, dark braids wore loosely woven maguey fiber; another girl with hair as yellow as wheat wore rags that had once been a holy bison robe.

So these are the bandidos in the hills, Cimarron thought with disappointment. They're only a gang of kids. But they're well-armed kids.

"Hey, where's everyone else?" Stether was looking around for the young people who had accompanied him in the attack on the supply depot in Reynada.

"Not back yet," a girl with long black braids answered.

"Don't worry, Stether," said a boy with red hair, who Cimarron figured to be about twelve. "They'll be along soon."

As if in response to the boy's prediction, the woman Stether had called Iphigenia ran into the cavern, laughing. She was tall, graceful, and as dark as roasted coffee beans, with large, round brown eyes and pale rose-pink lips. Her long hair curled around her head and shoulders like a black aura. She wore a necklace of feathers, stones, and shells and a short leather tunic that revealed the well-developed muscles of her arms and legs.

Great Houston's ghost, I should've known she'd be mixed up with the kid, Cimarron thought when Stether ran to her and they kissed, embracing passionately, their lithe young bodies molding against one another.

Iphigenia set down her bow and quiver of arrows.

A resonant rhythm on *teponaztli* drums filled the room. The low but insistent pounding on the tree-trunk drums grew louder and faster until the air vibrated. Iphigenia began to move to the rhythm, jerking her body almost violently with each beat, moving faster and faster, spinning wildly around the room. She took Stether's hand, and he began matching her every movement as the drums grew louder. Someone picked up the rhythm on a guitar.

Others in the cavern joined in the wild dancing and lost themselves in the rhythm and motion, as though they were free—not trapped inside the earth. The sound grew louder and faster, making the room pulsate.

Someone sent up an eerie cry that was louder than the drums: "Yeeehaah!"

Cimarron had long ago learned the ancient battle cry of Pecos, handed down to each generation since humans crawled from the wreckage of the worldwide fire centuries before. He joined his voice with that of the kids as the dancing stopped.

Iphigenia ended her frantic movement and leaned, breathless, against a thick, live oak post. The room grew silent.

"Great shots, Iphi," Stether said cheerfully.

"When I saw the fire burning in Reynada, I figured I'd better be on the lookout. There were three of them on your trail. I tracked them from the time they rode into the hills."

"Don't know what we'd do without her," Stether told Cimarron. "This is Iphi. From Delta Territory, out east. She was," he lowered his voice to a bitter whisper, "a slave. And this guy saved me from getting caught in Reynada," he said, by way of introducing the newcomer to Iphigenia and the others. "He's okay. By the way, what's your name, *old man?*" He let his already slow Pecos drawl linger in emphasis on the last two words and broke into a boyish grin.

"Cimarron Langtry. Pleased to make y'all's acquaintance." He reflexively reached for his hat to tip it but remembered it was more than likely already in the gulf, being nibbled by redfish.

Iphi took his left hand. "Welcome. And thanks for bringing this *boy* back." She grinned at Stether.

Cimarron grimaced inwardly but smiled anyway. "I'm the one who should be thanking you. You're a damn good shot."

"I learned to shoot before I could talk," Iphigenia answered softly. "I had to."

Stether was bouncing on the balls of his feet, as though he were about to start dancing again. "Where are the others?" he asked. "Boots and Jess and Terra and Velez?"

"Not back yet," came the answer again from a small boy with golden-blond hair.

"They'll be back soon. I know they will. Back in Reynada, the old man here and I heard the Clanker's supply depot burn," Stether said, looking at the eager faces around him. "Came down practically on top of us."

Several of those assembled uttered the sacred cry, "Yeeeeehaah!" again, at confirmation that the target had been successfully hit.

Suddenly, however, the cries turned from joy to anguish. A muscular boy with shoulder-length white-blond hair staggered out of a mine tunnel across the room from Cimarron, his young face a mask of tragedy. He was stumbling because he carried a heavy burden.

"Jesse!" Stether and Iphi both cried out to the blond boy. "What happened?"

The boy carefully laid his burden at Stether's feet. It was the body of another, younger boy. "They were waitin' for us in Tombstone Canyon. It was a trap. Terra and Velez're dead." Jesse fought back tears. "I brought Boots through the east shafts. He died in the tunnel he and I dug together last spring."

Cimarron was startled to recognize Jesse's distinctive accent— he was from Tesharka. Guess I shouldn't be so surprised, he thought. There must be some folks in Tesharka who don't like the way things are. But I sure never met one before.

"Oh, Jess, no," Iphi said, laying her hand on the blond boy's shoulder consolingly.

Jess took her hand and squeezed it, then quickly let go. His father was Cal Olivera, the general who had been wiped out along with all his men by the Prophet and his forces at Isleta, a man beloved by the guvnor—and the rest of the powerful men—of Tesharka. But Jesse had despised his father and everything he stood for, preferring the life of a runaway in a gang of orphans in the Blackhawk Hills to a life of privilege in the capital. Now, as he looked at his dead friend, Boots, everything he had done against his father's world—running away, striking out by damaging Confederation property—seemed pitifully little.

A girl with long black braids held a torch near the two boys, and everyone gasped when the light fell upon Boots. He was a beautiful child, certainly no more than twelve years old, with a round face and skin the color of red clay, framed by gold ringlets. His clothes were no more than torn rags and scraps of prairie dog and rabbit skins.

Stether knelt beside his dead young friend. "I swear on St. Elvis's grave, we'll get back at the Clankers for this," he said emphatically. Iphi stood at his side, her left hand on his shoulder, her right on the handle of her short bronze knife.

Jesse's voice was so low only Stether and those close to him could hear. "Forget getting back at anyone. Get everyone out of here. Someone must've ratted to the Clankers. They must've gotten their hands on one of our people and forced him to talk. The whole army'll be out here any minute."

"*Verdad*. You'd better get these kids away from here." Cimarron dropped to one knee beside Stether and the others. "What's your back-up plan for when you have to leave these tunnels and caverns?"

"Here it is, old man: We kill as many Clankers as we can before we go down."

Cimarron grimaced angrily and reached for the steel knife.

Iphi embraced Jesse. For a moment, the blond boy let his hand touch her curly black hair. Stether noticed and frowned darkly, but said nothing.

"There's got to be a better way, Iphi," the blond boy said. He leaned against her for a moment, then broke and ran from the cavern.

A faint wailing, like the wind on the prairie, suddenly claimed the group's attention. Cimarron could tell from the looks on the faces of the children that the sound was a warning of attack.

A sentry was blowing a conch, the shell that contained within it the roar of the wind and the sea. The powerful blast on the shell was cut off, dying in a sound more like a shriek than an alert.

Another harsh warning was blown on a conch shell, this time much closer. That sound was cut off abruptly, too. Even the youngest children realized the sentries must have died at their posts.

Stether stood and announced calmly, "Y'all know what to do. You'll have to come with me," he shouted to Cimarron.

The young people were already heading off into different tunnels and mine shafts, in groups of three and four, when acrid smoke began to fill the tunnels.

"Fire! ¡Fuego!"

"The tunnels are burning!"

The children were running, the older ones trying to see that the younger ones were not left behind.

Cimarron snatched up the two children closest to him, a girl with straight black hair and a boy with red curls, who stood transfixed as long cracks formed in the rock walls.

Iphi grabbed Stether's hand and sped out after Cimarron. Stether instinctively grabbed up another child, a tiny spritelike girl with alabaster-white skin, silver hair, and amethyst eyes.

Cimarron saw one fast way out and was going for it. "Kid, this way! ¡Ahora!" Holding the two children tightly, he jumped into a deep shaft. Iphi was in right after him, pulling Stether and the younger girl with her.

The young people took off running through the labyrinth.

Thick smoke filled the tunnels, and Cimarron pulled his blue bandana over his face to keep from breathing the smoke and soot.

CHAPTER 4

ESCAPE

"I hope Ixtpan is safe," Angelina whispered. "I fear the soldiers in the bronze hoop armor might have found him."

"What's an Ixtpan?" Paradox asked in her squeaking, rasping voice.

"He is my friend and my guide," Angelina answered.

"Forget that overgrown gorilla," Matsemela snarled. "This is absolutely *the* worst experience of my life," he growled bitterly as he stood and stretched his large body in the dark, hollowed-out rock where Paradox had led them to hide from the cavalry. "Stuck inside a blasted rock with a screwball mystic and a lizard! And I want you to know, lady, that I hold it against you and that rodent-brained giant. . . . What kind of mess have you two gotten me into?"

Every muscle hurt, and the mercenary had not been able to sleep. In spite of his long years, selling his sword to the highest bidder under no discipline but his own, he retained certain reflexes from his days in Ngamon's army on his home continent of Afria, one of which was to be alert while in the territory of mortal enemies. Decades of drink and what could delicately be called fast living had not eroded reflexes that had become as much a part of him as his nearly black skin, and his training could still override his exhaustion and even his anger. The main body of cavalry had headed east toward Reynada hours before. But not for one moment during the long night had Matsemela stopped watching and listening for soldiers who might be scouring the area for survivors of Comanche Springs, all the while cursing himself for accepting his job of providing protection for Angelina and Ixtpan. He was, somewhat to his own regret, proud of one thing in life, and that was his professional reputation. It was known among the mercenaries on two continents that Matsemela Nyakir had never taken a job he didn't finish. That stubborn pride had him stuck now. He had sworn to get Angelina safely to Epitaph, and he would have to see it through. He did not want any of his old friends, the most hardened and skillful mercenaries in the known world, saying that he walked away from a job. Of course, he reminded himself, his friends did not know Angelina and Ixtpan, not to mention the talking lizard, and could not possibly appreciate what he was up against.

I figured those two for loco the first time I set eyes on them, he thought of Ixtpan and Angelina ruefully, rummaging among his pockets and remaining pouches for his flask. Matsemela had dropped his spear and his precious sword during the scuffle in the ill-fated Armadillo Saloon. He had, however, managed to hang on to his flask, his goatskin canteen, and the pouches containing his maps, which had all been slung over his shoulders when the fracas started. "Do-gooders. Bah! Nothing but trouble," he growled, his thick lips twisted in an expressive snarl. "You get mixed up in things that're none of your damn business!"

"If you are so unhappy, why don't you just head back to wherever it is you would rather be," Angelina answered sharply. She had been unable to sleep in the small, enclosed space and was tense and jumpy. "You say what's happening in this land is none of our concern. Well, go on about your business. Stick your head in the sand. Pretend nothing's happening. Pretend history can't touch you."

"History has touched me—and now it can damn well leave me alone." Matsemela pushed his way around Angelina so he could follow the itzaur out onto the mountainside ahead of her, cursing in a language neither of the others recognized, although they did understand the gist of his sentiments.

Paradox smoothed her very wrinkled calico skirt and took stock of their position and circumstance. "How did I do it?"

"Do what?" Matsemela snarled.

"Get hooked up with you two. You're about as much fun as the circus in Quintanaroo."

"I've been to the circus in Quintanaroo, and I had a great time. What's the matter with you, you . . . you lizard?" Matsemela was becoming more irritated by the minute. Exiting their rock hiding place had not improved his mood in the least.

"For one thing, I'm no more a lizard than you are a monkey." She scrunched up her finely scaled, round face as though seriously considering the idea. "And you wouldn't like the circus so much if you had to be *in* it, bozo. Which, come to think of it, isn't such a bad idea. The manager's name is Montoya. Tell him Paradox sent you."

Matsemela tried to shove Angelina aside to get at the itzaur, but the healer managed to restrain him.

"¡Alto!" Angelina's green eyes flashed in shades of purple in the golden light. "Paradox saved us from the army."

"What?" Matsemela roared. "I'm the one who got you out of that third-rate cantina that's now a barbecue pit, lady!"

"Silence!" Paradox froze against the hot canyon wall, as did Angelina and Matsemela.

"There's something ahead of us. Stay back." Paradox lifted her calico skirt and pulled out a short knife she had worn tied to her muscular green thigh. She continued edging along, sensing the presence of the large creature nearby. It could be a bear or a cougar. She regretted getting hooked up with the humans, who were likely to be of little use in a crisis.

She crept around a bend, gesturing to the two humans to stay back. The woman seems to have good instincts, but you couldn't count on their kind, she knew. Blasted humans. The best of them get themselves killed as early as possible in life. Of course, they don't have much of a life span, anyway, poor things. Worse, they just weren't old enough as a species to *understand* anything yet.

The hot rock feels good, Paradox thought. The same genes that had given Paradox green scaly skin, a bulging forehead, two strong legs on which to stand upright, and clawlike fingers, had given her a love of warmth. The humans aren't doing so well in the heat though, she observed. It's all those silly clothes they wear. Of course, if I looked like that, she thought, I'd cover up as much as possible, too.

Paradox still wore her blue calico bonnet, since even a thick-skinned itzaur needed protection from the sun over western Pecos. She had, however, ditched the uncomfortable cotton shirt and now wore only the blue calico skirt, the fringed buckskin vest, and a pair of brown leather *huaraches*.

"Where are you leading us, you demented reptile?" Matsemela demanded in a loud whisper.

"*Sssss*," Paradox hissed, her narrow tongue sticking out through her thin green lips.

* * * * *

Ixtpan crept along, inching his way over a brown boulder, then slipping down to the ledge below. He sensed the presence. Two humans and something else, something that he could not communicate with. Like a reptile, he thought, as thousands of years of instinct took over and his body tensed with fear. No crocs out here. Gilas and iguanas do not reach such a size. Armadillos weigh a ton. You can hear them coming a mile away; they make more noise than a herd of bison. This thing is not that big, and it is silent, whatever it is. And not exactly reptilian.

Ixtpan was a man of science, and he had never believed those legends about monstrous reptiles in the Terlingua Mountains, not for a minute. But it occurred to him that in these mountains so far from all civilization, he should be prepared for *anything*. And, as a man of spirituality, he knew the Terlingua Mountains could well be alive with creatures of the spirit world and ancient gods. Ixtpan took the stone axe from his belt with his left hand and drew his short iron sword with his right. He stepped around the corner of the rock wall and found himself looking upon a creature who could only have come from hell.

"*Yaaaaaaaaahh!*" screamed Ixtpan, jumping back so far he landed on the rim of the ledge and had to quickly steady himself by flailing his long arms to keep from falling down the mountainside.

"*Eeeeeeeeeee!*" cried Paradox at the sight of Ixtpan, leaping about five feet up, then landing in precisely the same spot.

"Ixtpan!" Angelina called out, running toward him, her arms outstretched.

"Damn," said Matsemela. "I was hoping we'd gotten rid of King Kong here." He gestured at Ixtpan, who had by then grabbed Angelina's hands and been pulled back from the precipice.

Ixtpan caught Angelina up in his arms and spun her around, her long black hair flying around her. Then his dark eyes fixed on Paradox. Angelina felt him tremble.

"Evil!" said Paradox, her knife drawn, crouched to spring at her enemy.

"Angelina, what a relief to find you. And what in the name of the gods is that?" Ixtpan asked uneasily, gesturing at the enraged itzaur.

"Her name is Paradox. She is an itzaur. It seems they are more intelligent than we knew." Angelina laughed and hugged Paradox.

"I know the thing is an itzaur. What I mean is, what is it doing with you two?" The giant cast accusing glances in Matsemela's direction.

"*She*. Not it. *She* saved our lives . . . ," Angelina said.

Then Matsemela interrupted Angelina. "Saved my . . . uh . . . foot! Damn thing is leading us who knows where. Probably to hell. . . ."

"You ingrate! You overbearing oaf!" Paradox was hopping up

and down, swinging her knife, her blue calico skirt flying up and
down. Her large, round black eyes flicked back and forth from the
mercenary, of whom she was not fond, to the giant, of whom she
was naturally afraid.

"It talks! These lowly creatures can't talk!" Ixtpan's bronze skin
had paled noticeably to a sickly gold hue.

"The hell I can't, dumbo. We never have any reason to speak to
a species so far beneath our own!" Paradox was still yelling and
still jumping up and down.

Ixtpan still hung back from Paradox. And Paradox was ready to
spring at Ixtpan.

They all stared at each other for a minute in silence. Then Ixtpan intoned solemnly, "The Ancient Ones wrote: Beware the
great reptiles!"

"This one is hardly great," Matsemela snorted. "What's the
matter with you? You chat with animals three times your size as if
you were at a tea party in the capital, and now something you
could swat like a mosquito scares you witless! This is it. I've finally
seen everything." He sat on the cliff and took a long drink from his
silver flask. "Where the hell have you been, anyway?"

Ixtpan drew himself up to his considerable full size, his bronze
face set in a mask of disdain. "I, *cabrón*, have been searching
the region for you while you apparently have been sitting
around . . ."

"If we do not have time to aid a wounded man, we certainly
have no time for this useless talk," Angelina interrupted angrily,
knowing that the conversation could turn into a fatal delay. "The
copper-haired colonel and his troops may be in these mountains,
looking for us."

"*Verdad.*" Ixtpan glared at both Matsemela and Paradox. "But
we have lost all but one of the camels, and mine will be of no use
from here on. This ground is too rocky for the beast this far west.
Worse," he stopped, looked angrily at Matsemela and snatched
the flask out of the mercenary's hand, "we do not have much water. And no salt."

"Hey!" Matsemela protested, grabbing at thin air for his flask.
"Wait a minute."

"From here on, water is more precious than gold," Paradox said
solemnly, indicating agreement with Ixtpan.

They looked at the great purple, red, and gold peaks of the
Terlingua Mountains ahead of them. There was little green on the
horizon, because there was too little water in those mountains to

support any but the hardiest desert plants.

"Precisely." Ixtpan was momentarily disconcerted by agreeing with an itzaur. He sniffed Matsemela's flask. "By all the old gods, this is foul."

Angelina took stock of how much water—and other liquids— they had, and the result was not encouraging. Matsemela had a goatskin canteen of wine in addition to the half-full flask expropriated by Ixtpan. Ixtpan had a large skin canteen barely a third full of water, and a hemp bag with four prickly pear *tunas*. And she had a goatskin canteen of water and a gourd filled with *posole*. The other supplies had been lost at Comanche Springs. These supplies would not get them through the Terlingua Mountains.

"Maybe I can help," Paradox offered.

"Grrrrr!" commented both Matsemela and Ixtpan.

"That is enough!" Angelina's tone was sharp, so sharp it actually startled Ixtpan, who had known Angelina since she was a child and had never seen her so fierce. "In the Old World, humans placed themselves above all other creatures—and they destroyed themselves and their world completely. We will treat Paradox as an equal."

"Never before in my two hundred and fifty years have I heard words such as yours from a human," Paradox said solemnly to Angelina. "Humans generally have *no* perspective."

"Two hundred and fifty years?" Matsemela thundered.

"For my kind, I am young," Paradox insisted in a condescending tone, her green nose in the air, "barely past my adolescence."

Angelina shot Matsemela a look that dared him to interrupt her again. "We must work together if we are to survive." Her green eyes filled with tears, her fingers clutched the butterfly-shaped amulet with the turquoise spiral. "We must reach the Prophet. Ixtpan says only he can save this land."

"I've had enough of this," Matsemela bellowed. "What difference does it make if one more prophet dies? It's not as if the world hasn't had enough of them. And what the hell good have they ever done any of us? Stop talking in riddles and myths and try making some sense." He rolled his eyes to heaven in silent prayer for the impossible. He had never heard such nonsense as these people were talking, and he was getting madder by the minute.

Ixtpan sat and leaned wearily against the stone of the mountain. Clearly they weren't going anywhere until some explanations had been offered. He fought off the urge to take a long drink of Matsemela's wine.

"In the San Cris Mountains northwest of here, a young man lies ill, in pain, dying from an ailment for which there seems to be no cure," he said simply.

"People are sick everywhere. So what?" Matsemela grumbled.

"True enough, and if that were all there were to the story, we would not be here. But there is more. His name is Falling Eagle, or Cuauhtémoc in his own language, though now many call him the Prophet. He was born in the Valley of Mexico twenty-one years ago. His parents moved north when he was an infant, and he grew up in the ancient city of Zuni, west of the San Cris Mountains. As a boy, he wandered often in the mountains alone, as if communing with the spirits of the land. And as a boy, he first fell ill with the malady that plagues him, being stricken for days and weeks at a time with agonizing pain that has aged him far beyond his years.

"At seventeen, he began preaching among the western tribes, telling them of the importance of the land, their land, and how it must be protected from invaders who would come from the East. And his prophecy came true within a month. The Tesharka Confederation cavalry reached the eastern edge of the San Cris Mountains, devastating the ancient city of Tucumcari as they came. At Isleta, a surprise awaited them. Young Falling Eagle, at the head of an army of hundreds of warriors, destroyed four companies of cavalry. Since then he has defeated them again and again. But his illness worsened. Eventually he was unable to lead his people, and at Black Mesa they suffered a terrible defeat. Now the Confederation cavalry is marching northwest toward Epitaph, an archaic pueblo long hidden by perilous mountains, where Falling Eagle and his people have taken refuge. The illness leaves him delirious and in agony for weeks, often unconscious. His followers fear for his life. He himself has prophesied that he will not live out this year."

"So Angelina's going to heal him as she healed that saddle-tramp back at the river, right?" Matsemela adjusted his bone-and-leather helmet to relieve the headache the conversation was giving him.

Ixtpan sighed wearily and wiped his bronze face on the sleeve of his white robe. "Falling Eagle *must* live." At least, he thought, until his destiny is fulfilled. "Only he can keep the Confederation out of the San Cris Mountains, and it must—it *must* be stopped before it goes any farther west."

"Why?" Paradox asked. "It's come this far already."

"Because in the San Cris Mountains lies something the Confederation must not find, something Guvnor Baines Winchester already knows of and is determined to possess."

"What?" Matsemela and Paradox demanded simultaneously.

"The Fire God," Ixtpan answered solemnly.

"Huh?" asked Paradox.

"Winchester is a superstitious man. He is counseled by an astrologer priest named Zumarraga Apocalypse, a man of great and ancient knowledge—but also a man of great evil, a servant of an ancient God of War. Apocalypse has been searching for the Fire God himself for many years. I know, because I've had run-ins with him and his henchmen more than once in my own quest to find the Fire God. Apocalypse has apparently told Winchester the legends of how the most ancient race of humans, my own people, the Paleoricans, left behind idols of the Fire God that could unleash the power of the god himself."

"And," Angelina added, "if the Fire God, the god my people call Tezcatlipoca, is freed from the idol, Ixtpan says everything could be destroyed. *Todo.*"

"You have all been in the sun too much," Matsemela said quite calmly after a prolonged silence, withdrawing another corn shuck cigar from one of his pouches. People like the woman and the giant were always looking for a metaphysical angle to everything. He had known their kind before and preferred to avoid them. "Seriously. I know things haven't gone smoothly among us, but I'm not trying to . . . well . . . argue with you. I say this for your own good: You are completely loco. It's time to find some nice mountain where you can rest. Take some time to think. Meditate. I've heard it said there's hope for all but the most criminally insane." He cast an eye at Ixtpan with the last phrase.

"Frankly, I'd like to say all this talk of ancient gods and idols is a little silly," said Paradox.

There is, Ixtpan thought, so much more I dare not tell them, but they would never believe me. He knew even Angelina could not comprehend the full magnitude of the danger they faced. He gave in to impulse and grabbed Matsemela's flask from his belt, removed the pottery stopper, and had a stiff drink. He then passed the flask to Angelina, Matsemela, and Paradox, who all did the same.

"You find it silly, Paradox, because you do not understand," Ixtpan said. "The idol is not the god. The god is the power of matter itself exploding, the ultimate fire. He lies not in the idol but in a rock far beneath it."

"*God in a rock?* You idiot!" Matsemela jumped up and tried to swing at Ixtpan, his brown eyes bulging with rage. But Angelina and Paradox restrained him.

It took a moment for Angelina and Paradox to calm Matsemela enough for Ixtpan to continue.

"Yes, my friend, the God of Fire dwells in a rock. A rock my people—who destroyed themselves by releasing him—knew as matasol. Your kind call it uranium."

"Oh, no!" Paradox squeaked, her round black eyes growing wide, her thin lips pinching together. "Not uranium!"

Ixtpan continued the tale to the wild-eyed Matsemela and the thoughtful itzaur. "Uranium has imprisoned within it a fire that can scorch the earth, burn the air, and vaporize the water. If the Confederation releases the power in the uranium beneath the idol, civilization, such as it is, could be destroyed, and Tezcatlipoca, the God of War, will triumph, as he has many times in Noramica."

"From what I can tell—and I've spent twenty years here—civilizations have been chewing themselves up and spitting themselves out on this continent for a hell of a long time. So what?" Matsemela smiled, relieved. What could any of this nonsense possibly have to do with his life? "How about if we just get the hell out of here?" he offered, thinking that if he could only humor them for a while, he could make his escape from the bunch of locos while they slept or meditated or whatever it was they did.

"There will be no escape," Ixtpan said, as though he could read the mercenary's thoughts. "If anyone disturbs the idol, people across the continent could die in the fire that comes forth. If the idol is powerful enough, then the sky will grow dark with soot and ash and dirt, and the light of the sun will be blotted out, as if the sun had died, and in that darkness even more will perish. Whole races and species could vanish."

"It has happened before," Paradox said sadly. "More times than you know."

"I fear, Paradox, that I know only too well that it has happened before." Ixtpan's lips were downturned in despair, making his long face look even longer. Angelina took his hand and squeezed it tight.

"My race, too, knows of the power within uranium," Paradox said sadly. "Ixtpan speaks the truth. Ignited uranium burns like the inside of a star. It could set off earthquakes. Mountains could crumble. *Oh, no!* The San Cris Mountains are too close! We've got to stop those Clankers! My own home could be destroyed!"

"Home?" Matsemela and Ixtpan both asked incredulously.

Paradox sat with one hand rolled in a fist beneath her narrow chin, saying nothing. She knew very well what could happen when the sky went dark and the land turned cold.

Matsemela looked disgusted, taking the whole story to be nothing but the insane ramblings of two seriously ill individuals. Angelina was staring sadly at the red sun shining over the Terlingua Mountains. Ixtpan had buried his face in his large bronze hands.

Paradox looked from one to the other. "If this prophet can help, then I say let's go. I'm coming along. This is too important to be left up to humans."

"Paradox," Ixtpan mumbled, uncomfortable with addressing an itzaur, "the Confederation army is looking for us. They know we intend to get to Epitaph."

"How the hell do the Clankers know about us?" Matsemela asked suspiciously. "And what do you mean—us?" he added.

"Because of what happened in Nueva San Cristobal . . ." Ixtpan looked at Angelina, who met his dark eyes without flinching. Only Ixtpan's large hand on her shoulder kept her from trembling. "Because of what happened in Nueva San Cristobal, both Zumarraga Apocalypse and Baines Winchester know of Angelina's own great powers. And they will move heaven and earth to find her. That's why I hired you, Matsemela . . . and to prevent what happened in Nueva San Cristobal from happening again."

"You had better be specific," Paradox prodded. "What happened in this place, Nueva San Cristobal?"

Ixtpan opened his mouth to answer, but Angelina spoke first, her voice firm, almost hard. "On our journey north, Ixtpan and I traveled by sea. We put in at the town of Nueva San Cristobal, on the coast. There I healed a child who had fallen from a cliff and was near death. The people of the town tried to burn me as a *bruja*. They called me 'witch' and lit a fire around me."

"How'd you escape?" Matsemela asked.

"Look at me," Angelina answered softly. "How much do you think I could fight a mob?"

"But you're here." Paradox stated.

"I am here because of a miracle. The people of Nueva San Cristobal, thinking themselves holy servants of their god, dragged me to the stake in the middle of their town square. They held Ixtpan tied with strong hemp ropes, forcing him to watch while they bound me to the stake and piled the dry mesquite limbs high around me." She shuddered visibly, remembering the hands tearing at her, the ropes cutting into her flesh. It was the first time she had seen the lust to kill in the eyes of others. Looking into the eyes of those people, smelling the scent of the killing frenzy of the mob, she had finally understood what her people had fled so many centuries before, when they took refuge far from the eyes of others of their own kind.

She swayed and Ixtpan put his large arms around her to support her, saying, "Angelina, you don't have to tell them all this. The oaf and the creature can see you survived. How you survived is none of their business."

"Ixtpan, *compañero*," Angelina answered, "they deserve to know the whole truth. And I need to face it. Maybe then I will no longer see those people's faces in my dreams."

"Angelina," Paradox said, taking the woman's small hands in her own green ones, "you don't owe me any explanation. Really. I'm just glad you got away."

"I did not get away, Paradox. They lit the ceiba wood they had piled around me. The flames started slowly then suddenly burst up high. My hair caught fire. I could feel the flames touching me."

"What did you do?" Paradox asked, breathless with curiosity, her round black eyes bulging with interest.

"This had better be good," said Matsemela, rolling his dark eyes.

"I called out to the God of Air, Quetzalcoatl. Not to save me, but to acknowledge with my last breath the ancient beliefs of my people." She closed her eyes, her long black lashes dark against her olive skin. "And then the wind came."

"Huh? said Matsemela, rubbing his face in exasperation. "Wind? I must've heard wrong—"

"No, Matsemela, you heard me. The wind came up out of the south and brought the rain to put out the fire. Not the usual soft coastal rain, but a savage downpour so heavy it was blinding. The people began to scream and cry and flee. An old woman freed Ixtpan in the confusion and panic, and he cut me loose and carried me out of the city. I swear to you," she said, looking at Paradox, "that I do not understand it myself. I was saved, but not by my own powers. I was saved by the wind."

"That," said Matsemela, "is the silliest thing I have ever heard in my life."

"There is more," Ixtpan added. "When we put in at the port of Laredo at the mouth of the Rio Bravo, we overheard some people in a cantina saying that survivors of a great disaster at Nueva San Cristobal were arriving in makeshift boats, all with a tale of horror to tell, a tale of a witch who had brought the wind and the rain and the earth to destroy Nueva San Cristobal."

"What do you mean 'destroy'?" Paradox asked.

"Just that," Ixtpan answered heavily. "Nueva San Cristobal is no more."

"Because of the rain?" Matsemela asked. "How the hell much rain was it? "

"Enough, *cabrón*, to cause a mudslide in the mountains above the town. Nueva San Cristobal was buried under tons of mud."

Paradox looked quizzically at Angelina. "That's quite a trick."

Angelina's eyes filled with tears. "I swear, Paradox, I did not cause that destruction. I know I did not. I would have lost my healing powers if I had caused a human death, and I have not. And yet. . . ."

The tears ran down her face, reflecting the sunlight like tiny crystals on her golden brown skin.

"Don't cry, Angelina," Paradox said, putting a green arm around the *curandera* consolingly. "It was just an accident. A fluke. You didn't cause it."

"If you believe one word of any of this, you're dumber than you look," Matsemela snapped at the itzaur.

"Whether you believe us or not, the danger for Angelina is very real," Ixtpan said sadly. "Word of the miracle at Nueva San Cristobal soon spread. People throughout the southwestern part of this continent have heard the tale—among them Baines Winchester and his priest, Zumarraga Apocalypse. I know Apocalypse. I've run into him on some archaeological digs." He grimaced, remembering the man who had made him feel he was in the presence of evil itself. "And I know that what he was searching for is the Fire God. He has had his agents looking for it for years. I know, because I have run into them, too, in my own search for the horrible idols left by my race. Apocalypse knows Angelina could stand between him and the power he dreams of possessing, if she can heal Falling Eagle so he can lead his people to defend Epitaph. He has, through that superstitious fool, Winchester, arrayed the power of the Confederation against her. Now Winchester is reinforcing his army in Reynada for a drive west—to capture Angelina and kill Falling Eagle and his followers. And to seize the Fire God for Zumarraga Apocalypse."

"So why don't we just hide you?" Matsemela asked Angelina. He believed none of the nonsense about the rock called by that strange name, "uranium," and, consequently, was absolutely unconcerned about it. Hell, he knew every precious stone there was, and he had never heard of this one. Nor did he think one crazy priest in the capital could be any threat. He had, on the other hand, accepted the job of protecting the woman, even if she was insane, and it ran against his sense of honor as a mercenary to simply abandon her. I'll give this lady one last chance to wise up, he thought to himself. "I know lots of places *no one* would ever think to look. . . ."

"Winchester has spies everywhere," Angelina said, her green eyes meeting his gray ones. "And he is aided by the supernatural powers of Apocalypse, who has his own spies and agents. They will find me sooner or later, no matter where I go." Her left hand closed over the turquoise spiral amulet she wore on a silver chain around her neck, her long midnight-black hair hanging around her shoulders like a black silk shawl.

"We itzaurs know a thing or two about catastrophic destruction ourselves," Paradox said thoughtfully, frightened by the unquestioning acceptance of fate she saw in Angelina's green eyes. "And I'd hate to see that happen. I can help you. I can lead you to a place where we can get water. It's only a three days' climb into the mountains from here. We can make it that far, can't we?"

Matsemela looked skeptical, while Ixtpan's long face was a portrait of despair.

"Of course we can make it that far," Angelina said, revitalized with hope. "There is no point waiting around here."

"Just a damn minute." Matsemela was furiously pulling maps out of his pouches. "According to my maps, there's no water in these mountains. We don't take another step until you tell us where the hell you're taking us."

"Oh, no," Paradox said coyly. "That would spoil the surprise. Hey, look at me. I need water, too. I wouldn't steer you wrong."

"I say we follow Paradox." Angelina felt the itzaur might be their only hope of survival. "Your maps, Matsemela, will not do us much good here. Wandering aimlessly in land such as this is certain death. And Paradox doesn't look suicidal to me."

"You're right about that," Paradox snorted, but she was thinking, I must be suicidal or I wouldn't hook up with this bunch.

Matsemela and Ixtpan looked at each other, shrugged, and then fell in behind Angelina and Paradox, each of them cursing or praying in a long-dead language.

* * * * *

Cimarron put the children, Maria Diaz, who was nine, and Bren Mahoney, who had lived twelve summers, down for a moment, advising them to stay inside the sheltering walls of earth. He pulled down the dark blue bandana that covered his mouth and nose and crawled out the camouflaged entrance to the old mine shaft.

"It's still night. First thing that's gone right since I laid eyes on you," he grumbled to Stether as the black-haired youth followed him out of the tunnels. At first he couldn't see anything and figured it was just a dark night. But this was too dark for night. Darker than in the deepest valleys between the high sierras. Solid black all around. No moon. No stars. He gulped the air and choked as it burned his throat and lungs. He realized that the light of the stars was being blocked by thick smoke from the fires still burning in the hills.

Iphi emerged, coughing and gasping, still holding the white-skinned little girl with silver hair and amethyst eyes. The child was named Tatiana, called Tati, and though she was smaller than the other two children, at fourteen she was older. Tati pulled a silver knife from her belt.

Stether ran ahead with a bodark bow and a hackberry arrow in his hand as defense for the others. Cimarron picked up Maria and Bren, his companions staggering after him. He stumbled, fighting disorientation, and was reassured when he caught a glimpse of the moon through the clouds of smoke and ash. Cimarron had a rough idea where they were from the moon's position. And he knew that soon the bright red rays of the sun would light up the eastern horizon. He hollered, "Try to find cover!" Then he doubled over, coughing, and had to set Maria and Bren down again. In spite of his blue bandana, he had inhaled a lot of smoke and ash. His long brown hair was covered with gray dust, and his cotton shirt was so soaked with sweat that it clung to his body.

"I'll never be able to smoke again," Stether moaned, choking on soot between words. Iphi, too, was struggling to breathe, coughing deep and hard.

"Cover! Pronto!" Cimarron heard the horses and the clatter of bronze hoop armor and knew from the sound that the Clankers were almost upon them. The three of them felt their way to a

black wall of rock, and they dove behind it seconds before four soldiers rode by on horses only a few feet away.

Stether grabbed Cimarron's torn shirt and jerked him close.
"I'm going to hide the kids in the rocks then draw the Clankers
away from them. If you don't have the nerve to help me, old man,
hide with the young ones."

"Listen to me, kid. I've been in worse trouble than this. We're
not dead yet." Cimarron reached out to the boy, but Stether
pulled away.

"You know, old man, *you* walked into this. I could've handled
those Clankers in Reynada." His face was covered with soot and
streaked with tears.

The conversation was silenced by the first rays of the sun turning the eastern sky red, then gold and pink, while the western sky
remained pitch black.

They hurried up the rugged slope, moving as fast as their tired
bodies could. They stopped to catch their breath on a high ridge.
What they saw below would haunt them for the rest of their lives.
The whole eastern side of the mountain, where the Clankers had
lit their fires, was a still-smoking mass of black earth and stone
streaked with red blood. It was hard to believe anyone had survived, but the sound of screams told them some had.

"Look!" Stether pointed to two four-man squadrons of cavalry
that were making their way up the western side of Cotula above
them. "They're picking up survivors." He paused. "The ones who
died in the first attack, they're lucky." He took Cimarron's right
forearm and clutched it hard. "We've seen what the Clankers do
to people . . . they've been tortured . . . mutilated. . . ."

"I know what'll happen if we're caught, ki—, uh . . . Stether.
So let's not get caught."

"*A todo costa,*" Stether answered, his blue eyes as cold as steel.
"At all costs."

They followed Cimarron and kept climbing in hope of finding
some means of escape from the relentless cavalry sweeps.

In the light, Cimarron remembered this terrain. He'd ridden or
run every twisted path through the Blackhawks when he was a kid.
I've always hated this place, he thought with a shudder, looking
over the landscape of black rock and deformed, twisted trees—
mesquite that grew like a spiked vine, nopal not green but blood
red, and retama trees that bloomed in the spring with flowers not
yellow but black. He and Apizaco and the others had hidden in
the Blackhawks during the rebellion. He knew there was a clearing

ahead, a wide, empty, blackened expanse on the western slope—
where they would certainly be seen by anyone looking.

Suddenly on the rock ahead appeared salvation. Or at least
maybe half a chance. It was a horse, a riderless chestnut sorrel with
a leather army saddle and bridle, its owner apparently having
fallen in the assault against the young people in the mines.
Though the reddish brown horse was already sweating and breathing hard, it presented, nevertheless, a big advantage over being
on foot. Vaquero wisdom held that a sorrel would die before tir-
ing, and Cimarron had never known vaquero wisdom, accumu-
lated by the great horse riders over many centuries, to be wrong
about anything. Maybe, he thought, just maybe this horse could
get Iphi and the children to safety.

"You two hang back under the bluff," Cimarron said to Stether
and Iphigenia. His lean, angular face was set in a hard grimace.
"Hold onto the *niños*. I'll get the horse."

Before either of them could say anything, Cimarron was running down the path. He ran and jumped on the horse in one
graceful, swift motion, his long brown hair flying in the wind. As
he hit the saddle, Cimarron noticed something he had not seen
from ground level—a squad of six heavily armed soldiers riding
down from the next ridge.

A sorrel was the best horse to run *at* an enemy. The vaqueros
had taught Cimarron that, too, and he had found it to be true in
his years of riding with Diego Laredo, who was famous for running
horses right at his enemies' archers.

Just as Stether and Iphi and the children started to run toward
Cimarron, he turned the horse, let out an exceptionally loud
"Yeeehaah!" and rode straight away from them, directly at the
cavalry squadron.

"You traitor!" Stether screamed, running and shaking his fist
after the retreating figure. But his words were drowned out by the
startled cries of the soldiers as they reigned in their equally startled
horses. "Oh, no!" Stether cried in anguish as he saw the Clankers
and realized Cimarron had drawn them away, giving him and the
others a chance to escape.

Iphi grabbed Tati, Bren, and Maria and yanked them behind a
gray granite boulder. Stether followed. "Why?" Iphi asked, her
tears turning the black soot that covered her face to a gray paste.
"They'll kill him."

"I figure it's what he wanted. *¡Vamos!*"

* * * * *

The six soldiers were startled for a fatal moment—for one of them—in which Cimarron threw his steel knife. The Clanker was dead before he hit the ground. The other five reined their horses and pulled back, which was just the opening Cimarron needed to break through. He and the golden red horse were off toward the open mountainside. The soldiers wheeled their horses and took off after him.

Cimarron and the sorrel made it down the mountain and kept going. Sure enough, the mustang was way past its limits and still going strong. "You're the best *caballo* I've ever ridden," he told the animal, which only snorted in response. He lay low on the horse's back to make himself a smaller target for the soldiers' arrows that whistled past him. He was drenched in sweat and covered in dust and dirt, but he felt absolutely nothing but the horse beneath him and the wind around him.

But the angry soldiers, one in particular, a rider on a calico stallion, were gaining on Cimarron and the sorrel. The stallion was fantastically colorful: roan, white, and red pinto in an elaborate pattern, with a red star between its eyes. Its rider was almost as colorful, a big man dressed in buckskin, with hair as gold as the sun at high noon hanging in thick curls from under a wide-brimmed white hat. He was swinging his lasso faster and faster, making the rope swirl in ever-larger circles.

The golden-haired rider threw the lasso, which quickly encircled Cimarron then tightened and jerked him off his horse. Cimarron hit the ground hard, so hard it knocked the wind from his lungs and sent shock waves of pain throughout his body.

"Good work, Amos!" a large red-haired sergeant called out. Amos Crimsonleaf was as lethal with a lasso as other men were with bronze swords and Osage bows and arrows.

Cimarron looked up to see about two dozen soldiers riding down off the next ridge and surrounding him, all of them pointing gleaming swords, spears, or knives at him.

The red-haired sergeant ordered, "Give up, barbarian, or die." He drew his black obsidian machete back to throw it.

"You got me, buckaroo." Cimarron raised both his hands to indicate his surrender. He lay flat on his back and watched the bright blue morning sky spin at crazy angles above him.

"Get the chains on this one," the sergeant commanded. "He's trouble."

Amos Crimsonleaf retrieved his lasso while another soldier bound Cimarron's ankles and wrists with bronze chains. As he retrieved his rope, his brown eyes met Cimarron's. Amos looked away quickly, startled by the smile on the prisoner's face.

*   *   *   *   *

The capital of the Tesharka Confederation at Arshal rose suddenly out of flatlands visible through the rising red and black dust that always hung in the air. The government of the nation of Tesharka and of the territories was run from a gigantic gray building of granite, a fortress ten stories high and covering two square miles. Fort Beau, as the Beauregard Winchester Memorial Fortress was called, was surrounded by a large city of one- and two-story wood plank buildings, some bare and some painted brown or gray or black. The barren red, tan, gray, and black land seemed to merge with constantly blowing dust that swirled in small twisters, like miniature tornados, across the horizon. Once the land had been hilly and thickly covered with pine trees. But since Baines Winchester's father, Gen. Beauregard Winchester, the first guvnor of the Tesharka Confederation, had stripped the land of the trees, the earth was so dry the topsoil blew away in the wind, filling the air and making Tesharka appear always to be in fog. And nowhere was the mist of dust thicker than in the capital city itself.

A thousand mounted soldiers wearing bronze hoop armor vests and carrying long steel swords ringed the city of Arshal. Each wore a blue bandana over his nose and mouth to prevent breathing in the dust. On a low hill just beyond the city, a hundred scaffolds stood. The bodies hanging from many of them were in the process of being picked clean by vultures. The small twisters of dust blew through the nearly deserted dirt streets. The streets were empty not because the town was small—it was a large city, the capital of an empire, home to people from across the continent—but because the Clankers ruled the town through terror. People stayed behind closed and barred doors as much as possible. Only a few slavers herded their chained human property through the dust-filled streets.

Fort Beau was in the center of the city, and from within its impregnable walls, Gen. Baines Winchester ruled his ever-expanding empire. His office was a hexagon-shaped room at the top of the fortress from which he could see the entire city and the lands beyond through eight large windows cut in the walls. Those walls, like the floor and ceiling, were made of polished black marble.

Also cut in the marble walls were shelves, all of them full, not with books but with bottles.

The walls of the highest office in the Tesharka Confederation were filled with bottles labeled in black: "Mother Baines's Snake Oil Elixir." Baines Winchester would have considered his grandmother, Annamay Baines, for whom he was named, to have been close to a saint, had he believed in saints. In any case, he revered her memory, named buildings and bridges for her in all his captured territories, and kept full stock of the patent medicine she had developed and sold out of a wagon across Tesharka one hundred years before. On each bottle was a label claiming the elixir would cure any and all ills.

The ministers, all twelve of them dressed in military blue with bronze hoop armor vests, long steel swords hanging at their sides, were gathered around a twenty-foot-long rectangular table of polished white onyx. At its head, in a high-backed white onyx chair covered with a bearskin, sat the most powerful man on the continent, pouring Mother Baines's Elixir into crystal goblets. The purple liquid seemed to glow with a light of its own from within the crystal. It was the ritual with which the guvnor began each meeting of his ministers.

"This stuff keeps me young!" Baines Winchester exclaimed after downing a shot of the elixir. He did in fact look a good thirty years younger than his age, which was seventy-nine.

Baines Winchester, a big man with a fleshy face and large ears, had not been content with the complete rule of his own territory. At the age of twenty, he had embarked on a campaign of conquest and acquisition that had created the largest consolidated power north of the Rio Bravo since before the Great War a thousand years in the past. He was a man born to power, the son of the man who had created the nation of Tesharka out of the ruins of the eastern quadrant of Old World Texas—Gen. Beauregard Winchester, a legend in his own time. Baines Winchester was known for being extremely persuasive, able to get total agreement from his ministers and military officials easily. The secret of his persuasive abilities lay in his vast network of spies. Baines Winchester knew everything anyone close to him did—everything. There was no indiscretion that did not reach his ears, and he used the information that constantly flowed in his direction to great advantage.

At his side sat his astrologer and confidant, Zumarraga Apocalypse, wearing not military blue and bronze but a long black cape covered with tiny diamonds that looked like the night sky strewn with stars. When he swirled it around himself, it was as though he were wrapping himself in the night. Apocalypse was a tall, slender man, with long silver hair, black eyes that burned like hot coals, and skin the color of golden wheat. His shoulders were hunched and he was slightly stooped with age. He sat at the table, disinterestedly filing his long crystal fingernails to sharp points using a lava stone. There was a smell about him of sickly sweet incense and the other ministers all tried to sit as far from him as possible because of the cloying odor, and frankly because they were terrified of Zumarraga Apocalypse, who was believed to have great magical powers derived from diabolical rites of blood sacrifice.

Winchester was dressed in the garb of a common soldier—blue cotton shirt and pants, bronze hoop vest, bisonhide boots. A wide-brimmed white hat hung from a wooden hook on the wall behind him. Though Baines Winchester clearly enjoyed the trappings of office, he had never been much for what he considered to be flashy clothing. He was contemptuous of the fastidious fashionableness of some of his ministers and generals, particularly Col. Reno Bismark.

Winchester's amber eyes always twinkled, giving him a benign look even when he was ordering the enslavement of whole nations or the extermination of entire tribes. He was so good-natured, he took even his enemies by surprise when he struck like a rattlesnake. He appeared positively jovial as he passed the goblets of snake oil elixir to each of his ministers on this late afternoon as the sky grew darker with the always-blowing dust.

The ministers each downed the foul-smelling purple liquid in one swallow—all but one. For a new minister called Joton Sycamore, from Pecos, it was his first cabinet meeting, and he had never before tasted or smelled anything so vile as the elixir. He quickly choked on it, spitting the purple liquid onto the white onyx table.

A hush came over the room as Baines Winchester's face turned as purple as his grandmother's patent medicine. All the ministers except Zumarraga Apocalypse moved back from the table, all of them wanting to get up and run, but none of them daring to. Zumarraga Apocalypse did not move. He continued filing his long crystal fingernails to very sharp points.

Baines Winchester stood and drew a long steel sword with a golden handle from its sheath. He touched the tip of the blade with his fingertip. The blade was so sharp that just a touch drew blood.

"Your Honor, please," Joton Sycamore said, still choking on the snake oil elixir. "It's one of those things you have to develop a taste for. I'll get used to it . . . I swear!"

"No, boy, you won't!" Winchester swung the steel sword and stabbed Joton in the heart, right there at the table. Baines Winchester tolerated no one who could not swallow his grandmother's medicine, not for a minute.

No one said a word as blood spurted everywhere, splashing all the ministers and Zumarraga Apocalypse. The ministers were too preoccupied with pretending not to notice the bleeding corpse at the table to observe Apocalypse wiping the blood off his robe with his fingers and then licking them clean.

"All right, down to business," Baines Winchester said, sheathing his sword and sitting back down at the blood-splattered white table. "We got a report that that young bastard Bismark wiped out a bunch of savages and escaped slaves at Comanche Springs. Just as old Apocalypse predicted, the planet Mercury was in the right aspect to the planet Jupiter." He downed another swig of Mother Baines's Snake Oil Elixir. "Ah, that's good!"

"Great!" "Excellent!" exclaimed the ministers as a group. Zumarraga Apocalypse said nothing, his face turned down toward the white onyx table so that his long silver hair fell forward, hiding his face completely.

"Never liked that sumbitch, Bismark," the guvnor said. "I don't trust a man who dresses that well. But the boy's a damn military genius, one of the best I've come upon in all my years. He's gonna find that Epitaph place and kill that prophet and all his dadblamed followers and send me the witch and the Fire God idol old Apocalypse here wants so dang bad. Young Bismark's gonna make me the most powerful sumbitch in the world." He laughed as though he had just told a great joke, and the ministers to a man laughed with him.

Big John Cloudcap, the minister of state, cleared his throat and said, "If you don't mind my asking, Your Honor, what's so all-fired important about this witch and some old idol? Isn't getting rid of that prophet and putting down the western rebellion the main thing we're after?" The minister, who was called "Big John" because of his power in the government, not because of his height, which was about five feet, was famous as a military strategist. "Why don't we just torch Epitaph as soon as Bismark's scouts can find it and get on with moving our troops south into

Durango?"

"Good question, boy," Winchester responded. "Apocalypse, you want to answer that one?"

"Yes." Zumarraga Apocalypse raised his head, and the ministers sat so still and quiet that a pin could have been heard dropping. The priest's eyes burned red, like glowing embers. "I will explain to these . . . gentlemen why we must have the witch and the idol. The Prophet, whom we all agree must die, suffers from a lingering illness that weakens him and makes him unable to lead his people. The *bruja*, what you call a witch, has within her the healing magic of an ancient god. If she reaches the Prophet and heals him, he will be strong when our forces attack. But if he is dead, his people will run in panic before our troops. Clearly she must be stopped. And, if possible, she must be made to use her powers for us." His thin lips turned up in a slight smile while the ministers nodded in agreement.

Baines Winchester poured himself another shot of snake oil elixir and lit a big corn shuck cigar, taking a long, deep drag on it and blowing the smoke directly in the face of the minister of health.

Apocalypse continued, his long, thin fingers clasped tightly in front of him on the white table, his crystal fingernails shining in the sunlight that lit the room through the eight large windows.

"As you all know, in my long life I have studied all the ancient races of this land and assimilated their lore and their wisdom. I have explored their ruins, translated their few surviving writings, and made a thorough study of all the old cultures, many of which reached a far greater pinnacle of knowledge than we have. Long ago, another race lived on the continent of Noramica: the Paleoricans. Theirs was a highly developed society, a golden age of science. Their greatest achievement was harnessing the power of the god they called the Fire God. They found the power of the god manifested in a stone known to us as uranium. They built idols of their god that contained within them the uranium, the key to unlocking the greatest power in the universe, and a mechanism to ignite it and set off a fire that would make the fires of the greatest volcanos pale by comparison. When the Paleoricans perished, they left behind these idols, scattered about the continent, hidden deep beneath the earth's surface and inside mountains. I have dedicated my life to finding these idols, for he who controls the Fire God controls the world."

"With all due respect, sir," the minister of finance, a tall, thin, bald man from Muskogee, said, "but isn't this all just barbarian superstition?"

Apocalypse smiled. "No, you simple fool. I am a priest of the God of War, and my god has granted me the power to look into the past. *¡Mire!* Look." He pulled from inside his diamond-studded black robe a large obsidian mirror with a silver handle and held it up for all the ministers to see. Baines Winchester had already seen the pictures in Apocalypse's dark mirror, so he stared out the window, smoking his cigar and watching the blowing black dust swirl around the city below.

The ministers would no more have let on that they figured Apocalypse to be insane and his mirror with the moving pictures to be a cheap trick than they would have let themselves choke on Mother Baines's Snake Oil Elixir, particularly not with Joton Syca-more's body still slumped in his chair. They looked into the black mirror, each biting their tongue to keep from laughing. But then in the mirror they began to see swirling lights. The lights cleared and they saw a picture of a city like none they had ever seen or even imagined. It was a large city, seen from the air as through the eye of a bird, of tremendous buildings that rose to the heavens. Then through the swirling clouds a giant silver bird appeared. The bird dropped something on the city and in an instant there was a flash of light from the mirror so bright, the ministers all shielded their eyes while Zumarraga Apocalypse laughed. When the sharp light dimmed, the ministers saw in the mirror a growing mushroom-shaped cloud of fire where moments before a great city had been. Then the mirror went black. The ministers let out a collective gasp.

"Now you have seen the Fire God unleashed in the past. And the past is the future," Zumarraga Apocalypse said, looking at all of the ministers with unconcealed contempt in his black eyes. "As I told you, he who controls the Fire God, controls the world. And I mean to control the Fire God—for my venerable patron, Guvnor Winchester, of course."

The ministers were breathless from what they had seen and sat staring blankly at the astrologer priest who was the power behind the guvnor.

"At the archaic pueblo called Epitaph, one of the Paleorican Fire God idols lies hidden in a *kiva* dug beneath a room deep be-low the earth's surface. I have narrowed it down to that area through my investigations and with the aid of my magic mirror, which reveals both the past and the future. The Prophet and his rabble have taken refuge there. I have sent messages to Colonel Reno Bismark and General Absalom Ironheart, telling them where to find the god and instructing them to secure it above all else." And, he thought to himself, I have also sent a message to my disciple, telling him, too, where to look.

"When we take Epitaph, we must take the Fire God. Then the power of the sun will be unleashed upon the earth. And then the rebellions will end once and for all, as they must if civilization is to come again to this continent." He knew he was not lying. If the Fire God were unleashed, the rebellions would end—no one would dare oppose an army with such power. Zumarraga Apocalypse was certain his God of War would be pleased.

The guvnor eyed all the ministers carefully, which made them all profoundly nervous. "Ever see a flash flood in the hill country, boys?" Winchester asked. The others were too intimidated to answer with anything but shakes of their heads. "Well, I've seen a flash flood. Like we say down home, the creek's risin'. You can a have a creek bone dry one minute, and it starts risin' slowly. The next thing you know, you're being swept away. Well, that's like what's happening out west with this rebellion. The creek's risin' in the West. And if we don't sandbag it good, we'll be swept away. That's why I've directed Commander General Absalom Ironheart to pull his army out of Delta and head west, to back up Reno Bismark and see to it we put an end to this prophet and all his heathen followers once and for all—and to get this damn Fire God idol and bring it to me."

The green-haired minister of culture asked, "But would that not leave our forces in Delta severely weakened if Ironheart pulls out?"

"Apocalypse here, the founder and high priest of the Church of the New World, tells me the stars say the time is right to concentrate our forces out west and get all these problems out there taken care of once and for all. Ironheart and Bismark can find Epitaph, kill that interfering prophet and his rabble, and mop up the Comanches while they're at it. The Comanches've been giving our boys in the army too dang much trouble. After they finish off the Comanches, then the army—I figure it to be at least ten thousand strong at that point—can head south to help out my old friend, General Carlos Cortezhijo de Huerta against the bandits in Durango. Durango would do well to come under the . . . uh . . . protection of the Tesharka Confederation. And poor Huerta's damned old; probably won't be around much longer. It's time we take those folks in Durango under our wing. We've got to get moving on that one fast, while that Diego Laredo's still around causing trouble near our border and we've got a good pretext to intervene."

"How can you be so certain it will all go as you plan?" the nervous minister of information asked.

"Oh, I have my ways, boy." Winchester grinned broadly. "I have allies. Some no one would ever suspect. Before this is all over, I'll have that witch in my possession. From what I've heard about her, she should sure help keep things going our way once I persuade her to use her powers for our benefit." He laughed and took a drink of Mother Baines's Snake Oil Elixir. "And you know, boys, I can be damn persuasive."

At that moment, Joton Sycamore's body toppled from the chair and hit the floor with a dull thud, sending more blood splattering on the other ministers. Baines Winchester laughed heartily while the twelve ministers laughed nervously. Zumarraga Apocalypse smiled to himself, knowing that he would soon see his god, the God of War, the god some called Tezcatlipoca, victorious. Tezcatlipoca demanded the sacrifice of human lives, and Zumarraga Apocalypse routinely gave his god just that. As soon as the idol was in his hands, he would give his god a sacrifice like none in a millennium.

CHAPTER 5

THE CHOICE

Well, it won't be long now 'til I see Reno, Cimarron thought, as calmly as if he were evaluating a game of *pelota*. I wish I could've controlled the circumstances a little better. If Apizaco could see the mess I've gotten myself into, he'd just say, "*Asi es la vida.*" Such is life. It had been Zaco's answer to everything that happened in those last months of his life. To battles lost and friends dead, he would only say, "*Asi es la vida,*" with that somber smile of his. Cimarron wondered what Zaco would think if he knew their old friend Reno was a Clanker colonel.

The copper chains around Cimarron's wrists were cool even in the hot room. His dark eyes, shadowed in gray from pain and exhaustion, were fixed on the bronze sword with an entwined lily and a serpent carved in its golden handle, which lay on the dark wood table in front of him, easily within his reach. Am I supposed to be so afraid of him that I'll kill myself rather than face him? he wondered. It would be just like him to want a rematch of our last game—now that he has an army and I'm alone.

The days Cimarron had spent in a small, dark adobe cell had been hard on him, but, all in all, he looked a lot better than he had since crossing the river. The bruises had faded unnaturally fast. A military blue cotton shirt and pants had replaced the torn clothing he had worn from Durango. However, his feet remained in his bisonhide-and-crocodileskin boots, only because he had fought like a madman when two orderlies tried to take them off him. Copper chains shackled his hands and feet.

The orderlies had found the turquoise the *curandera* left in his pocket, and one of them had taken it. For a moment, as he watched the man put the small blue-green stone in his own pocket, Cimarron felt a wave of overwhelming despair.

He leaned back in his chair, still drained by the events of his return and the days he had just spent in a cell, awaiting the return of the colonel. Colonel Bismark was on his way back to Reynada after courageously turning back an army of a thousand mounted "savages" at Comanche Springs, on the edge of the Terlingua Mountains to the west, or so word around the post had it.

Cimarron observed that Reno had done all right for himself since turning to the other side. There was no question that Bismark had built up the Confederation's military power in Pecos. Cimarron wondered if his old friend was planning to help old Huerta's *federales* against Diego Laredo. He grimaced at the thought of Diego and his ragged vaquero army up against Bismark's modern, well-equipped cavalry. Diego was a great fighter, but would he be able to survive an assault by the most powerful force on the continent? He'd have about as much chance as an armadillo in a snake pit, Cimarron figured.

There was only one door to Cimarron's cell, and it led to the fort's courtyard, where there were always dozens, maybe hundreds of soldiers at any one time. Not good, he figured, estimating the odds of getting out of the room—much less out of the fort.

He noted that the room looked more like a library in one of the big haciendas in Durango than a colonel's office: a wall of bookshelves lined with volumes bound in leather, maguey parchment, and feathers; cane chairs covered with bisonhide; and a big table of carved almost-black mahogany. Papers and maps, a pottery jar, and a silver tray—on which sat two mugs and a glass bottle labeled "Mother Baines's Snake Oil Elixir"—covered the table. Near the tray lay the bronze sword with its decorated golden handle.

Reno must be itching for me to pick up that sword, he thought with a bitter smile. Why else would it be right there where I can reach it? Even with my wrists shackled, I could grab it and lunge. He'd take the risk just for the fun of it, knowing I'm trapped like a bull in a ring. It would be just like him.

A gilt-framed portrait of Guvnor Winchester, a man with a large, fleshy, wrinkled face, a big nose and even bigger ears, and wearing a wide-brimmed white hat, hung on one wall, and a rough map of Pecos and the other territories—Brazos, Muskogee, Delta, and Smokey Mountain—hung on another. All of the territories surrounded the nation of Tesharka.

A big window in the thick adobe wall was open to the west, on the courtyard. Cimarron could see a few horses tied to a hitching post outside. Next to the horses, two camels that had obviously been driven too far and too fast were tied. The leather saddles and the feathers hanging from the bridles looked familiar.

Could he have arrested her . . . them? Cimarron wondered. If they had had a run-in with him, they're dead now. He closed his brown eyes.

As suddenly as a thunderclap over the open range, the wooden door banged loudly against the adobe wall as it swung into the room. The sound reminded Cimarron of the cracking beams in the mines. In spite of the chains around his wrists, he clenched his fists tight, as if he were getting ready for a fight.

Col. Reno Bismark filled the doorway. He was taller than Cimarron, well over six feet, with very broad shoulders and muscles that bulged through his blue cotton uniform. He had grown his copper hair long and wore a mustache and short beard, but otherwise had not really changed much in the past five years. He was dressed in the uniform of a military commander: a vest of bronze hoop armor over a dark blue jacket with gold buttons, blue cotton pants, and gray bisonhide boots. The gold braid of his rank trimmed his shirt-sleeves, and a long two-edged steel sword hung in an elegant silver scabbard from his waist.

Cimarron looked at the most powerful man in Pecos and remembered the boy that Bismark had been—running after a *pelota* ball, dripping with sweat and flushed in the heat, as determined to hit the rubber ball as if it were a personal enemy. Looking into the colonel's sharp blue eyes, Cimarron realized Bismark wasn't really any different from the boy he had known in childhood, the boy who hated with a murderous passion anyone who beat him at anything.

"Cimarron Langtry! Great Sam Houston's ghost, I thought you were dead!" Bismark said jovially. If he had expected to be greeted with the sword, he did not show it. "I couldn't believe it when I heard you were back. Of course, I sent for you right away, rather than leave you in that hot cell to rot until you're hanged. Now you can explain to me personally what the hell you're up to."

"All I'm up to is passing through my hometown, old buddy. Anything wrong with that?" Cimarron's voice was steady but a little groggy. He was having a hard time focusing, and the colonel's bright hair looked like a flame in the wind to him. But, in spite of it all, he smiled for all the world like a man who, having already had a few drinks too many, had just run into an old friend in a cantina.

Bismark sighed and shook his head. "Old buddy—" He spoke the words with clipped sarcasm. "That depends on why you've suddenly developed this hometown spirit." He laughed loudly and sat heavily behind the massive table. He did not touch the sword that lay across the table, within both his reach and that of his prisoner. "And here, all these years, I've thought you were dead. I . . . well . . . I *almost* grieved over you. We did have some good times, remember?" Although Bismark's parents had emigrated to Pecos from Ohi when he was a young boy, Bismark had never quite lost his northern accent. At the moment, the accent grated on Cimarron's nerves.

"Yeah. Lots of ball games." Cimarron wondered if he was going to be executed because of an old sports rivalry. *Pelota* was a game that aroused both crowds and players to real passion and genuine rage. He and Reno had been captains of rival teams when they were kids. Even through his strong memories of the failed rebellion, he still remembered the bitterness of those games. Reno Bismark did not like to lose, as Cimarron had found out, pinned on his back in a dark alley with Bismark hitting him again and again after losing a big game. Cimarron remembered, too, the realization he had then, as he looked up at the twisted smile on the flushed face of the older boy who was beating him unconscious, that Reno Bismark enjoyed hurting people.

I changed my mind, Cimarron. I don't like to lose, and the rebellion's losing. I'm not going to stay here and wait to die with the rest of you fools. Are you going to kill me for that?

The memory made the air catch in Cimarron's throat, as though it would strangle him. He had let the man walk away because they had been together when they were hardly more than children—to live to help the conquerors of his own people.

"So tell me. Where've you been all this time, amigo?"

Cimarron did not hesitate or otherwise betray the emotions that clouded his mind. He knew that if Reno realized he was working for Diego Laredo, he was in deep trouble. The colonel would force him to reveal everything he knew about Diego and his vaqueros.

"Running buffalo way down south," Cimarron answered coolly. "That's where I've been. You should see the herds down there in the mountains. There're so many bison, the herds look like moving black clouds on the land. Check out the boots, man." He raised both feet, even though they were chained together at the ankles, and set his well-worn boots on the mahogany table.

Bismark rose to his feet angrily. His face darkened. He gestured wildly at the dirt- and soot-caked boots, sputtering, unable to speak.

Cimarron obligingly removed his feet from the table. "I've been riding the range with the vaqueros, driving the bison to market. 'Cowboys' you'd call them up here."

"Is that where you got this? From the cowboys?" The colonel reached into his jacket pocket. He withdrew his right hand, and in it he held Cimarron's steel dagger—the one the *curandera* had given him.

Cimarron had not seen the steel knife since he killed a Clanker with it before his arrest, and he choked back a curse at seeing it in his enemy's hand.

Bismark touched its sharp blade and whistled with admiration. "I hear you killed one of my men with this."

"I did." Cimarron knew a dozen Clankers had seen him throw the knife at one of their number, and there was no point in trying to deny it.

"You've just confessed to a hanging offense."

"Yeah, I suppose so." Cimarron was remembering chasing a large rubber ball through the streets of Pecos with Reno and Zaco and their other compadres when they were about twelve. It's damn funny, he thought, how things turn out.

Bismark continued examining the knife, tracing the carving on its handle with his long, thin fingers. "It's a relic of the Old World, the Late Classic Age, unless I miss my guess, and a deadly one at that. I suppose you need it to . . . well . . . mend fences?" He raised one copper-colored eyebrow to emphasize the question. Bismark's azure eyes darted from Cimarron to the knife and back.

"It was a gift from a friend."

"Someone who liked carrying a deadly weapon?"

"Just someone who wanted to help me."

Bismark struck a flint and lit a half-burned tallow candle in a golden candlestick sitting in the bookcase, then brought it to the table. He held the blade in the flame, absent-mindedly twisting it as it turned gray then brown then red-hot. "You're going to give me some straight answers." He paused, moving the red-hot blade menacingly in Cimarron's direction, then added, "There's a lot unfinished between us, remember?" He looked for fear in the other man's eyes, and, to his displeasure, did not see it.

Cimarron remembered too well the old rivalry—not just *pelota*, but far more deadly—the rivalry between he and Bismark for the love of the same woman, the beautiful young Comanche, Topsannah Morales. He remembered her as if it were only yesterday—the feel of her long black hair cascading around his face. There had been a lot of women since Topsannah, but Cimarron had loved none of them. Most of them he had already forgotten. Topsannah alone had stayed in his heart—along with the pain of her leaving him. He remembered how much Reno Bismark had hated him for having known Topsannah's love.

Cimarron looked at the knife and the candle flickering beside it. His eyes as black as the night sky, he said, "I'll tell you everything I know. But it's not much."

"I know you'll tell me. First, how did you get mixed up with those little vipers hiding out in the Blackhawks?"

"I didn't get mixed up with them. I just ran into them. It was all a mistake."

"Apparently *you* made the mistake. They're dangerous, murdering, thieving criminals. Don't be fooled into thinking otherwise because they're young. But you were dangerous at an early age, too. How old were you back then, when we both left Reynada? Eighteen?"

"Yeah. Something like that. Only a couple years younger than you. And you'd seen your share of fighting by then."

"That I had, old buddy. And now I've seen my share of fighting for a hundred lifetimes." Bismark set the knife on the heavy table's dark surface. "The fact is, I've found it damn profitable." He pulled a gold flask from his left hip pocket, removed the clay stopper, took a long drink, then reached across the table, offering the flask to his prisoner. "Have some *mezcal*. Go on, take it. You're going to need it." He laughed as if he had just told a good joke. He had hated Cimarron Langtry for a long, long time, and now he was going to have his vengeance. He had planned to have it on this day, but now, as he looked at Cimarron's haggard, hardened face, another idea formed in his mind.

Cimarron chuckled, too, but then was wracked by painful coughing. His lungs still burned from the smoke and dust he had inhaled in the mines. He took the flask in his bound hands and drank the smooth, burning liquid.

Bismark opened a leather envelope that lay on the table and took out three pieces of yellow maguey parchment. "Prove to me that your heart is in the right place—on the side of our duly constituted government—and I'm willing to be merciful for an old friend. Show me that you'll cooperate by identifying these rebels. These are sketches drawn by artists after hearing eyewitness descriptions of the leaders of that gang. I want you to tell me if you saw any of them."

"Look, I didn't get a good look at many of them. . . ."

Bismark waved his hand to silence his prisoner. He held up a rough charcoal sketch on maguey parchment. The figure was of a young man with long, dark hair and a long scarf tied around his head. A copper spiral earring hung from his left ear. Even without the details, the drawing would have been a pretty good likeness of Stether.

The kid wouldn't have used his real name, anyway, Cimarron

thought. And they know him. Old Reno wants him badly, or he wouldn't push me to help nail him. "That's the little bastard that got me into this mess!" he yelled, his dark eyes flashing like those of a wild mustang. "Have you arrested him yet? Stether Delgado, he said his name was. Where is he? *I've* got a score to settle with that one!"

"Calm down. No, we don't have him in custody. Not yet. What about this one?"

The sketch was of a woman, tall, with muscles so exquisite that the charcoal could hardly evoke them. The black charcoal had colored her completely in the drawing. Her hair was black and hung in a thousand tight curls around her head and shoulders.

"Who's she?" Cimarron asked.

"She's from Delta, a mosquito-infested pit of place if you ask me. As vicious a killer as has ever walked the streets of Pecos."

The sketch did resemble Iphi, and there was no doubt in Cimarron's mind that she was the one Bismark wanted and that Bismark already knew her name. He obviously knew something of her history.

"*Si*, I saw her. Really spooked me, to tell you the truth. I think the kid . . . Stether . . . called her Iphi."

"Good. How about this one?" Bismark held up a sketch of a tall, slender boy with long blond hair.

It was Jess, the boy who had carried his dead friend into the cavern. *I reckon I shouldn't seem too cooperative,* Cimarron thought. *Reno'll never believe it.* "Can't say as I saw him."

"Are you sure? Before you answer, think about what I can do to you if you don't cooperate."

"Do whatever you damn well want, I still haven't seen him."

Bismark looked thoughtful, then produced one more maguey parchment. "And this one?"

The sketch was unmistakably of Boots.

"Yeah, I saw that one. Boots they called him."

"Oh?"

"Kid made an impression on me." What he said was true. Cimarron knew that no matter how long he lived, whether it was another minute or a hundred years, he would remember the innocent-looking boy with curly hair who had died in the mines.

Bismark shook his head and clicked his tongue in mock amazement.

"I'd watch out for that one . . . Boots." Boots was dead, but Cimarron knew his friends who survived would find a way to avenge his death. It was the way of their people for more than a thousand years. The descendants of the Texans, like their forebears, were vengeful. Once the blood debt had been made, the people of Cimarron's homeland would pursue vengeance no matter how long it took or how much it cost them.

"Don't worry, I'll catch him and kill him. It's just a matter of time," crowed Bismark.

"Don't be too sure. The kids say Boots is protected by the spirits of ancient Texas. To their way of thinking, he'll never die."

"Rubbish! Texas is only a myth, and a myth born in a dead world at that."

"History hides in myths, Reno," assured Cimarron.

"Superstitious fools make up all kinds of nonsense about the Old World to justify clinging to their savage, barbarian ways. They'll all die, and soon! And so will anyone else who thinks he can stop progress."

"Progress?" Cimarron watched Bismark's copper eyebrows knit together in anger at his comment.

"Yeah, progress. I'm helping forge a nation that can change this continent from a backwater of bickering tribes living on dreams of a dead past into a real power in this world. Hell, I'm proud of what I'm doing."

"I can understand how you see it, Reno. Really, I can."

Bismark looked surprised. He became more thoughtful. "You know, I figured you must've died in Reynada during the last days of the rebellion. Didn't you want to throw your life away for a lost cause?"

"I see the choice you made's turned out all right for you."

"Yes. I met up with the Tesharka army at Ozona after I got out of Reynada that day, the day you let me go. General Rancon took me in at once and I told him exactly where to attack to finish off the last pockets of rebels. Soon I was on my way up the ranks."

Cimarron's heart pounded so hard that it hurt, and the room seemed to spin around him. So Reno had personally advised on the last assault on the city—the assault in which Zaco had died, the resistance with him. Cimarron felt his blood run as cold as mountain stream water. I let Reno go, he thought, and Zaco died because of it. "You always did have an eye for an opportunity," he said.

Bismark got up from the chair, walked around and sat on the edge of the desk, next to Cimarron. "That I do." He took a drink from the ornate gold flask and held it for Cimarron to take another drink. "And why should I have stayed here and fought and died for nothing? I *knew* the rebellion was lost!" He slammed the flask down on the table. "You know, things could be a lot worse for Pecos if someone else were running the place! I *saved* Reynada!"

"Saved?" Cimarron forced a note of contempt out of his voice.

"Did you see all those people in the streets of Reynada? Well, they're *here*—not digging mines in the North or picking cotton in Delta like thousands of others. So the Confederation takes a few slaves. So what? The army didn't leave a person alive at Santamaria. Not one. Would that have been better for Reynada? To be destroyed? *I* saved Reynada! Me. Not you and your crazy friends."

"They were your friends once," braved Cimarron.

Bismark, his face red with rage, stood next to Cimarron. "When I was too young to know better. What counts is that Pecos is alive."

"Right. And I'm alive like you, Reno. I got out before the end, too."

"Well, you were always a smart kid. It would've been a shame if you'd died for nothing. I take it there's no hard feelings about how it all ended."

"It was a long time ago."

"You know, I still remember how you helped me out. You didn't have to let me walk away from Reynada, particularly when there was already bad blood between us."

Cimarron winced, thinking again of Topsannah.

Bismark observed his reaction, then went on. "Without you, I wouldn't be what I am today. That's why I'm willing to help you now. You're up against some serious charges—inciting rebellion, aiding fugitives from justice, not to mention killing one of my men. And the people of this territory would cheer me on if I had you hanged for it. But I reward those who help me, Cimarron, and you sure did help me once."

"Forget it."

"So tell me again, what were you doing with those young thugs?" Bismark picked the steel dagger up from the table and paced across the room.

"What is it you want me to say? That I didn't like seeing a couple of your boys in bronze go after a kid? Hell, it was my first day back in Reynada. First time in five years." He fixed the colonel with his steely gaze. "And I see these two big guys on this one kid. How do I know the kid's loco? Hey, I'm on my way north. I just wanted to pass by the old hometown. *Es todo.*"

"Do you honestly expect me to believe you've come back to Reynada out of some kind of hometown sentiment? I want to know why you're here." He threw the knife, and it whistled a fraction of an inch from Cimarron's left ear and struck the table. Cimarron did not so much as bat an eyelash.

"I have a different life now, Reno. The world we grew up in is gone, as dead as the Old World's cattle. Sure, I fought in the rebellion. I was young and idealistic. I thought Pecos should be free, like Texas was. Independent, not run by some old general from a place five hundred miles away. But the rebellion's over. It was over a long time ago. We lost, and I've gone on with my life."

"Doing?" Bismark turned and crossed the room again.

"I told you—running the bison to market hundreds of miles south of here, in Durango. You know that area?"

"I've heard plenty about it. Seems to be a lot going on down that way, with that bandit, Diego Laredo, running around loose. Keep talking."

"I'm checking out opening buffalo trails all the way from Durango to Abilene, like in the old stories of the cattle trails in Texas. Farther even—across the Sea of Grass maybe. Me and my people—the people where I've been working—thought we could open the old trails up again. I'm supposed to check out Abilene to see if we can set up some business. That's it. That's the story. *¡Palabra!* On my word."

"It looks as if I'm going to be checking out your new home in Durango myself soon. Old Huerta, down in Durango, has asked us for military aid against that bandit, Laredo. And who knows, maybe it's time for the Tesharka Confederation to just annex the whole region. I'm heading down that way as soon as I tie up some nasty business out west." Bismark's bright blue eyes narrowed thoughtfully. He pulled the knife out of the table. "And you can forget about checking out Abilene. It's not there anymore."

"More of your work?" So it was true, Cimarron realized. Bismark was going to Epitaph. Then he was taking his army to Durango.

"Yes. And I'm proud of it. I am absolutely certain I've done the best thing for the people, and I can say that in good conscience. I suppose you hate me for it."

"I want the past to be over, that's all, Reno. Just for it to be over."

"So you finally figured out you were wrong. That's good. I

mean, after all, the Confederation is the future. A person would have to be loco to fight it." Bismark lit a corn shuck cigarette with the candle. He offered it to Cimarron, but Cimarron shook his head, refusing it. "Whatever happened to that crazy kid you grew up with? Apizaco was his name. Is he still alive? I can still remember him out there in the square, saying that you all would fight off the Confederation army." He smiled openly, pleased with the dark look that crossed his old friend's face when he mentioned Apizaco, and, as he did, the sunlight reflecting on his copper hair seemed to Cimarron to give him an aura of pale flame.

"He's dead. Now let the past alone. If you're going to kill me, do it and get it over with. But leave the games on the ball court."

Bismark's face flushed with anger. He leaned heavily on the table's edge and grabbed Cimarron by his collar, pulling him close until the two men were eye to eye. He held the steel knife directly before Cimarron's heart. Cimarron's dark eyes met the colonel's without a blink.

* * * * *

In the killing heat of the mountain days, the travelers knew they would not last long if Paradox did not find her promised source of water soon. They were drained and beginning to stagger in the heat. Though they were all used to walking for great distances, both the path and terrain had become treacherous. Though the days were hot, the nights were cold enough to freeze fire. The travelers climbed up canyons and over mountain passes, seeking shelter in caves and behind walls of rock with only some beaver-tail cactus for food and liquid.

Ixtpan felt in his tunic for the oscelotskin pouch where he kept his small calendar stone. He was also carrying his longbow and arrows and his buckskin canteen, which had been emptied the day before.

Angelina carried her pouches of stones and feathers around her neck and slung over her right shoulder, along with her now-empty goatskin canteen. Over her left shoulder she carried an empty gourd—the four travelers had finished the *posole* the day after they left Comanche Springs. She had lost her green shawl in the fracas at the Armadillo Saloon.

Matsemela carried his leather map pouches—maps of the whole world, he claimed—and a good brass compass. That compass had gotten him across the Sahara Grasslands, through the jungles of Azan, and across the East Ocean, even through the Swamp, and he felt—secretly, of course—that it brought him luck. He also carried his large but empty goatskin canteen. Ixtpan had returned the empty silver flask, which Matsemela carried in his belt as an omen of undying hope.

Though he had his bronze knife, Matsemela had left his spear at the table and dropped his gold-handled sword when he grabbed Angelina during that nonsense in Comanche Springs. Now he cursed her and himself both. The sword would have been more use to him. He'd had that sword, with its beautiful golden handle and the carving of the lily and the serpent, for better than twenty years. His old commander and friend, Ngamon, had given it to him after the battle at Yiketi, just south of the Grasslands. Matsemela felt as if he had lost his right arm. Come to think of it, that sword meant more to him than anyone he had ever known.

Paradox carried nothing but her knife, which was more often in her hand than in her belt.

Between the two great mountain ranges lay arid, open land, sparsely populated and traveled by the most dangerous and desperate people in the world. Matsemela knew that he and his companions would be running into all sorts of desperados—fugitives and adventurers, smugglers and priests, prospectors and spies, soldiers of fortune and guerrilla fighters, bounty hunters and army scouts, as well as the nomadic horsewarriors, such as the Comanches that lived off the bison herds on the Sea of Grass. It would, Matsemela knew, be the most dangerous part of the journey. It was still to his advantage to stay with the others, at least for now. If either the Comanches or the territorial cavalry attacked, *he* had a better chance in a group.

Although, *this* group might be the exception, Matsemela thought, looking at Paradox ahead of them and shaking his head sadly. A lot of good the giant and the lizard would be in a fight. No, he'd stick around for a while yet. For the woman. And because he could sure use the money he'd get paid for getting them to Epitaph. *If* there was an Epitaph. The place was probably just another crazy frontier legend.

"It's just ahead," Paradox called out in her rasping, high-pitched voice. "Follow me!" In spite of the heat and dehydration, she practically jumped up and down as she ran.

"May all the ancient gods protect us," Matsemela muttered.

"Amen," said Ixtpan.

Matsemela actually jumped about half a foot in the air in surprise. Ixtpan had never once agreed with anything he'd said. If

Matsemela had commented on a clear, cool day being pleasant, Ixtpan would have spoken at some length about the virtues of a rainstorm. Angelina, too, was surprised, and was not sure if agreement between those two was a good sign or an ill omen.

All three suddenly realized they had lost sight of Paradox and ran to catch up with her. They were standing right where they had last seen the excited itzaur, among boulders large and small, with a break of piñons ahead of them.

The round green head popped up through the rocks and mountain scrub practically beneath Ixtpan's feet, causing him to jump back in indignant horror.

"Down here," Paradox called out joyfully.

What followed was a long trek through a dark tunnel with Matsemela and Ixtpan both cursing every step of the way in a number of obscure and ancient languages. After about an hour in darkness, Ixtpan asked, "Am I going mad, or is there a light ahead of us?"

"No doubt the fires of the deepest pit of hell itself." Matsemela had his knife in hand.

Ixtpan drew an arrow from his quiver and raised it to his Osage longbow.

"Put away the weapons," Paradox said cheerfully. "You all are really lucky. Only a handful of humans have ever seen what you are about to see."

Matsemela and Ixtpan both shuddered in unison. Ixtpan's normal curiosity for exploring places was tempered by his distrust of the itzaur.

They followed the growing light until they came to a large opening in the mountainside and found themselves on a stone landing a half-mile wide. All three humans were too astonished to speak. It was surprisingly as bright as day inside the great mountain.

The whole inside of the mountain had been hollowed out, leaving an opening to the sky above. The sun lay directly overhead, and an immense stretch of open land lay ahead of them. There, inside the mountains, were small orchards and fields and a city carved in the rock walls of the inside of the mountain itself. The three humans were frozen in amazement.

"Wake up! What's the matter with you? We're here!" Paradox yelled. "This is it!"

Angelina screamed. The others followed her gaze to their right. They clung to one another and drew back from the edge of the rock landing.

There stood a creature more terrifying than any they had ever seen, dreamed of, or could have imagined. It was a gigantic lizardlike monster, easily ten times Ixtpan's height and more than that of a couple of bull mastodons. In fact, its two muscular legs alone were taller than Ixtpan. The gray-green monster's mouth was open in a terrifying grin that revealed its sharp teeth— unmistakably the teeth of a flesh eater. Its small black eyes were set near the top of a lizardlike head, which was the size of a full-grown ox. Its skin was reptilelike scales, and it stood on two tremendous, muscular legs. Its two arms were outstretched, the clawlike hands grabbing for anyone entering the mountain sanctuary. But for the sharp, frightening teeth, it could have been Paradox, had she grown about seventy feet taller and about two hundred times heavier.

Matsemela stepped in front of Angelina, his dagger ready. It was futile, but *he* would not go down without a fight. He looked at the dagger, which had killed many humans, and knew it would be nothing but a nuisance on the order of a mosquito bite to a creature the size of this one. In all his travels across the known world, he had never seen anything like it.

Ixtpan, too, realized they were doomed, that no arrow could fell the hideous lizard. The scholar in him wished he could learn more about the great creature that was like so many fossils he had unearthed in his work. It's so fascinating! he thought. What a dreadful time to die! *I've* just made the greatest find in paleological history!

"You human fools! It's a statue! It's not alive! He's Tyran the Seventeenth. He supervised a lot of the original building of the city." Paradox was more than a little exasperated with the slow-witted bunch. "He's been dead for *millions* of your years. Just think of him as a big welcome mat. Come on and meet the family."

"Those giant lizards have been bone and dust since before the Great War!" Matsemela's voice was strangled with astonishment.

"By the Serpent's tail feathers!" Ixtpan exclaimed, looking at the formidable statue. "These things have been extinct a lot longer than that."

"What you are seeing," Paradox explained patiently, as though to a mule or some creature of equal stupidity, "is the here and now, and we'll talk about this lizard nonsense later. There's water down there. Let's go!"

The three humans looked beyond the massive statue of the late Tyran XVII, on a city as majestic as any on the face of the Earth.

Towers and temples and dwellings, all carved in the rock wall of the inside of the mountain, were spread out before them. High above, the great white clouds looked like balls of cotton against the bright blue sky, framed by the dark mountain walls.

Where the mountain had been cut away, the strata of earth could be seen in distinct lines on the rock walls—the history of the world preserved in stone. Each line was a record in stone of an epoch when living creatures had been born, lived on the Earth, and then been swept from its surface.

A narrow blue river flowed around the city, and along it were small green and gold corn fields, a loquat grove, and small fields of other crops. The citizens of the world inside the mountain, not knowing themselves to be extinct, strolled leisurely along walkways of black onyx, white marble, and red granite. Here and there parents were strolling, pushing their children in wooden carriages. Groups of children ran through the pathways. Some residents of the hidden city rode horses or donkeys. They were all, of course, itzaurs.

"These are my relatives. Welcome to the city of Itzamma, our capital. Whoopee!" Paradox practically sang.

"Where have you brought us, you miserable . . . ?" Matsemela grabbed Paradox around the neck with both hands and began strangling her.

Paradox managed to utter something like a squawk before her face started to turn blue. Angelina grabbed Paradox by the shoulders and tried to pull her away from Matsemela. Ixtpan moved to help the warrior—no, Paradox—but couldn't decide.

A high-pitched wailing went up from the city. The sound cut through the cavern, through the inside of the mountain, through their brains. The three humans looked out on the mob heading straight for them. Matsemela and Ixtpan let go of Paradox, who went flying into Angelina, knocking both of them down.

Paradox got up slowly, dusted herself off ceremoniously, and offered Angelina her hand graciously. Angelina took Paradox's hand and stood. She walked beside Paradox to the edge of the landing and looked out, with Matsemela and Ixtpan scrambling right behind them.

Roughly a hundred citizens of the hidden city were running in their direction, long blue and white robes flying around their bodies like the mist in the hill country. Some wore tunics of silver and gold and carried crystal clubs. They were all yelling and, apparently, were all very, very angry, squawking and shaking their claws.

With a great cry, Matsemela leapt in the air and landed in the midst of his startled attackers—a phalanx of demonstrably flesh-and-blood itzaurs.

Matsemela held his own for a minute, until a green itzaur bit his ankle while another pounded a crystal club against the back of the warrior's head. Matsemela went down and was immediately surrounded by half a dozen itzaurs. One, a thin brown itzaur about five feet tall, jumped on his stomach and prepared to skewer him with a quartzite spear.

"No! Oh, no!" Paradox screamed in horror, as others of her species jumped onto the ledge and grabbed Angelina and Ixtpan. "Oh, no! I can explain!"

"You'd better be able to explain, you traitor!" The itzaur who spoke was short, as short as Paradox, but he was easily as wide as he was tall. His tunic was made of squares of dark blue lapis and moss-green jade held together with delicate bands of silver. The sharp-edged quartz machete he waved also commanded attention. He gestured with the machete toward Paradox, and two itzaurs seized her, too. "You know that the penalty for betraying the holy city of Itzamma is death."

Under the bright sun that they had known all their lives, the humans were taken under guard to the city that had been hidden from the eyes of all but a handful of their kind for the entire human history of the planet.

* * * * *

The colonel and his old friend stared each other down for a few very long minutes. The steel dagger was still poised before Cimarron's heart.

Bismarck finally said, "Okay, old buddy, this is it." Cimarron still did not flinch and kept meeting the colonel's steady gaze. "You're in the army."

Cimarron couldn't help flinching at that. His dark eyes opened wider. "Huh?"

"I know I could have you flogged and hanged at sunrise. Or worse. But instead, I'm drafting you." He laughed heartily at the look of horror that spread over Cimarron's sun-bronzed face.

"Drafting?" Cimarron broke out in a cold sweat, and his hands began to tremble. "You mean . . . like *in* the army?"

"You get the idea. But take it from me, boy, you'll like it. You'll get to travel. No more worrying about the buffalo market.

And you'll be on the military payroll right away." He set the knife down and took a key from his belt. "Well, you tell me. Do I take off the chains so we can talk about the job, or do I tell the boys to get a noose ready for a hanging?"

"Since you put it that way, let me loose."

"Done." Bismark released the chains and Cimarron rubbed his sore ankles and wrists. The colonel wondered when Cimarron would make a grab for the sword, or if his old friend was smarter than that. He hoped Cimarron would play it smart, because he wanted to have him around for a while before he killed him. He did not just want to see Cimarron die. He wanted to see Cimarron completely *broken*.

"Mind if I stand? You run a cramped jail around here." How fast could I get my hands on the sword on the table? Cimarron himself was wondering with icy determination. He figured he could grab the sword and lunge in one motion, turning to take Bismark off guard. He was glad for the sun shining through the window behind him. Always strike with the sun behind you, to blind your enemies, Diego had said many times. But Cimarron also knew Bismark had set him up and that the only thing he could be sure of when he made for the sword was that, whether or not he killed Reno Bismark, he was also killing himself, as surely as the sun would rise from the east.

Then he remembered the sight of Apizaco's blood running into the dust in the street in Reynada. Hold that thought, he told himself, and it will be easy.

"Be my guest," Bismark said. "You'll need to be in good shape for what I want you to do."

Good, Cimarron thought, eyeing the sword. Keep him talking, distracted, not watching my hands. "What do you want from me, Reno?" Cimarron was standing a few feet from the table, facing Bismark, with one hip cocked higher than the other, as all cowboys did when they stood still. One lunge was all he would have.

Bismark's mouth opened in a boyish grin. "You should enjoy this assignment. You've always liked the ladies. There's a woman involved." He took a drag on his cigarette and looked out over the courtyard through the large glass window.

Cimarron took one step closer, letting his right arm swing back and his hips swivel slightly to the left, going into a swing that would give him the momentum he needed.

The colonel went on. "She's a witch, a *bruja*. *Curandera*, I guess I should say, to be polite. One with great powers. She's

heading for the San Cris Mountains to help that heathen chief
that the rabble there call their prophet. Rumor has it that he's
dying, which, to tell you the truth, would save me a lot of trouble.
I am going to destroy that rabble-rousing prophet and put an end
to these blasted rebellions once and for all. Obviously, the last
thing I want is for the witch to heal the bastard—not that I believe
in that kind of hocus-pocus. But I've got to stop her. I'm supposed
to take her alive if possible, dead if necessary. She's an odd-
looking one by the description, not like anyone I've ever seen on
this continent, and people here are every mix of color imaginable.
I hear this one has funny-shaped green eyes that change colors in
the light, and she wears a dozen heathen amulets."

Cimarron froze.

"The guvnor himself gave me the assignment of destroying the
Prophet and putting down the rebellion in the pueblos out west.
And there's something more, some old idol that Winchester
wants that's supposed to be out there in the San Cris Mountains."

"An idol, Reno? Is Winchester crazy?" Cimarron returned to a
relaxed position.

"Yes, you could call him crazy. He's got this astrologer, a man
named Zumarraga from down south where you've been. Zumarraga's got him believing all kinds of nonsense. And Zumarraga's
convinced him that if he has this silly idol, of something called a
'Fire God,' he will be able to conquer the whole blasted world.
But Winchester's the guvnor, and I'm a military man, which
means I follow orders. I'll get him the damned idol and the
woman—and kill the Prophet. Besides, I can't start the drive
south of the river until I finish up at Epitaph. And I have to go
south. We can't have that bandit, Laredo, operating freely so near
our borders, now can we? Any fool can see that intervention will
be necessary. And the Confederation will be needing new resources, especially gold, and I hear there's a lot of that in Durango, not to mention more slaves."

"What does this have to do with me?" Cimarron turned casually from Bismark and the sword.

"The Prophet and his people are holed up in some old city
called Epitaph. We haven't been able to scout the place—it's out
in the San Cris Mountains, and you know they've never been
mapped. Only a handful of people have ever gone in there and
lived to come back and tell about it. I can promise you, I've got
agents working on finding the place right now. That's where you
come in. You're going to scout for the cavalry. Once we get west of

the Terlingua Mountains, our lives will depend on having good scouts. You used to be a hell of a tracker. Tracking's a skill that a man doesn't forget, so I'm willing to bet you still are one of the best trackers alive." Bismark was pouring brandy into two pottery mugs, so he did not see the expression that for a moment darkened Cimarron's face. He handed a mug to his prisoner.

The words sounded hollow, like rain falling on a log, empty, distorted, to Cimarron. He looked down into his drink, thinking of the great tracker who had trained him—Dezcalzo Two Creeks, killed by drunken Clankers when he intervened to save a young woman of Reynada from their attack.

Cimarron had started tracking when he was seven years old, when Dezcalzo Two Creeks had taken the young orphan along with his own son, Apizaco, to scout a trail for some adventurous settlers traveling west beyond the Terlingua Mountains on the far western frontier of Pecos.

Over the next few years, Cimarron had scouted the open land more times than he could count—for buffalo drivers, prospectors, settlers, and warriors. He had traversed much of the land from northern Pecos to the southern sierras. He owed Dezcalzo Two Creeks many, many debts. "What's this really about?" he asked casually. "Doesn't Winchester already have more women than he could ever . . . ?" Cimarron gripped the mug tightly, the lines of his angular face hard but unreadable.

"I don't know the whole story. You know how communication is out here so far from the capital. But the rider who brought the guvnor's orders said this woman could summon the wind itself, that when the people of Nueva San Cristobal tried to burn her as the witch she is, she called some wind god, and the wind came up and brought a hell of a rainstorm and put out the fire."

"So the wind blew? So what? Don't tell me you believe that kind of loco nonsense." It took all of Cimarron's strength to keep his hand from shaking.

"The witnesses—and there were a bunch of them," Bismark continued, "said this was like no wind they'd ever seen, at least according to the fellow who brought the orders. Those folks believe they saw the actual power of evil, that the woman could summon the powers of heathen gods. It sounds pretty far-fetched to me." He laughed. "But here's the part that's no laughing matter: It rained so hard on Nueva San Cristobal, a little town on the coast of the *Golfo de Huracán*, that it caused a mudslide the day after the witch and her companion fled."

"So?"

"It was quite a mudslide. It buried Nueva San Cristobal. The town's not there anymore, except for a few survivors who escaped in boats and canoes to tell their bizarre story. It's as if the earth swallowed up the town."

"How the hell do you know that?"

"I got it all from Winchester's messenger from the capital ten days ago. Winchester sent ships to Nueva San Cristobal from the port at Santone to check it out. The story's true, Nueva San Cristobal doesn't belong on a map anymore. If the woman caused all that . . . well, she sure must be interesting. And deadly." Bismark smiled. He liked things that were interesting and deadly.

"You say two men are traveling with her?"

"One's supposed to be a giant. Can you beat that? And the other's a mercenary, just a sword for hire. Matsemela Nyakir, no less. His ability—with a sword and with a bottle—are a matter of public knowledge. Of course, you can't believe everything you hear. Everything gets exaggerated on the frontier."

"What happens when we catch them?"

"Oh, we kill the two men, or sell them to the slavers if they're in any condition to be sold. Get rid of both of them quick. There's no reason not to. Neither one of them would be of any use to us. The main thing is to destroy the Prophet and anyone who might help him—and get the woman and that silly idol Winchester's astrologer is dead set on having. The message from the capital said it lies in a pit beneath Epitaph. Once we storm the place, it shouldn't be too hard to find." He swallowed his brandy and set the mug down hard on the table.

"Winchester must be as crazy as a jack rabbit that's chewed loco weed to believe in that stuff," Cimarron commented.

"Crazy or not, I follow orders. And you, old friend, are going to help me. When we're done out west, I'll be able to send my guvnor the woman, the idol, and the Prophet's scalp. I will then be next in line as commander general of the army of the Tesharka Confederation. Old Absalom Ironheart has been around too long. Once I have his job, I will have more power on this continent than anyone short of the guvnor himself, and that, buddy, is what I want. In return for your services, I'm willing to forget about you being arrested in the company of dangerous, thieving criminals. . . ."

Cimarron stared at the bronze sword lying on the dark wood table, feeling the strangely familiar sensation of time stopping, of a whole lifetime lived in a moment. He could kill and be killed right now and Winchester's army would still go after the *curandera*, with or without Reno Bismark. Not since the day he had lain wounded, praying for Apizaco to escape the Clankers, had he wanted anything as much as he wanted to pick up the weapon in front of him. But he could feel the *curandera*'s green eyes on him, begging for his help as though she were there. The woman had saved his life, the life he was about to throw away for one moment of vengeance. He couldn't just ignore the danger she was in. Maybe he could help her, slow the army down, warn her somehow.

He closed his eyes for a moment, feeling the warm sunlight through the window on his back. Then his angular face lit up with a big smile, he laughed loudly, and said, "By St. Davy's coonskin cap, blasted Winchester's got you out chasing women and old gods for him. I figured things had gone downhill in the last few years, but, Reno, that's plain pitiful."

"Don't press your luck. Baines Winchester has brought Pecos into the modern world, and I support him completely. I'm paid to do a job—paid well for it. If he wants a prophet and a giant and a mercenary dead, I'll kill them. If he wants some old statue of a dead god, my men will find the damned thing for him. And if he wants a woman with funny eyes, he'll have her, too." He laughed again. "Of course, I might have to see what's so special about this one myself before I turn her over to our beloved guvnor." He looked triumphantly at the sword on the table, one that his men had found in the ruins of Comanche Springs, the sword his prisoner had not dared touch, and he slapped Cimarron on the back. "You'll be on the payroll by sundown."

"Good. I need some money. And I want that steel knife, the sorrel mustang your boy, Amos, roped me off of, . . . and a hat. I lost my old one crossing the Bravo."

"You'll have the hat and the horse today. Oh, yeah, and this." He handed his new scout the steel dagger. "Since you've proven you aren't a threat—at least not right now—I have a surprise for you. Come out, Wyatt."

The bookcase opened and a slender man with curly brown hair, coal-black eyes, and sun-bronzed skin, wearing a Clanker uniform with a lieutenant's insignia, stepped from behind it, a long silver sword in his hand and a big grin on his face. He was slender, almost delicate-looking, though Cimarron sensed something as hard as steel in the man. Recognition was slow coming, but as it dawned, Cimarron's mouth fell open in surprise.

"Surely you remember Wyatt Fontana," said Bismark, "another Reynada boy. Used to play ball with us sometimes. Wyatt's my first lieutenant and right-hand man now. Isn't that right, Wyatt?"

"At your orders, Colonel," the officer answered. He smiled as if he were at a social gathering, and said, "I sure am glad you didn't go for that sword, Cimarron. I'd have hated for you and me not to have had a chance to talk. It's been a long time."

"Si, a long time," Cimarron said. "It's good to see you again." He took the other man's hand, as friendly as could be.

"It's good to see you still alive, Cimarron. Really, I mean that. Remember, I played on your pelota team a few times."

"Yeah. You did." And now you play on his team, Cimarron thought. He turned to Bismark. "You weren't taking any chances, were you?"

"Taking chances is for fools. But you made the right choice. I got quite a kick out of letting you wonder if you had a chance against me. But you were smart this time, old buddy. Let's hope you stay that way." When Reno Bismark laughed, his face lit up like the sun at high noon. "You know, Cimarron, I don't know when I've had such a good time as seeing you today. We'll have to get together on the court and play ball soon. It'll be just like old times."

"Just like," Cimarron said, his fingers closing around the carved ebony handle of the ancient steel dagger.

BOOK II

I, FOR ONE, BELIEVE MAN'S LIFE ON THIS CONTINENT
AND OUR NEIGHBOR CONTINENT TO THE SOUTH
IS MUCH, MUCH LONGER THAN HAS BEEN SURMISED.

LOUIS L'AMOUR
HAUNTED MESA

CHAPTER 6

THE WAY WEST

In the courtyard in front of the great temple, the three humans and Paradox were held under guard and surrounded by a crowd of at least a hundred gawking, chattering itzaurs, most of them green or brown, though there was a lot of variation in shading, from a bright gold hue to a dull gray. All stood erect on two muscular legs, except for the few old ones who leaned on their canes of gold or silver or green malachite. They were dressed mainly in opaque blue and white robes, though some wore military-looking silver tunics.

The rotund itzaur in lapis and onyx gestured toward the entrance to the massive temple, and four itzaur guards carrying crystal spears fell in behind the prisoners.

Matsemela started up the marble steps to the temple, ahead of Angelina and Ixtpan. Though he had been disarmed, his step projected the air of a man entering combat, and he was instinctively looking for a way to fight.

In spite of the obvious peril in which they found themselves, Ixtpan, now deprived of his longbow, approached the immense vaulted entrance to the great temple with something close to reverence. He was intrigued by antiquity itself, and this place was, to his trained eye, older than any place he had ever been, far older than the civilization of his own lost race, the Paleoricans.

The temple rose higher than any building Matsemela had ever seen, and he had seen some big buildings around the world. "A city of itzaurs inside a mountain!"

"It wasn't on any of your maps, eh, *compañero?*" Ixtpan did not bother to conceal the fact that at least one part of their predicament amused him.

Bright light and a heavy cloud of piñon incense enveloped them as they stepped inside the majestic temple. The bright sunlight from above was filtered by a tremendous round crystal window to intensify the light and to reflect the rainbow colors on the temple walls.

The high walls, Matsemela immediately noticed, were covered with solid gold and decorated with stunning mosaics of precious stones. Jewels on the gold wall formed portraits of gigantic lizard-like creatures like the one whose statue greeted visitors to the city.

"It's worth a fortune," Matsemela gasped, his dark eyes lighting up in ecstasy. "I had no idea the lizards were into something like this. I thought they lived in mesquite-and-mud settlements out on the desert."

"Clearly your assumption was in error," said Ixtpan.

"Shut up," snapped Paradox. "Look at the trouble you've gotten me into."

They were herded along into the temple by the ill-tempered itzaur in the blue and green stone tunic and an escort of guards.

The itzaurs were small, but, Ixtpan realized, they were clearly related to the great reptiles portrayed in stones on the gold walls, creatures once known, he believed, as dinosaurs. Vanished, yet walking the land again. "Did they get smaller over time?" he wondered aloud to Angelina, who was staring wide-eyed at the itzaur temple. "In millions of years, they would have evolved a lot. Evolution might have scaled them down to fit in a smaller world." In his work as an archaeologist, he had occasionally excavated the remains of great, sometimes monstrous, dinosaurs that long ago walked and even flew across the land. "Who ever would have believed it?"

"I'm not sure I believe it myself, and I'm looking at it," Matsemela replied tersely.

"Whether we choose to believe it or not," Angelina said, her eyes turquoise and purple in the crystal light, "Paradox's world is clearly real."

"Of course it is!" Paradox retorted. "Didn't I tell you it would be quite a surprise?"

The aisles were lined with itzaurs in white robes, with hoods up over their heads, the creatures' high-pitched voices united in chanting. Bronze gongs and crystal bells sounded in rhythm with the chants, and from the far end of the cavernous room came the piping of silver flutes.

The walk up the temple aisle seemed to the three humans and the one itzaur to take forever. They walked slowly, approaching what appeared to be a black altar on a stage or platform of quartz at the far end of the room.

A black-robed figure, taller than the other itzaurs, who ranged from four to five feet in height, stepped to the center of the stage and stood waiting for them, a six-foot obsidian spear held in its gray-scaled fingers. The figure's eyes were gigantic, great round crystal circles with obsidian balls in their centers, making him look rather like a large insect.

Angelina, Ixtpan, and Matsemela were aghast at the terrifying sight of the creature.

"You have entered the sanctuary," the gray-green figure intoned in a highly accented form of the Spanglish language of the frontier. "You have violated the sacred world of Itzamma. You have profaned the Temple of Creation." His long robe was made of hundreds of tiny squares of gleaming black obsidian held together by delicate silver clasps. The mineral garment moved with its wearer as though it were silk, shimmering around him with each angry movement.

"By *todos los santos*, the beast is wearing glasses!" Ixtpan exclaimed, realizing that the itzaur's bizarre, insectlike eyes were really not part of his body but were instead crystal disks held over his black eyes by gold wires.

"I have now," Matsemela muttered, "seen everything."

"Look, Jolosumu, if you'll just let me explain," Paradox said to the bespectacled itzaur, "I can straighten this whole thing out."

"You traitor," the black-robed one called Jolosumu answered, in a voice as cold as the wind off the ice mountains. The thick, clear crystal disks over his eyes gleamed in the light. "Yours is the worst crime of all. You are one of us, Paradox. You know the penalty for bringing a human into Itzamma. Take them to the dungeon while I plan their execution."

The companions let themselves be taken through a mile of long, twisting, cavernous hallways carved in solid stone and lighted only by torches, deep into the mountain, to a dungeon as dark as the heart of the universe and as ancient as the continent.

* * * * *

Cimarron nodded and touched the rim of his new broad-brimmed tan hat in greeting to Amos Crimsonleaf, who was watching from astride his pinto on a nearby brown and gold bluff. The hat was creased across the crown, in the style long popular in Pecos, where the past was never out of sight nor out of mind. The blond soldier made no move to acknowledge the gesture but kept right on staring off into the west. Ever since the army had left Reynada five days and one hundred and fifty miles before, one of four soldiers—one of them being Amos—was always near Cimarron and always had an eye on him. Any move Cimarron made to flee his officers would be stopped quickly and definitively with a poison-tipped arrow.

So Reno still thinks I might be up to something, Cimarron thought. He's right—I just wish I knew what.

The body of the army was about an hour behind them, and Cimarron was alone except for Amos. He rode his sorrel mustang higher into the hills near the ash and cinder remains of Comanche Springs. The land became more barren as they moved west, with hardly even a mesquite tree or a buffalo skull to break the monotony of the golden earth that went on as far as the eye could see. The foothills of the Terlingua Mountains were giant gray peaks that rose abruptly out of the desert. The path into the foothills was narrow and rocky, but Cimarron kneed his horse to keep going.

He was looking not only for some sign of the travelers but also for a way to escape from Bismark and his spies. He knew that if he managed to break and run, Bismark would have him hunted and killed. He would be one man against hundreds, although he was one man who knew how to live in this torturous environment for as long as was humanly possible.

To an experienced tracker, the routes taken by humans and animals were as clear in the dust, the dirt, and the crushed grasses as written words on parchment were to a scholar. Moccasin and boot prints, dead campfires, and broken branches, indicators known collectively to the tracker by the singular word "sign," revealed when the route was taken, the number of those traveling it, and sometimes even their purpose.

The sun was setting over the foothills of the Terlingua Mountains, and the sky was streaked with burning red and gold and laced with shades of pink and purple. Cimarron read in the dirt and dust that a large man, a small woman, and, of all things, an itzaur fled the destruction of Comanche Springs. He figured he knew who the woman and the warrior had to be. "Hell, a dog would've done them more good. Why in the name of all the gods would they have burdened themselves with a stupid itzaur?" he asked aloud. But clearly they had. The *huarache* prints were too short and the toes too wide to be those left by a human. No other living creature could produce a footprint like that.

They were here, he thought, the sign is unmistakable, and they got out before the town burned. But that doesn't mean they've survived in the mountains. They were obviously on foot, so they can't have gotten far, and unless they found water, they couldn't have survived long under this sun. They've been out here too long for there to be much chance of finding them alive.

Later, close to sundown, Cimarron picked up the travelers' path in the dust. They seemed to have emerged from a giant gray boulder. Something must've destroyed the other tracks, he thought. They sure didn't appear out of a rock. That's loco.

He rode on and found the physical evidence of a meeting between the warrior, the healer, the itzaur, and a large, almost gigantic, man wearing boots. There appears to have been a scuffle, Cimarron thought, noting the remnants in dust of Ixtpan's meeting with Paradox. But all four had gone off together toward the west, higher into the Terlingua Mountains, Cimarron estimated, about three days before.

The footprints got closer together as he went on. The travelers were tired, he could deduce, and slowed as they walked across this golden, sandy mountain path. They stumbled, and their steps were uneven, which meant they were out of water. He was glad the sun was burning blood red and low on the horizon, behind the jagged mountains ahead of him, that darkness was less than an hour away. If they were alive, the darkness would help hide them.

Cimarron took his skin canteen from his shoulder and drank from it, then took a piece of cornbread from his morral, the fiber bag containing a cup and rations that the soldiers and cowboys all carried hung around their saddle horns. He looked back over his shoulder as he chewed the hard, dry cornbread and caught a glimpse of Amos, just within firing range.

Suddenly, far ahead, in the great mountains to the west, Cimarron saw a guarantee that the army was going to be slowed down before long. Puffs of smoke rose on the side of a peak blurred by sunlight and distance, such that they looked like tiny clouds rising rhythmically against the blue sky. Talking smoke it was called. Smoke signals, a means of communication he knew well, a clear and public proclamation that a Comanche war party was gathering. Had he been inclined to pray, Cimarron would have thought the smoke signals, dim and remote though they were, were the answer to a prayer. His thoughts were abruptly interrupted by the sound of a running horse.

Reno Bismark reigned his silver-blue stallion to a halt beside Cimarron in a hail of flying gravel and dust. He inspected the faint remains of tracks in the dust. "Looks like we'll have them soon. Judging from how close together these footprints are, I'd say these folks are worn out good. They can't have gotten much farther north into the mountains. Hell, there's not much sport in a hunt this easy. And you, of all people, know how much I like a good fight. Don't you, old buddy?"

"Well, if you want a good fight, then this appears to be your lucky day, pardner." A half-grin flashed across Cimarron's dust-streaked face.

"It sure is," the officer grunted. "The fugitives are practically in my hands. I can feel it." He pulled out a blue silk handkerchief and wiped the perspiration from his face. He despised the heat and hoped that, once the campaign against the Prophet and the Comanches was over, he would never have to return to western Pecos.

"You're right, they are—or they were. When they passed this way, they were weak and on foot. Water is hard to come by in these parts. To tell you the truth, I doubt they could have survived in the mountains. More than likely, they died less than twenty miles from here. They just plain couldn't have made it any farther without water. Look at the mountains," Cimarron said, gesturing to the gold and red Terlingua Mountains ahead of them. "See any trees? Anything green at all?"

"Well, no. . . ."

"That means there's no water, which means that that woman Winchester's damned astrologer wants to meet must be dead, as well as the folks with her. The vultures've probably picked them clean and gone on. We could look for their bones out here forever and never find them. And, by the way, we're close to a lot more than that woman."

"Oh?"

"Look up there." Cimarron pointed to the puffs of smoke rising in the sky above the mountains.

"Read it," Bismark commanded.

"The gist is that the Comanches are up ahead, and *they've* scouted *us*. The war chief they call Bajo del Sol is gathering an army in the mountains."

"The one who wiped out old Colonel Dimit and his company at Tockto?"

"Probably. The one all the *corridos* are sung about. I've heard the songs about him in cantinas from here to Nueva Chihuahua. They say he's afraid of nothing under the sun. That's how come the name Bajo del Sol."

"Well, I'm under the sun, and he had damn well better be afraid of me. My troops can crush any band of savages. I'll meet up with that renegade, all right, and I'll carry his head on a pike to Reynada as a lesson to anyone who dares get in my way. And yours, too, if you make one wrong move. I'm going to give the order to make camp near here for the night, and I'll send out more scouts.

Men I *know* I can trust." He jerked on his horse's reins and galloped away in a cloud of red dust.

Cimarron watched the cottonlike puffs of smoke from the purple mountains, then turned his horse and rode back to camp, followed at a distance by golden-haired Amos Crimsonleaf on his pinto.

*   *   *   *   *

It took Cimarron another hour to lose Amos, and it wasn't easy. He slipped into a dry arroyo, then quickly got out behind an outcropping of large black rocks and doubled back up a shallow creek with just enough water to hide his horse's prints. He'd given some real professionals the slip in his time, and he had to admit that Amos was good. Too bad he works for Reno, Cimarron thought wryly. He was hoping to make contact with the Comanches as he rode farther north, climbing higher into the Terlingua Mountains. The mountains were rocky and barren, with only an occasional nopal or short mesquite tree along the mountain trail. On his right was a drop hundreds of feet down, into a canyon of red rocks below. On his left stood a wall of red and gold rock.

It happened sooner than he expected. His horse's ears pricked up, his first clue that he'd been successful. Cimarron reached for the steel knife and carefully pulled it from its sheath. He slowed the sorrel, listening and hearing nothing until the Comanche let out a war cry and jumped him from the rocks above, knocking the steel knife from his hand.

The Comanche had him off the horse and face down in the dirt within seconds. Cimarron twisted his body fast and painfully, throwing his attacker momentarily off balance. He rolled out from under the Comanche, who was on him again in an instant. The warrior had a long copper dagger, and Cimarron's steel knife lay in the dirt several feet from him. They struggled only a few feet from where the mountainside dropped off into a deep, rocky chasm.

Cimarron managed to dodge the blade repeatedly but with great difficulty, rolling toward the mountain wall and away from the chasm as he did so. His opponent was strong and fast, a tall man with rippling muscles that gleamed with sweat in the sunlight. He wore his silver-streaked black hair long and loose, as did all Comanches in battle, an eagle feather tied to a thin leather band around his head, and a buckskin breechcloth. He was older than Cimarron by a few years, enough to be more experienced as a fighter but not enough to be slower or weaker. Cimarron knew he had to get the Comanche's dagger—or get his own knife and get it fast—or he was done for. He swung at the warrior and missed. The gleaming copper dagger plunged toward him.

*   *   *   *   *

Deep inside the earth, in a cell cut from the solid mountain rock, Paradox explained the history of her people to her amazed companions.

"We're no animal upstarts like you. We've evolved as a species and as a civilization, not underground but inside the ground, protected by the greatest mountains in the world, for more than sixty million years. Of course, it took almost forty million years to get to the point of building cities and whatnot. We still had quite a lot of evolving to do. I mean, you don't go from roaming around, grazing and hunting, to this," she said, waving her right arm in a broad arc to indicate the city of Itzamma, "in a few thousand years. No indeed. But after the Holocaust, our Holocaust, that is, when a meteor struck and the Earth burned then turned dark and cold, most of our ancestors died within the space of a few years. Well, it was traumatic. You don't just get over cosmic catastrophe overnight. After the Holocaust, we decided to accept the protection of the Earth and live inside the mountains. It had the added advantage of keeping us away from the life forms that came along later."

"I am an archaeologist," Ixtpan protested, "and something of an amateur paleontologist, if I do say so myself, and in all my years of scholarship and exploration, I have never come upon anything to indicate that any species ever survived so long. The creatures from whom you claim descent—dinosaurs as many humans have called them—vanished from the face of the Earth—"

"Don't be silly. If you learn nothing else here, remember this: Nothing in the world vanishes forever. Nothing."

"You're wrong. Many species and races have gone extinct."

Paradox had to turn her round face up at a ninety-degree angle to look Ixtpan in the eye. "Some have only slipped beyond your view. The possibility of return is always present, in the Earth itself and in the genes of the species that come later. You yourself are a member of the indigenous human race of this continent, a race long extinct but brought back to life by a combination of forces during the last Great Human War."

Ixtpan's dark eyes were closed, his voice very low. "I am, as you say, of the race that evolved here, from this land, the Paleoricans. Our name in your language is People of the Earth. Later races called us Quinametzin. My ancestors were giants, as I am, compared to the humans who came to Noramica thousands of years later across the land bridges and oceans from the other continents. My ancestors, too, could levitate stone to build great pyramids—the first pyramids, greater than any of those of the later races."

"And where, pray tell, are these great pyramids?" Matsemela asked icily.

"There are many on this continent," Ixtpan answered. "And on the other continents where we established colonies. But the Earth transforms everything, and in more than thirteen thousand years, they have become covered with layers of rock and earth, so that now, to you, they appear to be mountains. Only the trained eye, such as my own, can discern the difference. And they are sealed by the Earth itself. Even I cannot move enough stone to clear away the tons of earth and enter one of them."

"If your ancestors were so great, what the hell happened to them? It's not like there are a lot of you running around now." Matsemela did not believe a word of Ixtpan's story, but he could not resist asking the question.

"My people, like later races, were cursed by a fondness for the God of War. They fought among themselves for lands, for markets, for political control. From what I can discover, our world was much as the world is today—though I would give—" He closed his black eyes. "—anything for one glimpse of that world. I have spent my life trying to discover just one bit of evidence of what Paleorica was like." Ixtpan opened his eyes, though his gaze seemed fixed on something far away. "Because some of my race survived the Great Holocaust—our Holocaust, that is—tales have been passed down of what happened at the time of the ending. At the height of our great civilization, a high priest named Beelzebub Darkmirror discovered the secret of the Fire God, who can ignite the essence of matter itself that lies within the silvery-white element, uranium."

Paradox grimaced.

Ixtpan continued. "Darkmirror constructed altars to the Fire God that in reality housed a means of releasing the massive energy of the uranium in great explosions. He claimed they were for self-defense against others of our own kind. And one day, Beelzebub Darkmirror, whether to gain power over someone or thinking his own nation was under attack, or because he simply went insane, lifted one of the idols from its pedestal and set in motion the mechanism to release the Fire God from the uranium. Fire like the heart of the sun exploded across the continent, igniting other Fire

God idols as it burned. The sky went dark from the earth thrown up in the air by the force of the explosions. And then the land turned cold, so cold that the northern quadrant of the globe froze with unnatural rapidity and the ice mountains began to grow. The world of thirteen millennia ago was in an interglacial period, but the Fire God ended that. The sudden dark and cold brought on another round of the last Ice Age, and those who survived the initial Holocaust perished, along with many of the native creatures of this land."

Paradox listened carefully. "I know what you mean, to wish that for just one moment you could see a world that's gone. I would love to have seen the world of my ancestors, giants who made the earth tremble with their footsteps!" Her green face lit up with a rapturous expression as she imagined how wonderful it would have been to be seventy feet tall.

"It has," Ixtpan said, "been the greatest dream of my life."

"If your race got wiped out, what're you doing here now?" Matsemela asked Ixtpan.

"It was a miracle of the gods," Angelina answered earnestly, laying one small hand on Ixtpan's wide shoulder.

"Actually, it had more to do with commerce than gods," Ixtpan responded. "My ancestors traded with colonies across the roof of the world. When the last period of the Ice Age struck suddenly after Beelzebub Darkmirror set off the idols, about two dozen of my ancestors were flash-frozen in the northern glaciers. There they were trapped in a sort of suspended animation until the Great Fire that destroyed the Old World more than twelve thousand years later—the most intense fire since the Paleorican Holocaust—freed them from the ice and brought them back to life in an instant of blinding energy.

"The dazed and confused survivors of a dead race, my grandparents twelve times removed, made their way back to their ancient homeland. They found all traces of their world were gone, as if erased by time. They found the remnants of other civilizations, many of them splendid, that had died, apparently one after the other. They were horrified, of course, to discover that so many millennia after Beelzebub Darkmirror blew himself and the rest of his own race to eternity, his example had not been heeded. Consequently, the Paleorican survivors set about trying to find out what had gone wrong with these later-evolving humans to cause such continuing destructiveness. That is why Paleoricans have been, in our short return to this world, among the foremost archaeologists and historians of this continent. And let me tell you, from what we have been able to put together, human history has been one long downhill slide."

"Apparently so," Paradox said.

Ixtpan added, "When I die, my race will be extinct. I am the last of the Paleoricans, although I myself, for all my years of exploration and research, believed your kind to be so."

"Don't be so sure about being the last of your race. This continent does not like to give up anything. And about us," Paradox said, "you humans needed to believe we were extinct, because you were terrified of anything you could not understand, particularly anything bigger than you. And we once were—" A look of great longing passed across her face. "—much bigger than you. We are the source of half your mythology and a good number of your religions. Of course, all that was before your last Great War, where you yourselves, not nature or the gods, almost made yourselves extinct. You split two of our mountain sanctuaries wide open with your bombs. . . ."

"What is a bomb?" Ixtpan asked.

"Oh, my stars, you don't know about bombs. Hmph. And you call yourself a historian. The humans of the days before the Great War had created great birds of steel that flew higher than the eagle, higher than the giant birds of our own past. From their steel monsters they dropped instruments of destruction that they called bombs, made from that element that contains what you call the Fire God: uranium. That's what your Fire God idol is—a bomb, an atomic bomb. Where the bombs fell, the earth burned, as did everything on it. The whole sky turned gold and red and filled with gigantic mushroom-shaped clouds of fire. Then darkness covered the Earth and did not lift for fifty-two years, as though the sun itself were dead."

"August Thirteen, A.D. Two thousand thirty-nine." Ixtpan spoke the cryptic words bitterly.

"And what's that supposed to mean?" Paradox asked.

"That is the last recorded date of the Old World. August Thirteen refers to the thirteenth day of the eighth month in a calendar based on twelve months to the year. And A.D. Two thousand thirty-nine was how they designated the year. The last day. The day they dropped the bombs from the giant silver birds."

So after decades of scholarship and exploration, Ixtpan knew why the Old World had died. Its people, too, had discovered the secret, and they had used the uranium. His blood ran cold with the realization. But the humans of the last civilization of the Old World had unleashed the Fire God through bombs they made themselves, not from a Paleorican idol. And uranium, he knew from his own excavations, was plentiful in the earth west of the San Cris Mountains. That must be, he reasoned, where the people of the Old World got the uranium to make their bombs. And if the Clankers got hold of the uranium, they might someday learn how to make their own exploding idols.

"After the mess you made with your bombs, we figured we'd better keep a closer watch on you. So, in order to know and evaluate what you were up to, we sent agents among you as servants and slaves. Many of them who live among you as your servants or your pets are, in reality, older, wiser, more experienced, and better educated than you. Like me," Paradox said.

"Traitor. Viper. Spy," Matsemela roared as he grabbed Paradox by the throat.

* * * * *

Cimarron threw all his strength and weight against the Comanche warrior with such force that he knocked the man over backward on the hard, rocky ground. He was fighting on blind instinct, with the fierceness that had kept him alive through dozens of hand-to-hand fights, soaked with sweat in the blistering sun and breathing heavily from the exertion. They rolled in the dirt, trading blows, Cimarron struggling to keep from being stabbed. He drew back his right fist and, when the warrior raised his right arm to block the punch, Cimarron struck the man hard in the jaw with his left. The move caught the warrior off guard, and Cimarron pinned him down and struck him hard again and again. The man's fingers loosened around his dagger, and Cimarron grabbed it, raising it to stab his enemy.

With the blade only inches from the Comanche's chest, Cimarron stopped, his hand suspended, shaking. It took all his strength to stop himself from killing the other man, and he trembled from the effort. Fighting had become an instinct to him and rage a normal state of mind over the years, so much so that once the rage was triggered, he couldn't stop himself from acting on it. But he looked into the man's eyes and saw too many Comanche friends from his youth in Pecos looking back at him, and the eyes of too many dead Comanches out on the grass plains.

"Do it, coward," the warrior growled in Comanche, his dark features contorted with hatred for the Confederation army scout.

Cimarron took a long, slow breath then threw the knife away. It clanked loudly as it struck the red rocks nearby. He moaned softly as he realized what he had done. He knelt beside the surprised Comanche, his sun-bronzed skin suddenly sickly pale.

The knowledge of what the Clankers had done to the Comanches was seared in his heart like a brand. To Cimarron's way of thinking, the horsewarriors had been victims of the Confederation's expansion as much as Pecos had. Six years earlier, he and Zaco had accompanied their friend, Topsannah Morales, the daughter of a Comanche princess and a gambler from Durango, to visit her mother, Morning Star, at an encampment at Dry Creek, a five day ride north of Reynada. It was early spring, and the land was ablaze with bluebonnets and the red, yellow, and orange flowers called Indian paintbrush. The *huisache* trees were covered in thick gold flowers, and the yucca were blooming with their flame-shaped white flowers. On that trip north, the world had been a beautiful place, but it was about to change for all three of them forever.

Before they arrived, the Comanche village had been visited by a company of Clankers under the command, they were later to learn, of the infamous Gen. Absalom Ironheart, the man who had directed the conquest of Delta Territory in the East. The smell of death reached them even before they caught sight of what was left of the once-peaceful village. The tipis were torn and burned, their poles snapped off, the bisonhide remnants blowing in the prairie wind. And there were bodies everywhere.

In his dreams, Cimarron still heard the sound of Topsannah's wrenching scream when she found her mother's body in the creekbed. Morning Star had died trying to protect the children from the swords and knives of the soldiers. The creekbed was littered with the bodies of dead children.

Zaco kept watch, making his own decisions and plans while Cimarron held Topsannah tight all night long, restraining her to keep her from harming herself in her grief. Though Cimarron had kept her physically alive through that night, he knew, too, that the soul of the carefree, city-loving young girl had died there at Dry Creek. And within a few months, she was gone from his life.

Cimarron had known many Comanches. He had loved a Comanche woman. He had already killed more men than he could remember, but he could not kill this warrior on this day, not even to save his own life. I've thrown it all away, he thought. All of it.

"Why, Clanker?" the warrior demanded contemptuously,

quickly rising to his feet. His angry eyes were bloodshot from years of riding through sand and dust. "You won. You should have killed me. Have you no honor?" He grabbed his copper dagger and stood facing Cimarron with it.

The blood-red sun was starting to set behind the mountains, and the clouds were streaking across the sky as fast as a herd of buffalo on the run, lit up with streaks of gold, pink, orange, and purple on the wide horizon. "I'm no Clanker," Cimarron answered calmly in perfect Comanche, letting his eyes stray from the warrior just long enough for one fast look at the flaming Pecos sunset. "I've known some of your folks, and I've got no quarrel with you. There's no honor in killing someone who could be a friend." He got up slowly and offered his hand, knowing fully that the man would more than likely attack him again.

The warrior, after several painfully long minutes, stuck his dagger in his belt and took Cimarron's hand, staring hard into his eyes. "So why do you wear their uniform? Why do you scout for them?"

"That's a long story." When Cimarron smiled, his angular face lit up and he looked for that moment almost as young as he was. "Is it enough to say I'm glad to see you, amigo?"

"I am named Eeschatai," the Comanche answered, his eyes carefully studying the stranger. "I was named for the one who was a great prophet of my people in ancient times. You are a warrior, as am I, and I honor you for that."

"They call me Cimarron Langtry."

"For the shrine on the Rio Bravo?"

"Yeah. I don't know my real name—whatever name my own people gave me. Don't even know who my own people were. The fellow that found me, Dezcalzo Two Creeks, gave me the name I use. For that old shrine to the goddess of Old World Texas, Lillie Langtry. Had a strange sense of humor, old Dezcalzo did. He died a few years back. Clankers killed him."

"Is that why you are glad to meet me, Cimarron Langtry? Because you think my people will help you avenge this man who was like a father to you?"

"No, Eeschatai." His voice was hoarse, his eyes half closed. "Let's just say I think you and I can help each other."

"How?"

"I reckon y'all are going after the Clankers, probably in a few days' time, when they get farther into the Terlingua Mountains. Don't try to deny it." Cimarron smiled in response to Eeschatai's

unsuccessful attempt at what was called, in the idiom of the
frontier, a "poker face." There was to Cimarron no mistaking the
slight grin that played for the moment on the Comanche's lips
and the gleam in his black eyes. "I'll bet you could use a map of
the layout of the camp, the locations of sentries, things like that."

The rigidly held lines of Eeschatai's bronze face melted into a
big grin and he started to laugh. "Why do you turn on your own
people?"

"They aren't my people."

"If our warriors attack your army, they will kill everyone in a
blue uniform, including you. We plan to attack at night, two days
from today. Do not be in your camp on that night."

"I'll be there. I've got to be. There's something I can do that'll
make it a lot easier for you. In two days, at midnight, I'll
stampede the Clankers' horses for you. That'll be your signal to
attack. What happens after that . . . *quién sabe?* " He shrugged
his shoulders. "Just see to it that the Clankers aren't in any shape
to go anywhere else when you get through with them."

"We will do our best." The warrior studied the scout for a few
moments. "Do not forget this." Eeschatai stooped and picked up
the steel knife from the dirt and handed it to Cimarron.

As Cimarron walked toward his horse, he turned and called
out, "By the way, who's the chief of your tribe?"

Eeschatai mounted his horse silently, then said, "We follow the
lead of the warrior, Bajo del Sol, and, like him, we fear nothing
under the sun."

*   *   *   *   *

The red flames of the roaring campfire shot against the black
night sky, and fragrant mesquite smoke filled the air. Two corpo-
rals, both huge men dressed in buckskin and bronze hoop armor
vests, lugged a desert terrapin to the fire. Laughing, they swung it
over the coals then let it go. The big turtle hit the hot coals with a
loud crack. Soon the flesh inside its shell began to roast.

Cimarron sat alone, far away from the fire and the general rev-
elry around it. From a distance he watched the terrapin cook alive.
Two soldiers caught hold of the hot shell and flipped it over onto
its stomach. One of them swung a bronze axe into its back, cutting
a hole in the shell. Another one shook some salt and pepper into
the hole. The soldiers let their dinner continue roasting for another hour before they took it off the fire, cut it open, and devoured its insides under the light of the full moon.

A huge bison turned on a spit over a pit of burning mesquite nearby. The turtle and the bison provided a welcome relief from the usual army fare—salt beef, rice, beans, cornbread, and coffee—and many of the five-hundred-man cavalry unit were celebrating. Two deerskin bags were suspended near the fires, and the cooks used bronze tongs to pick up heated rocks and throw them in the water. The hot rocks made the water boil and when it did, they threw in the blooms of dagger and palma plants to cook.

All of the men were so covered with dust that they looked like the naturally mummified remains of Ancient Ones sometimes found in dry caves at high elevations. And they were sick of tasting the alkali the horses kicked up from the dry ground. As a consequence, they were all very thirsty. Bottles and skin canteens of rotgut whiskey and sour wine were passed from hand to hand around the campfires. Several guitars were being strummed, and flutes made from bone, wood, and—most highly prized of all—from rare Old World lead pipes were being played around the encampment. The women who followed the cavalry mingled among the men and danced to the many rhythms of the night.

The tension of the past few days was broken by the food, drink, and recreation. The terrain wore on the nerves as much as on the bodies of those crossing it.

There were half a dozen tents pitched for the officers. The men, of course, would sleep on their blankets in the field. The cavalry's hundreds of horses were constantly guarded. The remuda of horses would be a tempting target for the Comanches. Even the blood enemies of the great tribes of the plains acknowledged them to be the foremost horsewarriors on the continent.

"Don't you like *tortuga?*" Amos Crimsonleaf asked Cimarron as he sat on a rock a couple of feet away. He uncorked his skin flask and offered it to the scout. Amos was covered in dust, as they all were, but the gold in his hair showed through the grime.

"Thanks. No, I don't like turtle." Cimarron took a long drink and handed the flask back.

The sounds of the night were interrupted by a soft whistling sound that passed over the heads of Cimarron and Amos. The owl feather-tipped hackberry arrow struck Noji Aliota, the short, black-skinned corporal who had served fifteen years in the Confederation army, in the heart not fifty feet from where Cimarron and Amos were talking alone. He screamed, then fell dead. Twenty men scrambled for their horses to take off after the assassin whose arrow had cut down one of their number.

Neither Cimarron nor Amos moved.

"Wasn't he a friend of yours?" Cimarron asked.

"Yeah," Amos answered, still not moving. "But what's dead is dead."

"A Comanche fired that arrow," Cimarron said, not bothering to suppress the smile on his face. "But they'll never catch him. Whoever shot that arrow is long gone."

"We'll catch up with them soon enough," Amos answered.

"There are enough Comanches out this way to wipe out this bunch in one fight," Cimarron offered.

"Winchester's got a contingency plan," Amos shot back.

"What?"

"Nothing."

"Tell me, damn you." Cimarron grabbed Amos by the shirt and jerked him close. "Look, Bismark's got my life on the line out here, too, and I want to know what's going on."

"All right, you think Baines Winchester's so crazy that he'd have only one division out here?"

"No, I don't think he's crazy—at least not about military strategy. Hell, I should've figured it out myself." He released Amos. "Who's in command?"

Amos looked at his own dust-caked hands and did not answer.

"Come on, damn it. You've told me this much. There's nothing I can do about it, is there?"

Amos grinned. "All right. Absalom Ironheart, commander general of the whole Tesharka army, is less than two weeks behind us with an army of five to ten thousand soldiers. Ironheart's had lots of experience mopping up Comanches. There's no one better. I served with him myself six years ago, out here on the plains. I was with him when we wiped out the devils at Dry Creek. Satisfied?" He enjoyed watching Cimarron wince and wondered what nerve he had struck.

"Yeah, I'm satisfied."

Amos made two corn shuck cigarettes, carefully laying the fragrant tobacco in the shucks and rolling them slowly. He offered one to Cimarron, who took it, lit it off a nearby campfire, and took a long, deep drag. Amos lit his own cigarette off the same fire, saying, "Sorry if the news about old Absalom's got you upset, buddy."

"*Es nada,*" Cimarron answered, his eyes fixed on the faraway eastern horizon. "You know, the Comanches could wipe you all out before your Ironheart gets west of Comanche Springs."

"Maybe."

"Why're you doing this? What's in it for you?"

"I'm in it for the money. I got tired of herding sheep up in Muskogee. Besides," Amos took another drag on the thick corn shuck cigarette, "I like being a soldier. Hell, it's what I'm used to. Maybe you can understand that."

"Maybe."

Amos stalked off, leaving Cimarron to watch the burning terrapin and the barely glimpsed wisps of motion beyond the encampment, ghostly Comanche warriors silently circling the troops, while the coyotes howled at the moon.

CHAPTER 7

THE EARTH SPEAKS

Still shrouded in constantly blowing dust, Arshal was ringed by five thousand troops, five times the number that had guarded the capital city only a month before, when Guvnor Baines Winchester had ordered his commander general's armies to pull out of Delta and move west. The number of soldiers guarding the impregnable capital had increased since the insurrection in Delta three weeks before. No sooner had Absalom Ironheart withdrawn his army, than slaves from all across Delta had risen in rebellion. Ironheart was now well on his way toward Epitaph, double-timing his men in the hope of beating his young rival, Reno Bismark, there. In Delta, slaves were burning the cotton fields in open insurrection.

Inside the hexagonal office atop Fort Beau, Baines Winchester poured another round of Mother Baines's Snake Oil Elixir. "Well, boys," he said, "we've got to get some more troops to Delta to put down that damned slave revolt."

"How can we get more troops?" the nervous minister of commerce asked.

The dark sands of Tesharka, visible through the eight windows, blew around those in the conference room. To anyone below, the dark, blowing sands gave the government office the look of being suspended above the Earth on a sinister cloud. From the guvnor's office above, the blowing sands looked like swirling, dark waters, often turning in twisters, like whirlpools in a churning sea.

"By drafting them out of the territories, of course. Put out a call today for another ten thousand conscripts." Baines Winchester lit a cigar and puffed the smoke nonchalantly. "We'll have them by the month's end or there'll be some towns burned to ash!"

"Ten thousand more? There'll be rebellion. . . ."

"Let 'em rebel," Winchester answered defiantly.

"But if we take the troops out of anywhere else," Big John Cloudcap said, downing a shot of snake oil elixir with a smile fixed on his round face, "there'll be a rebellion there. We can't draft every man, woman, and child in every territory!"

"I damn well can if I want to," Baines Winchester responded, pounding his heavy fist on the table so hard that he caused elixir to splash from the goblets of several ministers.

"That will not be necessary." When Zumarraga Apocalypse spoke, the room grew as silent as a tomb and all the ministers looked nervously down at the white onyx table. "When our troops take Epitaph and seize the Fire God, the rebellions will end forever. No one on this continent, not in this world, will dare oppose anything we desire. All lands, all minerals, all people, they will belong to us. And we will usher in a new world of peace under the guidance of a powerful god, the ultimate God of War."

"No more draft?" Big John Cloudcap asked hopefully, his full-moon cheeks flushed red with excitement. He had come to dread the riots that always followed a draft call-up, since it was his responsibility to put the rebellions down. He was arguably the most unpopular man in the territories, and he was unable to go anywhere outside his own rooms in Fort Beau without a contingent of armed guards to protect him. He bore scars all over his body from narrowly failed attempts at dispatching him from the planet.

"No more draft," Apocalypse answered, with a smile forming at the corners of his thin lips. "With the Fire God, it won't be necessary anymore. We will have the ultimate weapon, and no one will dare to fight us. We will usher in a thousand years of peace."

* * * * *

Later that night, in a high stone tower that rose like a needle above Fort Beau, Zumarraga Apocalypse, in his diamond-dotted black cape, opened the door to his private rooms to two soldiers. They had in their custody a boy of sixteen who had been captured in the Blackhawk Hills of Pecos while fighting with a gang of young vandals. The soldiers wearily led the blond-haired boy into the dark room, lit only by five white candle flames. The candlelight reflected monstrously off the black crystal walls. The boy tried to struggle, but the soldiers, both expressing boredom on their faces, held him tight and dragged him to an altar in the north corner of the room. The altar was covered in colorful stone mosaic images of strange creatures and symbols. Above the altar hung a cross of iron, but its arms were twisted at grotesque right angles. The guards laid the boy on the altar and held him down while Zumarraga Apocalypse withdrew a long obsidian knife from a black silk case. The boy was a sacrifice demanded by his god, a sacrifice that would ensure him success in his quest for the powerful idol that would make his god triumphant in the land once again. It was the ritual sacrifice that had kept Zumarraga Apocalypse alive for fifteen centuries. He was confident that the ritual he practiced faithfully would keep him alive forever. The high priest of the Church of the New World raised his knife high above the boy's chest.

* * * * *

Baines Winchester could not sleep. He was alone in his private chamber, a great room two hundred feet across with walls of brown-striped white onyx. On one wall hung an elaborate gilt-framed portrait of his grandmother, Annamay Baines, an old woman in a white lace cap that tied under her chin. Remarkably she shared her grandson's features almost exactly, from the bulbous nose to the oversized ears.

The guvnor of Tesharka paced his room nervously, stopping a couple of times to pour a shot of snake oil elixir into a crystal goblet and drink it down. He gazed through a six-foot-high window of perfectly clear crystal, out over his capital city. The dirt streets, as usual, were empty, except for a platoon of soldiers escorting one hundred or so chained slaves on their way to Delta.

He couldn't sleep when he was worried, and most nights lately that's just what he was. He was worried about the uprising in Delta, about the situation in the West with that damned prophet, and about just how powerful the Comanches were. What's more, Zumarraga Apocalypse had him spooked with all his talk of Fire Gods. He had watched the pictures in the obsidian mirror and knew that he sure would like to have the weapon that turned cities into mushroom clouds of fire. He figured for certain that he'd be remembered in history if he got hold of a thing like that. But sometimes he wondered if Apocalypse was playing with a full deck.

He had witnessed Apocalypse's bizarre rituals many times. Seeing the old man kill people on an altar didn't bother him a bit, but he did think the astrologer got a little carried away at times with his own rhetoric. But it was, Baines Winchester firmly believed, Apocalypse's ritual blood sacrifice that had made him such a powerful man. He didn't mind letting Apocalypse kill all the slaves and prisoners he wanted. Hell, it saved the army the trouble. Apocalypse's ritual had bought him longevity, vigor, and power beyond his dreams. There was no question in the guvnor's mind that he owed everything to Zumarraga Apocalypse. And, of course, to his grandmother, Annamay Baines.

There was no doubt that things had gone his way since fifty-nine years before, when he had made a pact with the old astrologer priest. He'd come a long way from being Beau Winchester's scrawny little boy, the little boy who had been afraid of the dark and hated to be alone. Only his grandmother had understood, always taking him into her bed when he was a scared child in the night. Hell, now he was the most powerful man on the continent, maybe in all of history. "That's what I want, Grandma," he said aloud, toasting the portrait of the lady with a goblet of her infamous elixir. "To be remembered in history. And Zumarraga Apocalypse says it's in my stars that I'll be remembered for a thousand years."

*   *   *   *   *

The cell was carved from the solid gray granite of the inside of the mountain. It was dark, lit only by one small candle stuck in a white obsidian pot. The candle cast a frail, flickering light on the prisoners, who sat on the cold stone, leaning against the hard gray walls.

"I fear, Ixtpan, that neither of us will reach your Falling Eagle." Angelina whispered. Her normally golden brown skin was ashen, and her long black hair fell around her shoulders like a veil. Her eyes were deep purple in the candlelight.

"Yes, we will, Angelina," Ixtpan whispered. "No doubt the gods have directed us to this place for some reason." Hiding his own fears from Angelina, he glared hard at Paradox, who had, in fact, brought them to Itzamma. The giant wondered if they would ever see the sacred sunlight again, if there was any chance of fulfilling their quest. Well, he thought, the gods have directed my steps before. Perhaps there is some purpose in our being in this ancient city, a city half as old as time itself, he thought. He was more distressed about the great knowledge of the itzaurs he would not live long enough to learn than he was about actually dying. But there was Angelina to think of. He had promised the *tlamantinimi*, the Wise Ones of Tamoanchan—most especially High Priestess Xochi herself, a woman he had loved in silence with pure devotion for the ten years he had known her—that he would protect Angelina with his life. Now there was no way for even such a sacrifice to help the young *curandera*.

Angelina pressed her face against Ixtpan's chest and focused all her concentration on memories of her home. She used the vibrant images of the leaves and vines in the constant mist where the clouds met the sierras to shut out the darkness and growing evil she sensed drawing closer to her friends and herself.

"Yes, Ixtpan's right." Paradox was eager to be helpful, since it was she who had brought the travelers to Itzamma and their current predicament. "We will get out of here any time now."

"Ixtpan," Angelina asked, "can you make the rocks move?"

"Are you kidding?" demanded Matsemela.

"My race built great pyramids by levitating stone, you ignorant oaf. Were we surrounded by boulders, I could free us. But there is no stone here I can move, because we are surrounded by solid granite," Ixtpan answered solemnly. "I would have to be able to move the whole mountain, and that is beyond even my powers."

As he spoke, they heard the iron bar being raised. The gigantic stone door slid open, and they saw two dozen guards, all heavily armed, standing in the doorway and beyond into the hallway. Six of them pushed their way into the stone cell. Their leader, a silver-robed gray itzaur built essentially in the shape of a cube, followed them into the cell, and said to Angelina, "Come forth. Our leader, the High Priest, Jolosumu, demands your presence."

"No way." Ixtpan was on his feet directly between Angelina and the platoon of green, gray, and gold itzaurs. "She goes nowhere without the rest of us."

Matsemela took his place beside Ixtpan, hands on his hips and a snarl on his face.

The commander laughed. "Don't be fools. It's only the woman they want. And she is not to be killed. She is to be returned to her own people. Then we will free the rest of you to go on with your pathetic lives."

"No," Ixtpan protested, his face red with rage. "You will have to kill me to take her."

"Ixtpan, *por favor*. Do not fight. There are too many of them." Angelina stood calmly by the commanding itzaur, fingering a tiny pouch containing a purple fluorite crystal, the stone that nature had created in the shape of two joined four-sided pyramids.

Paradox started to move beside Ixtpan, saying, "That goes for me, too, you son of stegosaur—" Suddenly she stopped in mid-sentence and stepped instead next to Matsemela, a hint of a smile on her narrow lips and a plan going through her mind. "Well, maybe not so fast. Why die for a human, after all? Citizens, do your duty."

Ixtpan raised his right arm to strike one of the itzaurs, but Angelina grabbed it and stopped him. "Do not fight here where you cannot win. Remember, *compañero*, there remains much to be done."

The healer stepped toward the guard whose outstretched,

clawlike fingers reached for her. But as the scaly fingers brushed her skin, the guard, as much to his own surprise as that of anyone else there, found himself flying across the cell, toward the hard stone wall. His green head struck with a loud clunk. Paradox stood grinning, pleased with her quick throwing of the guard who was a full foot taller than she was, an unusual height for an itzaur, then quickly kicked another in the stomach, letting out a loud squeal she intended as a battle cry.

Matsemela, who when motivated could move as fast as an untamed mustang, had two more guards flying half a second later. Ixtpan used one itzaur as a battering ram to push the others back from the doorway. Angelina tripped another so that he hit the stone floor hard.

Matsemela knocked out two more with fast chops of his big fists and made it out into the hallway, roaring like an angry bull, straight into the six other itzaur guards scrambling to get into the fight. He had four of them on the stone floor fast. And, better still, he grabbed a slender silver sword off another before sending him flying head over heels. Using the sword to hold back the others, he screamed, "Angelina, come to me! Now!"

Angelina ran toward Matsemela.

Suddenly one of the itzaurs grabbed her. The itzaur and Angelina struggled while four more guards engaged the others in fighting. Angelina broke momentarily from her attacker.

"Here!" Matsemela threw the long silver sword to Angelina and she caught its diamond handle perfectly.

The itzaur was about to spring at her, but he froze, seeing the weapon in the woman's hand.

Angelina raised the sword to use it, but then hesitated, staring at the weapon she held. Then she dropped the sword. It clanged loudly against the hard stone.

"No!" Ixtpan screamed. "Angelina!" He called her name in a heartbroken wail as Angelina stood silently, letting the itzaur guards bind her wrists and ankles with golden chains.

Reinforcements arrived, and they quickly returned the prisoners to their cell. Angelina was led away.

Back in the dark cell, Paradox moaned, "Why didn't she kill the son of Gila monster? Why?"

"She won't," Matsemela said, shaking his head sadly. "Crazy, plain crazy." He touched the side of his head to indicate insanity.

"She is not crazy, you insensitive buffoon," Ixtpan responded indignantly. "She is only following the way of her religion. She has taken sacred vows never to take a human life. Angelina comes from a race that long ago pledged to engage in no form of human sacrifice. For them, that came to mean that those in spiritual leadership must kill no other human, under any circumstances. Angelina has great powers of healing—as even you must admit, Matsemela. . . ."

"Yes, I admit it. Hell, I saw her fix that saddletramp—"

"If Angelina takes a human life, she will break her holy vows and lose her powers. Her life is consecrated to the God of Life, from whom her powers come. No, Angelina would die before she would intentionally kill."

"That," said Matsemela bitterly, "is just what's going to happen. She's going to die because she wouldn't kill. Not to mention that we're going to die, too." He looked accusingly at Ixtpan. "Where did she get her crazy ideas, anyhow?"

"That, amigo, is a long story," Ixtpan said in a voice filled with sorrow. "But since we aren't going anywhere for a while—if ever—you may as well hear it. It begins with a race of people that once dominated the continent of Noramica an eon ago—"

"The damned thing about this blasted continent," said Matsemela dismally, straightening his leather-and-bone helmet, "is that nothing is ever over! Nothing is ever just dead and gone in Noramica. You can't turn around without running into the ruins of some long-gone civilization or another! How the hell many of them have there been?" It was less a question than an accusation. "I never should've left Afria. At least there you don't get confused about what the hell millennium it is."

"The power of creation on this continent is very strong," Ixtpan responded, his eyes narrowed with annoyance, "and it never gives up. Here, time is an unbreakable cycle endlessly repeating, as though the Earth itself remembers its past and compels its children to live it out, again and again."

"What does all this ancient history have to do with Angelina?" Paradox demanded, tears forming in her round eyes. She feared what might be happening to the young woman of whom she had grown fond.

Ixtpan slammed his fist into the gray wall of solid stone.

*   *   *   *   *

While the travelers were imprisoned in Itzamma, the Confederation army moved steadily westward and had pitched camp only forty miles east of the hidden itzaur city.

Reno Bismark sat at a pine table inside his large tent during the heat of the afternoon, studying maps of the area. The army was in territory of which no known maps of any detail existed, and the colonel was forced to rely a good deal on his scouts, of which Cimarron Langtry was only one of several. Bismark was so hot that he felt the sweat rolling down his neck and chest, his uniform stuck to his body, and his copper hair was as wet as if he had been caught in the rain. Of course, he had seen no rain since he and his troops had left Reynada. "Damn this land!" he grumbled aloud. "It's not fit for man and should've been left to the coyotes and mesquite." He reached for his pottery mug of water and found it empty. "Here, boy!" he called out, clapping his hands together loudly as though summoning a dog.

A gray itzaur about four and a half feet tall, wearing a small version of the blue military uniform, including the bronze hoop armor vest, scurried into the tent. He stood in front of the colonel, his head humbly bowed low.

"Water!" Bismark ordered, pointing to the mug. He had had this itzaur houseboy for a month now and found him smarter—and less ornery—than most humans. The itzaur could understand certain commands and carry out simple tasks. He never talked back or acted insubordinate, and he tolerated the desert heat well—better, in fact, than many people. All in all, the itzaur the colonel had named Fred—for a friend of his who had died in the massacre at Isleta—was working out much to his liking.

Fred ran for the blue-and-white porcelain water pitcher that sat on a small table in the tent's far corner, but his gait slowed as he returned to his owner.

"What's the problem, Fred, old boy? Hurry up!"

Fred slowly poured the water, for the first time looking Reno Bismark in the eye.

The colonel was unnerved. "Do I need to have the doc take a look at you?" Bismark asked, reaching out to feel the creature's forehead for signs of fever. He felt none, then he picked up the mug and brought it to his lips.

"No, sir. Actually, if I may, I would like to have a word with you."

Reno Bismark spit out the water and dropped his mug to the ground, the precious water within spilling on the soil. "What in the name of . . . ?" He jumped to his feet and reached for his sword.

"I realize you are surprised, sir," Fred said, taking a step backward, "that I can talk, but if you will listen, I think you and I can be of great benefit to one another."

"What could you possibly . . ." Bismark drew the sword and swung.

"Wait!" Fred screamed in a high-pitched squawk, jumping out of the way of the blade by barely an inch. He knocked over the table and a bottle labeled "Mother Baines's Snake Oil Elixir," sending a purple liquid pouring forth from it. The elixir bubbled and steamed menacingly on the ground.

Bismark aimed the sword straight at Fred and began chasing him around the tent.

"The woman you want . . ." Fred was running so hard that it was hard for him to get out more than a phrase at a time. "The healer!" He threw himself flat on the ground, dodging the slashing sword.

Bismark stopped, his sword barely half an inch from Fred's chest. "What about the healer?"

"I know where she is." Fred was gasping, staring straight at the steel sword point, his large, round black eyes twice their normal size, his gray skin as pale as an unbleached cornhusk. "I can get her for you."

"Get up, Fred," Bismark said, lowering but not putting away his sword.

Fred got up slowly and dusted himself off. He shook himself, squared his shoulders, and with almost regal composure drew himself to his full height. "My name is not Fred. It is Xichendary. I can give you the woman if you meet my terms."

"Talk." Bismark reached for his skin canteen of *mezcal*. He did not like to drink much on the trail, particularly not in hostile country, where rebels or Comanches were as likely to show up over the next ridge as a tumbleweed was to roll in the wind. But on this day he took a long, deep drink of the smooth golden liquid. "Tell me what a lizard like you could possibly know about the witch." He took another long swallow.

"My people and I are *not* lizards. We are an ancient race that was here long before your kind crawled out of the muck, and which will survive your own. I can deliver the woman and her companions to you, provided, of course, we can work out an agreement that is satisfactory to us both."

"I'm sure that can be arranged," Bismark said. "I want the woman alive and unharmed." He grinned. "Well, at least not seriously harmed. Go ahead and kill the others if you want. They're of no use to us. All right, Fred, I am prepared to offer you ten thousand jadas for her, enough to make you a rich man." He stammered self-consciously. "I mean a rich itzaur."

"Fool, what are more stones to us? And my name is not Fred. What I demand in return for the woman is that you begin secret negotiations between your government and my own to establish trade between our peoples."

"Trade? What could you possibly have to sell, some dead flies or whatever it is you creatures eat?"

Xichendary reached into his uniform pocket. He held his tightly closed clawlike fist out to Reno Bismark. Then he opened his hand. "We do not eat dead flies." In the itzaur's fist were five round gemstones, each about half an inch in diameter, each of them flawless.

Reno Bismark quickly identified a diamond, a ruby, an emerald, a star sapphire, and an amethyst in the itzaur's hand. "I think we can work something out, Xichen . . ."

"Xichendary. And what we demand is that your army stop here. Go no farther into these mountains."

"Got something to hide up there?" With gems like these, Bismark thought, I'll bet you have a lot to hide. And where these stones came from, he realized, there were sure to be more.

"No, of course not. But we do not intend to have humans swarming like locusts out here, carrying your plagues and your eternal destruction. I will deliver the woman and her companions to you at this time—when the full moon is highest in the sky—two nights from now. Do we have a deal?"

"Give us the woman and these mountains are yours for as long as the mountains stand and the rivers run. You have my word on it."

* * * * *

In the army camp, the animals began going wild, the many-colored horses neighing and running about wildly, the black and gray mules kicking and braying, the tan camels trying to break free from their tethers. The wind was blowing up from the south, as though in protest against what was coming.

Cimarron knew what was going to happen, because he had seen the animals act that way before—just before he saw hundreds of people and animals die in Zatecas when the earth shifted. Friends in Durango believed the quakes were caused by the God of War, Tezcatlipoca, to whom human lives were sacrificed in ancient times. It was Tezcatlipoca who made the mountains rumble and moved the earth itself. Cimarron felt the tension building in the earth like some immense, sinister force of destruction. But he had also learned in the earthquake-prone region south of the Rio Bravo that there is no place to hide from the earth, so he sat watching the campfire, smoking a corn shuck cigarette, and waiting. Well, Tezcatlipoca, he thought, if you want human sacrifice, I guess you'll get it now. Does the day ever come when you've had enough?

The sound started out in the mountains. It was louder, deeper than the sound of a buffalo stampede. Then the earth began to shake. The soldiers screamed and ran as though there were somewhere they might be safe, though, of course, there was not. Some of the animals broke free and ran madly through the camp. The brown canvas tents collapsed. Men were knocked to the ground by the trembling earth. Dust rose in a stinging red cloud.

Cimarron still did not move but sat watching it all, a somber smile on his face. He took another deep drag on his cigarette. The jarring motion finally threw him to his knees, then the earth split open only a few feet away—and the crack spread and deepened as it came steadily closer to him.

As the earth opened up, Cimarron began slipping into the growing chasm, his fingers instinctively but futilely grabbing at the loose sand and stones.

Even with the earth still shifting, Wyatt Fontana, Reno Bismark's lieutenant, ran toward the cleft in the earth. His face was streaked with red dirt, and he shielded his eyes from the dust in order to see. He had seen Cimarron pulled into the rift as though by some gigantic hand. Wyatt threw himself to the shaking ground and reached for the man just beyond his grasp. "Take my hand!" Wyatt screamed over the roar of the earthquake.

The earth shook even more violently. Cimarron reached for Wyatt's hand but couldn't quite connect, then the earth jerked violently again, and he slipped deeper into the chasm.

Wyatt inched closer, his right hand still outstretched. He leaned over the edge of the crevasse and reached down to Cimarron, the sweat on Fontana's face running in streaks through the dust. "C'mon!" he yelled.

Cimarron strained with all his strength and reached for Wyatt with his left hand. Just as another tremor shook them, the lieutenant's fingers closed over his own. In spite of the horrendous shaking, Wyatt, who, as Cimarron had assessed, was a lot stronger than he looked, held onto Cimarron's hand. Both men slipped farther into the chasm.

As Wyatt was leaning over and the ground was shaking, an amulet on a leather cord fell out of his shirt, hanging down so that it was directly in Cimarron's face. As Cimarron felt the earth dragging him to his death, he found himself staring into a lead medallion in the shape of a cross, the ancient symbol of the unity of the earth and the spirit. But the arms of this cross were twisted at right angles.

Finally, after long, long minutes, the shaking and groaning stopped and the air was filled with an eerie silence and a cloud of red dust stirred up by the quake. The soldiers could be heard as they cried out, looking for their friends in its aftermath. Wyatt pulled Cimarron out of the gash in the earth and helped him to his feet. Both men stood facing each other, trembling from the earthquake's force and coughing from the dust in the air.

Cimarron clasped Wyatt's hand. "*Muchas gracias.*" He lowered his voice. "I'm mighty beholden to you. Now tell me why. You didn't risk your life to help me because we played a few ball games together when we were kids. You haven't even spoken to me since that day you were ready to kill me in Reno's office. Why do you care what happens to me?"

Wyatt's voice was little more than a whisper. "Believe it or not, back there in Reynada, when we were kids, I kind of admired you . . . you and Zaco. I didn't like . . . what happened in Bismark's office that day . . . but what could I do about it? You know what they do to soldiers who don't obey orders." He looked furtively around to be certain that everyone else was occupied with the earthquake and no one had heard what he had said.

"Yeah, Wyatt, I do know. In any case, I'm mighty grateful to you."

"If only things were different . . ."

"Cimarron!" Reno Bismark's deep voice called from a nearby group of men gathered around the wreckage of the whiskey wagon. "Get over here. I need to see you right now! I want you to scout us a new campsite fast! Away from this damn place! The land will be too unstable around this chasm when the aftershocks start." He yelled loudly to everyone who could hear him, "Get your stuff together and move out!"

"One of these days, Wyatt," Cimarron answered softly, ignoring Bismark and the flurry of activity around him for the moment, "there'll be a way to make it all different, but folks like you and me're going to have to face up to what has to be done." As he turned away, he wondered if he could trust Wyatt. No, he thought, no matter what he did for me tonight, he still works for Reno.

I am going to make it all different, Cimarron, Wyatt thought, putting the amulet back inside his shirt, where it would not be seen again, caressing the twisted cross with his short, sun-bronzed fingers as he did so. He was relieved that the symbol, the emblem of his religion, the Church of the New World, seemed to have meant nothing to Cimarron.

The army actually suffered little damage in the earthquake, whose epicenter was deeper in the Terlingua Mountains, because it had camped in a large open area where nothing could fall on it. Several men and horses died by falling into the newly formed trench in the earth and a barrel of whiskey broke when it fell from the wagon carrying it. The earth had moved, but its movement had cost the Tesharka Confederation army very little.

* * * * *

While Xichendary was revealing his true nature to a mightily surprised Reno Bismark about forty miles away, Ixtpan was telling Angelina's story to his fellow prisoners.

Ixtpan folded his long arms solemnly across his chest. His bronze skin glowed in darker shades of brown in the light of the small candle, and his thick black and gray hair stood straight out around him, making him look slightly mad.

"Angelina's history is interwoven with the history of this land, inseparable from it, and to understand her, you have to know something of its history," Ixtpan explained.

"Three thousand years ago, the greatest civilization in the history of post-Ice Age Noramica was created between the two great mountain ranges known as the Sierra Madre in the Valley of Mexico. It was called Teotihuacán." He spoke the name with reverence. "The name means 'the place where humans became gods.' It was almost true. The city was unlike any the world has ever known. It was a vast city of tens of thousands, with two great pyramids and exquisite buildings and temples, most important being the Temple of the Feathered Serpent. Teotihuacán spread its culture, language, and religion over thousands of miles, not with warfare but with the power of its highly developed civilization, great wisdom and knowledge of things both material and spiritual, and with a positively remarkable ability in the area of commerce. For more than eight hundred years, longer than any other civilization in the history of Noramica, Teotihuacán survived in peace and prosperity and became the mother of all the other civilizations on this continent. But, about twenty-three hundred years ago, the city died in flames, as if struck down by the God of Fire himself." Ixtpan shuddered, thinking of long-empty streets and majestic, deserted pyramids, his narrow eyes half closed. "The land sank into a Dark Age of confusion, isolation, and barbarism."

"Only twenty-three hundred years to go," Matsemela snarled, closing his eyes as though to go to sleep.

"Then, two hundred and fifty years after Teotihuacán burned, a great prophet, a prince, was born in the Valley of Mexico. His mother, Chimalman, was descended from the people of Teotihuacán, and she practiced their ancient religion. The prince took the name of one of his mother's gods, Quetzalcoatl, in the old language, or, as we would say now, Feathered Serpent."

"Not this again!" Matsemela roared, his eyes wide open again. His brow was creased so deeply that it formed a ridge against his bone-and-leather helmet. "Every time we're in trouble, you start with gibberish about flying snakes!"

"Hush!" Paradox's voice was high-pitched but nonetheless formidable enough to silence Matsemela temporarily. "I want to hear this."

"Prince Feathered Serpent, according to the ancient codices and legends, had fair skin and a long black beard, both most unusual for a man of his time and nation, and he always dressed in black. He was a great warrior and a man of great spirituality. He transformed the world of his time and," Ixtpan sighed, "affected the course of history on this continent irrevocably. He directed the building of a new city, called Tula, or Tollan, the Place of Reeds, in our language. Tula became one of the wonders of the Ancient World, a city of wondrous pyramids and temples and gigantic statues of warrior women with shields shaped like butterflies, who still stand guard there as though protecting Quetzalcoatl's city until his people return. The people of Tula were called 'Artisans' because of their unparalleled achievements as artisans and builders, but later races called them Toltecas, or Toltecs, which meant 'artisans' in their languages. The Tolteca civilization stretched from south of what is now the *Isla Quahtemal* to beyond the northern San Cris Mountains."

"Where do we get to the part where this history lesson has to do with Angelina?" Paradox demanded impatiently, clenching and unclenching her blue calico skirt in her fists, her green face twisted with frustration. She was growing more impatient with the giant's tale of ancient gods. The humans' gods, she had observed in her time outside Itzamma, did little but get them in trouble.

"I'm coming to that," Ixtpan said wearily. "Prince Feathered Serpent, like the god for whom he was named, was aligned with the power of life and creation. But the religion of his time was dominated by the worship of Tezcatlipoca, or Dark Mirror, the God of War, who demanded human sacrifice." He paused and took a deep breath. "But Prince Feathered Serpent brought back the old religion of Teotihuacán, which forbade human sacrifice. For a time, he was successful, and Tula became the center of one of the most glorious civilizations in all history."

"As human civilizations go, of course," Paradox mumbled, stroking her narrow green chin.

Ixtpan continued as though he had heard nothing. "Prince Feathered Serpent was unjustly driven from Tula by the priests of Tezcatlipoca. With some of his followers, Feathered Serpent journeyed east to the *Golfo de Huracán*. There he built a raft of serpents and set fire to it. After swearing to his weeping followers that one day he would return, he jumped onto the burning raft and was consumed by the flames. According to the legends, his burning heart rose into the heavens and became the planet Venus, commonly known to us as the Western Star or the Morning Star."

Paradox mulled over Ixtpan's tale. "You humans are simply driven to destroy yourselves, as well as each other. You do have vivid imaginations, though. Claimed he'd come back from the dead, did he? Hmph. Even we can't do that. Don't tell me anyone ever believed that nonsense."

"You would be surprised how much that one prophecy has affected the course of human life on this continent. The next great nation to emerge was that of the *Mexica*, best remembered by the name Aztecs. The Aztecs came out of the North about one hundred years after the Toltecas were destroyed. They built yet another glorious city of pyramids and temples and waterways filled with floating islands of thousands of flowers. Two hundred and seventy years later, the cycle was repeated. The Aztecs were themselves destroyed because their ruler, the *Uey-Tlataoni*, or Revered Speaker, Moctecozuma, believed a bearded, fair-skinned, heathen from across the Eastern Ocean—a man whose name has been forgotten by history—was the returning god, Quetzalcoatl. Moctecozuma let the invader and his army, known as *Spañols*, enter

his capital city, Tenochtitlán. Because of the old prophecy of Quetzalcoatl's return, the Aztecs were slaughtered and Tenochtitlán,
the most beautiful city in the world of its time, was destroyed.
And that defeat changed the history of the continent for five hundred and twenty years."

The Aztecs had lost, Ixtpan thought, but not without a fight.
Moctecozuma had surrendered everything, but his seventeen-
year-old nephew, Cuauhtémoc, Falling Eagle, had led a heroic
resistance, with his city already in ruins, his people dead in the
thousands—and he had paid a horrible price for it. The young
warrior had remained alive in the hearts of the people of the continent as an inspiring example of courage and self-sacrificing
devotion long centuries after the *Spañols* had been forgotten.

Ixtpan was possessed of a sorrow so deep that it hurt in his
bones. He thought of his friend, Falling Eagle, the shaman who
the people called the Prophet, and what those events fifteen hundred years before had meant to him. "There have been many who
believed—and who still believe—that Quetzalcoatl will return.
Angelina is one of them."

"That's absurd, you useless airhead!" Matsemela hissed.
"What could any of this long-winded nonsense about dead empires and dead princes have to do with Angelina?"

"It has everything to do with Angelina. She practices the ancient religion, Quetzalcoatl's religion."

Matsemela's eyes reflected the flickering candlelight. "And
why, in all hell, should Angelina take up the religion of a bunch of
weirdos who vanished a couple of thousand years ago? Why
should she believe some poor demented lunatic is going to live
again? It makes no sense, not even for someone as strange as
Angelina."

"It make perfect sense, *cabrón*," Ixtpan responded, his voice
echoing in the small stone chamber. "Angelina is Tolteca."

*   *   *   *   *

The room was lined with blocks of rose quartz and lighted by
tall candles hung from the walls. The flames reflecting on the rose
quartz caused the entire room to glow in red and pink. Jolosumu,
now wearing a long robe of deep purple amethyst, sat in a high-
backed chair of carved green malachite. The flames reflecting in
his crystal glasses made his eyes appear fire red.

Angelina stood only a few feet from the itzaur. They were alone
but for two guards standing three feet from her on either side—

each of them carrying a three-foot-long obsidian spear.

"Well, female human," he said with a hiss, "you and your friends have actually come along at a good time for me. It's time we itzaurs look to the future."

"And what is it you seek for your future?" Angelina asked. Her long black hair cascaded over her shoulders and breasts and her eyes were purple in the candlelight. Her clothes were covered with dust from the journey.

"I am going to make itzaurs a force in this world. We are coming up from underground."

"But you say you want no contact with humans. That is why you imprison my friends."

"In politics, you say what you have to, then you do what you want. I used the citizens' fear of you to increase my power. Slowly at first, I will begin introducing the idea of our having some contact with the humans. I can mention the benefits of trade or sharing information about the conditions of the Earth."

"You lied to your own people."

"Yes." Jolosumu's thick glasses bobbed on his nose. "I've been planning something like this for years. I already have agents among the humans."

"But if the humans find this place, they will destroy you and your world. What do you think will happen when they see your riches?"

"None of them will see Itzamma. We will never allow that. But we will establish embassies and centers of trade in the human world, and from there begin our strategy of conquest. My assistant, Xichendary, has been serving one of the human colonels, the one called Bismark, for some time now. It seems this Bismark," he shuddered as though describing something repugnant, "wants you in his possession very, very badly. I have sent a messenger to Xichendary to tell him to reveal himself to Bismark and to offer you to the humans."

He smiled, pleased with the balance of it all. "And, in exchange, we will begin private talks on establishing diplomatic relations between our nations. But as one of our conditions, we will demand the humans leave these lands near Itzamma as soon as we hand you over."

"Remember that humans have covered the Earth while you have hidden inside it." Angelina's green eyes were narrowed like those of a jungle cat.

"We were here before you, and we will be here when you are

nothing but vaguely interesting fossils," Jolosumu responded, his
hands on his hips. "And you, personally, will be on your way to
becoming a fossil pretty soon—along with your friends."

Angelina turned as white as the onyx walls and reached for one
of her small pouches of stones. She fingered the small turquoise
and silver beads through the fabric and drew strength from them.
"Do not be a fool. The humans will keep no bargain with you.
They keep no bargains even with their own kind. To trust any of
them is to condemn yourselves."

"We will take precautions against any treachery on their part.
We have weapons that you cannot imagine."

Angelina felt her blood run cold.

"In any event," Jolosumu continued, pushing his glasses back
up on his nose, "in the short run, we will keep our part of the ar-
rangement and deliver you to this Bismark. My trusted lieutenants
will take you to him tonight. By the way, tell me, why does this
Bismark want you so badly? What heinous crime have you committed?"

"I represent something that people like him have feared for a
very long time," Angelina answered, her fingers holding tightly
the butterfly-shaped amulet with inlaid turquoise spiral. "Something that will survive no matter what they do to me."

*　*　*　*　*

"It is all my fault that Angelina is here. It was I who discovered
the existence of the long-lost Tolteca survivors when I was doing
archaeological work in the ruins of the old capital of Tula twelve
years ago. I unearthed ancient stone tablets, long hidden from the
eyes of succeeding conquerors, buried deep in the caves that lie
beneath Quetzalcoatl's old pyramid. On those tablets were
carved, in hieroglyphics, tales of the events of Tula around the
time of Quetzalcoatl's defeat and banishment. One tablet re-
ferred to the many followers of the deposed priest who left Tula
with him long before the city was burned by barbarians of the
North, called Chichimecas."

"Seems there've been a whole string of invasions in this continent's history. Did anyone ever consider putting up a wall?" Matsemela muttered.

"There would be no wall high enough, my friend," Ixtpan answered. He went on with his narrative, his fingers tracing the out-
line of the jade calendar stone in his pocket. "Those Toltecas who
followed Quetzalcoatl went farther south to build a new Tula. I

traced the survivors—expecting to find some interesting ruins of Toltec origin, something I could present at the next convocation of Noramican archaeologists. But, to my astonishment, after tracing them through ruins, legends, myths, and folk songs over the course of two years, I found them still alive. They live in a small but elegant city called Tamoanchan, high in the cloud forest of the island you know as Quahtemal. The people there still call it Quahtemal, or Guatemala, as it was known for many centuries. It was there that Angelina's people found refuge two thousand years ago, when the island was still connected to continental Noramica." He buried his face in his large hands and sighed.

"Go on," said Paradox coldly, her round black eyes burning, her fists clenched tightly. "At least we've gotten to Angelina in this story. So what does all this mean for her in the here and now?"

Ixtpan raised his head and continued. "After Prince Feathered Serpent was deposed, the Tolteca nation continued with their wars and with their human sacrifice, and within a hundred and fifty years, they had vanished, to become the most famous lost race in the history of the continent. And the God of War continued to dominate the land, as he still does. But the memory of the Toltecas and their achievements has never died. According to ancient prophecy, they will one day return to reclaim their lands. And even with the destruction of Tula, the old religion—Prince Quetzalcoatl's religion—survived, changed and hidden among the later peoples, but still very much alive.

"Over the centuries, those Toltecas who went south from Tula with Quetzalcoatl were forced higher and higher into the most remote mountain cloud forest, always fleeing the war-cursed civilization that had destroyed their prophet and their world, fleeing more wars and more waves of invaders. They intermarried with members of other mountain tribes over the years and with refugees from the other world who stumbled upon them over the centuries. They took in some of the Aztecs who fled the *Spañols* and learned of the tragic role the belief in the Toltec god had played in the fate of that later race.

"And the Tolteca survivors, with those who joined them, kept to their old ways and religion. Through their traditions and beliefs, perhaps aided by the mysterious energies unleashed by the weapons used in the Great War, they developed their powers."

"Do you mean to tell me that it's because of some half-baked mystic a couple thousand years ago that Angelina could heal that saddletramp?" Matsemela demanded.

"*Si*. In a way, that is precisely true. Angelina is what she is because of what happened a long time ago. Prince Feathered Serpent was a great healer, the one who first developed the healing arts, and his people continued his tradition. Angelina is what has come out of two thousand years of that tradition."

"Then why isn't she in the cloud forest where she belongs, where she might be safe from the army and the uranium, instead of running around with the likes of you two?" Paradox asked.

"She insisted on coming," Ixtpan said, leaning his tall body wearily against the stone wall. "I have friends among the rebels in the San Cris Mountains—I met them when I was doing archaeological work in the area, searching for the Fire God idol. When I met Falling Eagle, the rebel leader the army is so eager to destroy, it was like no other experience I have had in my life. . . . He *is* a shaman. His is an ancient, highly developed soul, but he suffers horribly from an illness no one can heal. And he guards the Fire God. I went to Tamoanchan, a month-long journey by horse and ship, to ask Angelina to come with me. I never should have done it, but I was desperate. Falling Eagle needed a healer, and Angelina has healing gifts unlike anything I have ever seen."

"Why are her powers so special?" Matsemela asked.

"As it was told to me, when Angelina was ten years old, she fell from a cliff and struck her head. Her breathing stopped, and the most powerful healer in the village pronounced her dead. When her parents went to prepare the body for burial, though, she astonished them by sitting up, fully healed and alert. It could, the Wise Ones agreed, only have been a miracle through the divine intervention of their God of Life. Her parents told me later that the child who woke up after the accident was very different from the fun-loving daughter they had known up to that time.

"It was once said by High Priestess Xochi, who trained her, that Angelina had become someone else. She suddenly abandoned the usual activities of childhood and began spending all her time praying, meditating, and learning the ancient healing arts in the temple of Quetzalcoatl, at the center of the village. But the Wise Ones said it was as if she already knew everything they had to teach, as if the ancient wisdom had been born in her. When she was twelve, a friend of hers, a boy her own age, was mauled by a mountain jaguar. She healed him using the techniques she had been taught, but with a power beyond anything anyone had seen among her people in generations. At fifteen, she healed a woman who was bleeding to death in childbirth. And at eighteen, she healed a man who had been so badly hurt in an earthquake that his family had already begun funeral preparations. I witnessed it myself." She was delirious with fever for days after the strain, Ixtpan thought, his dark bronze fingers gripping the cloth of his brown cassock, his narrow, slanted eyes filling with tears.

"She was willing to come here because . . . because of who Falling Eagle is—one of the greatest spirits this land has ever produced. He is the last Aztec *Uey-Tlatoani*, or Revered Speaker, reborn. Because of the role her own people played in his destiny, she feels it is her duty to try to heal him.

"But the most powerful man on this continent, Baines Winchester, now knows of her powers and is determined to capture her. Winchester is advised by a priest named Zumarraga Apocalypse, who is given to listening to prophecies and who is well aware of the ancient promise of the return of Quetzalcoatl and the Toltecs and even more aware of the way ancient prophecies can fuel rebellious movements. Both men will stop at nothing to destroy Angelina, and to destroy her people if they find out what she is. Between the army and you creatures . . . uh . . . itzaurs, it looks as if I've only brought Angelina to the frontier to die."

At that moment, the earth began to shake, at first slowly, then with great violence—a result of the same earthquake that would come close to taking the life of Cimarron Langtry, forty miles away.

"¡Mi Dios!" Ixtpan exclaimed, as stones started to fall from the walls and a roar like that of stampeding bison filled the air.

"Oh, my stars!" Paradox rasped, covering her head with her arms. "It's another infernal earthquake!"

The walls started falling in around them.

* * * * *

Angelina was just being escorted out of Jolosumu's office, to prepare for her journey to the army camp, when the ground beneath her feet began to tremble.

When the earth began to shift, the itzaurs started squealing in panic. Angelina jumped past her guards with speed and agility. Even as the earth moved she ran, holding up her green skirt, leaping over cracks that appeared at her feet. The itzaurs were too occupied with dodging falling stones to chase her, so she had a good head start. The groaning of the earth and the screams of the itzaurs echoed throughout the enclosed city as stones fell.

It was not the opening to the hidden city that Angelina ran for, but the tunnel leading to the dungeon. She had lived her life in a land where the earth shook often, something that gave her a temporary advantage over the itzaurs.

Angelina made her way to the tunnel, jumping over stones, narrowly avoiding falling rocks, her long black hair flying around her. Her golden brown arms and legs were cut by the small rocks that filled the air. As the shaking and rumbling ceased, a platoon of guards was on her trail.

Angelina ran, dodging arrows and spears.

Suddenly she screamed and stopped, horrified by what remained of the dungeon. Where her friends' cell had been there was now only gray stone rubble, rocks broken on other rocks. There was no sign of life.

She ripped one of the small pouches from her neck and pressed it to her lips. Inside were a clear crystal for the energy of the stars, a tiny purple-and-white shell for the life energy of the sea, and a chunk of turquoise, Quetzalcoatl's stone. She threw the pouch into the broken earth that had become her friends' tomb, crying, "*Adiós, compañeros!* I will see you in the next life!"

CHAPTER 8

TOGETHER

Throughout the city of Itzamma, everyone was bustling around, trying to repair the considerable damage from the earthquake. Most buildings remained intact, protected by the strength of the mountain, but many statues and columns had fallen and lay scattered in gigantic pieces all over the city. Shattered precious stones lay everywhere, making the square and walkways look like a broken mosaic of a thousand colors.

In the confusion of the aftermath, none of the itzaurs thought to investigate the damage to the dungeon. Consequently, none of them noticed when, a full day after the quake struck, at the end of the dark, mile-long tunnel leading to what had been the dungeon, a great gray granite slab covered with many chunks of stone began to rise slowly from the pile of broken rocks on which it had fallen. At first it moved by tiny fractions of an inch, then, as though the force below it were growing stronger, more rapidly.

When the granite slab reached a height of half a foot above the rubble, a pair of round black eyes peered out from beneath it. "There's no one around," a small rasping voice whispered.

"Are you sure?" a deep voice grumbled irritably from below the slab. "You've done nothing but lead us from one disaster to another! There's probably a damned army of lizards out there waiting for us!"

"I'll prove it's safe. I'll go out first."

A soft, accented voice said, as though the speaker were under such strain he could barely talk, "I cannot . . . hold this stone . . . much longer. ¡Ahora, Paradox!"

Paradox squeezed cautiously out of the narrow opening, scraping her scaly skin and tearing her blue calico skirt as she did so. She emerged finally, wriggling her way out of the stones. Looking around, the itzaur saw nothing but broken rubble where once the dungeon and passageway had been—and no guards. "Come on!" she whispered loudly. "Let's go!"

"Get that rock up higher. I'm getting out of here," came the rumbling voice from below.

"Leave Ixtpan alone," Paradox snapped at Matsemela, who was, of course, still hidden beneath the stones. "It's taken him hours to get us this far!"

"Seems like days," Matsemela retorted.

"I will have you know . . . that levitating stone . . . is no easy matter." Ixtpan groaned as the granite slab moved another two inches upward.

"Here, let me help," muttered Matsemela, gasping the words under the weight of the slab.

In another hour, the stone was high enough for Matsemela to climb out. He then, with what he considered the useless assistance of Paradox, helped hold the stone while Ixtpan climbed out. No sooner were Ixtpan's tremendous feet through the opening in the stones, than the whole pile collapsed with a great crash that filled the air with gravel and dust.

"All right, how do we get out of here?" Matsemela demanded. He felt for his bone-and-leather helmet. It was askew. He took it off and inspected it with his fingers, allowing his short, curly black hair to frame his dark face. The helmet—one he'd brought from Afria twenty years before—was hopelessly damaged. He tossed it in the rocks without a second thought.

"Follow me," Paradox said, starting off down a long, dark hallway filled with only the gods knew what kind of debris.

"Not a chance," Matsemela responded.

But Ixtpan reluctantly agreed that Paradox did have the best chance of getting them out of the hidden city, and so they followed her, making their way carefully down the long, dark hallway from the dungeon. Paradox took them through a confusing maze of tunnels, each narrower than the last.

It took another full day of following Paradox through the twisting tunnels of Itzamma, crawling over broken stones, dodging patrolling guards, before the companions finally located a way out—an entrance to the ancient tunnels not used in a millennium on the far side of a great mountain. Now all they had to do was figure out where they were and how to find Angelina, not to mention avoiding the itzaur patrols and the Confederation army itself.

*   *   *   *   *

The army encampment was spread over a solid mile of golden earth and under golden skies and little else, near the Terlingua Mountains. The soldiers set up the new camp under orders from their commander, Col. Reno Bismark, who, for reasons of his own, chose to camp for two days, as if he were waiting for something. In the center of the camp was the colonel's tent. At the east end was a remuda of four thousand horses, a vast treasure in the

West. Both the horse herd and the camp itself were heavily guarded.

Two days after the earthquake, Xichendary and his two assistants delivered Angelina to Reno Bismark. The meeting was held in secret, in the dead of night, and Angelina was brought surreptitiously into the camp on horseback, swathed in a colorful Comanche blanket. She was taken directly to Reno Bismark's tent.

Xichendary pulled back the red and yellow Comanche blanket, and there stood Angelina, her eyes burning deep purple in the dim light of a small fire and the one tallow candle on the pine table.

Reno Bismark's eyes opened wide, and his whole body tensed at the sight of her. He actually stifled a gasp. She was, he realized, a woman of stunning, although unusual, beauty—small, with delicate features and high cheekbones, golden brown skin, and the strangest violet-green eyes he had ever seen.

"So this is the woman the people say can heal the sick and summon the rain," the colonel said, his voice low with menace as he looked slowly and deliberately over the young woman standing bound before him. As he stared at her, her almond-shaped eyes seemed, to him, to change color to a golden green, and for a moment he could have sworn he was staring into the eyes of a jungle cat. He had never, in all his travels, seen anyone with eyes like hers, and he wondered what exotic race could have produced her and what powers she might indeed have. "We could do with some rain out here, *señorita*. How about rustling us up some?" He laughed at his own joke.

Angelina only stared back at him silently. The expression on Reno Bismark's face as he thoroughly and coldly looked her up and down, made her cringe inwardly.

"As we promised," Xichendary responded. His black obsidian cape fell back, revealing the itzaur's gray face.

"You have kept your bargain and now we will keep ours," the colonel said. "Trade negotiations begin four months from this night in Retama City, a ghost town twenty miles south of here. Is that agreeable?"

"Yes. We will have a delegation of trade ministers there. And what about your army staying out of the Terlingua Mountains?"

"We have to pass through these mountains to reach our destination, to put an end to the warfare in the San Cris Mountains. But once we've fulfilled our mission and peace is restored, these lands will be yours forever. I swear it on my honor as an officer of the Tesharka Confederation army."

The itzaurs left and made their way back to the hidden entrance to Itzamma, never suspecting that yet another soldier followed them, carefully mapping the route.

* * * * *

The light of the fire and two torches cast distorted, monstrous shadows of those inside on the colonel's tent. The land was hot, even at night, and the colonel sweated uncomfortably.

What is she? Reno Bismark wondered, looking at her eyes, which seemed to change to deep purple in the firelight. The fact that she might be dangerous only made her all the more compelling to him. All in all, things were going very much his way, and he radiated good cheer, his fair complexion and copper hair practically glowing in the firelight. "What's your name, sweetheart?"

"In this land I am called Angelina, and that is the name by which you may address me. And I am not a 'sweetheart.' I am a priestess."

"I guess we'll see just what you are before too long."

"No, colonel, you will never see what I am."

"By the way, I'd like you to meet the man who helped track you and your strange friends through this desolate wasteland, my dear Angelina." Reno Bismark opened the flap to his bisonhide tent. "Come in, come in," he said to someone outside, beyond Angelina's vision."

Cimarron was dressed in his own version of the military uniform—the blue cotton shirt and blue hat, though his hat had a very unmilitary hawk feather in its rattlesnakeskin hatband. He wore no bronze hoop armor vest, in spite of the protection from lances it could have offered him. His long brown hair was tied back with a thin strip of beaded leather. And at the moment his normally bronze skin was as pale as dead buffalo grass. He froze where he stood when he saw the woman sitting on the ground, her hands tied around the tent's center pole behind her.

Angelina's face was scratched and bruised, her white blouse soiled and torn. What was left of her green skirt hung in shreds. Her arms and legs were cut and bruised.

Cimarron's expression betrayed nothing of what he was feeling. It took all the self-control he could summon to keep his hand away from his knife, to keep from going after Bismark at that moment. Such an action would only get him killed and possibly Angelina as well. He needed some plan if he was to help her.

In spite of her battered condition and helpless position, Angelina looked like some wild predatory creature of the night. Her thick black hair hung loose around her face and shoulders. She was seething with rage at her captors, her skin pale, her cheeks flushed, her lips twisted in just a hint of a feline snarl. And there was a hollow quality in her gold-green eyes that he had not seen the day he looked into them as he lay dying beside the Rio Bravo.

"Allow me to present *Señorita* Angelina." Bismark gave his scout a hard pat on the back. "Well done. Well done. You helped us get out here where we could find this lady. Good job. Angelina, my dear, this is Cimarron Langtry, my scout. Cimarron and I were childhood friends, weren't we, buddy?"

Angelina's eyes met Cimarron's in a silent recognition, and she was racked with both fury and sorrow. Can this really be what is intended? she wondered. What had it all been for? Because of an ancient prophecy? To protect an old idol of stone? To help a man who might—or might not—be able to stop the Confederation army? It all seemed pretty empty to her as she looked into Cimarron Langtry's emotionless face. She had given him life—so that he could deliver her to her enemies. The ways of her people ran deep in her, but now their beliefs and their gods seemed very distant.

Except for Tezcatlipoca, the God of War, who could move the mountains, the sorcerer who came to Earth on a spider web from the heavens at the beginning of time. He seemed for the first time very real to her. And very close.

The Wise Ones in the city of Tamoanchan had warned her when she left with Ixtpan that she was going out into a land where the God of War had triumphed two thousand years before. She had never really known hatred before, but at that moment she hated the copper-haired colonel. And she hated Cimarron Langtry, who had betrayed her gift of life.

Her hatred was almost palpable to him. "Yeah, Reno, that we were. Friends a long time ago." Cimarron wished not for the first time that he had died back then, a long time ago, with his friends. *It's living that takes courage, not dying,* hermano, Zaco had said to him—before he died. *You've got the courage to survive.* Do I? Cimarron wondered.

Angelina sensed pain from the scout and found that odd. The man had obviously fulfilled his purpose and would no doubt be richly rewarded. She thought of Ixtpan's words as he hung the silver and turquoise medallion around her neck before they set out from her village: *We, all of us alive today, are only living out an ancient saga, one beyond our understanding. Our destiny was determined long ago, my dear Angelina. As the Ancient Ones believed, we are but players on Tezcatlipoca's stage.* And the part of this player was to deliver her to her executioner.

Cimarron let out a low whistle of physical appreciation in Angelina's direction. "Something else, isn't she? Guess I see why old Winchester wants her so bad." He relaxed, standing with one hip cocked higher than the other in the vaquero manner.

"Yes, I do, too. I surely do understand why Winchester wants her, special powers or not." Bismark's blue eyes eagerly followed the slight curves of Angelina's slender body. "I know I'm going to enjoy taking this one to Tesharka." The colonel knelt on one knee next to Angelina and touched her left shoulder with his right hand. "Where do you come from, *señorita?*"

"I come from another world, *salvaje.* A world alien to you, where life is sacred."

Bismark's face clouded in anger at the insult and vague reply, but his grin quickly returned. "I'm sure you will tell me all about it in time, my dear. We're going to have a long journey east together, you and me. Yes, I've decided I'm going to deliver you personally to our beloved guvnor. Believe me, I'll bet you'll come to enjoy our time together. I know I'm a lot more sensitive to a woman's . . . needs . . . than old Winchester. Be a good girl, and I promise your captivity won't be so bad. By the way, what do you know about some old idol called the Fire God?" His long fingers began stroking her long hair.

Angelina's eyes looked black, the dark pupils open so wide that they nearly covered her green irises, and Cimarron could have sworn he saw flames within them. A strong wind came up out of nowhere, like ghostly howling, blowing sand against the sides of the tent. "Touch the Fire God and you destroy yourself."

"You'll have to try your barbarian superstition on someone else. It doesn't scare me," Bismark responded.

At that moment, Wyatt Fontana entered the colonel's tent. His eyes went immediately to Angelina.

"Well, Wyatt," Reno Bismark said, "this is the woman we've been looking for. Unusual, isn't she?"

"That she is," Wyatt responded, still staring hard at her. "I imagine there's no one quite like her in the world. The guvnor'll be mighty pleased to know she's in custody and on her way to Arshal." He had reason to believe that Zumarraga Apocalypse, the founder of the Church of the New World and close confidant and advisor to Guvnor Baines Winchester himself, would be even more pleased. "Congratulations, Reno," he said, "you'll get a promotion for this. I'm sure of it." He nodded to Cimarron and, without another word, left the tent.

"Wyatt's a strange man," Bismark commented, "but he follows orders, and that's what counts."

Bismark again reached for Angelina's long black hair. She hissed words in a language neither he nor Cimarron understood.

"Colonel," a voice with the slow, soft accent of Delta Province called from outside the tent, "we picked up a prisoner out on the desert. You'd better take a look at this yourself, sir."

"*Tanto mejor, señorita*," the colonel said. "All the better if you and I conclude our business later." Bismark stepped outside the tent and exclaimed, "Well, if this doesn't beat all! You're the second man lately to come back from the dead!"

Cimarron ran to Angelina, bent over, and whispered, "I'll help you. I swear it. *¡Palabra!*"

"*Al parecer*, it is your destiny to destroy me, vaquero."

Before he could respond to Angelina's bitter remark, Reno Bismark opened the tent flap and jerked his new prisoner—a large, black-skinned man dressed in bloody rags—inside. Cimarron instantly bent to kiss Angelina hard and rough on the mouth.

Bismark hollered, "Get away from my prisoner, scout!"

Cimarron pulled away from her, laughing, and said, "You know I never was one to pass up an opportunity with the ladies."

Angelina spat in Cimarron's face, and he drew back from her, startled. Then she cried out in anguish when she saw who the prisoner was. "Matsemela! No!"

Reno Bismark laughed heartily, slapping Cimarron on the back again. "How well I know about you and women, Cimarron. I remember how you and Topsannah used to be. Remember that night I stumbled over the two of you—" The words died in his throat when he saw a dark look cross Cimarron's face. "Sorry, old buddy," he said with needling insincerity. "Another bad memory? Whatever happened to the half-breed? Or do you know?" He watched Cimarron carefully.

"I don't know. I don't know what happened to her after she left Reynada." Cimarron wiped his face on his shirt sleeve, trying desperately to fight off the images that filled his mind. He knew he was seeing Angelina and Reno right there in the tent with him. But he also saw in his mind—as clearly as he saw the bruises on Angelina's face—a tall, graceful young woman with shoulder-length black hair named Topsannah, which meant "flower" in

Comanche. He felt Bismark's blue eyes staring into him as though trying to read his thoughts.

"I'll see you in hell, you lowlife saddletramp," Matsemela growled at Cimarron. "I should've killed you that morning beside the Bravo." Blood dripped from cuts in his forehead and lips. His lower lip and right eye were swollen, and more blood flowed from a wound in his right arm.

Reno Bismark looked the ragged Matsemela over critically. "Where is the gigantic companion you're supposed to have? Corporal," he called out, "be on the lookout for an unusually tall visitor."

"Don't worry," Matsemela snarled, "he's dead." If the warrior felt any emotion whatsoever, he betrayed none.

"¿Verdad, Matsemela?" The sight of Matsemela had given Angelina hope that perhaps the others, too, had survived the earthquake.

"Sorry, but the big guy's gone. And the lizard. In the quake. I saw a whole stone wall fall on them.

Angelina could not conceal the grief that overwhelmed her. She hid her face behind her loose hair.

Although Cimarron wished desperately for some way to comfort her, he knew he had to stick to his plan.

Reno Bismark looked thoughtful for a moment, then spoke sarcastically to the mercenary. "You'll be joining 'em in the hereafter. Tonight. It's been a long trek out here, and these silly stories about the rabble's prophet having magical powers have got some of the men spooked. They need something to occupy their minds. I'll order a pyre built. We'll have to use mesquite. It's about the only wood in these parts, and, besides, it'll be a fragrant way to die." He chuckled at his own joke. "I'll have the cook grill some rattlesnakes and bison steaks at the same time. Take him away—and make sure he's bound so tight he can't possibly get loose," the colonel directed a gawky young private with spiked brown and red hair.

Then the colonel turned to Angelina and said, "Of course, you will want to watch your . . . escort die. Perhaps you can heal him faster than the fire can burn him. Or will you call the wind to put out the fire? You're not likely to be able to bury us in a mudslide out here." He laughed long and hard, slapped Cimarron on the back again, and said, "C'mon, amigo. I want you to get some more tracking in today. We still have to clean out the rebels at Epitaph. Keep up the good work and there could be a sergeant's stripes in your future. How'd you like that?"

"I reckon it's all falling into place," Cimarron replied, following the colonel out of the tent, risking one fast backward glance at Angelina. She returned his gaze with one of pure, unforgiving hatred.

*   *   *   *   *

"Listen, I know what I'm doing," Paradox insisted vehemently. "I can get into that camp without attracting attention. Humans never pay attention to an itzaur, since they don't expect us to be able to do anything but fetch and carry for them."

They were hiding in a break of mesquite near the army camp, and Ixtpan grimaced as he pulled a mesquite thorn from his ankle. His white tunic was a tattered mess, and he was filthy, streaked with dirt and dried blood.

"I got you out of Itzamma, didn't I?" Paradox, too, was none the better for the earthquake and the days spent escaping from Itzamma and locating the army. Her buckskin vest and calico skirt hung in remnants. Her *huarache* sandals were so torn up that they were held on her feet by only a few remaining strips of leather.

"You also got me *into* Itzamma, remember?"

"All right, all right, hold a grudge," Paradox said with a sniff, wiping a smudge of dirt from her green face. "But you've got to admit, Itzamma's quite a place. And I think we make a pretty good team, you and me. You can raise stones and talk to animals, and I can travel unnoticed among the humans. It was great how you found us out from the birds where they had taken Angelina, and then called up those mustangs to get us and Matsemela here, near the army camp. It only took us a day and a half."

"Yes, but where is that miserable mercenary? He claimed he was going ahead to scout the camp, but he's been gone too long. The man has probably taken off and deserted us. I tell you this, Paradox, if I ever set eyes on Matsemela Nyakir again in this life, I will strangle that *cabrón* with my bare hands."

"It was pretty rude of him to go off and leave us—if that's what he did."

"It is just like him." Ixtpan's long face turned very sad. "You know, Paradox, you do not have to go along. Angelina is *mi amiga*, and I am the one who got her into this situation. She is my responsibility."

"I'll do what I can for Angelina. She's an exceptional human. And besides," Paradox added sadly, "I like her. She is the only human who has ever really treated me like I was the same as her, not some inferior animal who can't think or feel just like you humans do. She reminds me of my sister."

"Sister?"

"Senjella. She was a few years older than me. She was so wonderful, so educated and thoughtful, always teaching me things I didn't know. It was Senjella who first got me interested in the human world. She died fifty or so years ago from the plague. I was abroad at the time, working for a human family in Abilene."

"I am sorry, Paradox." Suddenly Ixtpan cried out, "Oh, no!" He paled, his black eyes opened wide in unmistakable horror.

"What is it?" Paradox hopped upward, hoping to see what had so distressed Ixtpan.

Ixtpan grabbed her by the scruff of her neck and jerked her back down, saving her from revealing herself to the nearby Clankers. "Look there," he whispered, trembling hard, "in the center of the camp." He pointed through the trees.

Then Paradox saw it. The soldiers were busily building a pyre around a high stake. They were going to burn someone. "We've got to move fast," Paradox said, starting to burst forth from their hiding place.

"¡Silencio!" Ixtpan clasped his large hand over Paradox's mouth. "Listen!"

"I don't hear anything," Paradox managed to squeak through Ixtpan's fingers.

"Horses. Hundreds of them. Maybe thousands. And they're coming this way."

* * * * *

The waning moon cast a pale silver light on the encampment, making the land look silver and the mesquite black. The cavalry soldiers were relaxed, preparing for a meal and an execution, confident that victory lay just over the horizon.

Cimarron managed to give Bismark's spies the slip more easily than usual, since the soldiers in the camp were so relaxed. He silently and separately killed two guards to get to the tent where Matsemela was being held, and he kicked their bodies beneath a supply wagon after taking both their bronze knives, sticking one of them in his leather belt and the other in his right boot.

He knew he was greatly increasing his chance of getting caught by freeing the mercenary, but he felt he had no other honorable choice. To do otherwise was totally against his Pecos ethics. The dark-skinned warrior had been one of the group that had saved

Cimarron from Clankers the night he had crossed back into Pecos, and he would do what he could to help the man. To repay blood debts—whether of gratitude or of vengeance—was ingrained in the sense of honor that ran deep in the people of Pecos, a trait traceable in legend and anthropology to the religion of Old World Texas.

Furthermore, he needed the mercenary's help.

Cimarron crept up silently behind Matsemela. "Don't say a word," he whispered, his knife at the mercenary's throat. "I'm going to cut you loose. Trust me."

"How in the name of all the devils you border rats call saints do you expect me to trust you?" Matsemela said in a low growl.

Cimarron faced the man and lowered the steel knife.

Matsemela's dark eyes, even the one half closed by swelling, were wild. His hands, arms, legs, and feet were tied with strong hemp ropes to a large wooden wagon wheel, which was itself roped to the tent's center pole. "You're Bismark's scout. Whatever happens to us is your fault."

"I know how it looks, but I'm telling you, I want to help." Cimarron's hoarse voice was hardly more than a whisper. His gaunt and angular face was set, hard and jagged, as if it were carved in stone. The pale moonlight made the blond streaks in his hair look silver, giving him the appearance at that moment of being very, very old. "There's no time to explain. We've got to free Angelina . . ." Cimarron knelt on one knee and cut the first strand of one of the ropes that bound Matsemela's right foot to the wheel.

"How do you know you won't be the first one I kill, cowboy?"

Cimarron cut the rope around Matsemela's left foot. "Because you want to live. If you try to kill me, I'll fight you. Then the Clankers will come, and you and I'll both die. Doesn't seem to be much point to that, does there?" Cimarron cut the rest of the ropes around the mercenary's right foot. Then he stood and cut the ropes that restrained Matsemela's arms, releasing him completely. He made no move to get away, nor did the mercenary. "You know, Reno and his boys are going to burn you alive tonight if you don't hightail it out of here. Now, you can go get Angelina or you can just look out for yourself—but do something before Bismark barbecues us both."

The wind was getting stronger, blowing hot out of the south, kicking up the biting red dust against the sides of the tents. And, as always, the coyotes howled mournfully at the moon.

"What are you up to? There's no way to get to her. There are guards around that tent—and at least a couple thousand soldiers in this camp. It would be suicide to try."

"Then you go on and I'll get her. But do me one favor."

"What is it?"

Cimarron answered sharply. "Stampede the horses. Then grab one and head west fast. Once the horses stampede, you won't have much time to get away." He handed Matsemela one of the long bronze knives he had taken off the dead Clankers.

"I'll get out of here, all right. About the horses—I'll do what I can," Matsemela said gruffly, sticking the knife in his leather belt.

"Whatever the woman is to you, surely you can't want her to be Bismark's prisoner. I know him. He's cold and he's cruel and he'll do anything to anyone to get what he wants. Just do this one thing. Give her that much of a chance." He turned his back to the warrior, but Matsemela grabbed him by the shoulder.

"And what are you going to do? Run away?"

"I said I'll get Angelina, and that's what I'll do." His voice was as hard as steel, his brown eyes fierce with soul-deep determination. "You were right about one thing. Whatever happens to her, it's my fault. If I'd done what I should have a long time ago, none of this would be happening." Cimarron slipped away into the darkness as the wind wailed and the dust blew in small twisters through the camp.

* * * * *

Cimarron crept slowly, painfully, on his stomach toward the tent where Angelina was being held, moving as soundlessly as a Comanche. He slipped up behind both of the two guards stationed on opposite sides of the tent, and quickly and silently slit their throats with the steel knife. With bloodstained hands, he cut a two-foot slit in the back of the tent and crawled inside. The only light came from a small fire that burned near the center of the tent and from one candle on a small wood table. He stood very carefully, braced for attack.

Angelina lay as still as death on a bison robe, her long black hair a disheveled storm around her, her hands tied to the tent's center pole. At first, Cimarron feared she was dead, but then she moaned and tossed her head from side to side.

The cry, "Stampede!" went up, and Cimarron smiled and hoped the mercenary had made good his escape. The noise from outside grew louder as the soldiers tried to catch the stampeding horses. Then there were other sounds—arrows, thundering hooves, and screams reaching a deafening crescendo. He knew from the sounds that the Comanches were attacking.

The noise echoed in Cimarron's mind as he ran, knife in hand, to Angelina. He was only inches from her when he felt the sharp tip of a knife press against his lower back.

"That's enough, buckaroo. Hold it right there. One move and you're dead."

*   *   *   *   *

About the time Matsemela reached the edge of the camp, he realized it was surrounded by hundreds, maybe thousands, of mounted Comanches just beyond the vision of those in the camp. The army scouts, apparently, were all dead and hence had been unable to give warning. As a result, the Clankers had been encircled. "Great! Is this part of that loco cowboy's plan?"

The thundering of hundreds of Comanche horses sounded louder than the roar of the earthquake that had shaken the mountains two days before. Flint, copper, and bronze-tipped arrows filled the air. Footsoldiers and cavalrymen hit the ground, dead.

Before long, the Comanche warriors were in the camp. Many dismounted and plunged into hand-to-hand fighting, using tomahawks, lances, and axes against the soldier's knives, swords, and arrows. The cavalry, taken by surprise, fought with a vengeance.

The mercenary quickly found himself being pushed back into the camp, away from the attacking warriors. At least, he observed, none of the Clankers noticed him, seeing as they had their own problems at the moment.

He intended only to keep moving, to stay alive and get out of the fighting somehow, then escape into the desert. The Pecos desert he had so recently cursed seemed like a paradise at that moment, with people dying all around him. The last thing he wanted was to get involved in the fighting, but a Confederation soldier came straight at him with a silver sword and Matsemela had no choice. He managed to kill the man with the bronze knife that Cimarron had given him, then he picked up the silver sword and, laughing and whooping as he swung it, joined the battle.

Matsemela moved steadily toward the western side of the large camp, from which he judged he would be most able to escape from the carnage that had nothing to do with him personally—except that he happened to be in the middle of it. He hated the Clankers and hoped to see them whipped, but he didn't particularly care for the Comanches, either.

He was not far from the outskirts of the battle when he was startled to hear an eerie, terrified scream—not from one man, but
from many simultaneously. Both Comanches and Clankers began
fleeing an area not far from him, racing back into the thick of the
fighting as though to escape some greater danger. Matsemela
ducked behind an overturned wagon, seeking protection from
whatever new horror was heading his way.

Peering over the rim of the wagon, he confronted a startling
sight—a gigantic, almost spectral figure clothed in white rags,
brandishing a long, two-sided bronze sword and riding straight
into the battle on a midnight-black horse. Combatants on both
sides scattered in the demon's wake.

"¡San Zapata! It's Ixtpan!" Matsemela jumped up from behind
the wagon, yelling, "Hey! Over here!"

He ran a hundred feet or so before Ixtpan heard that familiar
deep voice over the ruckus of the battle. He reined his horse to a
halt, waving the sword around him to hold off both Clankers and
Comanches. "So there you are!" he called out, and a horse, a
graceful silver stallion whose rider lay dead, went immediately to
Matsemela's side. The mercenary jumped on the horse's back.

"This way!" Ixtpan called, turning his horse to head deeper
into the camp, desperate to get to Angelina.

"Are you crazy? I'm getting out of here."

"What about the money you get if you finish the mission,
cabrón?" Ixtpan stabbed a soldier who was coming at him with a
bronze axe and turned back to the mercenary all in one fluid
move.

"Keep it."

"I'll double it if you help me get Angelina."

"No!"

"Triple."

"Done."

"Let's go."

"Not so fast. How do I know you can come up with the three
thousand jadas?"

Ixtpan scowled, his dark eyebrows knitting together with rage.
He reached inside his torn robe, took out a small packet wrapped
in ancient leather, and handed it to Matsemela.

Matsemela opened the packet and saw there two gold coins with
designs on their surfaces unlike any he had ever seen: an eagle
perched on a nopal with a serpent in its beak. "These aren't jadas,

you swindling—"

"Those, *cabrón*, come from the sacred times. They are the coins of the Ancient Ones, known as pesos. Each of those is worth a thousand jadas on the black market—there's no coin more valuable in the world. Take them. You get the rest when we get Angelina to Epitaph."

Matsemela pocketed the coins with a smile. From that moment on, he fought beside Ixtpan as they made their way through the battle, searching for Angelina.

*   *   *   *   *

The voice was high pitched and rasping, unlike anything Cimarron had ever heard in his life. The knife point prodded his back again. Hell, he was going to die, anyway; by all the gods, he'd get in a good stab or two first. He jumped around, swinging so his knife would connect with his opponent's body. But instead his knife connected with only air and he went sprawling on the ground with a thud.

Cimarron looked up and found himself staring at a four-foot-tall itzaur wearing a very tattered and torn buckskin vest and blue calico skirt. This itzaur had a ferocious look on its green face and was standing over him with a copper knife. It hissed at him and raised the knife. For the first time in his life, Cimarron was simply too astonished to react quickly.

"Paradox!" Angelina cried with joy.

"Angelina!" Paradox exclaimed, taking her eyes off Cimarron for a few moments. That was all Cimarron, who quickly recovered his senses, needed. He was on his feet and diving for Paradox, but the itzaur jumped faster and landed on his back, her copper knife about to plunge.

The *curandera* tried to get up, but was held by the braided rope that bound her to the center pole. She collapsed, her eyes fluttering open and shut. Both Cimarron and Paradox broke free and reached for Angelina, glaring fiercely at each other as they did so.

Suddenly a stone axe split open another side of the tent, and inside stepped what was to Angelina a vision from hell. It took her a full minute to realize he was a human and not some horrifying demon. Angelina shuddered at the sight of the man.

He was tall—not as tall as Ixtpan, but tall for a man of his time. It was the black scalp and the horns of a great bison he wore as a headdress that made him appear demonic. His long black and silver hair hung loosely from beneath the hideous headdress. He wore nothing but a leather breechcloth, and his dark skin was painted with stripes of black, the color of death. He carried a long, flint-tipped lance with eagle feathers hanging from it.

"Eeschatai!" Cimarron called out, grateful to see the warrior. "Get the itzaur!"

Eeschatai had entered the tent, hoping to find Col. Reno Bismark there. Instead he found himself confronting a strange assemblage—a woman tied to a tent pole and an itzaur that had apparently gone mad, along with the Confederation scout who had given the Comanches the layout of the Clanker camp. He grabbed Paradox by her vest and held her suspended in the air with one hand while swinging his axe at her with the other. Paradox was kicking, biting, and cursing in her own language in a fury while dodging the axe.

"No! *Por favor*, no!" Angelina screamed at Eeschatai.

"Wait!" Cimarron called to Eeschatai in response to Angelina's plea. The warrior stopped in midswing.

"Angelina!" Ixtpan yelled from the entrance to the tent. Matsemela had led him to Reno Bismark's tent, where Angelina was being held, and he was profoundly relieved to find her alive. Seeing Paradox in the clutches of the Comanche, he dropped the reins to the two horses he was holding and pointed his sword menacingly at Eeschatai. "Let her go or die, barbarian!"

Eeschatai, still holding the swinging itzaur, gasped at the sight if Ixtpan, then pointed his lance in the giant's direction.

"Ixtpan!" Angelina was overjoyed. "Matsemela!"

"Come on, lady," Matsemela said with a growl as he ran into the tent, "let's beat it the hell out of here. By all the gods," he started at Cimarron with disbelief, "I didn't figure you to still be alive."

"We're not out of here yet," Cimarron answered, getting between Ixtpan and Eeschatai.

Ixtpan froze for a moment in surprise as he recognized the vaquero. "You," he gasped, the words he had spoken that morning by the Rio Bravo reverberating in his mind. *After all, his destiny may one day be linked to our own.*

"*Si.*" Cimarron stood suspended, expecting Ixtpan to stab him.

"Leave the guy alone," Matsemela snarled at Ixtpan. "He's the one who cut me loose."

Eeschatai still held Paradox by her vest. He was confused by this unusual bunch of people, uncertain of whom he was supposed to be fighting. But he did owe some allegiance to Cimarron, whose information had been of immeasurable help to the Comanches in planning their assault on the Confederation cavalry. "Compadre?" he asked.

"I say we all get out of here together." Cimarron knew there was no point wasting time in trying to figure out Angelina's friends. He was grateful for the reinforcements. "The only chance any one of us has of surviving is getting away from the Clankers. And the only way to get away from the Clankers is through that battle out there."

Angelina turned to Cimarron. "What is it you want from me, Cimarron?" She pronounced his name *Cimarrón*, as they did in the South, the name meaning "untamed," which the Ancient Ones had given to both wild cattle and escaped slaves.

Cimarron stepped toward Angelina. Ixtpan moved to stop him but was restrained by Matsemela. "I swear, *señorita*, all I want is to help you. My friend, Eeschatai, will take you and your friends to where you'll be safe." He knelt beside her and cut the rope.

Angelina tried to stand, but her ankles had been sliced by the rope that had bound them and the circulation had been cut off to her feet, leaving her temporarily crippled. Cimarron had to catch her before she fell. She slumped into his arms and leaned against him for support.

"Get your hands off her, cowboy," Paradox snarled from where she hung, suspended. "Angelina, don't trust him. I found him coming at you with a steel knife."

Cimarron—not to mention Eeschatai—was still stunned by the talking itzaur, but there was no time to question its remarkable existence. Eeschatai dropped her to the dirt. "Speaking of the knife, I guess it belongs to you, *señorita*." Cimarron held the bloodstained steel knife out to her.

Ixtpan's knife, Angelina thought, seeing it in Cimarron's hand. "It belongs to him." She gestured to Ixtpan.

Cimarron handed the knife back to Ixtpan, who took it with a grateful smile.

"*Muchas gracias*, vaquero."

"It's I who should thank you," Cimarron replied, pulling the other bronze Clanker knife from his boot.

Paradox glared at Cimarron suspiciously as she picked herself up off the ground and dusted the remains of her blue calico skirt. She took Angelina's hand supportively. In her other hand was her copper knife.

"Let's go," Cimarrron said, taking Angelina's arm. "Eeschatai will get you out of here."

"No," Angelina said, fear evident in her voice. "We can trust none of the northern tribes. It was they who destroyed the homeland of my ancestors . . ."

"Eeschatai," Cimarron said, "is an honorable man, a Comanche warrior. Trust him."

"Trust him? How can we trust you?" Angelina asked. "You led the barbarian army to us, *verdad*?"

"Angelina," Ixtpan said, "we have little choice."

"Let's go." Paradox emphatically grabbed Angelina's hand and ran for the tent flap. Once Ixtpan started talking—even during a battle—they could be in for a long stretch of listening.

Cimarron and Eeschatai ran ahead of Angelina and Paradox, with Ixtpan and Matsemela following close behind them. Hundreds of people fought to the death all around them as they made their way through the battle.

* * * * *

Reno Bismark stabbed a Comanche warrior with the magnificent sword he had found in the ruins of Comanche Springs. He laughed as the Comanche doubled over, then dropped to his knees and fell face down on the bloodstained ground. The colonel's laughter was not his usual jovial outburst but was instead desperate and ragged. The Comanches had taken him by surprise, getting past all the scouts and managing to surround the camp before their presence was detected. And then someone inside the camp had stampeded the horses. An army unhorsed in western Pecos was a dead army.

He wondered angrily who the traitor might be, and the image of Cimarron Langtry immediately came to his mind. He had all along suspected Cimarron of being up to something, but he had thought his spies could take care of any problem. He cursed angrily, suspecting his old rival of having something to do with this potentially fatal defeat in which he found himself.

I should've killed you a long time ago, Cimarron, he thought. I tried to a long time ago. And, so help me, when I find you this time, you'll wish I had succeeded.

A Comanche came up behind him, stone axe raised to strike, but he was killed by a flint knife thrown by Amos Crimsonleaf. Reno called to Billy Ray Haggard and two other privates. They had consolidated a group of two dozen others around themselves and constructed a barricade of overturned wagons for protection.

* * * * *

The Comanches were everywhere, striking at anyone in a uniform, and that was gratifying to Cimarron Langtry, since he despised the Clankers with all his heart and soul.

The ragtag group fought its way through the besieged Clankers. Cimarron, Matsemela, Ixtpan, and Eeschatai killed several Clankers as they cut a path through the battle, protecting Angelina and Paradox as they went. Ixtpan proved invaluable, since many of the soldiers were simply so overcome at the sight of him that they turned and ran.

At one point, they were surrounded by a dozen Clankers and escaped only with the help of some friends of Eeschatai's. The Clankers were forced to fight the Comanches while the companions got away and were once again running toward the outskirts of the camp.

"There!" hollered a lanky soldier, recognizing Angelina. "Don't let her get away!" He fired an arrow at close range.

The arrow struck Matsemela in the arm, and the mercenary fell to his knees, cursing, as he jerked the arrow out. Ixtpan held back three sword-wielding Clankers with his long, silver sword while Paradox took a running leap and landed on the shoulders of a soldier who was about to strike Ixtpan from behind. The Clanker got a look at Paradox's green face as she stabbed him with her copper knife, and he died with a look of astonishment frozen on his face.

A bronze spear cut into Cimarron's left thigh, slicing into his flesh and drawing blood. He realized they were surrounded by another two dozen Clankers. A bronze-tipped arrow pierced his right shoulder, causing him to wince and fall to his knees. Angelina instinctively knelt beside him and tried desperately to pull him to his feet. The soldier who had slashed Cimarron moved in with a sharp two-sided steel blade for a killing stroke.

Paradox hopped between Cimarron, Angelina and their attacker, waving the bloodied copper knife and hissing ferociously. But the soldier's sword was longer than Paradox's arm and, consequently, she had no logical hope of stopping him. Nonetheless, like the saints of the Alamo, Paradox stood her ground, to Cimarron's amazement.

But, instead of striking, the soldier let out a scream and fell dead with a Comanche war lance in his back. The other soldiers turned to run.

An obsidian-tipped lance, dripping blood, slashed in an arc

past Paradox, right in front of Cimarron and Angelina. Angelina looked up and saw a tall, strikingly beautiful woman with dark eyes and shoulder-length black hair worn loose for battle, dressed in white deerskin. An eagle feather hung from her beaded leather headband. The woman raised her lance, the leather-and-stone-decorated lance of a war chief, and more than a dozen of her warriors drew in around them in a tight circle.

Paradox squealed loudly as yet another Comanche picked her up by her buckskin vest.

"Leave her alone!" Angelina yelled angrily from where she knelt beside Cimarron. Her fists were clenched tight, though she was, as always, unarmed.

The Comanche war chief wielding the lance had graceful, sinewy muscles and golden brown skin. The white deerskin she wore was trimmed with crystal beads that caught the moonlight and reflected tiny rainbows of light.

It couldn't be true, Cimarron told himself. She couldn't be standing there right in front of him. He fought for a grip on reality as hard as he'd fought the Clankers.

"Are you going to say you don't remember me, Cimarron?" the woman asked, lowering her lance briefly.

"Topsannah? How . . . ?"

She answered his question by holding out her hand to him. He took it and stood only inches from her. Then she put her arms around him and pulled him close. In the midst of a raging battle, the man in a blue uniform and woman in fringed deerskin embraced with a fierce passion.

Angelina and the others, including the other Comanches, stared in stunned silence.

Then Cimarron pulled away from the woman and bent to Angelina, saying softly, "It's all right. She's a friend. Topsannah Morales. Comanche." Cimarron's sun-bronzed skin had turned deathly pale. "I knew her a long time ago."

Topsannah's black eyes were cold and hard. She said, "Eeschatai, take Cimarron and the others back to camp. See that they come to no harm. I will join you later, after these intruders are beaten back beyond the eastern horizon. That's a promise, on my honor as a Comanche chief. And, Cimarron, I haven't forgotten—not anything."

"*Vamos*," Ixtpan said.

"Come on, Matsemela," Paradox squeaked.

Matsemela looked over his companions carefully. Then he took a good long look at the Comanche war chief. His arrow wound was bleeding but not dangerously. He felt a bit weak, but he knew he had fought in far worse conditions than this and lived to tell about it. "Matsemela Nyakir does not walk out on a fight," he said firmly. "I'm staying."

"No!" Angelina and Paradox cried.

"Good!" Ixtpan exclaimed.

"It's up to you, buckaroo," Cimarron said. "But we're leaving now. Take care of him?" he asked the woman he had once loved with innocent, youthful passion.

"We will treat him as one of our own if that is what you ask."

"*Si*, Topsannah, it is what I ask."

"Take care of yourself," Paradox said to the mercenary.

"My prayers go with you, Matsemela," Angelina said with tears in her eyes. Cimarron took Angelina by the arm and led her away from Matsemela.

"And mine." Ixtpan looked grim.

Hundreds of Comanche warriors rode through the now-burning ruins of the army camp. The flames shot higher and higher into the night, and the eternally dry sand became wet with blood.

*   *   *   *   *

Matsemela laughed with pure glee as he fired the last of a quiver of dogwood arrows he had yanked off a dead soldier, sending the missile into a corporal from behind a barricade of dead mules and horses. His wounds were painful, but they certainly did not keep him from getting into one of the best fights he'd ever been in. He could not remember the last time he'd had so much fun.

Topsannah was firing arrows with astonishing speed from behind the barricade. She let one of her ash arrows fly, then looked to the dark-skinned warrior and saw him to be out of ammunition. Without a second thought, she jumped over the barricade, calling out insults to the Clankers in Comanche, grabbed an iron spear from the hand of a dead soldier and a beaded quiver of arrows off one of her fallen tribesmen, and tossed the arrows to Matsemela. She turned in one swift movement, her black hair swirling around her, and cut down another soldier with the iron spear.

Matsemela stared at her in wonder, so transfixed by her that he was momentarily distracted from the fight. "Now *there*," he thought out loud, "is a real *woman*."

* * * * *

Billy Ray Haggard, the young man from Muskogee who had not so long ago wondered if he would be fortunate enough to see any action in the West, went down with an owl feather-tipped hackberry arrow, the kind preferred by the Comanches, in his heart. Then the Comanche who killed Billy Ray fell with a lariat around his throat, pulled tight until he was dead. The rider loosened his rope and pulled it from around the dead man's neck.

"Good work, Amos," Reno Bismark called out from behind an overturned wagon as he fired an arrow. "So both your buddies are gone. Sorry about that."

Amos dismounted and joined Reno and the others behind the barricade. "Never did like 'em much. Listen, Colonel, I think I can get us out of here. I've spotted a weakness in the Comanches' position. They don't have the east side of the camp as well covered. We stand a chance if we can get over there."

"If you get us out of this mess, I'll make you a lieutenant colonel and double your pay," Bismark answered calmly.

"Then follow me," Amos answered.

A group of two dozen Clankers formed around the colonel and his lieutenant. Together they fought Comanches straight across the camp, losing ten of their number in the process. Three times they had to take cover behind overturned wagons—one of them on fire—and regroup.

Finally they succeeded in getting to the east side of the camp and were about to make a break for the open lands beyond the campgrounds, when they were confronted by ten mounted Comanches. Amos threw his lasso and had one of them on the ground fast. The other nine Comanches rode straight at the Clankers. Reno Bismark quickly stabbed one who came at him, then another. Amos pulled another off his horse with the lasso and stabbed him. The remaining Comanches dismounted and fought Bismark, Amos, and the others hand to hand. Three Clankers died in the encounter—but so did all ten Comanches. Then Reno Bismark jumped on one of their horses and rode away from the camp, followed close behind by Amos Crimsonleaf and half a dozen others of his men.

* * * * *

Horses were running wild through the camp. Cimarron caught a white mustang and jumped into its empty Comanche saddle.

He reached down to Angelina, pulled her up in front of him, and kneed the horse to an even faster gallop.

Ixtpan summoned a black gelding with a white blaze for Paradox and helped her on it, then he mounted a silver-gray stallion. They took off, following Eeschatai, who rode a pinto, the favorite horse of the plains warriors.

Angelina had never seen a horse in her life until Ixtpan had taken her down out of the mountains. But she had learned to ride out of necessity, first horses and later camels, and now she could manage on her own. She had even come to appreciate their beauty, but at the speed at which they were traveling on these alien creatures, she was profoundly grateful for Cimarron's arms around her.

Eeschatai rode ahead of the others, clearing a path through the fighting with his stone axe. A soldier on a tremendous palomino came at Eeschatai, his long sword drawn and swinging. Eeschatai, to the soldier's great surprise, suddenly fell off his horse—or so it seemed. In reality, he caught the horse's mane with his right hand and slipped over its left side, holding on by the mane and his left leg. When he was alongside the soldier, he threw his knife from under his horse's neck. It stuck in the heart of the man and his body fell to the ground.

They were almost past the fighting when the horse Cimarron and Angelina were riding went down, an arrow in its throat. Cimarron pulled Angelina off and out of the way of the dying animal. He had one arm around her. With the other he waved his knife, keeping four attacking Clankers at bay. "When I make my move, run," he yelled.

Before Angelina could object, he threw her outside the reach of the attackers, then jumped straight at one of them. Cimarron stabbed the man and managed to kill him, but the other soldiers grabbed him. Two of them held him while another struck him repeatedly with his fists. He had already lost a lot of blood from the sword and arrow wounds, and the blows came hard and fast.

Ixtpan, Eeschatai, and Paradox formed a circle around Angelina and fought the Clankers encircling them. They struck down three of their enemies, but for every one that fell, two more joined the attack. Ixtpan cursed as a bronze sword cut deeply into his right shoulder. Paradox jumped in front of Ixtpan, calling, "Here!" as she threw her copper knife to Angelina. Paradox was fighting with a bronze sword that was heavier than she was, waving it wildly in a broad arc.

Angelina looked at the knife with wide blue-green eyes, and the wind blew up around her. A grinning soldier advanced on her with a long sword.

Then, with a savage yell, Wyatt Fontana jumped the man bearing down on Angelina. Paradox killed her opponent with a swift upward thrust of the long sword and ran to Angelina's side. Eeschatai and the wounded Ixtpan held more Clankers at bay.

Fiercely, with a long bronze dagger, Wyatt fought the soldier, a member of his own unit. Wyatt had the advantage of taking the man by surprise. He stabbed his opponent, and the man fell to his knees, a look of stunned disbelief on his young face. Then Wyatt turned to the men pummeling Cimarron. With a fast jab, he slit the throat of one of them.

When Wyatt stabbed one of the Clankers holding him, Cimarron got out from under another and dove at him with such a rage that he pushed the man's head hard against a limestone rock on the ground. He slammed the man's head into the rock again and again. He was trapped in a world of blood-red light, and there was an insistent drumming in his brain.

"¡Alto! Can't you see you have already killed him? You could have killed him ten times over!" Angelina was screaming, but her voice seemed unreal to Cimarron, as though he were underwater, drowning.

He heard Angelina pleading and felt her small hands pulling on his shoulders from behind. He stopped, looking at his blood-soaked hands. He felt her small hands on his shoulders and at that moment, the sensation seemed to be the only thing keeping him from madness. He sobbed out loud, dropped the Clanker, and reached out to Angelina. His hands dripped blood, and she drew back from him, horror evident in her face.

Eeschatai took hold of Cimarron, saying, "I've got a horse for you." He and Ixtpan had killed or scared off the rest of the Clankers around them, and for the moment the companions had a clear shot at escaping.

Ixtpan was summoning loose horses. He and Eeschatai already held the reins of two horses, one golden and one silver, both soaked with sweat from being ridden hard by fighting warriors.

"Take me with you," Wyatt said, his eyes blazing, his knife dripping blood from the Clankers he had stabbed.

"No," Paradox said, instinctively not trusting the man.

Ixtpan was leaning on Paradox, one of his large hands on her shoulders for support. He had lost a good deal of blood and was unsteady on his feet. "Paradox, the man saved Angelina."

"Look, you owe me, Cimarron." Wyatt's black eyes were pleading. "This time I've killed to help you. You know what Bismark will do to me now."

Wyatt spoke the truth, Cimarron knew. He did owe the man a great deal. "All right, come on," he said, staggering from pain and blood loss and from the magnitude of the fury that had possessed him.

Cimarron mechanically mounted the silver stallion whose reins Eeschatai held. The Comanche lifted Angelina into Cimarron's arms, then mounted the pinto. Ixtpan called another pinto for Wyatt and a black horse for himself. Paradox held the black horse's reins while he slowly climbed on, then she jumped up behind him.

* * * * *

The six companions rode from the camp where the battle raged. None of them spoke during the desperate hours-long ride across land whose barrenness was broken only by an occasional white bison skull or solitary mesquite tree. The only sound was the pounding of the horses' hooves.

The sun was rising over the eastern horizon, turning the clouds pink and gold above them. The morning light was comforting, reminding them all of the miracle of their survival, yet at the same time tormenting them with thoughts of the friends who might not see this new dawn.

"¡Aquí!" Eeschatai called out, reining his pinto to a halt in the middle of a level plateau. "This way!"

Cimarron reined in his horse behind the Comanche. Eeschatai dismounted, saying, "This is the place, my friends, the place of which the soldados know nothing."

"Where the hell are we?" Paradox demanded, jumping down from her horse.

"Follow me." The Comanche gestured to the level ground itself. Cimarron, Angelina, Wyatt, Ixtpan, and Paradox followed the motion of his hand across the broad expanse of the land, all of them at first unable to understand what he meant for them to see.

And then they saw it and stood breathless in amazement. As if a gigantic scythe had cut a deep wound in the earth, a tremendous crevasse lay in the high plateau. Anyone looking over the plateau would see nothing but level ground unless they were on the brink of the deep gorge. The dark chasm was hundreds of feet across.

The gorge's vertical walls appeared to drop at least seven hundred feet.

The limestone cliff was broken, so the footing of the steep, rocky incline was treacherous. The zigzag path into the canyon was so narrow that they had to walk single file, leading the horses behind them, taking every step with extreme caution.

"Amazing," whispered Wyatt. "No wonder we've never been able to find it."

"Is that the only way down?" Cimarron asked Eeschatai.

"*Si*," Eeschatai answered, "the only path. No one enters this canyon easily or quickly."

Cimarron was limping from the wound in his thigh and dizzy from loss of blood, but he noticed that Angelina's footing on the loose rocks was as good as that of Eeschatai, as though she were experienced with such terrain, and again he wondered where she really came from. And what she really was.

On the canyon floor, they were greeted by a sight so peaceful as to belie the warfare that was spreading across the frontier. A stream of clear blue water flowed through the canyon, and along its banks stretched bisonhide tipis scattered over about three miles. Smoke drifted upward from scores of small fires. Hundreds of colorful mustangs grazed on the grass fed by the stream. It was a vision as pure as the light that filtered into the valley.

Angelina suddenly felt as if she were on holy ground, a place blessed by the gods, like Teotihuacán and Tula, a center of spiritual energy on the continent.

"This is our home now, not the Sea of Grass, where our ancestors were born," Eeschatai said somberly. "Hoda Canyon."

* * * * *

While Cimarron and the others headed north into Hoda Canyon, Reno Bismark, Amos Crimsonleaf, and two dozen others rode back east, hoping to meet up with the companies under the leadership of Comdr. Gen. Absalom Ironheart.

"I sure as hell haven't come this far to have some feather-bedecked savages take everything I've worked for away from me," Bismark remarked angrily to Amos, as he kneed his silver-blue stallion to a faster gallop. "Or Absalom Ironheart, either. I'm going to be the one to wipe out those barbarians at Epitaph and the Comanches, too—even if I have to kill Ironheart and take command of his troops to do it." He paused thoughtfully, staring out over the vast horizon. "Yes, the Comanches, too. All of them.

Every last one of them. By the way, Amos, when did you last see Wyatt?"

"I didn't see him dead, if that's what you mean. But I didn't see him meet up with Cimarron, either." Amos absent-mindedly tied a loop in his lasso and tested the knot.

"The man could be dead, or he could be right where I want him to be—on the road to Epitaph with Cimarron and that witch. Wyatt, if he's still alive, is going to help me out by following Cimarron. He's going to be able to lead *me* right to Epitaph."

CHAPTER 9

THE JOURNEY

The sun was high in the sky, its penetrating golden rays shining directly into the deep canyon, as Ixtpan, with Paradox in tow, began exploring the Comanche camp. They had had barely three hours' rest, but Ixtpan was eager to look around. His sword wound had not been deep, and he had quickly recovered from its effects. There was a slight hesitation to his walk, and he would stop occasionally, overcome by momentary weakness, but he was propelled by his relentless curiosity.

Ixtpan, in the ragged remains of his white tunic and brown trousers, his thick hair sticking out all around him, and Paradox, her buckskin vest and blue calico skirt only remnants of what they had been, caused something of a stir among the Comanches.

Though the Comanches knew the old legends of an ancient race of giants, they had never seen—nor expected to see—a man as tall as Ixtpan. Nor had they ever seen a chattering itzaur. However, Eeschatai managed to allay the fears of his tribespeople by telling them of the heroism of both Ixtpan and Paradox in the battle with the Clankers ten miles south the night before.

"Ah, the horsewarriors!" Ixtpan exclaimed repeatedly as he inspected a bisonhide tipi painted with blue spirals and yellow serpents. "I have always wanted to know more about them!" He bowed from the waist to a Comanche woman just coming out of the tipi, carrying a large skin canteen to fetch water from the stream. The woman was so startled by Ixtpan that she dropped the canteen and ran back into the tipi.

"What's to know about them?" Paradox squeaked, taking two steps for each of Ixtpan's one. "They spend their lives chasing the bison and running from the Clankers."

"But, Paradox," Ixtpan responded, "their history goes back at least fifteen hundred years!"

"That's nothing!"

"Humph," Ixtpan snorted, taking Paradox's thin green arm and pulling her over to inspect some bisonhide war shields. The shields were decorated with colorful beads and paint, in the shapes of various animals whose attributes—such as the strength of the bear, the vision of the eagle, the endurance of the armadillo—the warriors sought to invoke. "Look at these. I can tell you a thing or two about the origin of these symbols. About three thousand years ago, . . ."

Paradox groaned but soon found herself ignoring Ixtpan's lecture and watching a group of Comanche children playing in the stream. They look so happy, so carefree, she thought, so unaware of what is happening outside of this canyon. The children reminded her a little of herself at a comparable age of sixty or seventy, playing with her older sister, Senjella, blissfully unaware of the world outside Itzamma and all its dangers. She smiled, but a tear came to her eye as she wondered if those children's parents had died in the battle with the Clankers, if the children themselves would live to adulthood.

Wyatt, too, was exploring the Comanche settlement, with its seemingly endless rows of tipis and its impressive horse herd. Even with the warriors in battle, there were another thousand horses in the camp. Among the plains warriors, horses were riches, and the Comanches of Hoda Canyon were the richest of all. He felt he was in a hostile place—with symbols of strange gods and spirits all around him. He shuddered inwardly, looking at the paintings on the tipis and the designs of the bisonhide shields, and he fingered the twisted cross he wore hanging unseen inside his blue shirt. He was consoled by the knowledge that now, at last, he knew where the Comanches had found sanctuary. He would bring the army of Tesharka here to this canyon, he told himself, and it would burn the heathens from the face of the Earth. And he would be, he knew, well rewarded by Reno Bismark, and possibly by the guvnor himself.

Angelina and Cimarron sat by the side of a small flowing stream, a tributary of the main stream that flowed through the canyon, while children of the Comanche village rubbed down their horses with dried grass. This tributary ran into a box canyon that ran off the east side of Hoda Canyon itself. They were alone, surrounded on three sides by high walls of gold, brown, and white stone. The box canyon was filled with cottonwood and live oak trees, and the sound of its cool waters relaxed them both and made the horror of the night's battle seem mercifully remote. Angelina had slept briefly there beside the water and she seemed revived, calm in spite of everything that had happened.

Cimarron had had no sleep. His eyes were bloodshot, his face a dark mask of pain. He had thrown away his blue army shirt, tossing it in a Comanche fire the night before, and had borrowed a fringed leather vest from Eeschatai. Angelina was cleaning his

wounds with water boiled in a skin sack with hot coals, and apply-
ing a poultice made from the sticky inside of the nopal cactus. He
had refused to let her use her stones and magic, because her rituals
made him vaguely uneasy. He had seen *curanderas* before, in Pecos and Durango, but none had the kind of power Angelina had.
Cimarron did let her clean his wounds to keep away the poison
they could unleash in his blood. He had seen many people survive
blood loss only to die from the killing fever that often followed a
wound.

"Why did you help me escape?" the healer asked, searching his
brown eyes for the answer as she bound the deep wound in his
shoulder with a clean piece of soft doeskin. "You betrayed your
own commander. You could have been killed. You will be killed if
the Confederation's soldiers ever catch you. I am no one to you. I
am not of your people or of your land."

"No, *señorita*, but you are someone to me. I'd have died beside
the Rio Bravo if it hadn't been for you. And he's not my commander. Bismark forced me to track for him . . . but I swear I only
did it because he was after you. I thought I could warn you in time
or slow the army down. I was lucky, real lucky, to meet up with
Eeschatai. I'm sorry there wasn't an easier way." He leaned forward, his right elbow resting on his knee, shielding his face with
his hand.

"You do not have to explain," Angelina said softly.

"Yeah, I do."

"Cimarron, you saved me—and Ixtpan and Paradox—and
Matsemela. I am very grateful to you. Forgive me for what I said
. . . what I did . . . in Bismark's tent."

"*Lo siento* for kissing you the way I did. I couldn't risk Bismark
realizing that I meant to help you escape."

"There is no need for you to be sorry." Angelina smiled, but
then she turned somber. "Cimarron, there is something I must
tell you. And when I have, you may be the one who is angry with
me."

"There is nothing that could make me angry with you, Angelina." His dark brown eyes stared at her, unblinking. "*Nada*." The
direct sunlight above them gleamed off the gold streaks in his
brown hair.

"I come from a place very different from your world, and I
know so little of life here. I have never known a man like you. . . .
Among my people, I am a priestess. I have taken sacred vows, dedicated my life to the practice of our ancient religion. . . ."

"I understand, Angelina. I respect your vows. I'd never ask anything of you. I swear by St. Davy's grave, I don't expect anything from you."

"There is more. I did not save your life by the Rio Bravo as you believe. Ixtpan and Matsemela killed the border guards. I cannot kill, not for anyone. I have the gift of healing, and if I take a human life, I will lose my powers. My friends fired at the men who were killing you that morning. They, too, are the ones to whom you owe your life. Forgive me for what I could not do." Her eyes seemed larger than ever, glowing golden green with a light from deep within her. She turned her head so that her long black hair covered her face, shielding her from having to see his reaction.

Cimarron gently took her shoulders in his hands, turning her to face him. "I remember you as clear as high noon sunlight, like some holy spirit, kneeling beside me. I was dying, and somehow, through some kind of energy that flowed through you, I was saved." He held her eyes locked with his own. "You gave me life, Angelina."

"I healed your wounds. I did not save you from those who caused them."

"You helped a stranger who otherwise would have died alone and unmourned. I'll do whatever I can to help you, Angelina. I promise you that. I'll stand by you until you're safe from Reno Bismark and all the rest of them. And I swear on my life, I would never do anything to harm you."

"I now know you would not, Cimarron, and I am grateful for what you offer. But I am going to Epitaph. It would be dangerous for you to go there."

"Then tell me why you're going there? This frontier is no place for a woman like you."

"But, Cimarron, you have never known a woman like me. There are many things I could tell you, but I do not know if you are ready to understand."

"Try me."

Once she told him, Angelina knew, he might turn against her, fearing her as had the people of Nueva San Cristobal. For all her uncertainty about him, she dreaded his reaction. But she knew in her heart that he deserved to know the truth.

"I am Tolteca, Cimarron. *Hija de Quetzalcoatl.* A daughter of Quetzalcoatl."

"*La leyenda,*" he gasped. The most enduring legend in the history of the continent. He had learned of the great Toltec warriors all his life. They had taken their culture across the continent, only to vanish in the mists of history long ago, before the Great War. For centuries, the return of the Toltecs had been prophesied. Diego Laredo's soldiers often invoked *las Toltecas* before going into battle, as had warriors of other now-lost civilizations. "It's not possible."

"No legend, Cimarron, a woman of flesh and blood, from a real place in your own time. Look at me. Am I possible?"

"You don't seem possible, not to me."

"Quetzalcoatl's children are still here, *mi amigo.* I am one of them. I am a priestess of the Old Religion, the religion taught by the Lord of Tula, Quetzalcoatl himself. Perhaps one day I will be able to tell you about it. I carry in me the gift of healing that Quetzalcoatl brought into this world. My god forbade human sacrifice, and so I will not kill, since all killing is sacrifice even if you pretend it is not by calling it war or vengeance or justice or something else."

"You are right about that," Cimarron responded somberly.

Angelina continued, her eyes turquoise in the sunlight. "My people are few, but we have survived for twenty centuries, while other empires have come and gone. As each empire has fallen, we have taken in a handful of refugees who fled south and, directed by the god of whom I am certain, found our city, Tamoanchan, high in the cloud forest of the *Isla Quahtemal*."

"What does this have to do with the Prophet?"

"The Prophet is a shaman. That means that he has lived before and that he remembers his past life and draws lessons and wisdom from his previous experience. We know who he was in his past life and we revere him as martyr to this land—"

"What past life, Angelina? Who is he? What is he to you?" Many people in Cimarron's time believed fervently in reincarnation, so the mention of someone's past life did not in itself surprise him. He personally, however, simply did not give a damn whether he had lived before or would live again.

"He was Falling Eagle, Cuauhtémoc in his own language, fifteen hundred years ago. And he is Falling Eagle in this life. He was the last *Uey-Tlatoani*—you would say 'emperor' in your language, but that is not all he was—of the Aztec people, just over five hundred and twenty years after Quetzalcoatl, our priest who became a god, died after promising his followers he would return someday. In that year, Ce Acatl, or One-Reed by our calendar, invaders from across the Eastern Ocean arrived on this continent.

The Aztecs at first thought their leader, a demon in disguise, was the returning Quetzalcoatl, and they let him come into their city, Tenochtitlán. But the invaders destroyed the city and killed its people by the thousands when he was only seventeen.

"Falling Eagle led a last great battle in the defense of this continent from those long-ago invaders. His people were armed with obsidian, while the invaders were armed with weapons of steel and magic weapons that shot death from sticks and great balls of lead from iron tubes. Ultimately, Falling Eagle surrendered himself to stop the slaughter of his people. In his past life, he was tortured horribly by his conquerors and finally burned to death at the age of twenty-one in a horrible sacrifice to their God of War. And it all happened because of his people's belief in the return of my god."

Cimarron was fascinated, perplexed, and worried. Angelina needed to be thinking more about her own dangerous situation than about things that had happened hundreds of years in the past, which all the magic in the universe could not undo. He had heard of the courageous young Aztec warrior, Cuauhtémoc, all his life—in legends, songs, among the vaqueros. According to the legend, Cuauhtémoc had spoken calmly of lying on a bed of roses while the conquerors held his feet in flames. But neither Cuauhtémoc's bravery nor his will to fight was, in Cimarron's opinion, likely to be able to help Angelina or anyone else now.

"He has been reborn," Angelina continued. "Falling Eagle has the wisdom of his experience—both in matters of the spirit and in matters of warfare. But he also feels the pain of that life. Ixtpan told me his story, and I knew I had to help him. In this year, Falling Eagle has passed his twenty-first birthday, and he has told his followers that he will not live out the year, that he will die at twenty-one, as he did before. Cimarron, perhaps I can save him. I know I can take the pain from him. And I must. I owe it to him because of who he is and because of what he must do now in this life. ¿Comprende?"

"Si, Angelina. I do understand. I come from Pecos, and I know real well what it's like to have to do something because of what happened a long time in the past. I mean, I can't let the saints of the Alamo down, now can I?" He laughed, realizing that the saints of the Alamo and Angelina's Cuauhtémoc had made essentially the same choice—to fight, not to win, not to live, but just to fight.

It was the first time Angelina had seen him laugh. When he

laughed, the jagged lines of his face relaxed, and she realized that this seemingly bitter, hardened man was really not much older than she was. "Ixtpan told me the story of your Alamo." Actually Ixtpan had called it a nonsensical fable, which she wisely chose not to mention to a man from Pecos.

"Then we can talk about it on the way to Epitaph. Look, I've got my own reasons for wanting to meet the Prophet. I don't know anything about past lives, Angelina, or things that happened a long time ago. With me, it's pure and simple—the Confederation conquered my homeland, and if this Falling Eagle can defeat the Confederation, I'm all for him. If you still want to go to Epitaph, I'll take you there."

"There is an ancient, evil power hidden at Epitaph. The Fire God himself is imprisoned there. And if the Confederation soldiers release him from his idol, my friend Ixtpan says there will be devastation like you and I cannot imagine."

"I've seen some devastation before, Angelina, and I'm not afraid of any god or any idol. My choice is made." Cimarron could not imagine that the talk of an idol to an ancient god was anything but archaic superstition. The only real dangers they faced, in his estimation, were the Confederation army and the deadly land itself.

"Then I would be honored to be accompanied by you, Cimarron Langtry. I admit I need your help." There would be, she knew, no way he would believe her if she explained about the rock called uranium and of the times when the Fire God burned across the earth and blotted out the light of the sun with dirt and ash and soot. She was not sure how much she believed of the stories herself.

A cry went up, a howling that at first they took for wails of grief. They jumped to their feet, Cimarron with his knife in his hand, expecting to see the attacking Confederation army entering the canyon. But when they looked in the direction of the narrow pathway, they realized the shrieks were of joy.

One by one, the returning Comanche warriors were leading their horses down the narrow path into their canyon sanctuary. They were a bedraggled lot, less than half the strength of the war party that had set out to attack Bismark's forces, bloodied, bruised, and dirty.

Some were wounded, bleeding; some had to be carried in the arms and over the shoulders of their companions; and a few were carried on stretchers. As the procession entered the valley, the children and old people who had stayed behind in the secure camp danced around them, singing ancient songs. Some took up the rhythm, beating carved stones against bisonhide drums.

The returning warriors and their families and friends embraced. Many, told that a loved one had not survived the battle, burst into tears and the wailing of Comanche mourning.

Cimarron and Angelina both watched, looking anxiously for someone they did not see among the survivors. As the procession slowed, the warriors who brought up the rear to guard against another attack began whooping, and soon all the tribes that made their home in the valley joined in a wild group dance.

Then they saw the last ones coming slowly down the narrow trail. A Comanche warrior wearing a rattlesnakeskin headband held the front of a stretcher. "Thanks be to the saints of the Alamo," Cimarron said when he saw Topsannah carrying the other end of a stretcher.

"No!" Angelina exclaimed. She started running, with Cimarron after her.

Ixtpan and Paradox ran to Angelina's side. Wyatt Fontana, too, approached the returning warriors cautiously.

Topsannah's strong voice called to them, "He's all right. This one is too tough to kill."

"By the Serpent's tail feathers, there is no getting rid of the man," Ixtpan groaned, though he hurried to see for himself.

Angelina ran to Matsemela. As soon as Topsannah and the warrior put the litter on the ground, Cimarron embraced her while Angelina knelt at Matsemela's side with Ixtpan and Paradox beside her. Wyatt Fontana, as always, looked on.

The mercenary was alive but unconscious, having apparently lost a lot of blood from a wound in his back. His chocolate-brown skin had a tinge of gray to it, and his brown eyes were closed. He was covered with bruises and swellings, and what had remained of his red and gold clothing after the escape from Itzamma had been further reduced to shreds.

"Great Tyran's ghost," Paradox said in a hiss.

"Perhaps some magic protects this man," Wyatt suggested, looking darkly at Angelina.

"The hell it does," Matsemela growled, opening his dark eyes. "The only thing that protects me is my sword—and this lady, of course," he added, gesturing to Topsannah.

Angelina cried out in delight at hearing the mercenary's voice, though she was most surprised to hear him speak so highly of anyone as he just had of Topsannah. She could not recall him saying anything good about anyone in the weeks she had known him.

Topsannah bent to check on the condition of the warrior. Her black hair fell against his chest, and her eyes, as black and as rich as Delta soil, stared into his own. Her oval face was scratched and bruised, her white buckskin clothing torn and streaked with dirt and blood; she still carried her beaded quiver on her back, even though all the arrows had been fired and not retrieved.

A big smile spread over Matsemela's face before he drifted back into unconsciousness.

Cimarron stared at Topsannah. "I've wondered so many times what happened to you after you left Reynada."

Her large, almond-shaped, dark eyes filled with tears. "I found my people. I had to, you know?"

"I do know, Topsannah. You made the right decision. And you're alive and free. It's more than I can say for the rest of us."

"You're alive and free."

"Am I?"

She pulled him close, her hands fiercely gripping the strong muscles beneath his sun-darkened skin. "Did they all die in the rebellion, Cimarron? All of the people we knew?"

"Most of them." He closed his eyes tightly for a second. "I'm glad you're alive, Topsannah, that you got out of Pecos in time. You look as though the years with the Comanches have been good for you."

"They have been years in which my people have been driven from the Sea of Grass and into a canyon to hide in the earth. I sure am glad to see you again, Cimarron. I give thanks to the gods of our tribes that you're alive and that you've come back."

Cimarron pulled Topsannah to him and held her tight.

So that is why I sense such pain in you, vaquero, Angelina thought, sitting on the ground beside Matsemela's stretcher, only a few feet from Cimarron and Topsannah. The lost rebellion, the dead you cannot forget—and something more, something in yourself you cannot forgive.

* * * * *

But for the small fires that burned throughout the Comanche village, the canyon floor was dark, its steep walls hiding all but a haze of gray moonlight. The Comanches were busy tending the fires, boiling roots, cooking bison steaks over hot coals, and preparing for a war council.

Cimarron sat alone in the darkness near the stream, smoking a corn shuck cigarette, the angular lines of his face set as hard as though carved in stone. Eeschatai approached him and laid a hand on his shoulder, saying, "Topsannah has requested that you and your friends join us for the council. We cannot allow you to vote, but, since you were so recently with the Confederation army, we think you may have knowledge that may be valuable to us in planning our strategy against the Clankers."

"I'd be honored, Eeschatai, and I'm sure the others will be, too. Will your chief, Bajo del Sol, be there? The old boy's the greatest war chief since the Old World god Kwahnah, and I sure would like to meet him. There must be a hundred different *corridos* sung about him in every catina from here to southern Durango." He laughed but then stopped abruptly as he saw the unmistakable sorrow in Eeschatai's eyes.

"Bajo is with us in spirit and in our hearts. He left this life thirteen moons ago. He fell in the fighting at Mud Walls. The Clankers fear him so much, we have concealed his death from them. Topsannah and I buried him high in the mountains that are sacred to our people—where the *soldados* will never find his body. No, Bajo lives on in all of us. Most of all in Topsannah and in their son, Texas."

"Their son?"

"Topsannah returned to us six years ago. She married Bajo soon after she returned. The boy, Texas, is five winters old. He's here in the camp. A fine boy. He will be a great chief one day—like both his parents. You will meet him after you have had time to rest. When Bajo died, Topsannah became our war chief."

"So, Topsannah Morales has become war chief of the Comanches." Cimarron let out a long, slow whistle. He remembered well that she could fight like the devil.

"Not only of the Comanches. Topsannah is war chief of all the tribes of the Sea of Grass that have not gone to the camp of that madman called the Prophet in the San Cris Mountains."

"Why don't the tribes unite with the forces in the San Cris? There's strength in numbers."

"*Si*, but their sanctuary, Epitaph, is a deathtrap." The warrior's gaze was downcast. "It is a tremendous pueblo of a thousand rooms that can be well defended, but it can also be surrounded and besieged. And if ever the army breaks into the pueblo . . . it will be a slaughter, like fighting in a honeycomb. You know no Comanche would ever walk into something like that. Not willingly. Comanches fight in the open air. We live and die in the open air."

"I understand your feeling, *compañero*," Angelina said softly. The two men had not heard her approach. In her torn green skirt and white blouse, with her long black hair hanging loose, she looked to them like some lost child-spirit. "My people, too, are nurtured by the open air."

"Then don't go to Epitaph, *hermanita*," the Comanche answered solemnly. "Epitaph is a cage for people like us. Don't let our enemies drive you into a cage."

They joined Topsannah around the low fire for the council meeting. Ixtpan and Matsemela were seated at her right and left respectively. No one had thought to invite Paradox, but she was there anyway, seated next to Ixtpan.

"How did you all get out of Itzamma?" Angelina asked her friends. "I thought you all died in the earthquake."

"Not me. It would take more than a few rocks to get me." Matsemela stated it as a matter of fact.

Ixtpan spoke up. "We come to be alive because of the ability of my race to attune ourselves to the vibration of the universe. So powerful is our syncrony with the universal vibrations that we can alter the relationship of objects to one another. By aligning—"

"He levitated the stones off us, is what he's getting at," Paradox put in, trying to expedite the situation. "The big guy just lifted the stones off, one by one."

"With his bare hands?" Topsannah thought she must have heard wrong—both about Ixtpan lifting the stones and that she actually heard an itzaur talk. Her long black hair hung in braids, and she wore a simple white buckskin tunic and trousers, and high-topped moccasins. In her hands was a braid of sweetgrass, which she was twisting absent-mindedly.

"Hands?" Paradox scoffed. "No. With that vibration stuff!"

Wyatt, sitting nearby, took a deep drag on an oak leaf cigarette and choked at Paradox's words. Cimarron raised his eyebrows in surprise.

Topsannah was utterly startled by the itzaur's speech. "What is this?" she asked, pointing a long, slender brown finger at Paradox.

"Don't ask," Matsemela said. "You'd never believe it."

"You must understand," Angelina said to Topsannah, seeing the war chief's expression of horror as she looked at the talking itzaur, "that Paradox comes from an ancient, highly developed race. You must listen to her as you would another human. And she's not a 'this.' Her name is Paradox."

"I am surprised," Topsannah responded honestly, "but I see the itzaur is intelligent. Go on, Paradox."

"I'll explain later," Paradox said indignantly.

"Once we found our way out of Itzamma, Ixtpan summoned up a couple of mustangs for us to ride and found an eagle to tell us which way Jolosumu's henchmen had taken you," Matsemela said. "Ixtpan's ability with languages sure does come in handy."

"It's amazing," said Wyatt, "truly amazing." A being who could levitate stones and talk to animals. Such a creature could bring him a rich reward from his commanding officer, even from his guvnor. But such a creature must be, Wyatt thought, the tool of the devil, the evil god who burned human souls in an eternal fire. And the devil's servants, he knew, like the giant and the lizard creature and the woman with the strange eyes, must themselves burn to purify the world. He fingered the twisted cross he wore.

Half a dozen Comanches, all dressed in beaded buckskin, chosen from their tribes to make policy and military decisions, approached and seated themselves around the fire.

The war chief studied the faces of those around her carefully, gauging their knowledge and their instincts. Six were warriors she knew well. And she had known Cimarron well at one time. The other newcomers were mysteries to her. Ultimately the decision of what to do would be hers, but she would evaluate the words of all those around the campfire.

She took some gray sage leaves from a leather pouch. One of the women handed her a long braid of sweetgrass. Topsannah put some to the sage leaves on the burning embers of the fire and soon the pungent smoke filled the air. Then she broke the braid of sweetgrass and laid it on the embers. Its sweet, pure smell mingled with the rich, musky sage.

Angelina understood what Topsannah was doing. In all the old cultures of the continent, the smoke of burning sage, sweetgrass, and, in Angelina's homeland, copal resin, was used to carry prayers to the gods. Topsannah's ritual awakened Angelina's homesickness, her longing for the temple at Tamoanchan, for the world she knew and understood.

Topsannah waved beaded eagle prayer feathers over the smoke. Then she filled the sacred pipe with tobacco and offered it to the earth, the sky, and each of the four primary directions before passing it ceremoniously among those gathered around her. "The Clankers will keep coming west. I have lived among the so-called civilized people of the continent, and I know the forces driving them westward. For many, it is greed and arrogance. But for others, it is desperation. The land grows drier with every summer that comes. The plague destroys whole cities overnight. Armies march from the Four Directions. The people are driven on, looking for food and land. Whatever the reasons, the army won't stop because we've won this battle. We must send delegations to Epitaph and Durango to investigate the forces gathered there—as to their strength and the possibility of alliances."

Cimarron started to say something, but held back.

"I say no," Parawah Crowfeather, brother of the late Bajo del Sol, said emphatically. "Never. This is not what Bajo del Sol fought and died for—for us to ally with the riffraff of the world. We fight for ourselves alone."

"He speaks the truth." Sara Bisonheart struck her left palm with her right fist to emphasize her point. Her face was deeply lined by years lived under the open sky. "Diego Laredo is a bandit who hides behind talk of liberation. And those at Epitaph have lost and lost and lost again, otherwise they would not have taken refuge in the city built by a dead race. Comanches need no one else. We stand alone."

"Comanches have died alone too many times." Eeschatai smoked the pipe slowly, watching the smoke drift up to the night sky, carrying prayers to the spirits.

Parawah's face was as red as molten bronze in the firelight, his eyes glazed with conviction. "Our Word Rememberers tell us that once, long, long ago, our people almost vanished from the Earth. They were hunted and killed by *Tejanos, Mexicanos*, Blue Coats, and Rangers until only a handful survived, until our enemies declared us extinct. But the memories were kept alive, and when the lights of the Old World went out, the Comanches and others of the old races returned to this land, our land." He looked long at Angelina and Ixtpan. "Just as the buffalo returned—greater and stronger than before. We will not be defeated this time. Never again."

"Then I suggest you find out just who's at this place called Epitaph and how strong they are. And I can tell you a thing or two about Diego Laredo, one of them being that he'd be a hell of an ally." Cimarron's dark eyes met Parawah's. "One coyote's not much trouble. But a pack of them are hell to fight. We've all got a better chance in a pack."

"No!" The warrior named White Bear stood angrily. "We fight

our own way. And our way has worked."

"Then why are you hiding in this canyon?" Angelina asked. "Were you not forced out of the lands called the Sea of Grass?"

The members of the Comanche council had hardly given any notice to this small woman who followed, they assumed, the warrior called Cimarron, and they were surprised when she spoke independently.

"Yes. Slowly we have been driven west by settlers and armies from the North and East. If it continues, we will be pushed to the Western Sea. And what then?" Topsannah demanded of Parawah and the others. "Where do we go then? Out onto the open sea to seek a new world?"

"We will be driven no farther." Parawah's sun-wrinkled face was set firm in determination. "I swear it on my brother's grave."

"Well, with all respect to old Bajo, and from what you all say, he must've been one hell of a guy," Matsemela said with sincerity, "lots of people've sworn on lots of graves, and all those vows aren't worth a blade of buffalo grass when your enemy has more troops and more weapons than you do."

"Those words are as true as any ever spoken." Cimarron knew what it was to fight with obsidian against steel, because he had done it in Reynada. It was defeat. It was watching his friends die.

"We want our people to survive, and to do that, we need more than hit-and-run victories. If Bajo were alive, he'd be the first to say so." Topsannah's voice was as hard as flint, though her oval face was strangely tranquil. "Sooner or later, the Clankers will find this canyon, and they will destroy our nation forever."

Parawah was adamant, his face set in rigid lines. "This canyon will not be easily attacked. Anyone coming in here will be cut to pieces by our warriors. And if you want allies so badly, Topsannah, then you go and get them. But the rest of us will stay and fight for our lands ourselves. Right here."

One woman sitting by the campfire had not yet spoken. She lifted the red-and-black woven blanket that covered her head, revealing long gray hair and a face as dark and wrinkled as old leather. Her name was Moon Shadow, and she was an elder of the tribe, one of the few old enough to remember the time before the Confederation had come, when the plains had belonged to the Comanches. "Yes, we want our people to survive," she said. "And to survive, we need far more than this canyon. We need the land itself. Without the land—without *this* land—the Comanche is as dead as the Old World. If the expansion from the east and from the north is not stopped, the day will come when the grasslands will be mesquite desert and the bison will be only bleached bones in the sand."

"Impossible!" snapped Parawah. "You dream too much, old woman."

"It has happened before," Moon Shadow said in a tone so cold it could have put out the campfire. "It has happened before. The Word Rememberers tell us of those days. And I have seen it in visions. Our ancestors lost the land and the land died. And when the land dies, the tribe dies."

Topsannah spoke authoritatively, her large black eyes burning like the embers of the fire. "The visitors among us are journeying to the San Cris Mountains to join with the Prophet and his forces. I want to go with them and then return to tell you what I find there. Only my life will be jeopardized by this journey to Epitaph—"

"No, mama, no!" A muscular little boy with long black hair ran and stood in their midst, his little brown fists clenched tight, his lower lip stuck out in determination.

"This," Topsannah said to Cimarron and the others, "is my son, Texas. His father was Bajo del Sol, my beloved husband. Texas has known five winters."

Eeschatai took the boy by the shoulders and said, "Listen to me, Texas. You are the son of two chiefs, and you must never for one moment forget that. It is you who must inspire others with your courage. I will go along to protect your mother. It is your duty to stay here with your tribe. One day you will wear the eagle feathers of a chief. You must be worthy of them."

Texas stood silently, his eyes flashing hatred at the newcomers who seemed to his young mind to be the source of this danger to his mother.

Topsannah took her son's hand and continued. "I ask Owl Feather and Running Wolf to seek out Diego Laredo in the sierras of Durango—"

"Not that bandit, Laredo," Ixtpan exclaimed. "I've seen villages across Durango that he's pillaged! An alliance with a criminal like that will destroy you."

"There's something y'all should know." Cimarron's voice was hoarse. He took a shuck cigarette that Eeschatai had given him from his pocket and lit it in the fire. "My name is Cimarron Langtry, and I come from Pecos. Five years ago, I fought with the rebels in Reynada. We didn't do so well." Several people laughed at the bitter understatement. Murmurs of sympathy were whispered all around him. The Comanches knew well from survivors they had encountered how terrible the repression had been.

"When it was over," Cimarron continued, "I ran down south. You know, when people from Pecos run, it's always south. It's something of a tradition with us." He laughed sardonically. "On the other side, I traveled around for a while. Then I ended up in Durango." He looked hard at Angelina, wondering how she would react to what he was about to say. "I rode with Diego Laredo for the past three years, in his army. And I'd do it again. They've got a shot at having something better in Durango, of not being governed by a rich old man who bleeds the country dry—but not if the Confederation intervenes with troops and weapons. That's why I'm here in Pecos—to find out if the western resistance can hold the Clankers, or if the Confederation is about to be heading south. And to try to cause the Clankers some trouble up this way."

So that's it, Wyatt thought. He's one of Laredo's bandits. There would be, he realized, a considerable bounty on Cimarron's head in Durango, which, after all, was really not so far away. And Reno Bismark would be eager to know his old friend had information about Diego Laredo and his forces.

"So you are really here as the agent of a foreign leader." Parawah drew his knife from its sheath. "Another reason not to trust you."

"If I can slow the Confederation down by even one day, I'm buying the lives of a lot of my compadres in the South, and I'm not ashamed of that." Cimarron watched the other man's knife, and his fingers inched closer to his own. His face was impassive, his eyes hollow, his cheeks dark and sunken.

"You would sacrifice your own people to protect your new friends, eh, amigo?" Parawah asked, twirling the knife so fast it made only one shiny blur in the firelight.

"Look, I don't know much about this Laredo fellow," Matsemela interjected, seeking to stop the impending fight, "but I've heard he's one hell of a leader, maybe better than Bismark, and if Cimarron here has been with him, that's good for us. We can sure use his help." He had heard, from other warriors throughout the South, of Laredo's ability in a fight. If Cimarron was one of Laredo's vaqueros, they were in better shape militarily than the mercenary would have thought. He extended his right hand to Cimarron, who shook it and smiled.

"This is disgraceful." Ixtpan put an arm around Angelina. "Congratulating that barbarian as if he were a hero for riding with the butcher, Laredo! Only you, Matsemela, would do such a thing! Do you not understand that we can't trust him? This Cimarron person is just using us to get to Epitaph to pull those poor souls into some crazy alliance with Diego Laredo."

Parawah twirled the knife and took a step closer to Cimarron. "Isn't that why you're here, Cimarron, to manipulate us into some kind of alliance with the bandit general?"

Cimarron took a long drag on the cigarette. In the firelight, his skin burned bronze. "No. And I'll tell you something else— Diego Laredo is no *santo*, that's for sure, but, no matter what you think of him, he could be a valuable ally someday. So I'd advise y'all to consider what I'm saying real carefully."

"We'll consider it. Only, you're the one who'd better be careful." Parawah made a slashing movement with his knife.

"*¡Basta!* Enough!" Topsannah drew her own knife. "These people are our guests here, and they will be treated as our own people. I have known Cimarron Langtry for many years, and I stand by him. Whatever reason brought you back to Pecos, Cimarron, I thank the spirits for it. I say it is time we send representatives to the north and to the south. We can't continue being isolated like this. None of us can."

Parawah said, "For now, I bow to the will of my chief. We will see what these alliances bring us."

Moon Shadow said, "It is as it must be. Owl Feather and Running Wolf will go to the sierras of Durango. Topsannah and Eeschatai will accompany the newcomers to the sacred San Cris Mountains. You will return and tell us what you find there, and we will meet again in council to decide what course to take. You must leave with the first rays of the sun—so until then, rest and prepare yourselves. The journey will be difficult in many ways. We will burn the sage and sweetgrass to send you strength and vision." She looked around, her old eyes daring anyone to argue. No one did. With a nod from Topsannah, she called out to some of the young people to gather supplies for the journey and to make tipis ready for their guests.

* * * * *

Topsannah was conferring with the warriors who would be leading the tribe in her absence. The others had retired to their tipis or were walking around the camp. Cimarron sat alone by the campfire with his face buried in his sun-bronzed hands. Eeschatai approached him cautiously and laid a hand on the younger man's shoulder. "*Comprendo*, amigo. It was a brave thing you did, speaking the truth. There is a bounty on your head, as there is on all of Laredo's *soldados*, from the Rio Bravo south to Oaxaca. In hard times like these, you make a tempting target. And may the spirits protect you from the Clankers if they ever find out you are in the country, working for Laredo."

"*Muchas gracias*," Cimarron whispered. "Most folks don't understand—not the situation I'm in, not the kinds of things that happen in a war . . ."

Eeschatai took a wooden pipe from his buckskin pocket and lit the tobacco in it. He inhaled the burning tobacco and passed the pipe to Cimarron, who took it and did the same.

"You called Epitaph a deathtrap," Cimarron said. "If you're right, we're all likely to die there. So why are you going?"

"To protect my chief. And because I made a promise to my next chief. The boy, Texas, will one day be the greatest warrior of our people."

"I'm sure he will. He's a fine boy, Eeschatai."

"*Si*, he is a credit to his parents and to our tribe. Already he is a straight shot with an arrow, and he rides as if he were born on a horse."

"I thought all Comanches were born on horseback!" Cimarron laughed, the hard lines of his face softening in the firelight.

"Practically. We live all our lives on horses. By the way, the children have prepared a tipi for you and your woman."

"*Gracias*, but Angelina is a priestess. She belongs to no man, certainly not to a man like me. I will stay outside her tipi, though, in case our enemies come."

Cimarron and Eeschatai found Angelina sitting by the stream with Paradox and Ixtpan, and they escorted her to a large sun-bleached white tipi painted with ancient symbols in blue and yellow. At least twenty cedar poles supported the tipi. They were covered by twenty bisonhides stitched together with the flesh side out. An opening about four feet high formed the door, its flap held back by a cedar pole. Inside the tipi were spread two piles of bison robes, near each other though not joined.

"*Está bien*, Eeschatai," Cimarron said, inspecting the inside of the tipi.

"Cimarron!" Topsannah called out as she and Texas entered through the flap in the tipi. Eeschatai excused himself with a smile at Cimarron, and left.

"We bring gifts for our honored guests," Texas announced formally. His dark eyes gleamed proudly as he laid a tan deerskin shirt and pants at Cimarron's feet.

Topsannah handed Angelina a short dress of fringed white deerskin trimmed with blue beads and a pair of knee-high white doeskin moccasins trimmed with silver beads. "You will need fresh clothing for the journey," she said. "And it is our way of welcoming you to our tribe. As far as we are concerned, you have a home with us if ever you want it. You are one of us now."

"Your welcome gives us strength for the journey ahead." Angelina took one of her pouches from around her neck. It was made of brown leather stitched with tiny black beads, and it hung from a strand of braided leather. "Inside are blue topaz to aid your communication with the spirits, a blood-red feather from the breast of a sacred quetzal, and a green sea snail shell, whose spirals symbolize the eternal cycles of life. Together they will strengthen the elements of your life force."

"The northern tribes call these bags of stones and other amulets medicine bags. I will treasure this one always."

Angelina hung the amulet over Topsannah's head. "I thank you for what you have done for me and for my friends."

Topsannah said nothing, her face impassive, watching Angelina as though looking for something in her catlike eyes.

"You have my gratitude," Cimarron said, shaking Texas's hand, then taking Topsannah's hand and pressing it to his heart. "Forever, Topsannah."

"I would do anything for you, Cimarron. You know that." Topsannah's eyes blazed at Cimarron, then turned to Angelina. "Heal your prophet, woman, and pray he can help us all." She turned abruptly and led Texas out of the tipi.

* * * * *

In the gray light that came before dawn, the riders headed north from Hoda Canyon. Cimarron rode a burnt-red sorrel stallion, the kind he preferred, with a black mane and tail. Eeschatai rode a colorful pinto. Angelina rode a graceful white horse, Ixtpan a sturdy bay, Paradox a small black-and-white palomino, and Matsemela a gleaming black stallion. Wyatt, who had insisted on accompanying the travelers, had a silver mustang he liked as much as any horse he had ever ridden. Topsannah rode her own beloved golden horse with a white star on its forehead. They all rode on leather saddles, all of which had been stolen off the horses of dead cavalrymen and all of which showed the effects of long and hard use.

The Comanches had given all their guests new buckskin clothing to replace their hopelessly damaged garb. Ixtpan rode in a tan, fringed buckskin shirt and pants, feeling like a true horsewarrior. Paradox was delighted at having received a new buckskin vest. She had liked her other one—and regretted having it shredded by the fallen and broken stones of Itzamma. She was also pleased by the short skirt of tan buckskin with blue beads and the thigh-high brown moccasins. Matsemela, on the other hand, was uncomfortable in buckskin. He found it too hot for the daytime climate, though he came to appreciate it at night, when the land turned cold. Wyatt felt unclean in the Comanche clothes, but he looked upon wearing them as a sacrifice he would have to make to fulfill the commandment of his high priest, Zumarraga Apocalypse. He put on the heathen garb so as not to arouse suspicion about himself.

Once they got up into the foothills of the San Cris Mountains, they began to see the rich green fragrant pine and fir trees, along with the red and gold mountain walls.

Topsannah rode in front, leading the way to the rocky paths up the mountains. Cimarron scouted ahead for food, water, and enemies or other dangers while Matsemela rode alongside the main group, his new ashwood bow over his arm. Eeschatai rode off to the west, then circled back and rode east, guarding the small party. Angelina hunted plants and roots that could be used for food or medicine. Ixtpan was mapping the area on deerskin with charcoal. Paradox was taking it all in with great interest, never having been this far west; and she hunted rabbits and squirrels along the way for food. Wyatt Fontana brought up the rear, keeping a lookout for anyone following them.

All of them but Angelina had gotten new weapons the morning they set out on their journey—bows and arrows, copper knives, flint-tipped spears. Topsannah had laughed aloud when Angelina refused the bodark bow and ash arrows offered her. The small, green-eyed woman refused even a knife.

Eeschatai protested, "But you cannot travel unarmed, *señorita*. We face many enemies."

"Just what I keep trying to tell her," Matsemela said, rolling his eyes in utter dismay that Angelina seemed to have learned nothing on her journey.

Cimarron had taken Angelina by the arm and helped her mount her horse, saying, "I have weapons enough to take care of us both." He carried a bodark bow and Osage arrows, a bronze sword with a mastodon bone handle, and two knives, one bronze and one silver. The knives he had taken off dead Clankers; one was tucked in his belt, the other in his right boot.

Topsannah had watched silently, her face impassive. Only Mat-semela noticed the way her lips pressed tightly together for half a moment.

* * * * *

The path was ancient, apparently having been cut through the mountains by the magic of the Old World. In places, for a few feet, it was actually smooth, having once been covered by a smooth surface. The old surface lay in chunks. As the group went higher, Topsannah led them away from the ancient roadway, onto a path cut by a now-dry river over millions of years. This path became narrow, so narrow in places that the horses could only pass one abreast.

They made camp on the side of a mountain, hidden among great red and golden boulders. They built no fire, even though at this altitude the nights grew cold, because its light would be too easily seen on the mountainside. None of them discounted the possibility that Bismark might have scouts already on their trail—or that someone else unfriendly to them could be near.

Eeschatai climbed to a higher promontory to watch for danger. As he watched and listened, he heard the low hoot of an owl. To the northern tribes, the owl's cry announced the coming of death. He sharpened his knife on a piece of brown flint until sparks flew off the stones.

* * * * *

Six days later, they were deep in the San Cris Mountains. Clouds as black as the far side of the moon came rolling out of the north, running across the sky, like a herd of bison gone mad, chasing away the white clouds and covering the blue sky.

With the clouds came jagged flashes of lightning across the sky and the answer of thunder so loud that it seemed to shake the mountains.

Angelina watched the lightning, like snakes of fire flying across the sky.

Ixtpan explained to Topsannah, "The lightning is the Feathered Serpent in flight, and the thunder is Tezcatlipoca, the personification of destruction, rumbling within the Earth."

"Don't pay any attention to him," Matsemela muttered. "He's always going on with this nonsense."

It was midday, yet suddenly, with astonishing speed, the land grew as dark as midnight. Rain began to fall in large, heavy drops that soaked them all to the skin almost instantly. Lightning flashed all around them, spooking the horses badly, and the thunder seemed to roar from inside the mountains.

"Get off the horses and find cover!" Cimarron yelled over the wind-lashed gusts of rain. "And tie the horses!"

"There's a shelter up above!" Topsannah pointed up the rugged face of the mountain to a ledge under a rock overhang. They all jumped off their horses.

"Go on, I'll tie the horses," Ixtpan yelled, grabbing the reins from Topsannah's and Angelina's hands.

Eeschatai hollered, "¡Rapidamente!" to Ixtpan as lightning streaked across the black sky. Ixtpan quickly tied the horses and started scaling the rocks.

By this time, the rain was a slashing torrent and climbing was difficult. Everyone was slipping, having a hard time holding on and climbing, as the rain made the dusty rock as slick as glass. Matsemela slipped and caught himself on a tree root. Cimarron handed him the bronze knife to cut handholds in the earth to get back up the mountainside. A bolt of lightning struck a pine tree not far from them, lighting up the land as if the sun had come to Earth. The tree was reduced to ash even in the driving rain.

Thunder shook the mountain and Angelina and Eeschatai both lost their footing and slipped, falling back down to the rocky path below. Cimarron let loose of his hold on the rock and jumped down after them. Ixtpan hollered, but his voice was lost in the deafening rain. Cimarron waved to the shelter, to indicate that the others should keep on—as fast as possible. Matsemela stuck the bronze knife in his belt, then helped Paradox onto the ledge.

"I'd better stick with Cimarron," Wyatt Fontana said, leaping down off the ledge.

"No!" Topsannah screamed. She, along with Cimarron and Eeschatai, knew the true danger of the heavy storms in the mountains: flash flood.

It came with a roar like an earthquake—a wall of water ten feet high roaring down the mountain pass, sweeping away everything in its path.

BOOK III

SHOWDOWN AT BIG SKY
DARKNESS AT HIGH NOON
KISS TOMORROW GOODBYE
THAT DAY COULD BE SOON

> ROBBIE ROBERTSON
> *SHOWDOWN AT BIG SKY*

CHAPTER 10

THE CATACLYSM

There were ten thousand of them, their bronze hoop armor vests and long bronze and steel swords gleaming in the bright light of the late afternoon sun. They were in formation, each battalion in perfect rows, riding past the reviewing officers on some of the finest fighting horses bred in the Confederation. The elite Paris Battalion of Tesharka raised its shining steel swords high. What steel the Confederation had, it gave to its fiercest warriors. Among them were men who had fought a hundred campaigns and never knew what it was like to lose.

Reno Bismark saluted Absalom Ironheart and rode his silver-blue horse along the assembled lines of cavalry. Bismark had a hard time concealing the contempt he felt at the sight of the upstart General Ironheart, a short little man with a long white mustache who was dressed more like a farmer than a military officer.

Bismark looked elegant as usual in spite of his recent ordeal with the Comanches. Ironheart, on the other hand, wore loose cotton pants, a long jacket, a straw hat, and, worst of all, he reviewed his troops while sitting sideways on his horse. "Old Rough and Ready" his troops called him. Well, Bismark did not know how ready the man was, but to call him rough was putting it politely.

"Pretty fair luck, I'd say, you meetin' up with us, boy," Ironheart said, chomping off the end of a corn shuck cigar. "After them Comanches bushwhacked you, you could sure be coyote meat by now." His laugh was a chickenlike cackle.

That laugh annoyed Reno Bismark, as did the general's rubbing in of his defeat at the hands of the Comanches. "But we aren't. And as sure as the sun rises in the east, neither are all of my men. I can promise you that there are other survivors. We'll pick them up on the way west."

"You understand, of course, lad, that you're under my command now." Absalom Ironheart intended to be the next guvnor of the Tesharka Confederation, and he did not want any competition from this young colonel, Bismark. He had to make absolutely certain that only he got the credit for the military victories that were about to be won. He would just as soon have left Bismark and his men to die in the desert, but he figured that that would look bad in front of the men, and, besides, word might get back to the guvnor.

"Certainly, sir. I wouldn't have it any other way." Reno Bismark grinned slyly at Amos Crimsonleaf, then added to General Ironheart, "At your orders, Commander. Together we'll wipe out the savages at Epitaph and the Comanches both."

"I guess you've got yourself a grudge against the Comanches now, boy," Ironheart said, a twinkle in his black eyes as he lit the cigar.

"That I do," Reno Bismark answered. "And I mean to kill every last one of them."

"Well, boy, I believe you're going to get that chance, thanks to my scouts. They captured a Comanchero, one of the half-breeds who trade weapons to the Comanches. Bring him over, boys!" he called to two of his soldiers, each of whom was holding the arm of a tall, dark-skinned man with a red headband holding down his long black hair.

The prisoner's face was cut and bruised, his eyes swollen. His shirt was torn and bloody. And as he looked at the two officers eyeing him, he turned as pale as buffalo grass.

"Within an hour, he'll tell us where the Comanches're hiding out," Ironheart said with a sly smile under his white mustache. "Get ready, Reno, boy. We're fixing to go after the Comanches."

Absalom Ironheart was wrong. The Comanchero held out for two hours before he broke down under torture and told the Confederation cavalry where Hoda Canyon was and how to enter it through the one narrow path to the canyon floor. He also told them where all the sentries would be posted. An hour later, the army, under a general and a colonel—one an old man, a legend on the battlefield for his refusal to take prisoners, the other a young man, famous for his military genius and his cruelty—was mounted and moving north toward the Comanche sanctuary ten miles away.

* * * * *

They came under cover of darkness, hundreds of them. They knew where the sentries were posted and they found them and killed them quietly, one by one. They knew where the path leading into Hoda Canyon could be found. A dozen men led the way, taking each step carefully so as not to loosen the rocks and make a sound. When they got to the bottom of Hoda Canyon, they started running straight for the horse herd.

Parawah had been unable to sleep. He stepped outside his tipi and stretched his long arms. It was then that he saw them. He gave the alarm before an arrow struck him, but it was too late. The first Clankers into the canyon stampeded the horses.

Within moments, the dark, peaceful canyon was the scene of a raging battle as the Comanche warriors struggled to defend their women and children. Moon Shadow, in a white buckskin tunic, grabbed the boy, Texas, who was staying in her tipi while his mother was away, and ran for the cliffs at the end of the canyon. The boy wore only a breechcloth and a fringed leather vest. Held tightly in his fingers was the eagle feather his mother had given him the morning she left with the strangers for the place called Epitaph.

Absalom Ironheart himself came swooping down on them, shouting obscene oaths and waving a long steel sword. Gone was the farmer's outfit. Now he was in military blue and bronze. He raised the sword to strike Moon Shadow, but Sara Bisonheart raised her bow and sent an arrow into his right arm.

"Ow! Infernal savages!" Ironheart roared.

But while he was pulling Sara's arrow from his arm, Moon Shadow and Texas got away and kept running for the canyon wall. Ironheart turned on Sara and cut her down with one sword blow. She fell, bleeding into the earth of Hoda Canyon.

Reno Bismark rode for the Comanche horses, Amos Crimsonleaf right beside him. He spotted the box canyon off the east side of the main canyon and whooped. "That's it! Just what we need! Herd the horses in there!"

Aided by a dozen other Clankers, Reno and Amos began herding the stampeding horses into the box canyon off the east side of the main canyon. It took them an hour, but they managed to round most of the vast and beautiful herd into the canyon. Then Reno and Amos started gathering tree branches and brush and piling them up at the entrance of the box canyon. Reno held a branch of a cottonwood tree high while Amos struck a flint and lit it. The dry branch flamed high in the dark night. Then Reno touched it to the pile of branches across the entrance to the box canyon and flames six feet high roared up in front of him. The Comanches' horses were trapped as the box canyon was engulfed in flame.

The Comanches had lost their horses. Anyone escaping from the canyon would be on foot in some of the most deadly terrain on the continent. Reno Bismark had his vengeance. As he surveyed the carnage in Hoda Canyon, Reno Bismark was a satisfied man.

All the women and children were scrambling up the cliff while the warriors covered their retreat. Moon Shadow dragged Texas over the jagged rocks. The boy never once cried out, not even when Moon Shadow jerked him up a rocky outcropping, scraping the skin from his knees. Confederation arrows flew all around them. Finally, gasping hard for breath, the old woman and the young boy climbed over the top of the canyon. Before them was open desert. They started running south.

Moon Shadow never stopped, and she never let go of Texas's hand. The child was all that was left of the future, and she would not let go of that.

* * * * *

Eeschatai sensed the water coming before he heard its shattering roar. He grabbed Angelina and held on to her, knowing well that there was not time to climb back up the steep rock wall to the safety of the ledge. He saw Cimarron jump down to the pathway and cried, "No!" too late. Not that the warning would have made any difference to Cimarron. Suddenly water as high as the trees was bearing down on them.

A round red boulder pulled loose by the flood was coming straight at them in the onrushing wall of water. Eeschatai pushed Angelina to Cimarron, who cried, "Eescha—" just as the boulder struck his companion. Before he could finish screaming the man's name, the water hit with the force of a buffalo stampede. And suddenly the pounding, raging rapids became Cimarron's whole universe. He saw Wyatt Fontana go under but was unable to help him. It was all he could do to hold on to Angelina and keep himself from drowning.

The bone-chilling current was filled with rocks and tree limbs that struck him, tearing and bruising his flesh. Dead animals—squirrels, foxes, and coyotes—floated past. A horse—his horse, alive and hopelessly fighting tons of unleashed water, went under and did not come up again.

Still the heavy rain fell in a hail of stinging drops. Cimarron locked his left arm around Angelina's waist and held on to her, fighting hard to keep them both above the ferocious flood waters. Together they kept up a constant, frantic battle that neither of them could sustain for long. Cimarron knew their only chance was his catching hold of a high tree or rock—and then being able to hold on. But it took all his strength just to keep the two of them from being pulled under by the torturous current.

The violent waters slammed Cimarron against the red, rocky mountain wall, tearing a deep jagged cut across his shoulder blades, and causing him to lose consciousness for a second. In that second, he loosened his grip on Angelina and the water wrenched her from his arms and pulled her under.

Cimarron dove after her, beneath the surface of the flood-waters.

*   *   *   *   *

On the ledge above, Paradox screamed and Topsannah shrieked a Comanche curse as, through the blinding rain, they saw the others covered by the raging waters. When the boulder struck Eescha-tai, it took all of Matsemela and Ixtpan's combined strength to keep Topsannah from leaping into the flood after her friends. They forced her back against the mountain wall under the rock outcropping. Insanely she lunged at them, trying to go to her companions, who, in both men's assessment, were more than likely past all help. Topsannah almost broke free, but Matsemela thrust her back, throwing his body against hers to keep her from leaping into the killing waters.

As the man and woman hit the rock wall behind them, it gave way. The three people and the itzaur fell into a deep hole in the side of the mountain.

They dropped at least ten feet then struck a rock ledge, which also gave way beneath them. They rolled down a narrow incline of astonishingly smooth stone, perhaps as far as one hundred feet, then dropped straight down another fifteen feet and finally struck hard rock.

Though they were all dazed and battered by the fall, they were quickly on their feet. It was pitch dark and cool inside the cavern—and the opening through which they had fallen was far above them. The air was stale and musty, indicating to all of them that the cave had been sealed off for a very long time.

"The way things have been going," Matsemela grumbled, brushing rocks and dust from his wet buckskin shirt and pants in the darkness, "this cave'll probably turn out to be the home of a family of grizzly bears, if not something worse."

"Oh, by the gods of our ancestors, they're dead," Topsannah groaned, slumping to her knees and burying her face in her arms. "Eeschatai and Angelina—and Wyatt. And Cimarron."

Paradox was shivering, and tears formed in her round black eyes. "No, they can't be dead. They can't be!" She stomped her moccasined foot hard, and rainwater absorbed by the leather splattered them all. "I won't have it!"

"*Mi dios*," Ixtpan groaned, leaning against the stone wall for support as he began to tremble. "Angelina."

"We don't know that she's dead." Matsemela felt around the stone walls, searching for a way out of the cave, his thick, dark fingers examining every inch of the stone. "What we need to do is figure out how to get out of this pit." He gave up examining the walls and reached out with both hands to the Comanche woman, whose presence he could sense in the dark.

Topsannah took his hands and let him pull her to her feet. She shook herself and stood rigid, her long black braids hanging wet, her soaked buckskin clothes clinging to her lithe, muscular body. "You're right, Matsemela. We've got to find something that will burn—and start a fire so we can have light to look around. Perhaps the way we came in is not the only opening to this cave."

They all began feeling in the darkness for something flammable and for rocks that could strike a spark.

Paradox found what felt like a tree limb. And Topsannah struck a stone—which her experienced fingers judged to be flint—against Ixtpan's steel knife until she got a spark. Even with such a tiny light, the walls of the cave into which they had fallen lit up golden—because, Matsemela realized almost instantly, they were filled with chunks of gold, shining like the light of a hundred fires. A hundred fires. The Lost Cienfuegos Gold Mine.

He was, he realized in that instant of gazing on those gleaming walls, in the richest gold mine he had ever seen or heard described in legend. Matsemela wanted to cry out, "Hallelujah! This is it!" but he knew that that would seem unpardonably unfeeling at the moment and suppressed the impulse. Damn, he thought. I've found the richest lost mine in the West. If there's no way out, this mine is nothing but a big gold coffin.

Others had been there before them. Paradox found a larger branch and lit it with the other. The flame flared, illuminating the entire inside of the cavern. There, lying on the floor or propped against the walls, were the skeletons of three other humans and another itzaur who had also found the Lost Cienfuegos Gold Mine. One of the humans was reaching out, as though his skeletal fingers were still trying to dig through the wall of stone.

"Conserve the light." Ixtpan's tone was solemn, almost funereal. "This cave is surrounded by solid rock. I can move stones one by one, but I cannot move the whole mountain. We may well be as dead as those prospectors." He pointed to the skeletons of those who had died without ever finding a way out of the gold mine.

*   *   *   *   *

Angelina opened her eyes and saw a rainbow high above her against a background of blue sky, red mountain walls, and tall green pines. She lay on the hard, rocky ground of a mountain path littered by debris from the flash flood, her white deerskin clothing wet and torn, her moccasins lost. Her long black hair was still damp and clung to her like wet silk. For a moment, she was lost in looking at the rainbow, free from the memory of what had happened. Then the memories came quick and hard. The water. Endless, turbulent water. Being ripped from Cimarron's arms and thrown into swirling darkness.

"Cimarron." She tried to cry out for him, but the sound came out as a feeble moan. She was barely able to move. Every muscle hurt from the pounding force of the floodwaters. She forced herself to roll to her right side. Topsannah's golden horse lay dead, tangled in the branches of a mangled pine tree. She rolled to her left. It was then that she saw him.

He lay face down on the ground only a few feet from her, so still that he did not appear to be breathing. His shirt had been ripped off by the flood. His body was covered with bleeding cuts and large purple bruises.

Angelina crawled on her knees to him, desperation overshadowing the pain in her body, blocking it and everything else from her consciousness.

But her bruised muscles contracted in painful spasms and refused to move quickly or easily. She dug her small fingers into the gritty, muddy sand that now covered the bare rock of the mountain clearing. All around them lay uprooted trees, boulders, and smaller rocks carried down from high in the mountains. She crawled through debris that left her hands and forearms and legs bleeding and raw.

She touched his left arm. His flesh was warm. Angelina pulled herself closer and leaned her head against his back and listened to his blood pulsing through his veins. She sobbed with relief and gently turned him over on his back.

Cimarron's battered face was streaked with dirt. There was a long, deep cut across the left side of his face. Both his eyes were swollen and ringed in black and purple. Angelina laid her head on his chest and cried, her tears washing over his body.

"*No llores*, Angelina," Cimarron whispered, slipping his bruised arms around her, his fingers tangling in her long black hair. "Don't cry. We're alive."

"Cimarron," she gasped, hardly daring to believe she was really hearing his voice.

He pulled her tight against him and closed his deep brown eyes. "*Gracias a la vida*," he whispered as his lips brushed her black hair.

* * * * *

"There's just no other entrance. The rock's solid all around," Paradox said dismally, her thin green lips turned down in despair.

Matsemela and Topsannah both agreed that they, too, found the cavern to be closed but for the one entrance far beyond their reach. "Even if I stand on the big guy's shoulders, I couldn't reach that opening. And even if we could get to the opening above us, we'd never make it climbing up that steep incline of slick rock we rolled down," Matsemela said. I'm going to die surrounded by more gold than I could spend in a lifetime, he thought bitterly. If Angelina were here, she'd say something about it being my destiny. He was, to his own surprise, very sorry she was not there, admonishing him about gods or some such silly thing.

"There must be a break in the rock somewhere, and we will find it. Then perhaps I will be able to move the stones and free us. We cannot abandon hope. Angelina needs us." Ixtpan was sitting silently in the middle of the cavern, praying for Angelina—and praying for the missing vaquero. He knew that the vaquero was Angelina's only hope of having survived the flash flood—and her only hope of surviving whatever else might be out there in the San Cris Mountains, from the Clanker army to hungry mountain lions. "But I have not the strength now, even if I found a place where I could levitate the stone. Perhaps by the time the sun rises I will be strong enough." He lay on the hard, cold cavern floor and closed his black eyes.

The others also were too exhausted to continue, so they leaned against one gold-filled wall and rested.

For long moments there was silence, which was finally broken by a high-pitched sob from Paradox.

Ixtpan took Paradox's green hand in his own, saying, "We do not know she is dead, *lagartija*. Perhaps the vaquero saved her. I did not trust him, I admit, but I do believe he would do anything for Angelina. We saw him dive beneath the floodwaters for her. *Puede ser—*"

"Cimarron," Topsannah said, "may well have died trying to save the woman."

Ixtpan shot the Comanche woman a dark look, his lips silently forming the word, "*Silencio.*"

"Whatever the hell's happened to them, there's nothing we can do about it." Matsemela settled his large body as comfortably as possible against the gold-filled wall. "Now get some rest so we can figure out how the hell to get out of this place."

Topsannah put out the torchlight. Paradox fell asleep, huddled against Ixtpan for consolation. Soon Ixtpan, too, was asleep. He moaned in his sleep and more than once called out for Angelina.

Matsemela and Topsannah were unable to sleep.

"You know, Topsannah," Matsemela whispered comfortingly, "things aren't so bad. We've been guided by the hand of destiny itself to the richest gold mine on the continent."

"Of what possible use could gold be to us?"

Matsemela figured the war chief must be in shock and that once they found a way out, the news would sink in and she'd be happy about it. "Hell, Topsannah, with all this gold, we'll be able to *buy* the Comanches a place to live in peace."

"I know this, Matsemela Nyakir: All the gold in the world cannot buy peace."

"I don't know about that. Enough gold could pretty much take care of any problem I can think of."

"There are far more important things in life than those that can be bought."

"Not in my book. Name one."

"Well, friendship. Love."

"Neither one lasts as long as a piece of gold."

"Tell me, does your Angelina love Cimarron?"

The mercenary was surprised, and not a little annoyed by the question. He wondered why this exceptional woman cared so much about the moody cowboy. "Yes," he admitted, "but I don't know if she realizes it herself. Angelina's in love with an idea, and people who fall in love with ideas usually miss it when love with a flesh-and-blood person comes along. Angelina's good at living in the past and in her own mythology—but not too good at life in the real world. I guess she's never had much chance to live in it, to be fair. But I do know this, that cowboy is in love with Angelina. If he's still alive, that is. Why the hell else would he have taken on the Clanker army to save her?" Topsannah said nothing. Matsemela took her hand in his own. "Tell me about Cimarron. You knew him a long time ago, right?"

She started to pull away, but, strangely, the mercenary's warm touch had a calming effect on her. She thought for a minute, then answered, "It was so long ago. Six years ago." Her voice had become flat, drained of emotion.

"Tell me, Topsannah."

Her long hesitation was painful to her and irritating to him. "I grew up with the Comanches, but I went to live with my father in Reynada for a while when I was sixteen. He was a gambler from Durango, my father was. He'd killed a man on the other side and hightailed it north, where he stayed the rest of his life. At first I didn't really fit in Reynada, though I did love that place. In Reynada, I was off the open land, which is like being a fish out of water for a Comanche. Then I met Cimarron. He was handsome and daring, and he talked of rebellion and liberation. We were so young." She paused and wiped a tear from her eye. "And then Dry Creek happened. My mother and her whole tribe were killed by Clankers led by Absalom Ironheart himself. I knew then that I had to go back to my people, no matter what. When I left, I knew I'd never see Cimarron again. So I never told him . . ."

"Never told him what, Topsannah?"

"About the child."

"What child?"

At that moment, a nightmare of Angelina being swept under the floodwaters woke Ixtpan, and he, too, heard Topsannah answer.

"His son. When I left Reynada, I was carrying his child. Texas is Cimarron's son."

Matsemela was speechless. That cowboy's life's been a real melodrama, he thought, biting his tongue to keep from saying something of the sort.

"Matsemela," she said, "promise me you'll never tell anyone what I've told you. It's only because I know they're dead and that we're going to die here that I can tell you. I don't want to die never having told anyone but Bajo and Moon Shadow. Only they knew the truth."

"Your secret is safe with me, Topsannah. And believe me, we're going to get out of here alive. But rest now. We have to save our strength to try to find a way out of this hole."

But is your secret safe with *me*, Topsannah? Ixtpan wondered. If Angelina and Cimarron are alive, I must tell her. I see the way she looks at that vaquero. She is my friend, and she deserves to know about his past with the Comanche woman and of the child they share.

Paradox was turned away from the others, facing the wall. They had all assumed her asleep. But Paradox slept fitfully, waking every few minutes from anxiety over her friends, and she, too, had heard Topsannah's secret.

*   *   *   *   *

Topsannah was awakened by the sound of digging and small stones falling on rock. "What is it?" she asked, unable to see in the darkness of the mine. "Matsemela? Ixtpan? Paradox?" She slowly stretched the sore muscles of her long, graceful arms and legs.

"Uh, . . . I was just digging around, trying to find a break in the rock so the big guy can move it." Matsemela quickly stuffed his bronze knife back in his belt and the chunks of gold he had pried from the mine wall in the pockets of his deerskin trousers.

"That's a good idea." Topsannah felt for the rock and steel knife to strike a spark. When she lit the end of one of the pick handles abandoned by the long-dead miners, she was greeted by the sight of Matsemela trying to force one last chunk into each of the two pockets in his rain-damaged buckskin trousers, both of which were filled to the point of being about to tear. For a moment, the war chief eyed the mercenary with anger, her dark eyes narrowed fiercely. Then she began to laugh.

"Look at it this way," Matsemela offered, "it shows my faith that we'll get out of here." Actually, he figured their chances of getting out were considerably less than those of an armadillo sprouting wings. He surveyed the inside of the cavern again.

"There must have been another way in here other than the entrance on the face of the mountain. It would have been impossible for anyone to climb out that way—ever. Maybe the way out is lost— and maybe it's here for someone who knows what to look for." Topsannah was embarrassed about crying in front of Matsemela the night before and was determined to be calm and logical. She had led battles of thousands of warriors against superior numbers and arms, and had been victorious, and she was not going to be daunted by the momentary problem of being stuck in a lost mine. She lit the other makeshift torch, lighting up the gleaming walls.

"We'll keep looking," Matsemela replied, absent-mindedly digging out another chunk of gold with his knife.

"Then let's look for rocks that we can move, not gold" Paradox was suddenly wide awake and furious with Matsemela for wasting precious time on that silly metal. She had never been able to understand the passion humans felt for that particular metal, and she had no patience with Matsemela's attitude. She adjusted her new buckskin skirt and vest and dusted off her new beaded moccasins while muttering to herself about fatal flaws in the human psychological make-up.

"Look at this! This damn piece of gold I pried out of this corner is shaped like a four-sided pyramid. What're the odds of that happening naturally?" Matsemela asked, holding a glimmering pyramid about three inches on each side in his right hand.

"None at all." Ixtpan snatched the shining object from Matsemela. He examined the object carefully in the light of the torch, brushing the dirt of centuries from its surface with his long brown fingers.

"Here we go," Matsemela said, disdain evident in his deep voice. "This guy's an archaeologist. He's always going on about pyramids and lost worlds and feathered serpents and stuff. Drives me crazy with it. A sad case."

"You are an ignorant *cabrón*," Ixtpan retorted, still intently studying the small gold pyramid, "who makes light of that which he does not understand."

"We Comanches know those stories of pyramids and feathered serpents," Topsannah said. "Often the essence of reality lies in such tales as those—"

"Look at this," Ixtpan interrupted, "there's no question this was formed by human hands. Nothing like this little golden pyramid appears in nature. Where did you find this thing?"

"Pardon me," Paradox put in testily, her thin green lower lip stuck out in a pout, "but it might also have been formed by itzaur hands. You humans aren't the only creatures around who know how to make things like this! And, judging by that skeleton in the corner, at least one itzaur has made it in here."

"You are right, Paradox," Ixtpan said. "I should not have made such an assumption. I am sorry."

Paradox was so surprised at Ixtpan's apology that she wondered if he was feeling well, or if perhaps the strain of their journey and the loss of their companions had finally caused the giant's mind to snap.

After a few moments of searching in the torchlight, Paradox found an indentation in the dark stone floor in the shape of a perfect pyramid. "Look! Here it is! The gold pyramid goes here!"

"Let me see that," Matsemela said, shoving Paradox out of the way and checking out the small pyramid-shaped carving in the stone himself.

Ixtpan inserted the gold pyramid into the hole and felt it click into place. At first nothing happened but the sound of metal against stone. He pressed the pyramid harder. And felt it slip perfectly into the rock.

As though moved by an unseen hand, a ten-foot high granite doorway three feet across opened in the wall. Before them was a pitch-dark tunnel. The air from the tunnel was bitterly stale and reminded Ixtpan of the air in pyramids and tombs that had been sealed for centuries.

"Well," Topsannah said, "we don't have much to lose. *Vamos.*"

"Of course," Matsemela pointed out, "whoever built this passageway could have laid all kinds of traps to protect the mine. Whoever they were."

"Or it could just be the passage to where someone lived, like a long hallway. In that case, there would have to be a way to the outside." Paradox was looking into the black tunnel, determined to reassure the others—and herself—that the tunnel could be a means of escape and not the path to some greater danger. "Perhaps," she added hopefully, hopping with forced enthusiasm, "this is an old itzaur home. Why, I might even have relatives up ahead! Let's go!"

"May all the ancient gods protect us." Ixtpan led the way into the tunnel, holding one of the torches ahead of them.

Matsemela was, predictably, less optimistic than Paradox as he followed Ixtpan. "This tunnel was dug a long time ago. Centuries—or longer. Even the face of the mountain changes in that amount of time. The exit could have been sealed before that screwy god Angelina worships was born—you know, the one with the funny name, ketzahl-something-or-other, the one who's a flying snake."

"Disrespect for the gods will not serve us well," Ixtpan intoned, turning around and glaring at Matsemela. "And I know full well that what once may have been an exit may now be blocked. But, as Topsannah says, we do not have anything to lose by going ahead. I am the last of my race, and I do not intend to simply lie down and die."

Topsannah held the second torch as the others felt their way along tunnel walls carved so perfectly that they were smooth to the touch. They went on for what Ixtpan would have estimated as nearly an hour before they ran into another stone wall that barred their way.

Matsemela cursed and struck his palm with his fist. "I'll be damned if we've come all this way to get stuck at a dead end."

Topsannah felt the smooth stone surface and found nothing. But on the floor at the foot of the stone her fingers traced the unmistakable pattern of a metal pyramid. She pressed it, and the stone door slipped slowly into the wall with a sound like the grinding of boulders against one another in a landslide.

A room opened before them. The torches flared wildly, illuminating a cavernous—and clearly inhabited—room.

"Great Tyran's ghost!" Paradox exclaimed in a high-pitched gasp.

"San Zapata!" Ixtpan's narrow, slanted eyes grew wide and almost round with fascination. He felt his heart pounding—not with fear, but with excitement. He had never seen anything like this room before in all his extensive archaeological excavations.

The vast room was cut from rock laced with gold, and in the torchlight the gold made the walls gleam in streaks like tongues of fire. The ceiling, which Ixtpan quickly deduced had been cut from solid, gold-flecked rock, rose at least thirty feet above them. There was a dark wooden table ten feet long, set with a golden plate, silver utensils, and a red carnelian goblet. A thick yellow tallow candle stood in a golden, three-foot-tall candlestick in the center of the table. There were four wooden chairs around the table and a long stone bench beside the wall to the companions' left. In the wall opposite them was a stone doorway. The most remarkable thing about the furnishings and utensils was their size, which, by human standards, was tremendous. The wooden chairs were six feet tall, and the golden plate a foot in diameter. The stone bench was at least eight feet long and the doorway was about twelve feet high.

Paradox approached the table. It was so high, she could barely peek over the edge while standing on her toes. She reached up and awkwardly tried to lift the carnelian goblet. The goblet was about a foot and a half high and Paradox set it down quickly with a grunt and a curse in her own language. "I don't think I want to meet the person—or whatever it is—that uses this stuff."

"I don't like this one damn bit." Matsemela's face twisted in a dark scowl as he evaluated the oversized furniture. "Not one damn bit. Whoever they are, they're bigger than Ixtpan, judging from the size of their furniture." Matsemela saw that inquisitive gleam in the giant's eyes and feared Ixtpan's archaeological obsession might get the better of him, and they would be stuck while Ixtpan examined the place. Matsemela was eager to find a way out so that he could begin transporting the gold right away and did not care who had once lived inside this mountain—unless, of course, they came back while he was there. He started toward the closed door on the far side of the room, Topsannah and Paradox right behind him.

Ixtpan lingered for one last look at the spectacular and mysterious room, thinking, Ah, this the great dream of an archaeologist's life! A new find! Something utterly unknown that may alter our whole conception of human history! What a moment this is! He clutched his heart in rapture, then turned to leave with the others.

At that moment, there was a great creaking sound of stone dragging against stone, and the twelve-foot door slowly began to open.

Paradox let out a high-pitched squeak. Topsannah gasped. Matsemela cursed. And Ixtpan stood frozen in a cross between horror and fascination as the creature entered the room.

Fully eight feet, it was taller than Ixtpan, with a heavy muscular build. It gave off a very strong and unpleasant odor that made Paradox wrinkle her nose. It was naked except for a breechcloth of gold beads. Its feet were tremendous, easily a foot and a half long. It stood erect on two legs like a man, and its long face and narrow, slightly slanted, dark eyes looked human—but its face and body were completely covered with long, thick, brown hair, almost like that of a bear. It uttered a menacing growl and pounded its huge fists against its massive, hairy chest.

Matsemela had never been one to wait to be attacked. He took a running leap at the creature, stabbing at it with his bronze knife. The creature jerked the knife from the mercenary's hand and threw it to the stone floor, grabbed him by his shirt and lifted him two feet off the ground, then threw him across the room. Matsemela hit the far wall with a thud and slipped to the floor, a dazed look on his face.

Topsannah went into a crouch, then sprang at the creature with her knife. The creature blocked her with a hairy arm so long that she was unable to stab its torso. Then it picked her up, too, and threw her against the wall. She slumped to the floor beside Matsemela.

"That's it, buckaroo," Paradox announced defiantly. "You don't hurt my friends and get away with it." She started striding toward the creature, but Ixtpan grabbed her by her vest to stop her. "Hey! Put me down!"

"No. I'll handle this." Ixtpan was determined to keep holding Paradox up in the air to keep her out of trouble.

"Greetings, amigo," Ixtpan began in Spanglish to the creature. He thought he would try a common language first. "We mean you no harm. We are lost, trapped *en su casa* by accident." He held up his free hand, palm upward to show he was not holding a weapon and as a universal gesture of goodwill. His other hand was taken up with holding Paradox, whose green fists were making punching motions at the creature.

The creature growled again, showing long, pointed teeth—the teeth of a meat eater. It took a step toward Ixtpan. Ixtpan stood his ground and Paradox continued with her jabbing motions, hissing menacingly at their adversary. The creature grabbed Paradox away from Ixtpan. Paradox screeched loudly and punched the creature in the right eye. It raised its arm to hurl her against the wall.

"Sasquatch!" Topsannah yelled. She and Matsemela were on their feet and at Ixtpan's side, all three of them about to jump the creature to try to free the helpless Paradox.

The creature froze in midswing, holding Paradox suspended over its head, her moccasined feet kicking at it in vain.

"Sasquatch," Topsannah repeated.

"Great St. Davy's cap, you're all crazy," Matsemela muttered. "Sas what?"

"Sasquatch," Topsannah answered softly, as the creature returned her steely gaze, still holding Paradox about six feet off the floor. "The name by which they have been known to my people for hundreds of years. They are the oldest of the races, and once this land was theirs alone."

"Well, well, Comanche lady," the creature replied in a voice so deep that it came out like a rumbling growl, "so you know what I am."

Matsemela had turned from his usual chocolate complexion to a shade closer to that of new wheat. Paradox stopped kicking and looked from the creature to Topsannah and back again, questioningly. Ixtpan stood frozen to the spot, his mouth hanging open.

"Yes," Topsannah replied calmly, "my people, the Comanches, have known your kind for many centuries. You are the hairy ones, the ones known for the huge footprints, who live in the forests and badlands."

"We know your folk, too," the creature responded icily. "And, as you can see, we prefer to keep a good distance away."

Ixtpan had sufficiently recovered himself to ask, "How is it you know our language?"

"We have, over the centuries, spoken with a few of your folks, enough to pick up the basic languages of this continent." The Sasquatch put Paradox down.

Paradox glared up at him, her green hands balled in fists on her hips, her thin lower lip sticking out. "Great Tyran's ghost, it's a Bigfoot!"

"Well, this is a hell of a surprise," Matsemela said. "A talking Bigfoot. I always thought they were just another silly Noramican legend. Of course, at this point, I don't see why I should be surprised by anything."

"We fell into this mountain from a ledge where we had taken refuge from a flash flood." Topsannah spoke quietly but firmly to the Sasquatch. "We must rejoin friends who were separated from us in the flood. We have a mission we must fulfill. *Por favor*, we must leave here. We were only searching for a way out when we found this room."

"Leaving is out of the question, ma'am," the Sasquatch responded, his black eyes burning like coals in his long, hairy face. "You've seen too much. You'd bring more humans back to take the gold from my home here. And they'd destroy my sanctuary. I can't have that."

"Nonsense," Matsemela assured the creature, "we'd never tell a soul." He was not lying—he had no intention of telling anyone else the location of the Lost Cienfuegos Gold Mine.

"It's true. We'd never tell anyone," Paradox added. "You may not believe this, but I understand your position more than you know."

"We know all about your secret world, little itzaur, so you can leave. I know you'll keep your mouth shut. But your friends here . . ." The Sasquatch shook his head.

"Now just a damn minute," Matsemela insisted, "you listen to me. You can't hold us here!"

"I'm not planning to hold you here. I'm going to kill you." The Sasquatch bared his sharp teeth and growled fiercely again.

Ixtpan stepped between the creature and his friends and drew his copper knife from his belt. "Then, *cabrón*, you will have to start with me."

The Sasquatch advanced on him, its mouth twisted in a hideous snarl, its long arms reaching out for his throat. Ixtpan stood firm and tried to stab at the Sasquatch, who quickly grabbed his knife and tossed it away. It clanked hollowly on the cold stone floor. The creature grabbed Ixtpan by the throat, shoved his back against the stone wall, and began choking him. Paradox took a running leap and landed on the Sasquatch's back. He brushed her off as if she were a mosquito.

The creature grabbed Ixtpan's throat again, then froze, staring hard at the giant for moments that felt like hours to Ixtpan and the others. Instead of choking Ixtpan, the Sasquatch took the giant's face in his hands and turned it right, then left, then pushed up Ixtpan's lip and looked at his teeth, rather as if he were inspecting a horse. Something that looked vaguely like a grin spread over his hairy face.

"What is the meaning of this?" Ixtpan demanded, his words garbled by the Sasquatch's fingers on his mouth.

"I believe," the Sasquatch finally said in a low growl, "we are cousins."

"¿Qué? What are you saying?" Ixtpan's heart was beating so wildly that he pressed one hand against his chest as if he could slow it down. "Cousins? What do you mean?"

"You're one of the Lost Brothers, the ones who survived the Holocaust that destroyed Paleorica, our old nation, a long time back. Your ancestors were of a Lost Colony. My old granddad told me the legends himself back when I was no bigger than this itzaur here. He said that back in the old days, some of our folks went to the top of the world to trade and explore—and got lost there after the Holocaust, which wiped out Paleorica like a cyclone whipping through a corn field. Good to meet you, little cousin!" The Sasquatch patted Ixtpan on the back so hard that Ixtpan nearly stumbled.

Ixtpan's bronze skin turned the color of cream, and he took a step backward, trying to catch his balance. Topsannah took his left arm supportively, while Paradox held his right hand.

"You know, Ixtpan, if you were covered with hair and a foot taller, you'd look just like him." Matsemela chuckled at the thought of a furry Ixtpan.

"In the name of the Great Spirit," Topsannah breathed, looking from Ixtpan to the Sasquatch and back again. Now that she looked closely, there was a resemblance in bone structure, facial features, and the texture of the thick hair of the two giants.

"Ixtpan?" Paradox tugged impatiently on his arm, wondering why he seemed to have gone into a stupor when here they were, about to be killed by a hairy Bigfoot. "Are you all right?"

Ixtpan answered with a stifled gasp. His long, thick hair, very much like the hair that covered the face and body of the Sasquatch, stuck out all around his face. His narrow eyes were half closed. Paradox tugged on his arm again, and all he could do was gasp again.

Ixtpan shook himself violently, clutching hard the hands of both Paradox and Topsannah. Then he let go and extended his own right hand to the Sasquatch, saying, "Cousin, this is the single greatest moment of my life."

The Sasquatch took his hand and shook it awkwardly, still looking Ixtpan up and down curiously, saying, "So the legend's true, after all. Hmm. I never took that stuff seriously. I always thought old Granddad liked the mezcal too much and he just made up those stories about a lost branch of the family tree. So some survived from the Lost Colony, after all. But something went wrong to deform you."

"Deform?" Ixtpan pulled himself up to his full height indignantly.

"Yes, deform. Where's your hair? You're practically as bald as an egg! And why're you so all-fired short?"

"It must," Ixtpan answered, "have something to do with all those thousands of years in the ice. Or perhaps the effects of the Great Fire that freed my immediate ancestors from the ice."

He stared at the creature, thinking, So this is what I am. Or what I should have been.

"Well, at least you're alive." The Sasquatch patted Ixtpan on the back again, this time consolingly.

"Not really, cousin. I am alive at this moment, but I am the last of the Paleoricans."

"In a pig's eye! There's a lot of us, thousands. We live, like the Comanche lady says, in the forests and mountains and badlands—as far away as these later races as we can get. After the old high priest, Beelzebub Darkmirror, destroyed our world with those blasted Fire God idols thirteen thousand and five hundred years ago, we gave up wanting cities and nations and all that fancy stuff that just got us in trouble. We went back to the simple life, back to nature, like life was meant to be. We tend to be solitary folk, and most of us like to live alone and keep to ourselves. The other races call us Sasquatch or Bigfoot or Yeti or any of a hundred other names. Fortunately folks from these later races take one look at one of us and run." His laugh was so deep that it echoed in the cavernous room. "That's the one thing that's worked out right for us—the rest of the humans keep their distance."

"Well, cousin," Ixtpan said, "I have sad news for you about the past we share and how it may shape the future. At least one of the Fire God idols survives. And a priest who serves the same War God as Beelzebub Darkmirror is out to get it. He has managed to send an army to take it from were it has lain all these millennia, beneath a pueblo called Epitaph in the San Cris Mountains.

"In case we all do not survive to reach Epitaph, I must tell you what I know of the Fire God. I have explored around this idol—carefully I can assure you, and I have also seen the remains of another Fire God idol I found some years ago in the great northern mountains. I have deduced something of how they are constructed. The idol lies in a *kiva*, a ceremonial pit, far beneath the surface . . ."

"Hell, cousin, you don't have to deduce! I'll show you how the idol is constructed," the Sasquatch said, leading the way out the huge stone door, the others right behind him.

*   *   *   *   *

The walls of the great stone room were covered in murals in paint whose colors still remained vibrant after untold centuries. They were pictures from the life of a civilization, a visual history. On one wall was a painting of a gray pyramid covered in tiles of a hundred different colors, with Sasquatch priests and priestesses in robes made of long green quetzal feathers arrayed on its steps. On another wall was painted a scene of a group digging into the mountain—possibly creating these very rooms and tunnels. Another showed an apparent ruler seated on a golden throne surrounded by others dressed in fabric made of stitched-together feathers. The last, the wall in which the door through which they had entered was cut, showed a stream running through a valley among the green pines and firs. Beside the stream sat a male and female, their arms around each other, their dark eyes glowing from across the centuries with love.

"They are the Ancient Ones of this land," Topsannah breathed. "We are in a holy place."

"This is the moment for which I have lived my life, and now I know why the gods have directed me to this place." Ixtpan was gazing on what he had searched for all his life—a glimpse of the

Paleorican world, the world that, had it not been for Beelzebub Darkmirror and the Fire God, should have been his. "*Dios*, do you know what this means? The history of intelligent life on this continent is far, far older and more complex than even historians such as myself have suspected."

"Not now." Paradox sternly cut off Ixtpan's ruminations. "We've got to find Angelina. She and that cowboy will be lost without us. And if we don't do something about that Fire God, we're all going to fry!"

"*Si*, I have seen enough. Whatever happens to me now, I am ready for it, because now I understand what I am." Ixtpan was glowing with pride and excitement. He stood tall, straightening the ragged buckskin clothes and smoothing his unkempt hair.

"Look here, cousin, here's your Fire God." The Sasquatch pointed to the murals of the pyramid. The others followed his long, hairy finger to a temple in the background of the painting.

The temple was a curved structure of stone. Inside, in its center, sat the thing that haunted Ixtpan's nightmares. It was only an idol, small and barely recognizable as a human form, a creature with a skeleton face, holding in one hand an incense burner and in the other a torch. Its arms and legs were bent in the middle at right angles, giving it the shape of a twisted cross.

"*¡Dios!*" Ixtpan gasped. "That's it!"

"This is the thing you're all so bent out of shape about?" Matsemela asked, wringing his hands with impatience. He was utterly bored with all the artwork and wanted to get going.

Topsannah looked questioningly at the painting. Paradox, too, stood on tiptoe, her thin green mouth hanging open in dismay.

"Just as I suspected! There is hope!" Ixtpan shouted exultantly. "*¡Mire!* Look here!" He pointed to the pedestal on which the idol in the painting sat, a long silver column about five feet tall, just like the idol at Epitaph rested upon. On the side of the pedestal was a turquoise spiral with a small lever. "This is just what I thought might give us hope!"

"That's the safety device," the Sasquatch said matter-of-factly. "Old Beelzebub Darkmirror was as crazy as a half-baked loon, but he wasn't stupid. He built some of these things over a deep pit, a thousand feet deep or so. The spiral emblem there is a lever; it's the way to send the whole thing plummeting, or at least that's how my old granddad explained it to me."

"Am I not right that this device could be the means of our salvation?" asked Ixtpan politely.

"Yep," the Sasquatch answered.

"I don't get it," Paradox said as she studied the painting, her green face twisted with apprehension.

"Look," Ixtpan explained. "The idol only covers the mechanism that would activate the uranium, the atomic bomb. But see here?" He pointed to the structure in the mural. Beneath the idol was a long cylinder encased in stone. "This is the thing that sets off the uranium." But below the mechanism, another far longer pit was open beneath the idol, separated from it by a thick sheet of stone. "Just as I thought, the whole thing—the mechanism, the uranium, all of it—can be sent plunging to hell."

"What good would that do?" Topsannah asked.

"If the uranium ignites far enough beneath the surface, it is possible that the earth will save itself by absorbing the fire," Ixtpan answered. "I suspected that was the purpose of the spiral emblem lever on the side of the pedestal, but, not knowing what activated the uranium itself, I feared to touch it."

"Good move, shorty," the Sasquatch said. "After all this time, who knows? It's possible any movement could set off the uranium. Touching that thing to send it falling could send you and everyone around to one hot eternity."

"As I feared," Ixtpan moaned.

"But you're right, cousin. If the uranium reaches its critical mass . . ."

"It's what?" Ixtpan asked.

"You'd never understand . . . the thing is, if it goes off far enough underground, you get destruction, all right. Anyone right above it is history. But you don't get the big bang, kiss-it-all-good-bye, mushroom cloud kind of thing that you do if that damned idol blows near the surface."

"We're in luck on that score," Ixtpan said, studying the painting intensely. "The pueblo at Epitaph is constructed above an older pueblo that now lies buried beneath the earth. The Fire God's *kiva* is beneath the original pueblo. It is already about two hundred feet below the surface."

"That's good. And having two pueblos, a ton of earth I'd bet, on top of it, might help contain the fire, too. It all depends on how it gets set off. Somehow you'd have to get it deeper before it blew up. Who knows, buckaroos, if this doesn't go well, we could all be looking at another round of the Ice Age real soon—like next week. I wonder if we've got any kinsman up north this time, cousin," Sasquatch said, slapping Ixtpan on the back. "Who knows, maybe we'll whip those Clanker varmints. But let's get going, or Epitaph will be our epitaph."

As the others followed the beast into another long, dark tunnel, Ixtpan turned back for one last look at the paintings of the Paleorican world. He thanked Angelina's god, Quetzalcoatl, for giving him a destiny that led him to the thing he had wanted most in his life. In that room, he felt something he had never felt before—a sense of belonging, of being at home. And above all, he felt hope.

Soon, after making their way through yet another long, dark hallway, they came to another stone door, which the Sasquatch easily opened, and found themselves in sunlight and fresh air and surrounded by tall, fragrant pine trees. They could hear mockingbirds in the trees and a mountain lion roaring somewhere off in the distance. Topsannah was so happy to be outside again that she hugged Matsemela spontaneously.

The mercenary pulled her close and whispered in her ear, "Whatever you do, remember this spot. Memorize every tree. That way we can come back for the gold of the Lost Cienfuegos Mine. And, Topsannah, all your secrets are safe with me. So I know I can count on you to keep our little secret."

"You can count on me for anything you ask, Matsemela."

Matsemela brightened and started to say something else but caught himself and stifled his own words with a cough. He was convinced the talk of the Fire God was pure bunk, that Ixtpan and the Sasquatch were loco, and that Epitaph sounded like a bad proposition all around. He told himself to ditch his crazy companions and get on with taking out the gold. But he looked at Topsannah and remembered how magnificently she had fought the Clankers. Well, he would not abandon the woman, not to two creatures, particularly not a talking lizard and a Bigfoot, not to mention the hopelessly insane Ixtpan. He would have to go along, at least for a while. Matsemela reached inside his deerskin shirt pocket and smiled as he felt the chunks of gold there.

CHAPTER 11

AFTERMATH

The mountain air was cool and filled with the scent of piñon and cedar as twenty people riding donkeys came upon the two young people lying in each other's arms on a debris-strewn path. There were broken branches, dead animals, and shattered stones along the path that had in ages past been cut through the mountains. The pine-covered mountain walls rose up straight around them. The people could see that the woman was alive by the slight rise and fall of her back. The man was as unmoving as if he were dead.

"Now who in tarnation are these two?" a white-haired woman in an indigo tunic asked, drawing a copper sword from a scarred and torn leather scabbard that hung from a lizardskin belt around her waist.

Angelina lay beside Cimarron, her head resting over his heart, her black hair covering his chest like a black shield. The northern accent woke her from a deep and dreamless sleep, and this time when she opened her eyes it was not a rainbow she saw—instead it was the points of a dozen gleaming black obsidian, red bronze, and gray iron spears.

Her golden brown fingers carefully felt the warmth and suppleness of Cimarron's flesh. He was alive. It was a miracle. She looked up the length of the iron spear closest to her, the one pointing between her eyes, and found herself looking into the deep blue eyes of a darkly weathered old woman with short snow-white hair. The old woman's long tunic was indigo cotton, and she wore an amulet of a bluejay wing feather, a tiny unopened pine cone, and a small chunk of red iron ore—all sacred to the ancient tribes of Tesharka—hanging from a thin black leather cord.

They were a mixed group of men and women of all colors of skin, hair, and eyes. Most wore fox, squirrel, or rabbit skins, though some, like the white-haired woman, dressed in ragged indigo cotton tunics and trousers. A man and a woman in tattered buckskin wore brown and white hawk feathers in their long black hair, as was the custom of many of the horsewarriors of the grassland.

"*Quién* . . . ? Who are you?" Angelina asked the old woman. She struggled to sit up, holding Cimarron in her arms, her long black hair covering his face, which was streaked with dirt. Her clothes of white deerskin were torn to shreds. "You speak with the accent of Tesharka."

"Who we are ain't none of your business just yet. First things first. Who're y'all two?" the white-haired woman retorted.

Angelina did not answer.

A pink-skinned man with arms as big around as tree trunks stepped closer, pointing his bronze spear at Angelina. He was dressed in a short tunic made up of squirrel and rabbit skins. "Talk up and make it fast."

Still Angelina said nothing. Her arms tightened around Cimarron and she prayed to her gods for protection. Then she felt Cimarron's body tense slightly and realized he was conscious, that he must be aware of what was happening.

"Hold on a minute there, Tyler. She don't know who we are, either. You always have been too dadblamed hotheaded. All right, girl. You're right about the accent," the old woman's voice softened, as did the lines etched in her face like arroyos in the desert. "My name's Loretta Daingerfield, and I come from Tesharka. But I been gone from there a long time. And don't jump to no conclusions about a person because of where they got born. Or no conclusions about the place, neither, just 'cause of who runs it. Tesharka wasn't always like it is now. . . . But you tell me, girl, what're you and your gentleman friend there up to in the San Cris? Haven't you heard these mountains are haunted?" She laughed, a strange, almost demented, laugh. "Where'n Tophet did y'all come from?"

"I come from an island far away," Angelina answered, "from a people who want nothing from you. You have nothing to fear from me." She turned to the one called Tyler. "This man and I can do you no harm. Surely you can see that."

"I'll ask one more time: Who are you and what're you doing in these mountains?" Tyler moved his spear tip over Cimarron's back.

"We seek the man they call the Prophet." There was, Angelina knew at that moment, no reason not to take the chance of revealing their purpose to the strangers. Perhaps they were followers of the Prophet themselves. "I know he is slowly dying, that he is racked with pain in his body and in his mind. I am a *curandera*, a healer, and I have traveled from far . . ." From across twenty centuries, she thought bitterly, her green eyes half closed. "From a place very far away, to heal him."

"There ain't no such person as this Prophet," the old woman said. But that was not the answer that flashed across her deeply lined face when Angelina spoke his name. "Just a story for the kids, that's all the Prophet is."

Yes, Angelina thought, they had found the people of the Prophet. "I come because your leader is dying. I can help him." She looked from one to the other, seeing no belief in their faces. "Please take us to your city. That is where you come from, no? The city called Epitaph? We are only two unarmed people. There are many of you and you all carry several weapons. You can kill us as easily as an eagle snatches up a rabbit any time you choose. What do you risk by taking us there?" Her eyes were pure turquoise, her lips pale. A breeze rustled through the tall pine trees, softly blowing her long hair.

"People like us don't take risks if we can help it," said Tyler. "Got enough trouble already. Problem is, we don't know who or what you are. Absalom Ironheart's army picked up the survivors of Reno Bismark's company. Our scouts say there's thousands of Confederation soldiers heading our way, so many, they outnumber us two to one!" He was screaming as he angrily recounted the forces arrayed against his people. "How do we know you're telling the truth? Can you prove what you say? How do we know you didn't bring the cavalry after us?"

Then, slowly, as if he had all the time in the universe, Cimarron turned over, taking Angelina in his arms as he did so. He looked calmly at the circle of people around them, his dark eyes hollow, his fingers locked for one precious moment in Angelina's long, silken hair.

"My name is Cimarron Langtry," he said very slowly, as though each word were spoken with great effort. He was tired to his bones and bruised all over from being struck by limbs and rocks in the floodwaters. He had heard Tyler say the army was still coming west, that Absalom Ironheart, the Butcher of Dry Creek, was not far away. And that Reno Bismark was still alive. "I come from Pecos, and I'm no Clanker. This is Señorita Angelina. We're on the run from the Clankers ourselves. If you are the people of the Prophet, then we're allies. If not, then I guess we're your prisoners."

"I say it's a trick," a gaunt, loose-limbed man in a coonskin jacket said. "A hoax. The Confederation government's already sent a dozen assassins, and we've found them all out and killed them. They know we need a healer, so they use this ruse to get in. Odds are, these two're spies—or assassins. Now I suggest you talk the truth pretty quick here, *chamaco*."

The band closed in tightly around Cimarron and Angelina, swords and spears in hand, pointing at them.

Tyler raised his spear as if to hurl it at Cimarron.

"No!" Angelina screamed. "Wait! Do you not know the archaeologist named Ixtpan?"

"Ixtpan?" Tyler hesitated. "Hell, everyone in these parts knows him."

"He is my friend," Angelina added quickly. "He brought us here."

"That's enough for me," Loretta said. "Ixtpan went on a mission to some island down south to get someone to help the Prophet. If she is the one he brought, then I say she's okay. Let's take these folks home. Sorry about all this. Let's get going!" Loretta said. "Everybody saddle up!"

From a ledge above, a man watched, unseen by those below. Wyatt Fontana had survived the flash flood by catching hold of a strong branch and managing to hang on until the waters receded. He had seen Cimarron and Angelina lying in the dirt from the ledge and had been about to approach them when the people of Epitaph had appeared. He had hidden behind a break of cedar and observed what had transpired. He had heard and seen everything. As Reno Bismark had predicted, Cimarron and Angelina would lead him right to Epitaph. And then, Wyatt thought, when the army storms the place, I will kill the witch who practices the heathen magic. And I'll deliver the Fire God to Zumarraga Apocalypse of the Church of the New World. With it, he will usher in a new age.

* * * * *

As they rode the gray and black donkeys up the steep mountain paths, Angelina, Cimarron, and the others passed piñon, juniper, and fragrant cedar trees, plus an occasional scrub oak or mountain mahogany. Water was no longer scarce, since clear streams flowed out of the ancient rocks. They found food easily, hunting rabbits and spearing fish in the streams. They easily gathered strawberries, raspberries, chokeberries, and the wild plums that grew freely in the high country. Grapes and currants grew along the streams.

For two days they rode, days in which Cimarron and Angelina's strength grew steadily, as did their concern for their missing companions. "We saw them make it to the ledge," Cimarron reminded Angelina again and again. "They were all above the floodwaters, except for Eeschatai and Wyatt." He had not known Wyatt well, and, had in fact, not been entirely sure what to make of the man who had saved his life more than once yet seemed so distant. But in his heart, he missed Eeschatai and grieved for the man who had in such a short time become a real friend to him.

Finally they entered a narrow pass between the peaks of two high pine- and fir-covered mountains. "Daugherty Pass," Loretta said. "That's Zapata Mountain to the left and Miners' Peak on the right. This is the gateway to Epitaph."

Both mountains soared to the heavens, like the sides of a great pyramid that should have joined at the top but did not. The peaks were separated by a gap a quarter-mile wide and half a mile deep, as if in ages past some great force had dislodged part of the mountain itself, leaving it forever split in two. And the sides of the sheer mountain walls where it had been split were burned black. Cimarron saw no boulders lying around, no overgrown piles of rubble, no clue as to what destroyed a chunk of a great mountain so completely as to not leave a trace. He remembered what Angelina had told him in the Comanche sanctuary about a Fire God with great power at Epitaph and wondered, staring up at the black walls of bare rock, if perhaps the story was more than antiquated superstition.

"It's a pretty wide pass," Cimarron observed, looking across the dead ground between the mountains. "It would slow an army down, but not for long."

"You're right," Loretta responded. "But this land has never been mapped by the Clankers, and these mountains around here are deadly. Only a fool or a demon could cross them. When the army comes, they have to find this one pass and they have to come through here. At least we know where to mount our defenses."

Cimarron agreed, looking up at the black walls of mountain on either side of him.

The peaks on either side were so high that only the sun's vertical rays reached the pass directly. The rest of the time, it was gray, dusklike, and cool.

Finally they emerged from Daugherty Pass on the east side of a clearing about four miles across, surrounded by a tight circle of high mountains that rose, first green, then blue, and then purple, around it. And ahead of them, in the dead center of the clearing, near a narrow, winding stream, was a city unlike any Cimarron or Angelina had ever seen.

They saw row upon row of shacks and tipis, easily half a mile in radius, encircling an enormous, ruined, red-gold pueblo that stood in five stair-step levels, some of them broken down, caved in by time and by the warfare of a forgotten age. It should, Cimarron thought, have been deserted long ago, like the pyramids of Old World Mexico. But, instead, there were hundreds of people going about their business on the various outside levels of the pueblo that, along with the city of shacks and tipis around it, covered roughly a square mile.

"It's like a honeycomb," Angelina said.

"Like a maze." It would, Cimarron thought, be a hell of a place for hand-to-hand combat. The idea of a battle fought in this tightly enclosed pueblo made him shudder inwardly. A death-trap, Eeschatai had called it.

* * * * *

Wyatt Fontana, unseen where he watched from the side of Miners' Peak, had found what he was looking for. He turned the horse he had recovered and rode south to find the cavalry. He could now lead them straight to the target. He smiled, secure in the knowledge that the high priest of his religion, Zumarraga Apocalypse, would richly reward him for the service he was about to perform for their god, a god known over the millennia by a thousand different names. To Wyatt Fontana, he was simply the God of War and he would give power and riches and immortality to those who gave him what he needed to survive—the sacrifice of human lives.

* * * * *

They rode slowly through the shack city, past rows of one-room houses and shacks made of mesquite limbs and pine or cedar planks, interspersed with occasional bisonhide tipis. People of every known nation or tribe on the continent looked at them curiously, and many called greetings to Loretta and the others.

"Not many years ago," Cimarron told Angelina in his slow drawl, "some of these tribes were blood enemies. I remember a time when the Athaba tribes and the folks from Pecos were killing each other. But here they're pitching their shacks and tipis right next to each other. I wouldn't've believed it if I hadn't seen it. Maybe there is something to this shaman of theirs."

"There is a great power here among them," Angelina responded. But whose power? she wondered, watching the questioning eyes of the people around her. Loretta had given her a long black cotton cassock to wear, since her deerskin clothing had been torn to shreds by the floodwaters. The large, dark garment made

Angelina appear even smaller than she was. Cimarron still wore his torn buckskin pants and, of course, his badly scratched bisonhide-and-crocodileskin boots.

Scrawny dogs, some of them part coyote, ran among the dwellings, chasing cats and chickens. A few goats and sheep wandered loose, of no apparent concern to their owners. There were even a handful of camels wandering around.

When the riders reached the end of the rows of dwellings, they came to an open square. It was not really shaped like a square—actually, it was more like a long rectangle—but throughout the entire Southwest of Noramica, the gathering place at the center of town had been called a square, or zócalo, since time immemorial and so it was called in Epitaph. This square was big enough for a thousand people to assemble on—though five times that number now filled the city. On this day, only a few children ran about the square, chasing a large black rubber ball. Six great mountains circled the level clearing where the pueblo and the village around it lay hidden. Being surrounded by the high mountains gave Cimarron an uneasy sense of being trapped—as did the crowd that was gathering around them. But he could see why Epitaph had been so hard to find.

Within minutes the square was filled with people, most of them gaunt and ragged, dressed in skins and patchwork cloth and maguey fiber, many of them with feathers in their hair, some with colorful paint on their faces. They had all lost everything or else they would not have been driven to take refuge in a long-deserted pueblo. Soon, Cimarron, Angelina, and their escorts were surrounded by a crowd of several hundred curious people. There was a low rumbling in the crowd as people wondered who the strangers were. With reports from scouts coming in by the hour that the Confederation army companies were moving inexorably toward Epitaph, the people were understandably suspicious and jumpy.

Cimarron had expected to find a well-armed fortress at Epitaph. What he saw was a ruined pueblo that had been long ago abandoned to the elements, filled with people who looked hardly able to defend themselves. Many, maybe half, were children and old people. There's no way, he thought, absolutely no way these folks are going to make it against the Confederation army. If their Prophet's so smart, he should be evacuating this place right now. Cimarron thought maybe some of these people would have a chance of escaping, of getting across Corpus Cristi Mountain on the north side of the pueblo and into the great mountains that were rumored to lie farther north, mountains which, it was said, dwarfed the San Cris. But he realized, even as the idea formed in his mind, that unless the Confederation was dealt a crippling defeat, it would keep expanding, reaching into the great northwestern mountains and beyond. To think that the people of Epitaph could inflict a defeat on the Clanker army seemed to him patently impossible. It was entirely likely, he realized in the flash of the moment, that the Tesharka Confederation would enslave the entire continent, crushing all resistance like a mountain lion devouring a rabbit, and then neither he nor anyone else—even a prophet—could do anything to stop it.

A large gray-bearded man, his long brown cassock flapping around his legs with each purposeful step, approached Loretta. His curly gray hair stood out like a round halo around his head, and his eyes were piercing blue, but bloodshot from a life spent in sun and dust. "Greetings, sister," he said somberly, with one hand on the silver handle of a long copper sword sheathed in beaded leather. "And who are these strangers?" At first glance, he took the newcomers for Comanches, but with closer examination, he realized differently. Something about the short, green-eyed woman spooked him.

Cimarron and Angelina looked filthy and bedraggled. Cimarron had lost his shirt, and the remainder of his deerskin clothing had been torn to shreds by the flood. They were both covered with cuts and bruises—yet glowing from the excitement of finally reaching their destination. Angelina took Cimarron's hand, and whispered, "*Gracias*, Cimarron, for bringing me here."

"*De nada*, Angelina," A half-smile softening the hard lines of Cimarron's sun-bronzed face.

"Found 'em up near Hermit Pass, Japhet," Loretta answered, her weathered, dark hand on Angelina's arm. "The woman, she's a healer. Ixtpan brought her here. I think we need to talk to Jayhawk and Kiri. Maybe they should see—"

"Enough, sister, until we are certain who they are. With our enemies practically upon us, we can't be too careful. Where is Ixtpan?"

"Lost, apparently," Loretta answered. "These two say they got separated in the flash flood a couple days back. But they say Ixtpan and some other folks were on a ledge high above the floodwaters. He'll probably be showing up any time now. You know that old buzzard, Ixtpan. He's probably digging around in the rocks somewhere, looking for some old relic or another. I tell you, the woman *is* a healer—"

"If we can believe what these strangers tell us." Japhet was responsible for the security of the pueblo, and he knew of the proximity of the army and suspected that Reno Bismark would find a way to place agents in their midst. He was suspicious of the two people who appeared so mysteriously with the Confederation army so near.

At that moment, they were interrupted as three riders on sleek black mustangs galloped into the square. The horses were soaked with sweat, having been ridden hard and fast.

"The army's comin'," one rider gasped. "Army's comin'! Be here before mornin'."

"We tailed the army up from White Sands." The other rider had dismounted. He was a thin man with red eyes and hair the color of wheat. His blue cotton shirt had faded close to white and was stained with sweat and dust. He wiped his brow, only deepening the furrows of dust.

"Looked like they knew right where they were heading," the third rider, a slender young woman with angry blue eyes and hair as yellow as corn, added as she dismounted.

"Someone's led them right to us, all right," a young man named Ginty said icily, glaring at Cimarron and Angelina. "And that someone is going to pay for it. I say hang them both now." Ginty pulled his bronze knife from his belt and pointed it at Angelina.

"It appears, boy," Japhet said to Cimarron, "that you are in one heap of trouble."

A low rumble went up from the crowd of frightened, angry people, and a hundred knives and swords were drawn.

Loretta stepped between the two strangers and the angry crowd, yelling, "That's enough, you damn fools! You're all acting like a bunch of frightened chickens!" Her manner was so forceful that the angry crowd drew back for a moment.

"*Por favor*," Angelina pleaded with the people of Epitaph, "just let me speak to your Prophet."

The crowd surged forward again, and a dark-haired woman handed Japhet two long ropes with nooses already tied in them. Japhet said, "Let's get this over with!"

"Cut it out." A slender young man with long blond hair stepped forward authoritatively. He was dressed in tan buckskin and wore thigh-high dark brown deerskin moccasins folded down to his knees. His bow was of Osage, and the quiver of arrows over his left shoulder was made from beaded brown deerskin. A bone-handled, bronze knife hung low on his hip. "We don't have lynchings at Epitaph." His voice, a slow Pecos drawl, seemed to Cimarron to echo off the surrounding mountains.

"Jayhawk, you've got a battle to get ready for. You go worry about the goddamned Clankers and leave the running of this pueblo to me. You know we can't trust any newcomers, not now! Don't you understand? Bismark has spies, scouts, assassins! We can't trust anyone, not anyone!" Japhet's face was burning red, and his eyes were bloodshot and ringed in black circles.

"You've gone mad, Japhet," the yellow-haired warrior named Jayhawk responded sadly. "Lynching people isn't what we're about here." His eyes were turquoise blue and around his neck, hanging from a thin strip of black leather, he wore a small gold, five-pointed star, the symbol of both Old World Texas and of the Republic of Pecos.

Cimarron stared hard at the symbol that had been on the flag in which his dead parents had left him wrapped, the symbol of what he had fought for in his youth, what his friends had died for. He remembered seeing that star on a wall in Reynada that first day he had come home after five years away. His arms tightened around Angelina.

"We'll see how much good your pretty ideas do us tomorrow, when the army gets here, Jayhawk," Japhet answered.

"I swear it by all the saints of the Alamo and on my honor as a man from Pecos, it wasn't us that brought the army here," Cimarron said.

"Saints of the Alamo!" Jayhawk yelled, slapping his knee. "You're from Pecos!" Jayhawk drew his own knife, pointed it at Japhet, and said, "You'll have to fight me first, Japhet. Folks from Pecos stick together. And it's high time the rest of ya'll learned that."

Japhet signaled for two of his lieutenants, both enormously fat men in coyoteskin vests, and each of them came and stood on either side of Jayhawk with their own bronze knives drawn.

"Stop! In St. Elvis's name, stop! I know the old man, and he's all right!" The youthful voice tore through the crowd like an arrow. All eyes turned. A fair-skinned, black-haired young man dressed all in black was running across the square. "I know him. He's on our side!"

Cimarron's bronze skin paled, and the lines of his face softened into an expression of utter disbelief. "It's Stether Delgado!"

The young man running toward him was, indeed, Stether Delgado, whom Cimarron had last seen in the hills of western Pecos just before he was captured by the Clanker army. Cimarron was so stunned at seeing the boy in Epitaph that he thought for a moment he must be losing his mind.

Stether stopped a few feet from Cimarron and smiled. "Good to see you again, old man."

"You're interfering," Japhet exclaimed indignantly to Stether.

"I'd have been dead a month ago if not for this guy. And he can ride like *el diablo* himself. It's loco to hang him."

"The whole damn Clanker army could come through here and wipe us all out while this foolishness is going on." Loretta put an arm around Angelina, who squeezed the old woman's weathered hand in gratitude.

"True enough," Japhet admitted grudgingly. "But, I warn you, Jay, if either of these people brings us or the Prophet any harm, I'll kill them both myself."

"Odds are, Japhet, we're all going to die tomorrow, and it doesn't much matter what you or them or any of us does. But to tell you the truth," he said to Angelina, "I don't know that Falling Eagle is in a condition to see anyone."

Jayhawk looked sadly at Angelina, thinking, It's too late. No matter what she can do, it's just too late. Then he led the two newcomers inside the ancient pueblo, the ruin of a forgotten past.

* * * * *

Jayhawk led Angelina and Cimarron into a dark, cool room inside the pueblo and offered them a place to sit on a cedar wood bench. The only light came from one small white candle in a wooden holder on the wall to their right. The golden-haired warrior took a skin canteen from a bison horn hook on the wall and offered Cimarron and Angelina some water, which they drank gratefully. Then he left them alone for a moment while he went to confer with the people who attended Falling Eagle.

Cimarron buried his haggard face in his hands. "Does your god protect us, Angelina? He must have some reason for keeping us alive . . ."

"For all of my life, I would have answered that it is not our right to question the will of the gods, Cimarron. But right now, at this moment . . . I do not know what I believe anymore. The world where all my beliefs made sense to me . . . it seems very far away now. In your world, the things I know do not make much sense. I wonder if I have been wrong . . ."

"No, Angelina, your faith gives you strength. Don't lose it now. Not now." Cimarron took her hand tentatively, seeking only to offer solace. Her small brown fingers gripped his hand hard.

"Hello, old man."

Stether had aged dramatically since Cimarron had last seen him only a month before. The boyish quality was gone like tumbleweed in the wind. His deep blue eyes were sunken, his skin pale and dried. His black hair hung loose, no longer styled with aloe gel. Only the golden spiral earring and the black clothes were the same, though the earring was tarnished and bent and the clothes were torn and dirty.

"Kid!" There were tears in Cimarron's eyes—as there had not been in many years—as he stood up and embraced Stether. "I didn't expect to see you again this side of hell!"

"And the last time I saw you, there was a whole Clanker squadron after you! What're you doing still breathing?" Stether gripped Cimarron's bare arms hard. "I was damned surprised to see you out there on the square!"

"Maybe there's a god who looks after loco vaqueros." Cimarron smiled grimly. "But where's Iphi? By St. Davy's cap, we can use her—"

"She's dead." Stether spoke the words without emotion. "We were holed up with a couple hundred others at an old mission called Katishya about two hundred miles southeast of here. An advance company of Ironheart's troops found us and killed everyone about three weeks ago. Only a few escaped."

"How did you get out?"

"Iphi and I were ordered to take the younger kids out. We did. Iphi died protecting the kids."

Cimarron winced, remembering the beautiful, dark young girl who could shoot an arrow better than most trained soldiers and who had loved Stether Delgado with all the passion of youth.

Stether continued. "Most of the others are gone now, too, except for me and Tati and Nat and Bren. We made it here. It was Jayhawk who found us, wandering, delirious, in the mountains. Lucky, huh?" He laughed bitterly. "Maybe some of the others from the old days are alive somewhere. ¿Quién sabe?"

"I'm really sorry Iphi's gone, Stether. She was something else."

Stether for a moment looked like the child he had so recently been, then the lines in his face set hard. "I wish it had been me, but it wasn't."

"Don't think that way, ki—Stether."

"Look, it's done. No point in talking about it now." His blue eyes were far away. "What matters now is that we break that damned Confederation army."

"I know, Stether. At least we can do everything we can to see to it there's a lot fewer Clankers after tomorrow."

"That we can. The ones of us who've stayed here . . . that's what we mean to do. Who's your lady friend?"

"This is Angelina. She's a *curandera*. Came here from down south to heal this Prophet who's supposed to be leading these people. This, Angelina, is Stether Delgado. He caused me a good deal of trouble a while back, but under the present extenuating circumstances, I'm willing to let bygones be bygones."

"Caused you trouble?" Stether retorted with a grin.

Stether led them deeper into the pueblo to a small room with an ancient altar, where candles burned to the goddess Tonantzin, the earth goddess whom the people called "Our Mother."

"You'll be safe here. I'll see about getting you some weapons."

Cimarron and Angelina sat to rest on the adobe floor in the small chapel. Cimarron put his right arm around Angelina's shoulders. "What I really want to do is get you out of here. These people can't hold off Winchester's army. Half of them are kids and old folks. What can their Falling Eagle do against thousands of Confederation cavalry, even if you do heal him?"

"Perhaps he can do nothing against them. But we are here and we must do the best we can."

Suddenly Angelina seemed very different from the frightened, fragile young woman Cimarron had laid eyes on only a month before. He knew from the legends that the Toltecs were among the greatest warriors in history and realized that she had within her their warrior strength. "Angelina, I don't want you to be a sacrifice to a future we may not have. I've seen too many blood sacrifices. Hell, I've made too many blood sacrifices." He paused, fighting a deluge of memories, his eyes dark with pain.

"Cimarron, I am alive in this time and place because of this man, Falling Eagle. I cannot expect that to make any sense to you. My beliefs are all I have, all I am, even if I have come to realize there is much more to the world than what I have been taught. I wish I could be more like the people of your world—I do—but I do not know any other way to live."

"Please." His fingers gripped her thin arms almost brutally. "Don't. I know it would be dangerous, but we'd have a chance of making it into the mountains behind the pueblo and getting to the northern—"

"I cannot walk away now. You know I cannot escape my destiny—any more than you can escape yours. There is something between you and the copper-haired colonel, something you would rather die than leave unsettled, no?"

"*Si, es verdad. . . .*" Cimarron's brown eyes were half closed, thinking of the childhood friend who had betrayed his own people, who had betrayed his own friends, all for the wealth and power their conquests could give him. He remembered the sight of Zaco's blood running into the dust.

"I saw it in your eyes that night in his tent. If you and I both had a way out of here right now, you would no more take it than I would." Angelina's eyes were a pure, deep green in the dark room. Cream-colored tallow candles burned on a wooden altar to an ancient, dark-skinned goddess in a long blue veil covered with golden stars.

"You're right. If you weren't here, I'd go looking for Reno and to hell with the consequences. Until I met you, Angelina, there wasn't anything in the world I wanted but vengeance. *Nada.* And I wouldn't have minded dying to get it. Frankly, I would've considered it a fair trade-off. But you are here, and if you'd leave with me, yes, I would leave."

"If you can turn away from confronting your Reno Bismark, do it. Leave here now. Live your life, Cimarron Langtry."

"Kiri sends for you," Jayhawk said, entering the doorway and interrupting their conversation. His face was drawn and pale, and his blue eyes were rimmed in red from days and nights of little sleep. "This is Delani," the Prophet's lieutenant said, indicating a white-skinned woman barely four feet tall, dressed in red fox skins the precise shade of her curly hair. "She will lead you to Falling Eagle. I pray you can help him and that he can help you."

Stether appeared with a bronze sword and knife for Cimarron and a silver dagger for Angelina. Angelina started to refuse the weapon, as she had always done, but then she hesitated. She looked hard at the silver dagger, then took it, stuck it in her cord belt, and started out of the small, dark room behind Delani.

As Angelina reached the six-foot doorway braced with ancient pine beams, she turned so abruptly that her long black hair swung around her like a fan unfurled, ran to Cimarron and embraced him, then just as abruptly turned and ran from the room after Delani.

For a long time, Cimarron stood staring after her, as if time had slowed and the Earth had stopped turning. She seemed to him to have been swallowed up in the darkness of the earthen pueblo.

"Come on," Stether said, taking his arm. "Let her fight this battle her way, old man. You and me can go take a look at the other battle that's shaping up. The Confederation cavalry's almost here. Ten thousand soldiers just about twenty miles south of Daugherty Pass. Some of their advance battalions are already at the pass."

Jayhawk explained, "A scout made it an hour ago, saying four of our twenty-person squads are fighting them at the entrance to Daugherty Pass, the entrance to this valley. The Clankers're going to have to come through there unless they want to come over some of the most brutal mountains on the continent." Jayhawk led the way to the roof of the pueblo's second level, from which they could survey both the preparations in the valley and the opening to the pass only two miles directly across the flat clearing from the pueblo. "They'll slow the Clankers down. But that's all they can do. The time we have to get ready is being paid for with the blood of some of our best fighters. By the way, the scouts say the one in command is a colonel with bright copper hair. Does that mean anything to you?"

Cimarron shook himself free of the sense of having stepped out of time, like breaking out of a fever or a nightmare. "Yeah, I know him. And I know how he thinks. Let's have a look."

* * * * *

Delani led Angelina deep into the pueblo, through a mazelike series of small, dark rooms, each about six feet high. The only light was from an occasional white or golden tallow candle suspended on a wall by a pine holder. Ixtpan must have had to stoop when he came through here, Angelina thought with a smile. Then they began to descend by means of pine ladders that connected each level of the pueblo, far beneath the surface of the Earth. "Where are you?" she asked the woman as they climbed down a fifth ladder. "What is this place?"

"Epitaph was constructed by a vanished race that built its pueblo on top of another, older pueblo, now buried beneath the surface of the Earth itself. And that pueblo, now so deeply buried, was built above a far older temple. We are going to the deepest level." Dalani led Angelina across a small, dark room and down yet another pine ladder.

When they had passed through six levels of adobe, they came to a landing of solid stone. Delani took a torch from the wall and lit it with a flint. The light flared off the dark walls of a long, arched hallway of stone. They began descending a long, dark stairway, and Angelina realized they were in a building cut from the earth itself. And here the cavernous stone ceiling towered high above them. This, she could tell, was a very ancient place—and a place that gave her a strange sense of foreboding. She followed Delani down the long hallway and then descended a steep stone stairway. At the bottom of the stairway hung a curtain of heavy brown buffalo robes, and from behind them came the soft hum of chanting and praying. The curtain opened, and a dark-skinned woman with cascading hair the color of pure gold motioned for the *curandera* to come closer.

The woman's cobalt-blue eyes examined Angelina closely, as though she were trying to divine something. Finally her lips parted in a slight smile. "I am Kiri, from the Cochiti tribe. You may enter Falling Eagle's chamber now."

The woman's gown shimmered with the color of seawater at sunset in the light of the torch hanging from the wall beside them. For just a moment, Angelina thought longingly of her island homeland. "*Gracias*, sister. I will do all I can to help him."

"I pray you can ease his suffering, but it seems the gods have already claimed his life. His energy is steadily failing, his pulse erratic. Unless you can make miracles, he will not live out this night." The tears that filled the woman's blue eyes glistened like clear crystals in the torchlight. Kiri stepped aside, holding the bison robe curtain open for Angelina.

The immense, round room behind the curtain was cut from solid sandstone, and its walls were streaked in colors of gold and yellow, orange and red, blue and purple, and black, each stripe a layer representing an epoch in the earth's history. The stripes seemed to Angelina to dance in the flickering light of a few torches and candles scattered about the room. The ceiling was fifty feet high, the room's diameter two hundred feet across. In the center of the room was a round ceremonial pit, called a *kiva*, dug into the earth and surrounded on its rim with red stones piled three feet high. An obsidian railing carved in the shape of twisting, interlocking serpents led down into the dark *kiva*.

Near the pit, a small fire burned, and the air was thick with the fragrant smoke of burning sage and sweetgrass. A silver-haired, fat woman and a skinny woman with long black braids knelt beside a man lying on a pallet of bison robes about ten feet from the

pit. A man in a buckskin breechcloth, his face and chest painted
with stripes of blue and green, sat cross-legged beside the pallet,
chanting in a language unknown to Angelina. He was breaking a
braid of sweetgrass to throw on the fire, as was customary to carry
prayers to the gods and to banish evil spirits. The three looked up
as she slowly came closer. Even from several feet away, she could
feel the draining energy and pain of the man who lay there.

His long hair was spread out around him like a distorted black
halo on a pillow of deerskin. "The flames," he moaned in a language similar to Angelina's own, writhing and thrashing. "Always the flames." He tried to scream, but the sound came out a
tortured groan. He sat up suddenly and grabbed the silver-haired
woman, his deep-set, almond-shaped brown eyes open wide.
Dark circles rimmed his eyes, and his cheeks were hollow beneath
his high, fever-flushed cheekbones. "Run, *hermana*," he rasped
desperately in Spanglish, "*las flamas* are all around you! Can't
you see the flames?" Then he fell back, gasping for air, his right
arm shielding his eyes.

Angelina was surprised by how young he was. He looked barely
twenty-one. What could this young man do against Baines Winchester and all his armies? she wondered.

"The flames," he moaned again. His dark brown eyes closed as
if he found even the dim torchlight painful.

"*Cuauhtémoc*," Angelina whispered as she took his hand,
speaking his name in the old language. She knelt at his side, her
head bowed. "It is a miracle I have found you. My name is Angelina Ixtacci. I am Toltec. I am a priestess of the god Quetzalcoatl,
and I have come here to help you."

After a moment of piercing silence, Falling Eagle opened his
eyes and looked straight at her. His deep-set, dark brown eyes
were the eyes of someone very, very old. "If you are Toltec, why do
you bear a name *en Español?*"

"I am Toltec, but we, like everything else in this world, have
changed over time." Angelina answered him in her Toltec language, an older version of his Aztec tongue, though similar
enough that he could understand her. He started to speak, but she
held a finger to his lips. "Let me explain. Refugees from other lost
nations have found and joined us over the centuries, all of them
fleeing some new conqueror, some new disaster. The name Angelina has been in my family for many centuries, since the last days
of what the people of this land call the Old World. It was the name
of a woman who was my ancestor. She came from the land far be-

low our mountain sanctuary, from the nation that was called Guatemala before the Great War."

"Guatemala," Falling Eagle whispered bitterly. "Yes, I know the land of which you speak. Too well. And I know that it fell to the *Spañols* long, long ago." He thought in silence for a moment. "So it is true what the great scholar Ixtpan said, the Toltecs have returned." He spoke calmly in a voice that sounded a thousand years old, in spite of his apparent youth.

"Yes. And at least one of us has returned to this land where no Toltecs have set foot in two thousand years."

"So the ancient prophecy is true after all—the Toltecs have come back to reclaim their empire." In spite of his weakness, there was a fiery anger in Falling Eagle's voice. He tossed and turned on his bed of bison robes, his fingers gripping Angelina's small hand as his dark eyes looked at her with mistrust. "I am sorry my late uncle, the *Uey-Tlatoani*, Moctecozuma, could not be here in this time to meet you."

The healer was drawn to his dark eyes as though by a magnet. She had seen those fevered eyes in her dreams, in the copal smoke that incensed the temple in her homeland, Tamoanchan, and in the eternal mist of the cloud forest. "Once all these lands—from the high sierra cloud forests of the South to far beyond these northern mountains—were Toltec. We had colonies here in the San Cris Mountains, many even farther north. But that was long ago," she said.

Falling Eagle stared at her. "We Aztecs built an empire on your land, and we believed you would come back and take what we had stolen from you." He gasped for breath, his eyes burning bright in the dim red light of the flames.

"You have stolen nothing. My people lost their own empire—because they served the God of War. As he always does, the God of War destroyed those who served him best. As our *tlatoani*, Quetzalcoatl, taught, those who make the blood sacrifice sooner or later sacrifice themselves."

Falling Eagle winced, not from pain but from memories of his past life. "Yes, I know that very well to be true. The Aztecs, too, served a war god, a god who demanded the sacrifice of human lives, and, in the end, he destroyed us."

Angelina continued softly, "My god, Quetzalcoatl, will return one day, and when he does, he will vanquish the God of War and reunite this continent, one land again. Then the blood sacrifice—whether it takes place on an altar or on a battlefield—will end forever. But, until that day, my people want nothing from the rest of your world but to be left in peace."

The young man began to laugh, and he laughed until tears rolled down his face. He began coughing, as though he were choking on smoke, and Kiri ran to his side, looking angrily at Angelina.

"Please," Kiri begged, "you're making him worse."

"Let her stay," Falling Eagle whispered, gently touching the golden-haired woman's hand. "I do not have much time left. And history has waited a long time for this meeting."

Angelina took the butterfly-shaped amulet with the turquoise spiral from around her neck and laid it over Falling Eagle's heart.

His fingers touched the spiral gratefully. He was gasping for breath, his face as pale as the mists of Tamoanchan. "I have seen this butterfly before . . . on shields of the giant stone warrior women who guard the ruins of Quetzalcoatl's capital city of Tula. My uncle, Moctecozuma, took me to see the ruins of Tula once, the year before the conquerors came. My uncle thought he was honoring a god when he opened our city to the invaders—but instead he was welcoming a demon who destroyed us. Because of the prophecy of Quetzalcoatl's return, our world died."

"Your world did not die. Your people survived in spite of the conquest. They still survive. Some of them fled south. And in the mountains of Quahtemal they found my people, and they stayed with us. Their blood runs in my veins. We know of the destruction of your city, Tenochtitlán, and of your people. And we know what the conquistadors did to you." Tears filled her eyes as she thought of the ancient legends of the valiant young *tlatoani* who was burned, hanging from a sacred ceiba tree. "Your people live on, in the land that was *Mexica* and across this land. In my own people. And you have survived in their memory while those who tormented you are long forgotten."

Falling Eagle stroked the silver butterfly, gazing into the turquoise spiral, and smiled. "If you know who I am, my sister, then you know I made the blood sacrifice to the War God myself. And I have paid for it, in that life long ago and in this one." Then his coughing started again, and he began to toss and moan. "Your god, Angelina, forbade human sacrifice, and he does not forgive."

Angelina helped him to sit up, and his coughing eased slightly. "My god does not condemn, either. You have suffered too long, Falling Eagle. It is time for your pain to end forever." The healer felt herself growing weak as she touched him. His weakness was draining her energy. She pressed the turquoise spiral to his lips—as she had done for Cimarron by the banks of the Rio Bravo one day that seemed to her so long ago—and her body shook from the force of healing power that flowed through her. "It belonged to our *tlatoani*, Quetzalcoatl, and he left it with my ancestors two thousand years ago, when he lit his own funeral pyre. Perhaps, in some way, he knew this day would come."

"I know this symbol, and I know your god." Falling Eagle's chest began heaving, and a glazed look came over his eyes. "He could not save me in my past life, and he cannot save me now." He began to moan and writhe.

Angelina took his head in her hands as he held the turquoise amulet. Suddenly, she began to feel flames around her, to hear them crackling, to smell the acrid smoke, to feel herself burning, as young Falling Eagle did. For a moment, the old terror of fire that had been born in her in Nuevo San Cristobal threatened to overcome her. But she held on to Falling Eagle, who moaned deliriously and thrashed about. In that moment, she knew a force beyond her powers was killing him—a force against which she was powerless. And Angelina knew that if she went on with the healing, she, too, might be dragged into a world of pain and agonizing visions—and even death. But she did not stop.

Then, in a vision, she saw the flames and felt them licking her hair, as in Nuevo San Cristobal. This place, though, was not Nuevo San Cristobal. Instead, they were in a jungle, surrounded by giant ceiba trees, and she was hanging over a burning fire. Around her, the people who had conquered her nation were laughing—all but one, a priest who begged in the name of a god he called Cristos that the fire be put out. The others seized the priest, and he was burned, too, begging for a cross that the conquerors would not give him.

She saw a light, not the flames around her, but a clear light at the end of a long, dark tunnel, a light that seemed to have no source.

But then, in the vision that was shared by Angelina and Falling Eagle, the wind came and grew stronger. The dust swirled up as the wind wailed and howled, and the land became dark. The rain began, a heavy, pounding rain that put out the fire.

Angelina screamed and collapsed on the floor.

Falling Eagle let go of her hand, shuddered, and fell back, gasping for breath. "The fire went out," he whispered in his own language. "The flames are gone. The ancient magic worked." And as the flames in the vision died, so did Falling Eagle's pain.

* * * * *

"The army'll be setting up to invade the clearing and surround the city," Stether said, pointing in the direction of the pass. They were standing on the roof of the highest level of the pueblo, from where they could see the clear land and perilous mountains around them. The one clear way to get to the city, Daugherty Pass, was plainly visible. The mountains shielding Epitaph looked like jagged, forbidding giants in the hazy light of dusk. "If the Clankers all get through, . . . from what the scouts are saying, there'll be thousands of Confederation troops in here. A third of our people are children. Others are too old disabled to fight."

Cimarron started to protest. "But they say there are thousands of warriors here. . . ."

"They're crazy," Jayhawk answered. "They think there are thousands more of us than there are because the Clankers had never been beaten before we whipped them at Isleta. They were just too damn used to winning every fight. They plain weren't expecting to be attacked from three sides by a bunch of howling rebels. Hell, it was their own panic that defeated them. There were enough of them to have wiped us out." He laughed, remembering the rout of fear-crazed Clankers. "The simple fact of the matter, pardner, is that if all of those Clankers make it in here, that's it. We're done for."

"Maybe I can help out," Cimarron offered, his brown eyes fixed on the pass from which Reno Bismark would attack.

"How?" Jayhawk asked.

"Give them something they're not expecting and use their own panic against them." Well, Diego, Cimarron thought, here's where we see if everything you taught me pays off.

"I hope you're satisfied."

The icy voice startled the three men who had not heard Ginty approach them.

"What the hell do you—," Cimarron began.

"I hear she's with him now," he said, grinning. "You thought you could assassinate him, and you were wrong. Dead wrong. It's the witch that's dying."

"Angelina!" Cimarron bolted toward the center of the pueblo.

"No! Don't interfere!" Jayhawk called, running after him. "Wait! Stop!" Jayhawk caught Cimarron by the arm.

"Take me to her now." Cimarron's angular face was set in rigid lines and his fists were clenched tight.

"Jay, don't do this to the old man," Stether said. "If you won't take him, I will."

"All right, come on." Jayhawk took off running, with Cimarron and Stether Delgado right behind him. Within seconds, they were climbing down into the chamber at the heart of Epitaph.

*   *   *   *   *

Angelina lay on the stone floor beside Falling Eagle's pallet, exhausted and drained. She took several long, deep breaths, then knelt at his left side, trembling and pale, knowing she had taken away his pain but had not healed him. He had, she could tell from her sense of his life energy, perhaps one more day to live. But she could also sense that the pain of the fires had finally gone out in his mind and in his body.

"You were very brave in the other life, Falling Eagle, and very brave to come back to this world."

"All I did in the past life, Angelina, was the best I could for my people." His voice was weak, but his skin had turned a healthy golden brown and his eyes were bright. "And that is all I am doing in this life."

He is delirious, Angelina thought. She touched his forehead but found it cool, the fever gone.

Falling Eagle took her hand in his own and smiled at her. "Soon I will see your god again. Again through the flames."

Cimarron came running through the bisonhide curtain at the foot of the stone stairway, with Stether and Jayhawk right on his heels. "Angelina, are you . . . ?"

In a corner, a golden-haired woman in a blue gown wept as though her heart would break.

Falling Eagle touched the turquoise amulet, his fingers caressing it. He smiled at Jayhawk and Stether. Jayhawk came to a sudden stop when he saw his leader sitting up, conscious and free from pain. He hardly dared to believe it.

Stether stopped abruptly and gasped, "St. Elvis's blue shoes! She did it! Your lady friend did it, Cimarron."

Angelina stood unsteadily and walked slowly to Cimarron, her arms outstretched. "I failed. I could not heal him." She leaned her head against Cimarron's chest, and then her legs gave out from under her. He caught her and held her close, his fingers locked in her shimmering black hair.

Falling Eagle's voice was strong. "You have given me another day of life, Angelina. And one day is all I will need."

Cimarron glared angrily at the man. "What the hell have you done to her?"

"I am Falling Eagle. And you?"

"Cimarron Langtry, from Pecos. I brought her here." He spoke bitterly, cursing himself for having brought Angelina to the poorly defended pueblo.

"I am all right, Cimarron," Angelina whispered.

"A god protects her, my friend," Falling Eagle said. "And that same god sent you to protect her and bring her to me, for which you have my gratitude."

"Jay! Jay!" a youthful voice screamed from the stairway.

The yellow-haired lieutenant ran toward the bison robe curtain that blocked the stairway from view and bumped straight into Ginty. The younger man was soaked with sweat and breathing like a horse that had been ridden too hard for too long.

"What is it now, boy?" Jayhawk demanded, wiping the sweat from his own brow with a red bandana.

"They're through, Jay! The Clankers've broken through! There's thousands of 'em streaming into Daugherty Pass. Tyler's taken a squadron to reinforce the pass, but he won't be able to hold them long. They'll be ready to attack us at daybreak, no doubt about it. There's nothing to going to stop them now."

Angelina leaned against Cimarron in deep despair. She had taken away Falling Eagle's pain, but she had only given him one more day of life. It seemed pitifully little with the armies of Tesharka getting ready to assault them. *As the Ancient Ones believed*, Ixtpan had said, *we are but players on Tezcatlipoca's stage.* She touched the pearl handle of the silver dagger in her belt tentatively at first, then she gripped it harder.

"And what of the squadrons that were to engage them in the pass?" Jayhawk asked.

"Must be dead, sir. There's no more resistance in between those two mountains."

"So our enemies are upon us. I have lain ill while they approached . . . and now it is too late to do anything but face them." Falling Eagle looked to Angelina for a moment like a lost child. "Jayhawk, assemble everyone in the courtyard in one hour. I will address my people for the last time. Come with me," he said to Cimarron. "And you, Angelina. But first, let me show you something."

He pointed to the northern wall, where a ten-foot-long red-and-black Comanche blanket hung. "Behind the blanket is a door. Through the door is a long tunnel leading a mile underground and then up into Corpus Cristi Mountain, directly behind the pueblo to the north. It is a dangerous and ancient path—but it may be your only hope." For the first time in two months, Falling Eagle stood. Kiri handed him a long robe of sky blue and helped him put it on, fastening it with a shell-shaped gold clasp on his right shoulder. He stood straight and tall, a proud young warrior from a race of warriors, his golden brown skin shining in the firelight. He walked to the hanging blanket and pulled it back, revealing a massive stone door ten feet high, with a golden lever beside it. "Pull this, and the door opens."

"Why don't we just get everyone out of here now?" Cimarron asked.

"Because I cannot risk bringing so many to this chamber. And because the Clankers must not take this place. Soon you'll see why."

Then, taking a long torch in his hand, Falling Eagle led Cimarron, Angelina, Kiri, and Stether to the ceremonial pit in the center of the room as Jayhawk climbed the long stone stairway out of the chamber to confront the immediate military emergency. "It is called a *kiva*."

The *kiva* was about ten feet in diameter and was surrounded by a low wall of smooth red rocks. On one side, a stairway with a black obsidian handrail was cut in the stone, leading down into the pit. Falling Eagle climbed over the side, hiking up his long blue robe to his knees to do so. "A god that many have sought is down here." He started down the steep stairway, holding high the torch to light their way. "The Ancient Ones believed their ancestors had emerged into the world through these holes called *kivas*. They believed the *kiva* led to the underground where the gods lived. Many of those gods were not pleasant characters, the one who dwells here most especially." Kiri followed him down the stairs. As Falling Eagle looked up at her, her long golden hair seemed to light the darkness in which they were descending.

Cimarron leaned over the *kiva*. He had seen *kivas* before in other ancient pueblos when he was a young teenager, and he and Apizaco used to accompany Dezcalzo Two Creeks on his scouting expeditions in the West. This *kiva*, however, was much deeper than any he had ever seen before.

"Can you make it down?" Cimarron asked Angelina, noticing

how weak and disoriented she seemed.

"*Sí.* I want to see this god who destroyed the world of Ixtpan's ancestors." Angelina lifted her long black cassock up above her knees, climbed over the side of the *kiva*, and went down the stone stairway after Falling Eagle.

"Only a few people know this is here," Falling Eagle said, his voice echoing in the cylindrical chamber. "Your friend, Ixtpan, is one of them."

"You mean the people of Epitaph don't know what's down here?" Cimarron asked, carefully placing one foot ahead of the other.

"No. I cannot take the risk that one of them would try to seize the weapon that lies hidden here. Even before Ixtpan explained to me what it was, I knew it contained within it an evil power, and I have kept this place a secret from all but a handful of those closest to me."

When he reached the bottom, Falling Eagle hung the long torch in an iron ring on the stone wall. The torch illuminated smooth, curved walls of black marble and a floor of polished red carnelian tiles. In the center of the *kiva* stood the thing for which both Ixtpan and Zumarraga Apocalypse had spent their lives searching.

It was only a statue. It stood on a silver pedestal five feet high. The figure of the god was just three feet tall, bent and twisted, scarcely recognizable as human, holding in its left hand a torch. The idol was made of many precious stones—emeralds, rubies, sapphires, diamonds—and gleamed in a hundred colors as the light of Falling Eagle's torch struck it. The god's grotesque face, a grinning skull of diamonds and black onyx, was lit by a demonic emerald smile, and its eyes were blood-red rubies. The idol's arms and legs, twisted in the middle at right angles, gave it the shape of something Cimarron had seen before—the amulet worn by Wyatt Fontana: the twisted cross. Cimarron felt a tightening in the pit of his stomach.

"Ixtpan's Fire God," Angelina breathed. "Why have you not destroyed it?"

"Touch it and you may destroy us all, for if Ixtpan speaks the truth, beneath that stone statue lies a force like a serpent coiled to strike. And this serpent has a tongue of fire that could reach hundreds of miles."

Cimarron looked at the old idol and wondered if the story Angelina had told him could really be true, that this piece of metal and stone could cause a fire like the one that burned the Old World to ashes. He had seen the *tierras quemadas* many times in Pecos and Durango, he had seen the ruins around the holy Alamo in Santone. He wondered how this statue could turn Epitaph and the land for miles around it into one of those blackened, burned lands where any living thing would die. It's just not possible, he thought. Ixtpan must be crazy.

"There's no god here. Or weapon either." Stether's disappointment was evident in his angry blue eyes and the slight boyish pout to his lower lip. He had been hoping that what Falling Eagle was going to show them could be their salvation. Instead, it was only an old statue made of rocks.

"My young friend," Falling Eagle said gently, his voice echoing within the *kiva*, "gods are what you make them. And more than one race has made what lies beneath this statue into a god."

"What in St. Elvis's name is that thing supposed to be?" Stether asked, bored by the Fire God. He felt a certain fondness for St. Elvis, but otherwise, religion had never interested him much, and he certainly could not see what was so important about an ugly old idol.

"That, Stether," Angelina answered, "is the god who can kill the sun."

Cimarron was perplexed, as was Stether. All they saw was nothing more than a grotesque statue. Neither could he imagine that any real threat lay below them. Frankly, Cimarron thought, he would prefer to look into the military preparations far above them than to waste time with an idol. "With all respect—," he began, about to make his excuses and join Jayhawk.

"Stay, Cimarron Langtry. And you, Stether. I choose you and the woman, Angelina, along with my beloved Kiri, to be the ones to know the secret of the Fire God."

"All right, buckaroo," Cimarron said, "what's the secret? Is there more to the idol than it looks?"

"Yes," Falling Eagle responded. "As I gazed upon it on the first day that the gods directed me to it seven years ago, I knew in my heart that here lay an ancient evil. Ixtpan confirmed it for me. He had spent decades searching for the lost idols. He knew, as it had been passed down to him from those of his race who survived their own Holocaust, that what lay beneath the statue was a stone he called *matasol*, or uranium."

Angelina's eyes were dark violet in the torchlight of the dark *kiva*, and her skin was as pale as alabaster. "Ixtpan told me there is a mechanism within it that can set in motion forces that will release the fire within the stone. Cimarron, if the ones you call Clankers get into this pueblo, they will try to seize the idol. And, if they do, everyone here and far beyond may die."

"I'm having a hard time with this story," Cimarron responded calmly. "I mean, come on, what can be in a rock?"

"This rock holds within it the key to the birth of the universe and the forces that drive it. But the gods have forbidden it to us, and, to protect it, they have made it deadly, not only to those who handle it, but to all life on this planet."

"Why can't we just smash the damned thing?" Stether asked.

"No!" Falling Eagle cried with surprising force. "Touch it and you risk activating it."

"If half of what you say is true," Stether responded, "why haven't you evacuated Epitaph?"

"Had I not lain unconscious or delirious these past two months, I would have ordered an evacuation of the children and the old ones. But I would have asked others to stay and fight."

"What we're in is a situation kind of like the Alamo, Stether," Cimarron added, laying a hand on the young man's shoulder.

"What is an alamo?" Falling Eagle asked.

"A poplar tree," Cimarron answered with a smile. "And an old Texas legend, the point of which is that maybe you can't win a fight, but as sure as there's grass on the plains, you can take a lot of your enemies to hell with you. Maybe enough of them that they won't be able to win their next battle. Maybe you can't finish them off, but maybe you can weaken them enough so that someone else can."

Cimarron thought of Diego Laredo and his people in Durango. He could help buy them some time to consolidate their own strength and do everything he could to decrease the number of Clankers who would be going south . . . or anywhere else. It was what he had wanted to do when he came back to Pecos—that and vengeance for what had happened to Zaco. Well, he thought, I'll get everything I wanted tomorrow. If only Angelina were safe somewhere else, I'd be downright happy.

"What we will do is fight like devils. But the Clankers have us hopelessly outnumbered. The chances are that one of them will find the idol. If they do, there is only one possible defense against the fury of the Fire God—this emblem at the base of the pedestal." Falling Eagle pointed to the base of the silver pedestal holding the idol and there was a turquoise spiral, like the one on the

Toltec amulet that Angelina had given the Prophet, set in the archaic silver. "Ixtpan told me this emblem, when pressed, may send the uranium plummeting deep into the Earth, where, perhaps, the Earth itself can contain the fire."

"Why not try it now?" Stether asked.

"Because, Stether, Ixtpan may be wrong. And perhaps the device will not work and the fire will not be imprisoned, but will instead be set free. It is a terrible risk. No, we must only press this spiral if we have no other choice, if we know we have lost and the Clankers are going to seize the idol. If I must, I will risk using it tomorrow. I have burned before, and I am not afraid of the flames."

CHAPTER 12

THE LEGACY

In the square outside the pueblo, they gathered in the hundreds, the scattered peoples of an ancient continent under the silver light of the moon and the stars. The air was filled with the scent of piñon, sage, and sweetgrass as the sacred herbs were burned throughout Epitaph to carry prayers to the gods. They were men and women, old and young, with skin in every shade from ivory white to obsidian black, hair of black, white, gold, brown, yellow, red, blue, silver, and gold, wearing cloth or skins or woven vines and leaves.

They were Nacodo, Ufki, Zuni, Maba, and a hundred other tribes. The Ciowa and Athabas wore headbands of beads or snakeskins, some with feathers attached. Those from the northern plains wore war bonnets made of many brown and white hawk and eagle feathers. From the Southeast came the Ayette in colorful fabric turbans and the Balcons in their wide-brimmed hats.

They came from the cities like Nopal, Dry Gulch, and Reynada, in quilted cotton armor, in silver hoop vests, in buckskins, and in hopsack.

They came from Pecos, Delta, Muskogee, and even Tesharka, carrying knives, spears, and lances of bronze, copper, or iron. The defenders of Epitaph had weapons as advanced as steel swords—though there were pitifully few of those—and as primitive as stones—of which there were many.

And they all stood together to face the army that had driven them from their homelands. These people who still remained at Epitaph had been driven out before, but they would not be driven any farther. Here at Epitaph, they would make their stand and either keep the western lands free or die trying.

When the slender young man in a long blue robe, with a long green quetzal feather, the symbol of life, in his hair, appeared on the third-level roof of the pueblo, a murmur went through the crowd. Then a cheer went up as the people recognized the leader who had brought them all together, the man without whom they had feared they were doomed.

"He's alive!" Loretta, who was in the crowd outside the pueblo, sighed with relief to Tyler. "So the woman did it, you damned old fool."

"Sure as mesquite has thorns, she did!" Tyler slapped her on the back. "Now maybe we have a chance."

Tyler's words were repeated throughout the crowd as the sight of the Prophet standing well and strong gave the people of Epitaph the hope and the will they had been steadily losing.

Jayhawk stood at Falling Eagle's left hand. Kiri stood behind him, her golden-haired head bowed in prayer. Cimarron sat on the adobe landing just behind them, his knees drawn up to his chest, leaning back against the pueblo wall. Angelina sat beside him, her head resting against his shoulder and her long black hair falling over his chest. Stether was nearby, sitting cross-legged on the edge of the pueblo.

"Compadres," Falling Eagle began, speaking Spanglish fluently but rapidly, as if he found the language distasteful, "The guvnor of Tesharka says he's going to rule this continent, that his nation will rule for a thousand years. He does have a powerful empire and a great army. But on the continent of Noramica, everything changes. You call me Prophet. Well, here is my prophecy. As every other empire to rise on this land has fallen, so, too, will Tesharka, no matter what happens here tomorrow."

There was a commotion in the crowd as people wondered what their leader was talking about. The young man with the quetzal feather continued, his face serene, even radiant in the moonlight. "There is so much I cannot explain to you because I do not understand it myself. But believe me when I tell you that if the Clankers seize this pueblo tomorrow, there could be destruction on a scale you cannot imagine, and the land for miles around may burn in a fire like the heart of the sun. . . . You might have a chance of making it to the great mountains to the north," he said, gesturing to Corpus Cristi Mountain, behind him. "Go now, for by the time the sun rises, it will be too late. Or you can stay and fight. The choice is yours. But I must tell you this—not only must we keep the Clankers from this pueblo, we must keep them from the land to the west. The western land is sacred land. It has been since the beginning of time, when the gods left the secrets of the universe hidden in its stones. The Ancient Ones called Hopis once guarded that land from invaders. And, in an earlier time, my own people, as the Toltecas and Teotihuacános before them, protected that land. When invaders have taken the western lands in the past, they have harnessed the God of War. At this moment, it falls to us to stop these invaders. And to do that, I myself may be forced to unleash the power of an ancient and horrible god."

Falling Eagle expected the people to scatter like leaves in the wind, but there was no movement in the square below as every man, woman, and child stood firm. "Go on." In his past life, Falling Eagle had been the last ruler of a great nation, and in this life he stood with the same determination and nobility as he had at Tlatelolco. "Parents, if you will not leave, bring your children to me. I will see that they are protected as much as is possible. I swear that to you."

There was a bustle of activity in the darkness as parents began pushing their children toward the pueblo, bidding them to follow Falling Eagle's order and seek refuge from the destruction that was upon them.

Cimarron whispered to Angelina, "He must be going to send the kids out through that tunnel he showed us. I'll take you down to the tunnel and as far as that mountain behind us, but then I've got to come back. I can help them hold the Clankers off while the rest of you get away. Come on."

"No, Cimarron. I am staying. I can heal the wounded. I can help you." Angelina's voice was calm with a steely determination.

"No way." He stood and pulled her up beside him, taking her arm firmly, but Angelina jerked away from him.

"I have made my own choice!" She stamped her small foot hard, her eyes flashing the green of Falling Eagle's feather. "For myself, not for you or for my people or my god or anyone or anything else—just for myself. For eleven years, I have been the perfect little priestess, so holy and pure and above the things of the world. But now what I am is a woman, a woman who can do whatever she has to. It is *my* choice what I do, not yours, not Ixtpan's, not the Wise Ones, of my homeland. It is my choice and I have made it."

"I don't believe this superstition about the idol, but I know we're outnumbered by an army with more and better weapons than we have. Falling Eagle is right when he says everyone who's here could die tomorrow."

"My god, Quetzalcoatl, chose his own time to die, Cimarron, and I can choose mine."

Cimarron took a long, deep breath and laid his bronze hands gently on her shoulders. "All right, Angelina. But for now, for the rest of this night, come with me. I swear on my soul, I won't do anything to hurt you. I just want . . ."

"*Sí*, Cimarron. *Comprendo*." She took his hand and let him lead her inside the pueblo.

* * * * *

First light would come soon. The long night was nearly over. Will we still be here tomorrow night? Cimarron wondered as he gazed wearily out at the city from the pueblo rooftop. How many of us will still be alive?

Epitaph was dark but for a few candles and small fires burning throughout the pueblo and the shack city. In the city below, the people were preparing for the morrow. Some were leaving to escort the children to the relative safety of the deadly mountains. But most were staying to try to hold the Clanker army from taking Epitaph.

Cimarron took a black-and-orange pottery pitcher from a mesquite wood table, poured some water into his hands, and splashed it on his face. He liked the feeling of cold. It woke him up, made him feel more aware of being alive. It felt good.

They had climbed to the roof an hour before, and now Angelina lay, sleeping fitfully, on a bed of bison robes, her hair tousled around her. Cimarron poured some water onto a white cloth and washed her face. "You healed me—my body and my mind—Angelina, and what I've done is brought you into a trap." He thought her asleep and was startled when her small fingers grasped his hand.

"You did what I needed, Cimarron. And for your help I will be grateful for all eternity. Without you . . ." She sat up and laid her hand on Cimarron's arm. Her green eyes were half closed from fatigue yet still as vibrant as they were that day he'd first looked into them with what had seemed his last breath. "It is I who have brought you here . . . to die in this place."

"I brought myself here, Angelina. And we aren't dead yet. It's funny, but this is probably the last night of our lives, and it's the first time in years I've known what it was like to really want to live. I'm real glad to know what that feels like again—even if only for a few hours." He laid his head on her shoulder, his brown-and-gold hair mingling with her coal-black hair. "You know, I had a friend a long time ago—Apizaco his name was. Falling Eagle kind of reminds me of Zaco. If Zaco could see this place, I think he'd be proud of what we're doing. Knowing that makes me feel good, as if my life these past five years hasn't been for nothing."

"Tell me about your friend." Looking directly into Cimarron's eyes, Angelina was almost overcome by the pain she saw there. "Forgive me, I had no right to ask. . . . I only thought . . ."

"It's all right, Angelina. Maybe if I'd been able to tell someone about it a long time ago, I would've handled it better. But I just couldn't talk about it. Not with anyone, not in five damn long years." He took a shuck cigarette from his pocket, struck a flint, lit it, and took a deep drag. "Apizaco Two Creeks was my brother. My adopted brother. Zaco's father, Dezcalzo, took me in when I was a baby. I was an orphan he'd found in the ruins of a burned-out wagon. All he knew about me was that my parents, or whoever it was I was with, left me wrapped in the Pecos flag.

"Zaco and his father were the only family I ever had. Zaco was four years older than me. I looked up to him like he was St. Davy or somebody." He was at that moment remembering good times and the sharp lines of his face began to relax in the soft light of the half-moon. But then, as the memories came, his face hardened again, the creases deepening at the corners of his eyes and around his mouth. "He was involved with the rebellion before I was. Real involved. He inspired a lot of folks to fight against the Clankers, me among them. We had a lot of dreams. . . . We wanted to really change things, . . . not just in one city, but across the territory, across all the land that used to be Texas."

"Why did you make this fight you could not win, Cimarron?"

"So much was happening back then, Angelina. Topsannah's mother and her whole tribe were wiped out by Absalom Ironheart and his boys. I was with her when we found the bodies. Topsannah and I . . . were only kids, only seventeen. . . . She . . . she meant a lot to me . . ."

"I understand, Cimarron. I know a little of your world, enough to know that if you and Topsannah shared love, that is good. Do you not think I can understand that? Am I so distant? So different from you? So different from Topsannah?"

"Yes, I guess you can understand. *Lo siento.* I was afraid a woman like you would be shocked."

"I have been in your world for six weeks, and in that time I have been shocked by a great deal that I have seen and experienced. But I have not been shocked by love. What happened between you and Topsannah?"

"She left me. Just up and left one day. I knew after her people were killed at Dry Creek that she'd go back, that she'd have to go back and fight. I just wish . . . she'd told me she was leaving. I blamed the Clankers for what they'd done to her people, for what they'd done to Topsannah. I was so angry. And then Dezcalzo was killed two months after Topsannah left. That night, Zaco and I found the three Clankers who'd killed him and we took care of them. We left them hanging from a mesquite tree just outside of Reynada. It was kind of like a declaration of war."

Angelina noticed him shivering in spite of the heat. She wished desperately she could help him, but her healing could only stop physical pain, and Cimarron's pain was deep in his soul. She sensed, however, that until he could talk about his past, he could not begin to heal. "And then what happened?"

"The rebellion. It lasted three months, all across Pecos. We had the Clankers stopped dead there for a few days. But then they sent reinforcements from all over the damned Confederation. At the end, they were sacking Reynada. I know now it was Reno Bismark who told them where to strike to break the resistance." He shuddered. "We had been friends all our lives, . . . but Reno was always ambitious. And he had a cruel streak in him."

"I saw his cruelty in his eyes that night in his tent."

"The resistance was dying all around us, but Zaco and I went out to fight. A squad of Clankers on horseback sighted us and took off after us, firing arrows. I got hit in the back and was wounded pretty bad. We made it into an old church, and Zaco helped me up into the choir loft. But we heard the Clankers downstairs. I told Zaco to run, to leave me, that I wasn't afraid of dying. Zaco said, 'It's living that takes courage, not dying, *hermano*. You've got the courage to survive.' Then he jumped out the window of the loft, the Clankers took off after him, and he led them off down the street. They killed him."

Angelina felt him shaking, as though with fever. "Did you see it happen?"

"*Si*. I crawled to the window. I tried to go with him, but I'd lost a lot of blood. The arrowhead was deep inside my back, and I could barely move. I saw him leap up on a tile roof, and then jump straight at them. You won't believe this, but I swear he was smiling. He was holding an obsidian knife and, when he jumped, he landed square on one of the Clankers and killed the bastard. Then Zaco started running again, and they shot him down with a dozen arrows. I saw his blood running into the street. Then I passed out, thinking I was dying, too. But I didn't die." He covered his face with his trembling hands. "At least my body didn't die. My soul did. Zaco haunts me every day and every night of my life." His deep brown eyes were glistening with the tears he'd held inside for so long. "And I have wished for every one of those days and every one of those nights that it had been me they killed instead of him. Zaco made himself a target to get them away from me. If he hadn't, he might be alive today. Don't you see? I should be dead, not him."

Angelina embraced him, her small fingers caressing his gold-streaked brown hair comfortingly. "If you had died when he did, you would not be here now to help defend Epitaph. Were it not for you, I would be Reno Bismark's prisoner and Falling Eagle would have died last night. My life and those of the people here are your friend's legacy, just as your life is. Zaco wanted you to live, Cimarron. Accept what he gave you."

Angelina touched Cimarron's face gently, then she kissed him softly, and then almost fiercely, her arms encircling him, pulling him hard against her.

He pulled away. "Angelina, no. . . ."

"Cimarron, I know what I am doing, and I know what I want at this moment."

"Angelina, you don't know what you're saying. . . . I wouldn't . . . you're a priestess . . . a saint."

"No, I am not! I am a woman. As much as your Topsannah. Do you not see me as a woman? Do you not see me as flesh and blood? Am I just some useless spirit from a dead world?"

"No, but you're so innocent . . . so pure."

"I do not want to die so innocent, Cimarron."

As she spoke, the first golden rays of the sun came over Miners' Peak and Zapata Mountain on the eastern side of Epitaph, the direction from which the Clankers would come. Somewhere on the pueblo rooftop, someone was blowing a conch shell, the signal that the attack was about to begin. From the roof where he and Angelina sat, Cimarron could see the Clanker army, their banners and flags flying, the sunlight gleaming off their metal weapons, at the gateway to Epitaph, the entrance to Daugherty Pass.

"I'm sorry, Angelina, but it looks like time has run out for us." Cimarron kissed her gently at first, then with a passion as deep as the heart of the Earth. And then it was time to go.

* * * * *

The morning sun's first rays gleamed off the bronze hoop armor vests of the Confederation soldiers at the entrance to the clearing where Epitaph lay. The pass was filled with a thousand Clankers, with nine thousand more behind them.

The soldiers in their thousands massed in formation. They, too, came from across the continent, from all of the territories of the

Tesharka Confederation and beyond. There were battalions of savage Hanans from the northern Ice Mountains, Nevas from the west, Andos from the east, and Amas from the south, all lured by the need for money, adventure, or power—as well, of course, as those who had been simply drafted into the army of Tesharka. There was even a battalion of men who had ridden with Diego Laredo in Durango, but who had become disaffected with his tendency to share the proceeds of his daring robberies with the poor and who had come north to hire out as mercenaries in Baines Winchester's army.

"Whatever you do, find the woman, Angelina!" Reno Bismark had to yell to be heard over the sounds of horses' hooves pounding, metal clanging against metal, and warriors from across the continent singing and chanting. Using a soft brown rabbitskin, he polished the diamond blade of a long, silver-handled dagger. The dagger's handle was molded in a pattern of roses and stars. He and Amos Crimsonleaf were on foot inside the pass, far from the front lines, where they could hold a serious conversation without fear of having to dodge rebel arrows. "Capture her if you can. But if not, kill her." He handed Amos the diamond dagger, his blue eyes as cold as ice, his handsome young face rigid, and his jaw set tight. "And kill Cimarron Langtry."

"Yes, sir." The golden-haired soldier put the dagger into its jaguarskin sheath and tied it to his belt.

"And, Amos, . . ."

"Sir?"

"Be sure they're dead. Bring me their scalps."

"Understood, sir."

A battalion of cavalry went by them, two hundred men in bronze hoop armor vests on black horses with red and blue saddle blankets and black leather saddles. They were an elite battalion from Tesharka, all of them carrying raised steel swords that shone like fire in the golden morning light.

"I'd sure like to get a crack at Cimarron myself," Bismark said, eyeing the steel swords with a contented smile, secure in the knowledge that whatever weapons the people of Epitaph had, they could not possibly have anything stronger or more deadly than steel. "I should've just killed him when I first came back to Pecos, but I didn't." Reno Bismark pulled his two-sided sword from its gold scabbard and began polishing it with the rabbitskin. "There was something so . . . dead about him. I kind of enjoyed watching him, wondering when he was going to crack like a ripe watermelon, wondering what I could do to push him over the edge." He laughed, put the sword in its long gold scabbard, and mounted his silver-blue stallion. "After today, Amos, I'll be the next commander general of the army of the Tesharka Confederation. You've done a lot, been loyal. I'll reward you well. There'll be an extra five thousand jadas in your next pay."

"Thanks," Amos responded with a smile, adjusting his knife sheath, "I'll see you at Epitaph." All in all, he thought, things were working out well. He had already earned a raise and a promotion and now he had the promise of greater reward.

* * * * *

"There's no way." Matsemela surveyed the soldiers half a mile below him in Daugherty Pass from a rocky vantage point halfway up Miners' Peak. He, along with Ixtpan, Paradox, Topsannah, and the Sasquatch, were concealed from the Clankers' view by gigantic black boulders. "There's a few thousand of the swine down there, and I'd say that's too much even for us."

"If Angelina and Cimarron," Ixtpan said, casting an eye to Topsannah, "are in Epitaph, on the other side of this mountain—as the hawk and the eagle have told me they are—then we *will* go to them. And we must get to Epitaph. We must protect the *kiva* in the center of the lowest level of the pueblo. Remember that if you reach our destination without me. We must get to the *kiva*. We cannot use the pass since it is filled with the Confederation army, so it is a simple conclusion that we must cross the mountain."

"But these mountains are said to be almost impossible to cross." Topsannah, her long black hair hanging in two braids, looked up at the rest of Miners' Peak another half-mile above them, its black peak shrouded in flame-trimmed clouds, and she fingered the medicine bag that Angelina had given her. Then she looked down at the endless columns of Clankers below, many with gleaming steel weapons, and she prayed that if Cimarron were in Epitaph now, the woman healer had brought him happiness in the days before this battle.

"There's got to be a way," Paradox insisted, her neck craned so that she looked straight up at the barrior of jagged earth.

"Of course there's a way, you tenderfeet!" The Sasquatch—nicknamed Sas by his companions—failed to see the big difficulty and cursed the frailty of the later-evolved races. "It's not so all-fired hard getting up this mountain. You just jump the boulders." He illustrated his point by leaping about twelve feet up, practically flying over a ten-foot-tall boulder, and landing on the rocky ground with a loud thud and a spray of rocks and gravel. "See?"

"Great," said Paradox, adjusting the tops of her thigh-high moccasins in preparation for the climb. "You know, we can't all jump quite that far, Sas."

"Well," Matsemela added thoughtfully, surveying the rocks above them, "we've got the big guy here along to help out." He pointed to Ixtpan. "As we've all seen, he's got an unusual talent in the area of moving rock."

"Right," Paradox exclaimed gleefully. "He'll get us there. Won't you, Ixtpan?"

"Yes, I must. If the Clankers capture the Fire God, all will be lost. But I have an idea. Hmm . . ." He squinted his dark eyes, deep in planning his strategy as they made their way, climbing up the side of Miners' Peak, his torn buckskin clothes flapping around him but his bearing as regal as ever. "And," he said, turning around to face the others, "I sense the presence of some wild horses on this mountain. That will be useful! ¡Adelante!"

"I'm pretty good at moving rocks myself," Sas growled helpfully.

"Do you levitate stone, too?" Topsannah asked the Sasquatch as she tried unsuccessfully to move a half-ton black boulder that blocked their path, the graceful muscles on her brown arms and legs straining from the effort.

"I don't bother. It's too dadblamed much trouble." The eight-foot, brown-haired Sasquatch picked up the black boulder and moved it aside as easily as if it were a rubber ball while the others stared in amazement. "What're y'all waiting for? Let's get going, pardners!" He started up the jagged mountain face ahead of his companions.

Matsemela hesitated, looking down on the most monstrous army he had seen in his long life as a professional warrior.

Topsannah gently tugged him from the spot to which he seemed rooted as he considered the obvious wisdom of going in the opposite direction from the Clankers instead of toward them. "You've got to play the hand that's dealt you, Matsemela."

"We've been dealt one sure loser of a hand here, Topsannah. But, what the hell, let's go."

* * * * *

The tight phalanx of two hundred and fifty archers was at the entrance to Daugherty Pass, directly below where Ixtpan and his companions were climbing Miners' Peak. The archers were inching their way into the clearing as Epitaph's defenders fell before their relentless fusillade of metal-tipped arrows. From the low elevations of the pass came more arrows, many of them burning. The flaming arrows struck the tipis and shacks around the pueblo, and the ragged dwellings began to burn.

One such arrow, with its whole shaft afire, struck Tyler in the heart as he commanded the defense of the pueblo itself. He crumpled over.

"No! Tyler!" Ginty was screaming, tears running down his dirt-streaked face. He snatched up Tyler's bronze sword just as the line of cavalry broke through the ranks of Epitaph's defenders. He took out two of them before an arrow hit him in the back.

The first Confederation cavalry battalions began surrounding the city of Epitaph. The sanctuary had become a battleground.

* * * * *

Cimarron knew what to do as if by instinct. Diego had taught him a hundred times—do the thing they least expect. He shouted, "Yeeeeehaaaaaaaah!" and rode right at the infantry archers.

"Ready!" yelled a red-haired sergeant as the crazy battalion of people of Epitaph rode closer, their horses' hooves kicking up so much dust that they seemed to ride on the air. The attackers had appeared to him to come out of nowhere, striking the right flank of the cavalry. "Now don't fire 'til I say. The one in front makes a hell of a target, don't he? We'll turn this fool into a pincushion fast enough. Aim!" One hundred bronze- or copper-tipped arrows were aimed at Cimarron.

"He ain't turnin' back!" cried a corporal. "The bastard's headin' right toward us."

"Magic, that's what it is. He's worked a spell. They say that Prophet's a shaman. His people must be devils!" The soldier who offered that explanation was twitching like a gopher's whiskers, and his arrow slipped through his fingers.

"We'll see in a minute if this one can turn back arrows," observed another, only a second before the sergeant hollered, "Fire!"

A hundred arrows flew at Cimarron. None of them struck him, though many of those around him fell dead or wounded. He was riding too fast for anyone to take careful aim at him, and his surprising action of coming right at them unsettled the Clanker archers, affecting both their aim and their concentration. Still Cimarron kept coming, riding faster, faster, firing his own arrows and never looking back.

Stether rode from the south, leading another squadron straight for the enemy lines.

Cimarron, screaming curses as he rode straight at them, had the complete attention of his enemies. Consequently, they did not even notice Stether's charge and were taken by surprise to find not one but two squadrons bearing down on them from opposite sides of the valley. Though there were only twenty-five riders—most of them young people—in each group of attackers, the hundreds of soldiers who had felt invincible compared to the poorly clothed and armed rebels, suddenly realized their own vulnerability.

However, there was many a good shot among the Confederation army soldiers, and the charge cost Falling Eagle's army the lives of many of his people.

Still they kept coming. Cimarron's horse jumped over a rock-and-sand barricade, straight into the archers' ranks, his warriors fast behind him. The Confederation soldiers directly in his path broke and ran.

The warriors of Epitaph pressed the attack, but a fresh troop of Clankers was waiting, and from the two mountainsides, a hail of arrows rained down on them.

*   *   *   *   *

"We've got 'em trapped, sir. A rabbit couldn't get past us." The sergeant's narrow face was flaming crimson with excitement. His tan-colored stallion was sweating hard from having been ridden from the front lines back to Bismark's position.

"And the troops behind us? Are they so tight that no damn rebel can get through?" Reno Bismark asked as his silver-blue stallion bucked. Bismark's copper hair was uncharacteristically unkempt. His uniform was covered with dust, and there was a wildness in his eyes that disturbed all but those among his troops too dull-witted to notice it.

"Right. There's no way through here but under our best archers."

Reno Bismark laughed and shook the reins, and the silver-blue stallion took off for the entrance to the valley and the city within it.

*   *   *   *   *

Angelina's long black hair flew around her as she ran through the dark rooms of the pueblo.

"Angelina! Stop!" Kiri screamed after her, running to catch up. "Stay in the inner pueblo with us!"

"No! I said I would never use a weapon, but I was wrong. Now I am ready to fight with the rest of you." Her green eyes were frenzied, and her small hands clenched and unclenched.

"But you can heal the wounded!" Kiri grabbed Angelina by the shoulders, her blue eyes burning with desperation, her golden hair shining as though with a light of its own. "The more of our people we keep alive, the longer we can hold out . . . and the more chance we have of driving the invaders away."

Si, Angelina thought, I can keep them alive. Some of them. For a little while. In her ankle-length black cassock, Angelina looked like a small, trapped animal.

"Please. We need you. Falling Eagle needs you." Kiri took the other woman's thin shoulders and shook her. Then she let go and stepped back, her hands outstretched. "I'm sorry, Angelina. Forgive me. I know you want to be with Cimarron. I have no right . . ."

"No, I am the one who has no right," the healer answered. "I will do what you ask."

Her stones were gone, and the butterfly-shaped amulet, the symbol of the Toltec nation, was hanging where it belonged—from a silver chain around Falling Eagle's neck. Ixtpan, Paradox, Matsemela, and Topsannah were lost, perhaps dead. Cimarron would be leading a squadron in the battle. Falling Eagle would die before the sun rose again. And she had seen the Fire God in the *kiva* and understood what must lie within him, the element that Ixtpan had spoken of—uranium. Perhaps after this day, the sky would grow dark no matter how great their sacrifice.

*   *   *   *   *

Wyatt Fontana rode toward the pueblo on a black horse, cutting down three defenders with a long bronze sword as he did so. He had his assignment, and he was determined to carry it out. Zumarraga Apocalypse had sent him instructions by messenger—a man pretending to be a traveling peddler from Lanceville who just happened to run into the army on its way west—telling him where the Fire God idol lay: in a *kiva* deep below Epitaph. Fontana would find the Fire God and present it to the high priest of the Church of the New World himself. He fingered the twisted cross that hung around his neck and smiled. On this day, he would bring his god back into the world. And he would consecrate his triumph by making a blood sacrifice to his god—he would find the witch named Angelina kill her.

*   *   *   *   *

The pounding hooves of the cavalry's horses kicked up a thick red dust cloud, obscuring the view of the archers waiting in the shack city and on the rooftops of the pueblo. They held their flint-and obsidian-tipped dogwood and ash arrows, waiting for the attackers to come in closer, where every shot could count.

"Charge!" the cavalry officer in command shouted above the horses' hoofbeats and the screams of the wounded and dying. A volley of arrows fired from the fifth-level roof of the pueblo struck down several of those around the officer, and he veered sharply to the right to save himself from being cut down.

By the time they reached the shack city, the number of the first ranks of the invaders had been nearly halved, which meant that fifty of them had reached the city itself. There were another hundred right behind them, and hundreds more followed. If the main body of the cavalry was not cut off in the pass, Epitaph would soon be overrun.

Jayhawk, his long hair flying like a corn-yellow flag on the battlefield, fired an owl-feather-trimmed arrow as his pinto jumped the bodies of two cavalry horses. Soon both cavalry troops and rebels were engaged in thick and heavy hand-to-hand combat.

From on horseback, Cimarron jerked an arrow from a dead soldier's chest and fitted it to his own bowstring. As he fired his arrow, a Clanker spear cut his right thigh. He drew his bronze sword and killed the man. He was bleeding, but he had no time to bandage the wound and there was nothing he could do to stop the blood seeping slowly out of his body.

Fortunately he had an excellent horse, a sorrel stallion with the second sense that allowed some to move as one with their riders in battle. He barely had to press his knees against the horse's sides or pull the reins for it to react. Cimarron let an arrow fly and steered the horse straight for a line of archers. The sorrel never veered from the path.

It was the fifth line of archers he'd broken since the sun came up that morning, which already seemed a thousand years old—and, Cimarron noticed by the position of the sun, it wasn't even noon yet. He'd learned how to break a line single-handedly from

Diego Laredo, and he was glad for the time he'd spent fighting in the vaquero army. So, he thought as he fired another arrow that hit its target square in the chest, I went south to learn what I needed to know to come back here and live out this day. He thought of Angelina's talk about destiny, something he'd never particularly believed in, and laughed out loud at how his life had turned out.

He was proud of the way Stether had ridden, leading a ragtag squadron at the Clanker lines, deliberately showing himself at close range to draw their fire—and to open them up to an attack. The kid's all right, he thought. He's a Pecos boy, through and through.

Screams, harsher and more desperate than those from the general clamor of battle, arose from the massive pueblo, which was being assaulted by a whole platoon of Clankers on horseback. From where he saw them on the west rim of the valley, Cimarron turned his horse toward the city.

*　*　*　*　*

One of the Confederation soldiers fighting from behind some boulders near the opening of Daugherty Pass, a white-haired boy with bright citrine-gold eyes, fitted a flint-tipped arrow to his bodark bow. He was disturbed by a great rumbling sound and looked up. He screamed, but the others around him never heard his warning. It was silenced by a deafening roar that shut out even the other noises of raging battle. The boulder falling down the mountain took the Confederation soldiers by surprise. They had believed the mountains around Epitaph to be impassable and had had no thought at all of the possibility of any danger from above them.

"Must be hundreds of 'em up above!" screamed a panic-stricken man in a coonskin hat who gazed up in horror at Miners' Peak and the chucks of rock breaking away from the mountain's face.

"It's not possible!" a black-skinned soldier conscripted from Delta Territory yelled in response. "Nobody could cross that mountain! Nobody human, anyway!"

The tremendous boulder bounced like a child's rubber ball down the mountainside and crashed into the pass, killing twenty soldiers who happened to be where it landed.

A great scream went up among the Clankers.

"There *are* ghosts in these mountains! Or monsters!" yelled a red-faced lieutenant from Tesharka as he broke into a run toward the east—away from Epitaph.

"That's just barbarian superstition!" a colonel in a coonskin cap hollered, trying to stop others of his men who were following the lieutenant.

Another boulder crashed and bounced down the mountainside, this time crushing half a dozen soldiers.

"Can the Prophet bring down the mountains?" a white-skinned man from Balcon who lay beneath one of the boulders asked in his last breath.

Suddenly things took an even worse turn for the Confederation soldiers. A specter from hell appeared to come down the side of Miners' Peak. A tiny green creature firing arrows and yelling curses in a high-pitched, rasping voice rode on the bare back of a huge black stallion with a white star on its forehead. The soldiers felt the hair rise on the back of their necks. The creature was followed by a gigantic, hairy monster leaping down the mountain and stopping occasionally to pick up a boulder to hurl at the terrified soldiers below. The monster let out a growl so loud that the ground seemed to tremble. Whole platoons broke and ran east for the safety of the peaceful, empty desert.

A golden stallion came leaping over the rocks, running down Miners' Peak. From its back, a tall, muscular woman with long black braids fired off six arrows in less time than it took most of the soldiers to light a shuck cigarette. Five of her arrows struck their intended victims. Her sixth arrow took the bow out of the hand of the last. He spurred his mustang and fled.

A dark-skinned warrior, waving a gleaming bronze knife and laughing like a man insane, came riding down the mountain on a pinto. "Let's go!" the warrior yelled, kicking the horse's side with unbridled enthusiasm. "Run down the jackals! Stomp them into the ground!" His deep laugh could be heard over the screams of the dying.

A tremendous black boulder, much larger than the others, started tumbling their way, rolling over and over, bouncing off the ridges all the way down the mountain. With that, even more soldiers turned and ran away from the haunted San Cris Mountains.

A rumbling like from the inside of a volcano rose from the mountain, and a wall of rocks came down, crushing many of the cavalry forces still massed in Daugherty Pass and blocking the passage of any others. The survivors climbed over rocks, the bodies of their dead colleagues, and the bodies of dead horses, to escape.

The pass was sealed to rapid troop advancement, cutting off half the Clanker forces.

But five thousand of Baines Winchester's finest troops were already through the pass and besieging the old pueblo. The people of Epitaph were still outnumbered by trained soldiers with weapons of metal while they fought with weapons of wood and stone.

From the highest roof of the pueblo, Falling Eagle watched the battle in the golden, dust-filled light of the midmorning sun. He saw the dead, at least a thousand of his own people and as many of the enemy, scattered about the eastern side of the pueblo. Between the pueblo and Daugherty Pass he saw one fluid battle of thousands of combatants both mounted and on foot. He saw the wall of mountain fall and thanked the gods for the miracle. But he also saw how many Clankers were attacking the pueblo's defenders, and he knew it was only a matter of time before the attackers would be victorious. He wanted to go out and fight, as he had at Tlatelolco against the *Spañols*, whom he also had had no hope of defeating, but now he knew with certainty that his destiny would be played out in the *kiva*. He touched the butterfly amulet, then raised his arms to the heavens, to the gods, and screamed, "Save this land!"

The wind began to blow out of the south, softly at fist, then fiercely, and great black clouds rolled across the sky like a herd of buffalo on the run.

*   *   *   *   *

Absalom Ironheart cursed, his white mustache twitching furiously, as he narrowly missed being crushed by a falling red boulder. He was no longer dressed like a farmer, but was wearing military blue and bronze, his epaulets golden, the medals that covered his chest gold and silver. The commander general practically gleamed in the sunlight from all the metal he wore. He had forced his way through the lines and made it to the head of the troops when the rockslide hit. Now most of his own troops were cut off from the attack on Epitaph—as well as many of the cowards, he knew, who would have cut and run in fear. He had learned, over the years, that he could not trust the conscripts in a time of crisis. Ironheart was in a blood fury. "There will be no survivors here!" he yelled into the wind. "No survivors at all! You're all going to die! Just like those Comanches at Dry Creek! Just like the fools at Katishya Mission!"

He figured he would head on in to the pueblo and try to be the one to take the Prophet himself. And he would look for that Fire God that Zumarraga Apocalypse wanted. If the damn thing was so powerful, he'd just have to find it—and use it against the people of Epitaph.

* * * * *

The burning torches cast distorted and grotesque shadows on the adobe walls as more wounded were carried or dragged into the ancient meeting room that had become Epitaph's hospital and morgue. The room was deep inside the pueblo, on the ground level, so torches were necessary even as the sun neared its zenith. A few pine tables were scattered around the room, containing what remained of medicinal herbs and plants. The floor was covered with the bodies of the wounded lying on bison robes or striped wool blankets. An adjoining room was filled with the bodies of the dead.

Angelina sat on a blood-stained blanket, cradling a dying girl's head in her arms. The girl was no more than sixteen, and her brown hair was soaked and matted with blood. Angelina's black cassock was stained with it. Angelina no longer had the strength to heal anyone.

Earlier in the day, she had returned a dozen rebels to the fighting who had been more dead than alive when they were brought in. But now the energy was gone. It was all she could do to hold the girl. She fixed the image in her mind of Cimarron in that last moment as he held her in his arms just before he went out to fight, and she let it guide her like a beacon through a fog.

* * * * *

Half of the Confederation's forces had either retreated south or lay dead under the boulders of Miners' Peak by the time Ixtpan rode his silver mustang down to the fighting.

His horse went down, hit by a dozen arrows, but Ixtpan kept going on foot. He took a two-sided, long bronze sword with a copper handle in the shape of an eagle's wings off the body of one of the rebels. Since he was a head taller than the biggest men on the battlefield, he had the advantage of sighting any oncoming attackers before they saw him, and he got near the shack city before he was wounded. But a long copper knife struck Ixtpan just below the center of his rib cage. He groaned and sank to his knees, then forced himself up and kept going. He was certain Angelina was in the pueblo, if she were still alive. He had promised his beloved

Xochi, the high priestess of Tamoanchan, the one true love of his life, that he would protect Angelina. He could not fail now. He had to make it to the *kiva* beneath the pueblo.

My people created the Fire God, Ixtpan thought as he staggered onward. And now I must keep him from being released from the uranium beneath the *kiva*. As he could control the atoms of matter to levitate the stones, so, too, could Ixtpan slow the flow of blood from the wound—but he could not stop it. Any other human would have bled to death from such a wound within minutes. With Ixtpan, it would take longer.

*   *   *   *   *

Cimarron's leg felt as if it were on fire as he rode toward the pueblo. The wound in his thigh was slowing him down, no question about it. But there was no time to rest. He had seen Reno Bismark, whose bright copper hair made him extremely visible, heading for the pueblo. And Cimarron knew his childhood friend well enough to know he would be looking for Angelina.

Cimarron dismounted at the burning shack city and continued on foot. He had to stop and fight twice among the flaming tipis and shacks, but he managed to kill both attackers with his knife, quickly, on blind instinct. By the time he reached the square, the ground was tipping beneath his feet and there was a sound like an earthquake rumbling inside his head. He knew he was passing out and fought his own body harder than he had ever fought any enemy. Just let me find Angelina, he prayed, for the first time since the day he had watched Apizaco die. Let me find her before Reno does.

What did I do, Cimarron wondered, to anger the gods so much that they would make me face this kind of hell again? Whatever it was, punish *me* for it, not Angelina, he thought desperately. I've killed so many times, life and death are all the same to me. But she's never killed anyone. She has never taken the life of any living creature. Help her. If you're there, if there have ever been any spirits or gods of this land, please, help Angelina. He knew that Angelina would wait in the pueblo for him and that if he did not come, she would die there.

*   *   *   *   *

Stether Delgado, on foot and out of breath from running, caught sight of Absalom Ironheart near the earthen pueblo. The old general was hacking down opponents right and left with a gigantic two-sided steel sword, his blue uniform spattered with blood. He was bearing down on a woman cowering beside the pueblo, sheltering her young child. Looking at the man who wiped out the Katishya Mission, Stether thought of Iphigenia, who had given her young life that the children might have a chance to survive. Stether had only an old bronze sword.

He ran at the most feared general on the continent, waving his bronze sword and screaming, "Iphi!"

Absalom Ironheart struck him dead with the double-sided steel sword. The woman grabbed her child and ran, escaping the general, who, had it not been for Stether, would have killed them both.

Stether Delgado's blood ran into the dust.

* * * * *

The pueblo was only a few steps away. Cimarron could almost reach out and touch the adobe walls. That was when he recognized the boy dressed all in black dead on the ground. "Stether," he moaned, staggering to his young friend's side. "No. Not Stether." Tears filled his eyes as he thought of the young man, hardly more than a boy, who had so eagerly jumped a Clanker in the square in Reynada on that day he had first come home.

Then something hard grabbed Cimarron around his arms and chest and jerked him to the ground.

Amos Crimsonleaf, Cimarron thought, with his face in the biting dust, his arms pinned tight to his sides by the rope.

"Sorry about this, Cimarron. Nothing personal. It's just my job."

Amos's blond curls looked golden in the sunlight and reminded Cimarron for a moment of the boy, Boots, who had died in the mines outside Reynada. The boy had had golden curls, and he'd been dead a long time. The rope was pulled so tight that Cimarron felt as if it were cutting into him. The wound in his leg was hurting more from the fall.

Amos tossed the rope to wrap it around Cimarron a second time. Cimarron kicked out with his left leg and caught the soldier in the gut. Amos grunted and Cimarron sprang at him. Still bound by the rope, Cimarron threw his whole body at the soldier. Amos hit the pueblo wall hard and started to slump to the ground. Cimarron had the rope off himself in a second and lunged at Amos. But he saw the flash of a tiny star in Amos's hand and jumped aside just in time to avoid being slashed. It was the tip of a diamond dagger.

"Give up, Cimarron," Amos breathed, circling his intended victim, who was gasping and staggering. "You're already wounded. And tired. You know I can take you. Don't make it hard on yourself. It'll be fast, I swear."

Amos lunged at Cimarron, who barely dodged his blade.

Cimarron was weaving, unsteady on his feet, breathing hard in the smoke-filled air. He moved his own knife in rapid jerks as though his vision of Amos was fading.

Amos Crimsonleaf lunged.

Cimarron managed to jump out of his path, then swung hard at Amos. The blond soldier felt a swift jab to his left jaw and found himself falling fast toward the ground. He threw out his arms to break his fall, and as he did so he felt something sharp slide between his left ribs. In his last moment of consciousness, he knew it was Cimarron's knife.

"This," Cimarron said calmly, as he pushed the knife into Amos's heart, "is for Topsannah's mother." He took the diamond knife from the dead man's hand. "You know, Amos, I advised you a long time back to find another line of work. You should've stuck to sheepherding."

Cimarron kept the diamond blade in his right hand. He took one last look at Stether Delgado and whispered, "*Adiós, compañero,*" before he ran into the pueblo, where screams and curses echoed through the maze of rooms.

*   *   *   *   *

The wind blew harder and harder, and the sky grew dark with huge black clouds rolling out of the south, turning the land nearly dark in late morning. The Clankers looked to the heavens and became spooked by the sudden bizarre change in the weather.

As Ixtpan staggered, breathless, toward the ancient pueblo, forcing one foot in front of the other, he never once thought of the centuries past or of the people who had vanished from the pueblo so long before his own time. For the first and only time, the man who had spent his life obsessed with the past thought only of the present. The wind blew throughout the battleground, stirring up the blinding, stinging dust, and drove the black clouds across the land. Ixtpan wished for a moment that High Priestess Xochi could have seen those Clankers run before the boulders he and the Sasquatch, each in his own way, had hurled. And he wished so much that Xochi could have known his kinsman.

He caught sight of the Sasquatch—who was hard to miss as he towered two feet above the tallest warriors and because everyone, whether Clanker or a defender of Epitaph, ran at the sight of him rampaging across the battlefield. Sas hurled boulders and dead horses at Clanker archers. Ixtpan felt so proud of his relative, who had joined the battle of a race he disdained in order to save the land from the devastation of the Fire God.

Ixtpan whispered a prayer of thanksgiving as he felt the growing wind and looked one last time at the gathering clouds. He felt the earth beneath his feet and the wind around him, the earth and the air, the elements of life. He said very softly, as though to someone or something only he could see, "Now I know why I am alive in this distant time—to have had that one glimpse of the past and to help give this land a future. To testify that the ancient powers are real. ¡Adelante!"

* * * * *

Angelina lay unconscious among the dead and dying, her long black hair tangled, her clothing wet with blood, her delicate face as pale as ivory.

Only Kiri tended the wounded now. Her turquoise dress was covered with blood. Even her golden hair was stained with splattered blood. She was exhausted beyond knowing what she was doing. She mechanically brought them water and wiped their faces and lied to them that they would be all right.

The man at first appeared like any other victim of the battle. He was covered in dust, his clothes stained by dirt and blood and sweat.

"Lie down," Kiri said as she covered the face of the man who had just died. "I'll bring you water."

"Yes," the man answered. "Water."

He sat on a pine table cluttered with the remnants of herbs and roots that had been used to heal the wounds of those brought in earlier in the morning. He tried to wipe clean his bronze hoop armor vest with a piece of deerskin he ripped from the jacket of a dead Athaba warrior.

The golden-haired woman handed him a brown pottery pitcher, and he drank from it. "Much obliged," he responded, offering the pitcher back to Kiri. As soon as it was in her hands, he rose in one fast move and let go a hard blow to the side of her head. Kiri fell, unconscious, to the floor, and the pitcher shattered. "I won't kill you, lady, though, I'd lay odds my men will.

It's someone else I want." The man walked over to where Angelina lay unaware of what was happening around her. He laughed as he took the silver dagger from her belt and dropped it on the floor.

She was as easy to lift as a half-full bag of cotton. Reno Bismark carried Angelina out of the room and down a series of ladders, deeper into the heart of the pueblo. "No point making it easy for him," Bismark said aloud. "If Cimarron makes it here, I want him to be good and tired. And the last message from Winchester said to look for Apocalypse's Fire God in the lowest level of the pueblo, so that's where we'll go, Angelina."

It was not hard to find the way down. Bismark carried his prisoner down the pine ladders, five flights, to the stone level cut deep in the earth, then down the fifty-foot stone stairway to Falling Eagle's chamber. He brushed aside the bisonhide curtain and yanked it from the wall. He was stunned by the sight of the chamber. The cavernous room, with its strange pit surrounded by a low wall of stones in the center, was empty. A small fire burned near the pit, casting faint red shadows on the red walls, which were lit also by four flickering candles. The room smelled of burning sage and sweetgrass. Reno Bismark wrinkled his nose. He hated the sweet, earthy smell.

Bismark untied a thick, foot-long rope from around his leather belt and bound Angelina's wrists together as she lay unconscious on the stone floor. He laughed as he tied her hands to the obsidian railing of the stairway into the *kiva*.

Angelina opened her eyes, and the firelight flared, highlighting the young colonel in grotesque shadows. She gasped and turned as pale as death, realizing immediately that she was Bismark's prisoner. "Are you mad, Colonel? You know you will never get out of this place alive." Her violet-green eyes were narrowed, her muscles tensed, as she rose to her knees. She tried to stand, but the short rope held her tied, kneeling, to the obsidian railing.

"Oh, I'll get out of here alive, all right," Bismark answered, walking quickly around the room to be certain there was no other means of entry except the lone stairway, of which he had an unobstructed view from anywhere in the eerie, cavernous room. "You're going to be my hostage and get me out—after I kill Cimarron. And once we get out of this pit, you and I have some unfinished business, remember?" He knelt beside Angelina, lifted her head, and ran his fingers through her long, thick hair, twisting it and pulling it. "You got away from me once, but you won't again."

Angelina shuddered at his touch and struggled against the ropes that bound her hands. Her long black hair jerked around her shoulders like a snapping whip as she tried to free herself.

"You and Cimarron have caused me a great deal of trouble. And now you're going to pay for it." Bismark was yelling, hoping Cimarron would be in the pueblo and would hear him. "If Cimarron is still alive—and I'm betting he is—he'll come looking for you. He'd do anything to get to you, wouldn't he?" He smiled when Angelina winced and struggled harder against the ropes that bound her. "Of course, he will. He'll figure I've come for you, and he's got too much of that damned Pecos sense of honor to walk away from that. He'll have to come face me. Then he's going to die knowing I've got you, Angelina." He laughed, his fair skin the color of gold in the flickering light of the torches and small fire. "After that, you'll be my way out of this place."

Angelina sobbed, quit struggling against the ropes, and hung limp, realizing she would never be able to break loose.

Bismark leaned over the stone wall around the *kiva* and looked down. One torch burned on a wall halfway down into the *kiva*. He could make out something in the semi-darkness far below him. The torchlight flared and struck the idol, and the jewels that covered it gleamed in a hundred colors. "Well, well, look at that damned idol. Must be worth a small fortune. And the guvnor wants it so bad himself. This is my lucky day. I'll just pick that thing up and take it with me, along with you, Angelina—after I kill Cimarron. I've hated him for a long time—six years. Ever since Topsannah fell in love with him."

Angelina froze at the mention of Topsannah, and it took all her strength to mask her emotions from Reno Bismark.

"You have already hurt him more than you can imagine." Angelina closed her violet-green eyes and murmured a two-thousand-year-old incantation, remembering the pain in Cimarron's face when he spoke of his friend, Apizaco.

"Not enough." Bismark went on, his eyes constantly darting to the stairway that was the only entrance to the immense, dark chamber. He held his long sword ready to swing or stab. "And it all started because of a goddamned Comanche." He laughed insanely at the irony of it. "I was really in love with this Comanche girl, Topsannah Morales." He spoke her name as though it tasted sweet to him. "She was mine, too, until she met Cimarron and went blind to anyone but him. She was probably the only good and pure thing in my life. Cimarron deserves everything I'm going to do to him and more for what he did to her."

"What are you saying?" Angelina was taking slow, deep breaths. What else? she wondered. What else can this man do to us? "What could Cimarron have done to Topsannah?"

"He sent her out to the Sea of Grass, alone, in the middle of winter—when he knew she was carrying his child. I know, because I'd gone to see her, to try one more time to get her back. When I got to the shack she shared with that no-good father of hers, I heard the sounds of an argument and Topsannah crying. I listened outside a window at the side of the house. She admitted to her father she was pregnant with Cimarron's child. That drunk old bastard slapped her face, and she ran out the door, never seeing me there on the side of the house. And I never saw her again. She left Reynada that day. I imagine she died on the Sea of Grass that winter, and it was all Cimarron's goddamned fault."

She was carrying his child. The boy, Texas. A straight, sturdy little boy destined to be the Comanche chief. So that was the deep bond Angelina had sensed between Cimarron and Topsannah. The world seemed to spin faster and faster. Oh, Ixtpan, she thought, I have always believed what you taught me—that we cannot escape our destiny. Wherever you are now, *por favor, compañero,* help me have the strength to face mine.

In darkness, crouched at the top of the stone stairway that led to Falling Eagle's chamber, Cimarron shuddered and leaned, trembling, against the rock wall.

CHAPTER 13

DARKNESS AT HIGH NOON

The near-noon sun burned the same golden red as the burning shack city, bathing the pueblo in hot light the color of fire. Falling Eagle watched from the roof as the last defenders in the shack city broke before the onslaught of Clankers. Now the Earth would speak in a voice that would be heard for a thousand miles and a thousand years.

Falling Eagle sank to his knees on the warm adobe, overcome by the magnitude of what was certain to happen before the sun reached its apex, by the agonizingly vivid memory of his own defeat at Tlatelolco all those centuries in the past. Before, he had finally surrendered himself to his enemies to stop the slaughter of his people. No such sacrifice would do his people any good in this distant era.

He watched his valiant followers fall before the Clanker steel and iron for a few more moments, then he touched the quetzal feather lovingly and bowed his head in prayer. Suddenly, he heard a roar like that of some demon let loose from the underworld. There below him, just outside the main entrance to the pueblo, was a monster such as he had never seen, and he thought for a moment it must be some ancient God of Evil. The creature was easily eight feet tall and covered with thick, brown hair. He remembered the legends of the giant, hairy creatures of the wilderness, the oldest of the races, the Sasquatch.

The Sasquatch was holding off the invaders, fighting off five mounted Clankers with a two-edged steel sword. The flames from the burning shack city were drawing closer to the Sasquatch and the pueblo. Falling Eagle picked up the long obsidian lance that lay beside him and hurled it, killing a Clanker who was bearing down on the Sasquatch. The creature grabbed the lance from the dying man's body and threw it with a mighty heave into the next Clanker coming in its direction. It threw the lance with such force that it went into the man's chest and came out his back. The Sasquatch grabbed the horse of another soldier by the bridle and brought it down. But the fire drew closer to the Sasquatch and its opponent, and they disappeared in the flames. Falling Eagle did not see whether the Sasquatch perished or escaped the flames.

One hundred Clankers, screaming the names Tesharka and Winchester, broke into the pueblo. Falling Eagle ran for the *kiva*.

* * * * *

Cimarron's knuckles were white from the force with which he grasped the side of the stone stairway as he listened to the voices echoing from the room beneath him. The sounds of the battle, now inside the pueblo itself, drowned out some of the words, but he had heard enough. He had heard that Topsannah left him without ever telling him she was carrying his child. Topsannah's love for Cimarron had driven Reno Bismark to his betrayal of Reynada and his role in the assault in which Apizaco had died. And now Angelina would be the one to pay the price of Reno's madness.

Cimarron concentrated on everything around him as he tried to figure out what to do. Is this how the people who built the pueblo hundreds of years before had died, killed by others of their own kind? he wondered, listening to the screams, curses, and shrieks from the fighting.

"All right, Cimarron," Bismark yelled, his voice frenzied, "I figure you're nearby and you can hear me. I've got your girlfriend here, and if you want to keep her as pretty as she is right now, I suggest you get here quick."

Cimarron got up from his knees and stood straight. The wound in his thigh still bled and ached, but the thoughts that filled his mind shut out the pain. He put his right foot on the first step of the stairway. Well, Zaco, he thought, *asi es la vida.* Such is life. He took one step down.

"Vaquero."

The soft, deep voice came from behind him. Cimarron jumped and turned around, his copper sword drawn back to strike.

The large hand easily reached out to stop the sword blow. "*Silencio*," the giant whispered. "Or do you want to let that murdering jackal know we are here?" His hand was on a long, bronze sword he had taken from a dead Clanker.

"Ixtpan?" Cimarron breathed. "Where've you been?" He felt unsteady on his feet and leaned against the stone wall.

Ixtpan smiled as he remembered what he had said to Matsemela that day on the banks of the Rio Bravo: *His destiny may one day be linked to our own.* So, he thought, this, too, was true. Our lives *are* like strands of fiber interwoven on a loom.

"All that matters is Angelina. I know you will do anything for her. Is that not true?"

"Ixtpan, I will do whatever I have to for her." They spoke very softly. "What of Topsannah?" His voice wavered as he spoke her name. "Matsemela? Paradox?"

"Matsemela Nyakir is a hard man to kill. The Comanche woman is alive also, and Paradox. Or they were alive when last I saw them, only an hour ago. They are here, fighting."

"No . . ." St. Davy, he thought, why didn't Topsannah tell me about the child?

"We have made our small contribution to the battle. We have sealed the pass, and there'll be no more Clankers coming through it."

Cimarron embraced Ixtpan. In the darkness at the top of the stairs, his gold-streaked hair looked white and his angular face was lined with anguish. He looked to Ixtpan at that moment to be about twenty years older than he was. "Thank you, compadre."

"But I fear our efforts were not enough. We have bought some time, . . . but the enemy is upon us, still thousands strong. The time remaining to us is counted in moments. I will distract the copper-haired colonel while you get Angelina. When you come down these stairs, the colonel will be busy with me."

Cimarron grabbed the giant's right hand with his own. He held it tight and shook it, their thumbs locked together in the old Texas tradition. Ixtpan returned the handshake and made an ancient symbol for good luck—a closed fist with an upraised thumb. "Look, I'll take Bismark; you get Angelina and run."

"It is too late for that, too, vaquero." Ixtpan moved his left arm, which had been held across his chest, and Cimarron saw the red bloodstain slowly soaking the giant's tattered shirt.

"No, Ixtpan . . ." Cimarron's earth-brown eyes were circled in black, and his cheeks were so hollow that he looked almost skeletal.

"I will live long enough to do what I must. Take this." Ixtpan handed Cimarron the steel knife, the knife Angelina had put in his hand so long ago beside the Rio Bravo.

"*Gracias.*" Cimarron's fingers closed around the black ebony handle.

"And, vaquero, whatever you do, get Angelina away from here pronto. There is a tunnel behind a Comanche blanket on the north wall. Take her in there and run as far and as fast as you can and keep going. The tunnel will take you through the mountain directly behind the pueblo. And, no matter what happens, do not come out until you are at the far end of the tunnel. If it is raining, stay inside the mountain until the rain stops."

"Why?"

"Because if the Fire God escapes, he will poison the rain, and it will kill you just as if you had entered a *tierra quemada*. The land around here may be a *tierra quemada* after today. Just get Angelina as far away as you can. And, vaquero, tell Angelina I found what I was looking for. I am not alone in this world."

"Yes. I will tell her." If it's the last thing I do, he thought.

Ixtpan stepped onto the stairway, the bronze sword held high.

Reno Bismark heard a noise and looked to the stairway, expecting to see his childhood friend coming down at him. Suddenly he saw a man with thick, silver-streaked black hair coming his way, bounding the steep stairs three at a time. The colonel raised his steel sword—and found himself looking *up* into a pair of flashing black eyes and at a long, double-edged bronze sword in the hand of a man seven feet tall.

Bismark was startled—but only for a moment. His long steel sword connected with Ixtpan's in a loud clang. Angelina cried out when she saw Ixtpan, and for a moment she thought she must be seeing her friend in a death vision. As the swords collided again, then again, she knew it was real.

Though Ixtpan's steps were unsteady, his mind was sharp. He sensed each move Bismark made with the sword and blocked each thrust. But he was already severely weakened by the energy needed to stop the flow of blood from the wound he had taken outside the pueblo. He spun around, the sword swinging in an arc. Bismark had to jump to dodge it—and he also had to turn his back to the side of the room where Cimarron would appear.

At that moment, Cimarron jumped over the side of the stairway, a copper sword in his hand, the steel knife in his belt. Bismark's next lunge pierced Ixtpan's right side. Ixtpan fell to his knees, then fell face down on the cold stone floor.

Angelina screamed as Ixtpan fell. Cimarron's eyes desperately sought her—and he winced when he saw her bound to the *kiva*. She shuddered and turned white when she noticed Cimarron. Neither her magic nor her ancient faith could help Ixtpan, Cimarron, or herself. But now her strength was returning, and she fought her bonds like a wild animal. "Cimarron, no! Get away from here!" Her wrists bled from trying to break the rope that tied them. "Ixtpan! Ixtpan!"

Bismark turned toward Cimarron, the point of his two-sided

steel sword dripping Ixtpan's blood. "Somehow I've always figured it would come to this."

"Me, too."

For a moment, Cimarron's familiar slow, soft-spoken Pecos
drawl was unnerving to Bismark. "So this is where you want to
die? In the ruins of a dead civilization?"

"I reckon this'll do fine," Cimarron answered. For all of us,
Reno, he thought.

Angelina begged, "No, Cimarron! Get away from him!"

Bismark raised his long, two-edged steel sword, let out a savage
yell, and charged Cimarron, his great sword swinging, slicing the
air as it hunted for its target.

Cimarron matched him blow for blow, across the dimly lit room
and back again. But copper was no match for steel, and a hard
stroke by Bismark's sword broke Cimarron's in half. Bismark
laughed, his azure blue eyes bright with amusement, and ran
straight at his opponent.

*   *   *   *   *

Matsemela and Topsannah fought back to back, both using
swords they had taken from dead soldiers. They hacked at a dozen
attackers at once as they slowly inched their way to the pueblo. A
dogwood arrow with a flint tip pierced Topsannah's right shoulder, and she dropped her sword. Matsemela realized what had
happened, but he was in the act of fighting three swordsmen at
once and could not even turn to see how badly Topsannah was
hurt. He stabbed two of them and whirled, still fighting two
others, in time to see a sergeant lift a tremendous iron spear to
stab Topsannah.

Suddenly, the sergeant let out a howl, jumped straight up in
the air and took off running. There stood Paradox, with a wide
grin on her round green face and an obsidian lance tip in her
hand. She had struck with the sharp stone, which went neatly
through the soft leather of the man's boot and into his foot. Since
Paradox was only four feet tall and the sergeant was a burly man of
six feet in height, he had never seen her coming. The unexpected
wound had terrified him into retreat.

"Don't just stand there!" Matsemema bellowed.

Paradox let out a high-pitched giggle and struck again, this
time stabbing one of the soldiers fighting Matsemela in the back
of the knee with the lance tip. She quickly stabbed two more
successfully—all of them stunned into panic by the surprise attack

from beneath their line of vision.

The rest of the attackers took one look at the green itzaur in the fringed buckskin vest and ran. Matsemela grabbed Topsannah by the arm and pulled her to the pueblo with Paradox running after them.

Topsannah leaned against the adobe wall, gasping hard to get her breath. She pulled the arrow from her body and sank to the adobe floor. She was beginning to feel a growing numbness in her legs that told her with aching certainty that the arrow had been dipped in rattlesnake venom.

"Are you all right?" Matsemela asked, kneeling beside her.

"Sure," she said confidently. "It takes more than an arrow to kill a Comanche war chief." But her skin was turning deathly pale, and she was beginning to tremble.

"What is it, Topsannah?" Paradox asked, her copper knife in her hand, her eyes on the door to the room where they had taken refuge.

"Rattlesnake venom," Topsannah answered. "The arrow was dipped in rattlesnake venom. You all go on . . ."

"Hold her, Matsemela!"

Matsemela put an arm around Topsannah and held her steady while Paradox quickly slashed an X with her copper knife over the arrow wound in the war chief's shoulder. Then the itzaur began sucking the venom from the wound and spat it on the floor.

*   *   *   *   *

The two-sided steel sword struck the adobe wall with a thud as Cimarron jumped out of its path, missing the blade's edge by an inch. Cimarron had the steel knife out fast, and again he led Bismark around the room, always just out of reach of the steel sword. He couldn't get in close enough to strike with the dagger. One good throw was what he needed. But Bismark kept him moving too fast to aim. He had to get closer.

Bismark came in with a fast jab that cut Cimarron's left shoulder. Blood began to run down Cimarron's arm. Blood also seeped from the wound in his thigh.

Cimarron knew he had to strike fast. He took a long lunge toward Bismark. But he had lost too much blood, and his foot slipped and he staggered. The steel sword caught his right arm, causing an agonizing wound.

"Just think about it, Cimarron. You're about to die, and Angelina is mine. She'll be mine for a long, long time. Until I hand her over to Winchester. *If* I hand her over."

Bismark's face was flushed, his eyes wild. He was dancing about, jabbing the sword at his enemy.

As Angelina watched the blood flow from Cimarron's body, she was transformed by animal strength and rage. She fought almost insanely and suddenly the ropes broke loose from the copper railing. She fell backward and lay trembling on the stone floor.

"Angelina!" Cimarron yelled. "Run!" He lunged again, but Bismark struck quickly, and Cimarron's knife fell from his hand, skidding away. Cimarron dove for it, but the colonel jumped on top of him, turned him over, and put a knee in his stomach and the razor-sharp edge of the steel sword against his throat.

Cimarron winced and waited to feel the blade cut deeper. Reno jabbed his knee hard into his victim's stomach.

"I'll see you in hell, Reno," Cimarron said, spitting in his enemy's face.

Reno Bismark blinked for an instant.

At that moment, Cimarron felt the intricate spirals carved on the handle of the steel knife as it was miraculously placed in his hand. He didn't question the miracle, he just struck hard and fast, upward.

The broad smile on Reno Bismark's face seemed to quaver. The crazed eyes grew wilder and then froze. Instead of driving the sword into Cimarron's throat, he hung poised over his victim for a moment. The sword slipped from his hands. The ebony handle of Ixtpan's steel knife stuck out of his chest.

Bismark stared at the knife handle in surprise, then made a strangled, gurgling noise and fell sideways.

Cimarron maneuvered, grabbed the knife from Bismark's chest, and held it to strike again.

"Wish me peace?" Reno Bismark gasped, a strange, crooked smile on his lips, his blue eyes fixed on Cimarron.

"No." Cimarron struck hard again and again, and Reno Bismark died. Then Cimarron forced himself to his feet. A thin line of blood ringed his throat where the sword had cut him. Angelina was beside him, staring at her small hands, the hands, he realized that had given him the steel knife.

Angelina stood there calmly and steadily, her eyes gleaming violet-green.

Cimarron grabbed her and ran to Ixtpan.

Unbelievably, Ixtpan was still alive. He reached out and touched Angelina, who embraced him, crying, "I'll help you, Ixtpan, *compañero*. I'll heal you." She placed her hands over his heart. "I'll give you my own life energy."

"No, you will not, *mi* Angelina. It is too late." The giant reached out his huge right hand and held her left hand in it tightly. "Get out of here. Now. Take the tunnel. Run. Cimarron, . . . make her go. . . ." He was unable to continue, his chest beginning to heave, his breath coming in deep gasps.

"I will not leave you, Ixtpan," Angelina protested.

"Make her go, vaquero, . . . or my ghost will pursue you from the far side of hell." He tried to laugh, but it came out a weak gurgle, and blood trickled from the corner of his mouth. Ixtpan's dark eyes closed as his long fingers gently brushed his friend's tear-streaked face. He whispered, "Angelina, I am not the last Paleorican . . . not the last . . . Tell Xochi . . . live and tell Xochi . . . I love her." And then Ixtpan died.

*   *   *   *   *

Matsemela came bounding down the stairs two at a time into the cavernous chamber beneath the pueblo, yelling, "Thanks to all the gods of the Sahara, we've found you . . ." Once inside the besieged pueblo, the companions had not had a hard time finding the eerie stone room at the foot of the long stone staircase. Matsemela stopped abruptly when he saw Ixtpan lying in a pool of blood. His dark skin was streaked with ash and dirt, and his buckskin clothes were stained with blood and sweat and earth.

"Oh, no. Hey, the big guy's going to be all right, isn't he? You can fix him, Angelina. I've seen you heal people."

But Angelina was on her knees, slumped against Cimarron, crying softly and making no move to heal Ixtpan. Cimarron looked up at Matsemela and shook his head.

"Why not? You've fixed other people. Even that cowboy! Why can't you fix Ixtpan?"

"Because," a high-pitched, rasping voice from the stairway said, "he is dead." Paradox stood at the top of the high stone stairway, holding Topsannah's hand. In her other green, clawlike hand she held a copper knife. Paradox took a deep breath, squared her shoulders, and started down the long stairway.

"And so, apparently," said Topsannah, following behind Paradox, carrying a bronze sword, "is Reno Bismark. Good riddance." Topsannah was dizzy and kept one hand on the stone wall for support as she descended the long stairway. Though Paradox had sucked the rattlesnake venom from her wound and thereby saved her life, some of the poison had reached her bloodstream. Her vision was blurred and her head pounded. But there was no time to rest and recover.

Cimarron held Angelina sobbing in his arms as they knelt beside Ixtpan. Matsemela, Topsannah, and Paradox ran to his side. Topsannah silently placed one hand on Cimarron's shoulder, and he trembled and closed his brown eyes. Paradox, tears rolling down her green cheeks, hugged Angelina as Topsannah and Matsemela stood staring at Ixtpan's body. They were all startled by the sound of the soft voice.

"Get out of here, now, all of you." Falling Eagle stepped from the shadows at the foot of the staircase. "I have been watching our forces from the pueblo rooftop, and I can tell you they are broken, scattering to the mountains in defeat. The Clankers are overrunning the pueblo. The only way out now is through the tunnel."

Cimarron jumped to his feet, reaching for the steel knife as he did so.

"Falling Eagle!" Angelina whispered gratefully, as she rose to stand at Cimarron's side as straight as any warrior.

"If the Clankers're here, then come on, let's go!" Cimarron ran for the Comanche blanket on the north side of the great room. He jerked the blanket down, revealing the narrow stone door. He flipped the lever that opened the door, and Matsemela, Topsannah, and Paradox ran into the tunnel. Cimarron turned back to Falling Eagle and Angelina. But instead of running, Angelina knelt beside Ixtpan again, calmly uttering the ancient prayers for the dead—and the prayers for the dying—her long black hair falling over her shoulders like a mourning veil. Falling Eagle stood in the dark at the foot of the stairway, not moving, only staring at the *kiva* in the center of the room.

"Come on!" Cimarron yelled to the young warrior and to Angelina.

"No, Cimarron Langtry, I will stall our enemies here to give you time to get away. I fear the time has come to face the Fire God. I will give you as much time as Angelina's god allows me. Run. And don't stop running. No matter what happens."

"No! *Por favor*, no." Angelina grabbed Falling Eagle by the arms, shaking him. "Come with us."

"I cannot, *hermanita*. My destiny lies here in this dark room and in the flames that will come." His dark eyes were clear, his complexion golden brown, his black hair gleaming like obsidian. He was, in that moment, the healthy young Aztec warrior he had been in another lifetime.

"But you will die here," Angelina protested.

"I have died before, Angelina. Cimarron, take her now."

Cimarron embraced Falling Eagle for a moment, silently handed him the steel knife, his fingers lingering for half a moment on its carved ebony handle. Then he grabbed Angelina's hand and ran for the doorway to the tunnel. They were about five feet away when a voice from the top of the stairs stopped them.

"Hold it right there, Cimarron. You and the witch aren't going anywhere." At the top of the stairway a light flared as a torch on the wall was lit, and there stood Wyatt Fontana, his dark eyes blazing with madness. He held a long steel sword in one hand and a steel knife in the other, both of them gleaming blood red in the torchlight. His twisted cross amulet was outside his blue uniform now, and it shone in the light of the fire like the weapons. Holding his knife poised to throw at Angelina, Wyatt started moving inexorably down the stairway. "I understand there's something I'm looking for down here."

Cimarron froze. He had given the steel knife to Falling Eagle. Now he was unarmed, and Wyatt could kill Angelina with one deadly throw.

"If you want your Fire God so badly, he is below us. There. He is waiting for you." Falling Eagle stepped out of the shadows, and his slender brown finger pointed to the *kiva* in the center of the great room. A somber smile crossed his face. He knew by now that there were probably a thousand Clankers in the pueblo and directly outside it. Their shouts and screams echoed through the pueblo.

Wyatt stopped short, taken aback by the sight of Falling Eagle, who was to him an apparition of evil himself. Wyatt Fontana stared at the man who stood so calmly before him, thinking, Look at that bird feather in his hair. He's pure savage. His eyes moved to the *kiva*. So there it was. He had the idol, Cimarron, and the witch, not to mention Falling Eagle. His guvnor would reward him—and even more would Zumarraga Apocalypse reward him. He reached the stone floor and started toward the *kiva*.

Suddenly, Falling Eagle blocked Wyatt's path, smiling. The steel knife was pointed straight at his enemy. But then he saw the twisted cross amulet and realized the man was a disciple of the Fire God. He knew in that moment that the god would be released. "*Run!*" he screamed.

While Falling Eagle blocked Wyatt, Cimarron grabbed Angelina's arm and yanked her through the door. The door, made of solid stone three feet thick slammed shut behind them, and they ran blindly into the darkness through a narrow tunnel filled with stale air. In spite of everything they had been through, they ran as fast as they ever had in their lives, stumbling over loose stones, bumping blindly into the jagged rock walls, stopping only twice to gasp for air. They ran as if they were pursued by the fires of hell.

Falling Eagle knew he had to stall the Clanker so that Cimarron and Angelina could get far away. But is it possible to get far enough away from this fire? he wondered.

"The witch will not escape. There is no escape from my god," Wyatt said with a sneer. "You must be the barbarian who's caused us so much trouble."

"Yes, I am. And I have met your kind before." Falling Eagle smiled. "I have waited long centuries for a moment such as this. You, too, have lived and died before. Do you not remember?"

"I don't know what gibberish you're talking. I never set eyes on your heathen face in my life."

"Not in this life. And like the others of your kind, you are so much out of harmony with nature that you fail to remember your past lives. I do. I remember my other life—the life where a man like you burned me alive."

Cleverly the young man who remembered his past life so well, manipulated the Clanker so that his back was to the *kiva*.

"If I did, I'll be happy to do it again."

"This time," Falling Eagle said, "you, too, will be in the fire, *conquistador*." He lingered over the last word, turning it to a biting insult, then lunged at Wyatt with the steel knife.

Wyatt came at him with the steel sword, but Falling Eagle was faster and leaped out of its way. Again and again, Falling Eagle came close enough for Wyatt to strike, then leaped out of the way at the last instant, all the while waving the steel knife menacingly. Falling Eagle kept this strategy up for the length of time he estimated it would take Cimarron, Angelina, and the others to run at least a mile. For his part, Wyatt was in a blind fury.

Then, all of a sudden, Falling Eagle dove toward the steep stairway of the *kiva*, which was lit only by the light of the one torch hanging on the wall halfway down.

Wyatt Fontana was right after him.

Swiftly Falling Eagle covered the ground to the idol. Just as he was about to touch the spiral emblem on the base of the idol's silver pedestal, Falling Eagle felt a sword pierce his back. Wyatt stabbed him again. And again. Falling Eagle fell face down at the feet of the Fire God.

Then Wyatt turned to the idol.

So enthralled was the Clanker with the sight of his god, he did not see Falling Eagle reach out with his last strength and press the spiral emblem at the base of the statue's pedestal. The *kiva* gave a slight jolt and began to descend imperceptibly into the earth.

Falling Eagle smiled as he felt the *kiva* move. This death is easier than the last, he thought. And this time, the conquerors will burn with me. He saw a man with fair skin and a long black beard, wearing a long black cassock, reaching out to him from inside a bright, clear light. "Quetzalcoatl," he whispered. "Quetzal . . ." His eyes closed. This time, he would not feel the flames.

"It's mine!" Wyatt Fontana shrieked. "I claim this idol for Zumarraga Apocalypse and the Church of the New World! With this god the whole world will be ours!"

Wyatt was in such a state of religious ecstasy that he failed to notice that the stone *kiva* chamber was descending into the earth. Nor did he hear the footsteps on the stairs behind him as he delivered the fatal blow to Falling Eagle. He was so enthralled with the presence of his god, he did not realize someone was creeping up behind him.

Absalom Ironheart jerked his steel knife out of the lieutenant's back and wiped the blood off it on his own shirt-sleeve.

Wyatt slumped to the floor, his face ashen, his blue eyes round with astonishment. "Why?"

"Well, it wouldn't do to have a lieutenant seize this thing, boy. It's mine. And it's going to make me the next guvnor of Tesharka." Absalom Ironheart lifted the Fire God idol from its pedestal, his white mustache twitching with pleasure at having found the fool thing that his guvnor had made such a fuss about. He turned it around in his hands, shaking his head. "Damned if it's not an ugly thing."

"I put my god's curse on you." Wyatt Fontana was leaning against the silver pedestal, gasping.

The chamber had been dropping by inches. "What the hell?" Ironheart grunted as the chamber took a lurch and began to fall faster, dropping by feet.

The general was so agitated by the sudden motion that he did not notice that where the statue had stood there was now an opening, a hollow tube leading down into a mechanism far below. Absalom Ironheart did not hear either the whoosh of air rushing out of the tube, creating a vacuum inside, or the whirring of movement caused by the magnetic field he had disrupted when he seized what he believed was the Fire God. He was mistaken. The Fire God lay *beneath* the statue, at the end of the long tube, and through it a projectile of the silver-white element uranium was rushing at that moment, on its way to joining another piece of uranium and thereby reaching something neither Absalom Ironheart nor Wyatt Fontana could possibly have understood: the critical mass of uranium at which a nuclear reaction began.

The whole *kiva* glowed red and shook harder than an earthquake as the uranium exploded in fire like that at the heart of the sun.

*   *   *   *   *

The earth reverberated as if struck by the hand of a god, and the deafening explosion echoed for hundreds of miles as the uranium detonated in a gigantic burst of matter transformed in an instant into pure energy. The single moment in which the Fire God was released set off tremendous forces within the earth and the air. Beneath the ancient pueblo, rock melted into glass or evaporated into radioactive gases that escaped into the air.

Epitaph began to tremble, slowly at first, then more intensely. Terrified screams went up throughout the clearing in the circle of mountains.

But because Falling Eagle had activated the safety mechanism, the uranium had been hurled far enough beneath the Earth's surface that the earth itself could imprison the fire. There was no mushroom cloud of fire to scorch the earth, and the planet would not become locked in murderous darkness and cold, as it had in ages past, when the Fire God had burned across the land and filled the sky with ash and soot and dust.

However, the force of the blast was so powerful that the thousands of Clankers who had overrun the pueblo were killed instantly—as were the remaining rebels. Those not directly above what would in another time have been called ground zero, screamed in a frenzy of fear and ran for the mountains. It was good for them that they ran, because as the earth burned to glass below the pueblo, the already-shocked earth began to sink.

About half an hour after the blast, the pueblo collapsed into the earth, and then the earth itself gave way, imprisoning the fire of the uranium and taking with it all trace of what had been there—the pueblo, its defenders, a quarter of the largest army of the Tesharka Confederation, a statue of an ancient god, and a young shaman.

When the blast occurred, Cimarron, Angelina, and their companions were in the pitch-black tunnel inside Corpus Cristi Mountain, directly north of the pueblo. They were thrown to the hard ground by the force of the shock waves that tore through the earth. The explosion's roar seemed to go on forever as time came to a crashing stop.

The companions did as Ixtpan had told Cimarron, and they followed the dark tunnel through the mountain until they reached an exit on its far side. In the light of the sun filtering through the opening, they could see footprints in the dirt—a sign that the children who Falling Eagle had sent out of Epitaph the night before the battle had at least made it this far.

There was no rain falling when Cimarron stepped out into the world—a world not of darkness but of bright sunshine—so the others followed him out. He looked at the blue sky and gold-streaked clouds above and the green pine trees around them, and he took a long, deep breath of clear mountain air. He heard a mockingbird sing nearby and laughed with happiness at the sights and sounds of life. After the hellish blast that came close to shattering both his body and his mind, he had feared the Earth he had known would be gone forever. The land survived, he thought gratefully. The land survived.

They were determined to see what had become of the ancient pueblo. Without Ixtpan's help in summoning horses, it took them an entire day of hard climbing to reach the top of Corpus Cristi Mountain. From its rocky peak, they looked down at where the pueblo called Epitaph had been.

Topsannah moaned in horror and took Matsemela's hand. The mercenary turned as pale as buffalo grass and held Topsannah, his mouth open in disbelief. Angelina trembled and fell to her knees. Paradox knelt beside Angelina, taking her friend's hand in her own, and bowed her head. Cimarron stood behind Angelina, clutching her shoulders hard, as much to steady himself as to support her. What he saw took the breath from his lungs and made his heart stop beating. He had seen so much death and war and destruction in his life, they blended in his mind into one long blur of blood red. But he had never in his worst fevered nightmares seen anything like what lay below them.

Where the ancient pueblo had stood, there now was only a crater of golden sand a mile across and half a mile deep, as if a fist the size of a mountain had slammed into the earth. And there was nothing else. The green pine and cedar trees that had once lined the mountain walls around the pueblo all lay brown and uprooted, their dead tops pointing away from the valley as if in a warning, and of the birds, rabbits, mountain lions, horses, and other creatures that had made these mountains their home, there was no trace. There were no bird songs or bobcat growls or coyote wails. Not even the rustle of wings or the rattle of a serpent's tail. There was no sound at all.

"Ixtpan said there were more of those things," Matsemela said in awe, "that there are more of those idols out here somewhere. . . ."

"He is still waiting." Topsannah felt suddenly as if her knees would give out beneath her, and she leaned against Matsemela. "The Fire God is still waiting to escape from the uranium. But, perhaps from this great destruction," she added, "will come a warning that will protect this land from other invaders."

"Sure," Matsemela replied, in a tone far softer and more subdued than was normal for him, "what happened here will keep the human vultures away for a while. Until that lunatic, Zumarraga Apocalypse, or some other damned fool just like him comes looking for more of that rock that caused . . ." Words failed him, and he could only point mutely to the crater.

"This," Paradox said in a high-pitched, rasping whisper, "must never happen again. Whatever you humans do with your wars, *this* must never happen again."

The thought flashed in Cimarron's mind that he should be happy. His enemies were dead, the Tesharka army crippled. Yet, as he stared into that vast crater of sand, he felt nothing but sorrow that hurt to the depths of his soul. Then he looked to the white cloud-filled sky, toward the southeast—his homeland—and silently thanked his brother Zaco for giving him life—the life that had led him to bring Angelina to Epitaph to keep Falling Eagle alive long enough to save the land itself. *Asi es la vida*, he thought as his brown fingers locked in Angelina's black hair. Such is life.

Angelina took Cimarron's hand, and her green eyes, the color of the quetzal, the Bird of Life, filled with tears as she thought of Ixtpan, Falling Eagle, Stether Delgado, and all the others whose sacrifice had kept the sky from growing dark and the earth from turning as cold as if the sun itself had died.

EPILOGUE

The land looked black and silver in the light of the Comanche moon. Somewhere in the night, a lone coyote wailed mournfully and an owl hooted like a lost spirit.

The woman ran steadily in spite of her age, in spite of the murderous land, in spite of the dead she had left behind. When she thought of those who had fallen, she wanted to stop and grieve in the Comanche way, but she could not stop. Her purpose gave her strength. The boy had to survive. If they could reach the Sierra Madre, he would be safe. No army would follow the Comanches into the Sierra Madre, in whose vast wilderness whole races could disappear. Many of their people had fled south after the massacre at Hoda Canyon. She and the boy would find them, and they would find a way to live in the murderous mountains. And the boy would grow to be a leader of his people, as was his destiny.

It was of no consequence to the old woman that the great chief the boy believed was his father had, in reality, been a stepfather. Moon Shadow knew who the natural father of Texas was, because his mother had confided the truth to her during the boy's birth. She had met the man, Cimarron Langtry, briefly and had admired his courage and openness, qualities she was sure he had passed on to the son he did not know existed. And Texas had been raised by Bajo del Sol and Topsannah Morales, two of the greatest in the long line of Comanche chiefs. He would fulfill his purpose. Moon Shadow would see to that.

Though he was only five years old and all of his people were dead or dispersed, the boy was not afraid, not crossing the Terlingua Mountains, not crossing the Rio Bravo. He was the son of two chiefs, and he was afraid of nothing under the sun. But in his sleep, he cried as he dreamed of his beautiful mother. He wished very much that he could see her again, and he hated the strangers who had come and taken her from him. He vowed, with every step of his small moccasined feet, that he would find his mother. And he would, he swore, one day kill all of the men in the bronze hoop armor who had destroyed his world.

Sunrise was still hours away when they caught sight of the old mission.

The mission's adobe walls were cracked in many places. The old woman knew the building could well be deserted, possibly having been abandoned centuries before. Like the Alamo, it had been built in an archaic era by a religion and a government both as dead as the coyote and mastodon bones in the desert.

But there were signs of current habitation: a shack made of mesquite limbs daubed with mud, known as a *jacale*, two sun-bleached bisonhide tipis, and a small corral, also made of mesquite limbs, that held a bare-boned gray mare, two black mules, and a blue-haired goat.

It was possible that someone at the mission would betray them, but she and the boy needed water, and the presence of animals indicated a source of water.

There was a long, creaking sound as a tall, black-bearded man wearing a long, black cassock stepped outside. His black hair hung past his shoulders, and his skin was very fair, almost ghostly in the moonlight. He was carrying a yucca broom, which he leaned against the cracked adobe wall. "*Bienvenidos*," he said, smiling. "How can I help you, my children?"

"The boy and I need water, Padre." Moon Shadow looked the man over carefully. There was something oddly familiar about him, and she felt a sense of peace and safety.

"Come inside, *mis amigos*," he said, taking young Texas by the hand and leading him inside. "The Mission Santa Guadalupe Tonantzin does have water from a deep well. I can see you have traveled far. You may stay here for as long as you need."

"*Gracias*, Padre," Moon Shadow said as she followed him into the old mission. "We will only stop to take water. We seek others of our people who have fled into the Sierra Madre, and we must hurry on our way."

"These are very dangerous times, and this child must be protected, *mi hermana*," the padre answered. "And he will be safe here. This mission is a sanctuary. Welcome."

He made the ancient sign invoking the power of creation over them, moving his right hand in the pattern of a cross, a symbol dating back long before the fiery death of the Old World, the period believed to have been the Golden Age of human history. The horizontal bar of the cross represented things of the earth and flesh—things mortal—and the vertical bar represented those of air and spirit—the eternal.

ABOUT THE AUTHOR

Susan Torian Olan is a native Texan, with family from Goliad, Texas, scene of a battle in the Texas War for Independence. She lives in Dallas, where she is a typesetter and computer layout artist. She is the mother of one child, Anita Marie Olan, a student in art history. Susan Torian Olan firmly believes that Texas will one day be a republic again. *The Earth Remembers* is her first novel.